Readying Rilla

edited by

Elizabeth Waterston

Kate Waterston

Published by
Rock's Mills Press

Library and Archives Canada Cataloguing in Publication data is available on request. Contact us at customer.service@rocksmill-spress.com.

Table of Contents

To the Memory
of

Katherine Zoë Waterston

who died of a pulmonary embolism on November 9, 2015,
at the age of thirty-three.

Kate transcribed and clarified the manuscript of L.M. Montgomery's *Rilla of Ingleside*. Kate's father Dan and her aunts Christy and Jane Waterston helped me check and correct the transcript, line by line, against the *Rilla* manuscript. My friend Jen Rubio edited our work and designed and produced this book.

—Elizabeth Waterston
February 2016

L.M. Montgomery's Creative Path to Publication

L.M. Montgomery began writing *Rilla of Ingleside* on March 11, 1919, exactly five months after the Armistice ended World War I (*Selected Journals of L.M. Montgomery*, II, 309). Over the next two years Montgomery drove her pen over hundreds of pages, telling her story of that war: a story not about soldiers fighting and dying on Flanders fields, but about Canadian people struggling to "keep the home fires burning." Slowly she piled up 518 pages of hand-written narrative, almost every page refined by deletions and additions. Beside this manuscript she built another stack of 71 pages which she titled "Notes." Here she recorded longer second thoughts, designed to increase the realism or enhance the rhythm of the ongoing story. When the time came to type up a clean copy, she merged the auxiliary notes into the already change-laden pages and sent the typescript to her publisher, McClelland & Stewart.[1] They returned page proofs to her in March 1921, and on September 8th she received the printed version of the novel (*SJLMM,* III, 17). After that she made a bundle of her handwritten narrative and the extra notes, added a title page, a dedication and table of contents, and stowed it all away.

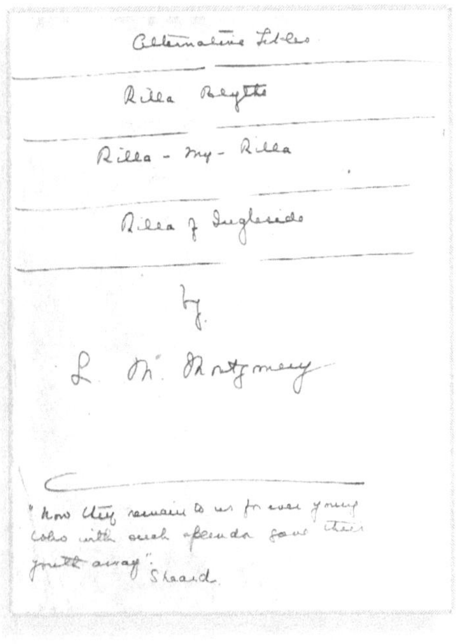

Alternative titles

Rilla Blythe

Rilla - My - Rilla

Rilla of Ingleside

by

L. M. Montgomery

"How they remain to us for ever young
Who with such splendor gave their
youth away".
Sheard.

That bundle was acquired by the University of Guelph in 1999. Its previous owner was a retired school teacher named Emily Woods. She decided that the manuscript ought to be made available both for lovers of Montgomery's work, and also for students of all literary creativity.

Each hand-written page also shows Montgomery's scrupulous self-editing. The manuscript is a piece of strong, clear writing, and also a tangle of deletions and insertions, second thoughts and coded references to late revisions recorded in the "Notes" pile. The first page of the *Rilla of Ingleside* manuscript appears in typical complexity:

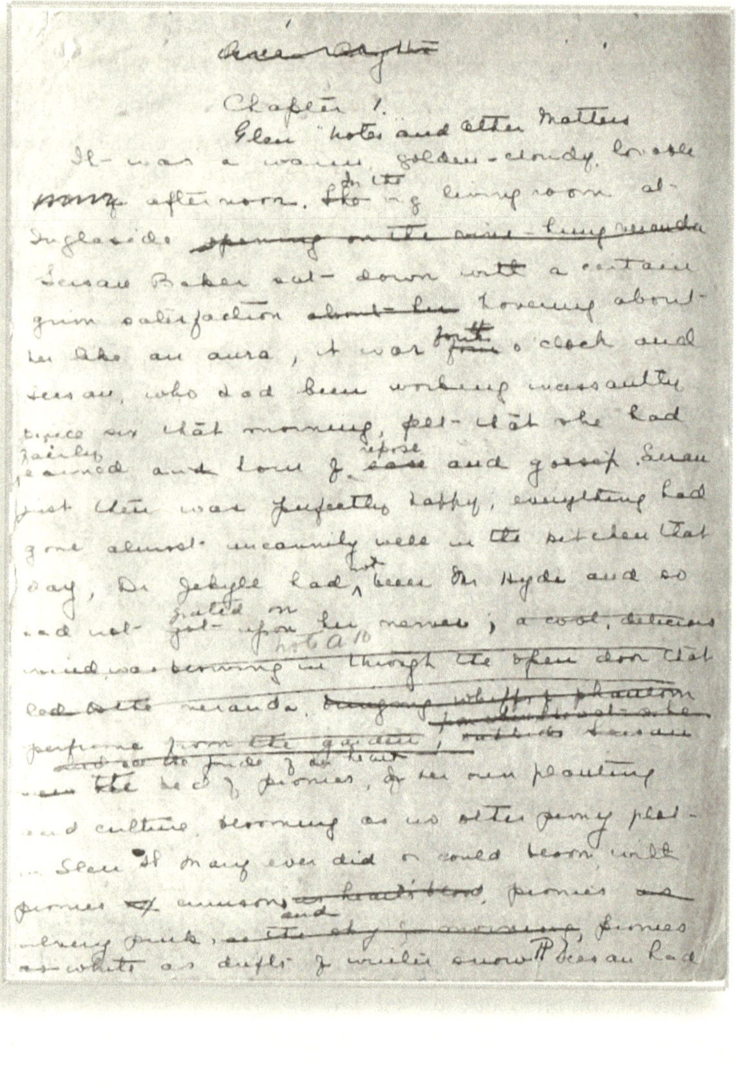

To make study of the manuscript easier, a computerized file was created in 2007 by Kate Waterston.[2] She input the *Rilla* manuscript, marking on-the-page deletions in strikethrough (~~deletions~~), and short insertions in carets and bold face (^**insertions**^). She left longer additions in their original place, among the separate pages marked "Notes." The first page of the manuscript appears in the computer file like this:

~~Rilla Blythe~~

Chapter 1

Glen "Notes" and other Matters

It was a warm, golden-cloudy, lovable ~~morning~~ afternoon. ~~The~~ ^**In the**^ big living room at Ingleside ~~opening on the vine-hung veranda~~ Susan Baker sat down with a certain grim satisfaction ~~about her~~ hovering about her like an aura; it was ~~four~~ ~~^4^~~ ^^**four**^^ o'clock and Susan, who had been working incessantly since six that morning, felt that she had ^**fairly**^ earned an~~d~~ hour of ~~ease~~ ^**repose**^ and gossip. Susan just then was perfectly happy; everything had gone almost uncannily well in the kitchen that day; Dr. Jekyll had ^**not**^ been Mr. Hyde and so had not ~~got upon~~ ^**grated on**^ her nerves; ~~a cool, delicious wind was blowing in through the open door that led to the veranda, bringing whiffs of phantom perfume from the garden, outside Susan saw ^from where she sat^ she saw ^could see the pride of her heart^~~ ^**Note A10**^ the bed of peonies, of her own planting and culture, blooming as no other peony plot in Glen St. Mary ever did or could bloom, with peonies ~~as~~ crimson ~~as heart's blood~~, peonies ~~as~~ silvery pink ~~as the sky of morning~~, ^**and**^ peonies ~~as~~ white as drifts of winter snow. Susan had

All the changes Montgomery made while writing and editing this page are logical and effective. It must be afternoon, not morning, since Susan the housekeeper would be too busy to sit down early in the day. The picturesque vine on the veranda, too romantic to suggest plain, practical Susan, must be moved to the next page where more sensitive characters will be introduced. As she composes, the author notices an inept phrase, "satisfaction about her," so she strikes out the word "about" and at once writes "hovering about her." Later, to further characterize Susan, she goes back and uses a caret (^) to insert stronger synonyms above the line of handwriting, to replace original words. "Repose" implies a stronger shift from fatigue than does "ease," and "grated on" is sharper than "got upon." The undeveloped reference to the bi-polar cat, Dr. Jekyll/Mr. Hyde, is a teaser, hinting at a mystery to be explored later.[3]

These are tiny changes, made probably during the first rush of writing. But farther down the page the author makes a telling cut: no delicious wind or wind-borne perfume for unpoetic Susan. She scribbles out three lines and inserts "Note A10" to signal that a reduced description of Susan's peony bed, saved among the separate sheets comprising her appended Notes, is ready to be inserted when she types the final copy.

The signal "Note A10" seems strange. Why is this first note not referred to as "Note A" since it is the first in the book? The answer is that Montgomery had created her own method of enumerating notes – a system deciphered years later by Dr. Elizabeth Epperly when she was studying the manuscript of *Emily of New Moon*.[4] The notes, Epperly discovered, were numbered in the order in which Montgomery composed them rather than in the order in which they would appear in the book. The first ones she wrote were marked A to Z. She went on from there to notes marked from A1 to Z1, then A2 to Z2, and so on until A10 to W10 (the final entry of 261 notes).[5] The indicator "Note A," although it does not appear in the manuscript until page 6, reminds the author to insert there the earliest item in her collection of Notes: a further description of the ominous cat mentioned at the outset of the story. On the other hand, the indicator "Note A10" is placed on page 1 to remind Montgomery to insert an effective phrase composed during final revision. It will tighten the portrait of a simple woman in a summer time of peonies and peace.

The first page of the manuscript ends with the deletion of poetic similes applied to the colours of those peonies, since these fairy-tale touches are inappropriate for Susan. Yet regarding the white peonies

Montgomery retains the comparison of white peonies to drifts of winter snow, a chilling phrase that prepares for the second page, where the impending war is first mentioned.

On page 2 the romantic vine-wreaths frame three more complicated people: Rilla, her older friend Miss Oliver, and her brother Walter. If Montgomery clarified Susan by chipping away poetic allusions, she made Rilla more real by addition. Revisions in the first account of fifteen-year-old Rilla add light emphasis on her promise of unusual beauty. The next additions give a more complex and comic impression of her nature by amplifying the sound of her voice, in a dialogue with Miss Oliver. A single page of the manuscript, page 22, is spiked with a sharp set of notes:

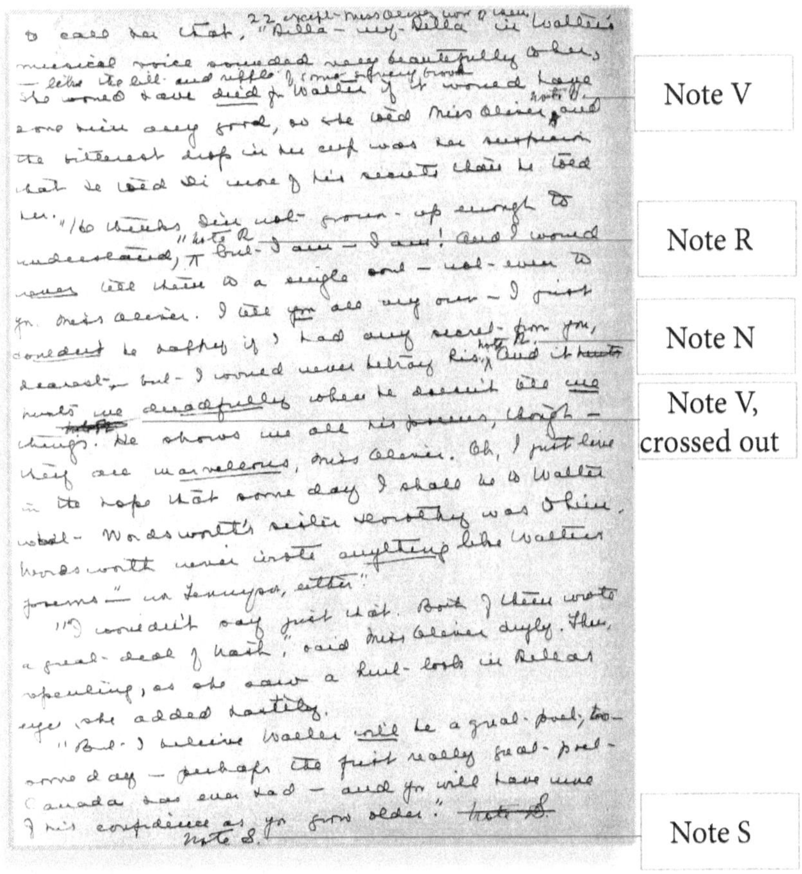

Pages 31–32 of the sheaf of paper marked "Notes" contain the corresponding snippets, to be added when the work is typed:

V. – i~~n italics, for Rilla~~ Rilla was fond of italics as most girls of fifteen are –

R. she had ^**once**^ lamented rebelliously to Miss Oliver,

N. ^**I tell him everything** –^ I even show him my diary.

S. "When Walter ~~had the fl~~ ~~was ill~~ ^**was**^ in the hospital with typhoid last year I was almost crazy," sighed Rilla, a little importantly. "They never told me how ill he really was until it was all over – father ~~said~~ wouldn't let them. I'm glad I didn't know – I couldn't have borne it. I cried myself to sleep every night. ~~Bu~~ as it was. – But sometimes," concluded Rilla bitterly – she liked to speak bitterly now and then in imitation of Miss Oliver – "sometimes I think ~~Rags~~ Walter cares more for ~~Jack Rags~~ Dog Monday than he does for me."

As each Note adds to the sound of her voice, Rilla's character becomes more contradictory: she emerges as shallow and self-absorbed but loving; sharp but guileless. Montgomery had moved beyond the charm of her Anne of Green Gables to a more down-to-earth awareness of adolescence.[6]

The character of Gertrude Oliver, on the other hand, is deepened not by little touches but some of the longest "Notes" in the list. Revising, Montgomery pours into these her own mysterious experiences of prophetic dreams. She adds some 200 words to the description of Miss Oliver's first dream, a Cassandra-like warning of the imminence of war and death. Later long additions deepen and darken the sense of Miss Oliver's character, her irony, her unhappy love story, her wry mockery of the Blythes' foibles.[7]

The story of Walter's response to militarism – "the blood and filth and misery of it all," leads Montgomery into more poignant notes. Sharpening her vision of a sensitive young man caught in the headlights of war, she writes Note Q2, which begins, "And a bayonet charge! If I could face the other things I ~~couldn't~~ could never face that. It makes me sick to think of it – sicker, even, to think of giving it than receiving it – to think of thrusting a bayonet through another man."

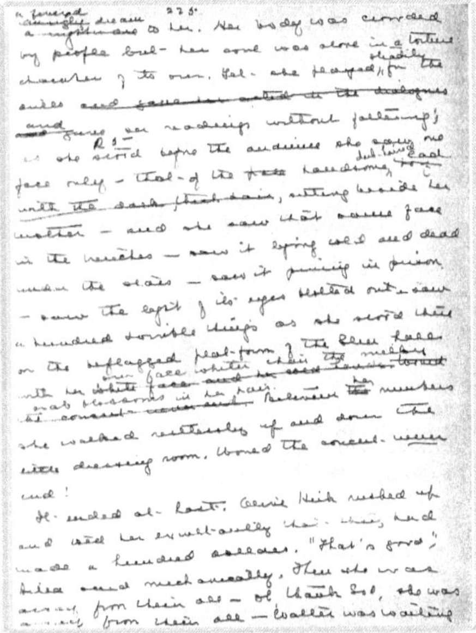

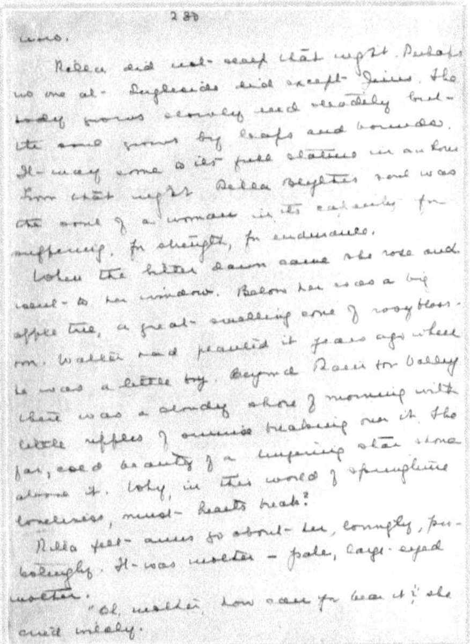

When Walter enlists, Montgomery, reporting Rilla's reaction, fills page 225 of the manuscript with a disturbed account that includes nine corrections plus an indicator "R5" that more is to be added from the appended notes. Five pages later she writes what will turn out to be the only page in the whole manuscript that has no corrections at all. The clean sure writing on page 230 reflects the calmness with which Rilla accepts her womanhood, "with its capacity for suffering, for strength, for endurance."[8]

With some difficulty Montgomery begins the account of Walter's heroism in battle: "~~In late Apr~~ ~~That week~~ ^~~In late April~~^ ^^**In May**^^." When Walter is awarded a Distinguished Service Medal, Montgomery reduces the drama by creating comic responses among the women back home, correcting the narrative as she writes: "'He should have had the V.C.' said Susan, and was ~~quite~~ very indignant over it. She was not quite sure who was to blame for his not getting it, but if it were General ~~Haig~~ she began ^**for the first**

time^ to entertain serious doubts as to his fitness for being Commander-in-Chief. Rilla was beside herself with delight . . . – it was Walter who had dashed ~~out of the~~ ^**back from the safety of the**^ trench to drag in a wounded comrade who had fallen on No-man's-land. . . . ~~What if a~~ What a thing to be the sister of such a hero!" Montgomery devotes three ancillary notes to the power of Walter's single published poem, "a short, poignant little thing ~~of only three verses; called 'The Piper'."~~. In Note X7 which is very hard to untangle, Montgomery calls it "the one great poem of the war." Finally she tightens the brief report of Walter's death: "When ~~the tel telephone rang that afternoon and the~~ her father, his face gray and drawn and old, came to her that afternoon and told her that Walter had been killed in action at Courcelette she crumpled up in a pitiful little heap ~~on the floor and spent~~ of merciful unconsciousness in his arms."

Meticulous revisions also clarify references to the wartime experiences of Jem Blythe and of Jerry and Carl Meredith. Inserted phrases in the story of Carl Meredith, facing a post-war world with gallantry although blinded in battle, echo phrases in her Journal entries about her half-brother Carl Montgomery, his leg amputated, but still cheery as a post-war visitor to Leaskdale (*SJLMM*, II, 229–31). Most memorable is the picture of Jem, returning from captivity "with a barely perceptible limp" to be greeted by Dog Monday, "gone ^**clean**^ mad with ^**rejuvenating**^ joy ~~and rapture~~."

That happy ending leads directly to the more romantic one that completes Rilla's story. In her final correction Montgomery weeds out a series of sentimental adverbs to conclude with a more evocative choice:

"Is it Rilla-my-Rilla?" he asked, ~~tenderly, passionately, with tender, passionate intonation.~~ meaningly.

Some time before Montgomery neared that conclusion, she delayed it by creating more and more lengthy Notes, indicated by the signals P8, U8, and especially W8. Curiously, "W8" appears twice, as the title of two of the longest Notes, both of them subsequently embedded in Note V8. The first Note W8 runs to 258 words. In it, Mary Vance discusses the amputation of her husband's leg with aplomb, before donning workman's overalls which shock the old ladies in this post-war world. The second Note W8 runs to 416 words. It tells of the time Whiskers-on-the-Moon got his comeuppance in a comic classroom scene. Note

V8 with its two embedded Notes W8 and W8-the-second runs to a total of 893 words, to be inserted in the final typescript in Chapter 26.

Kate Waterston, surprised by such unusually long late entries while inputting her version of the Notes, also noticed an arithmetical sum entered in the margin of page 42, opposite Note A7, a little more than halfway through the 71 pages:

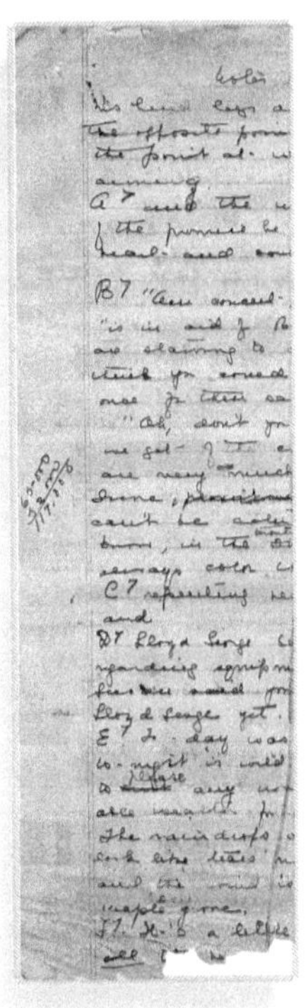

65,000
52,000
117,000

Kate reasoned that 65,000 was roughly the number of words in the narrative up to that point (around 300 words to a page, for 217 pages). The total of 117,000 was the desirable word-count for a full-fledged novel such as Montgomery's previous best-sellers: (roughly 390 to 400 manuscript pages). This meant that there were 52,000 words (173 pages) to go. An easy way to enlarge the final count without tinkering with the current draft would be to assign new and longer entries to the Notes pile. This seemed to suggest that the longer notes at the end were make-weights, filling out the novel to a saleable length.

Montgomery certainly needed to produce a sellable commodity. Ten days before beginning *Rilla*, she worried as she did a financial accounting of royalties "earned by my pen." (*SJLMM*, II, 308). Less than two months after the published copy of *Rilla* arrived she was anxious again; "If I can get along until spring when the Rilla reports come in I ought to come through all right" (*SJLMM*. III, 19).

But concerns other than royalties were in play when she wrote those long late notes. In them she shared with fans of her earlier books a child-like joy in surprises. She also added, for all readers, comic twists that might soften the harrowing effect of reading about war. In that 839-word Note V8, she switched wicked Whiskers-on-the-Moon and nasty Mary Vance into lighter roles as the story neared an end.

Close study of the manuscript and notes in all their entangled complexity clearly shows that aesthetic considerations were at least as important as pragmatic ones. The first fine frenzy of storytelling had produced a virtuoso display of sober reportage lightened by charm and humour. The insertions and deletions enhance the first draft with subtlety, delicacy, a fine sense of rhythm, and an unceasing quest for both precision and suggestiveness in choice of words. Unending lessons in creative editing can be gained from close attention to all the changes made by L.M. Montgomery.

Learning such lessons is not a privilege we will be granted by most modern writers. They push buttons to cut, copy, paste and delete, in order to produce a strong and shapely work. But their admirers will never be able to note and relish the moments when inspiration or ingenuity made a good book better. They have destroyed the log of their creative voyage. Luckily, the manuscript of *Rilla of Ingleside* lets us trace the path a creative writer travelled on the way to publishing her novel.

Elizabeth Waterston

Notes

1. There is no known copy of the Rilla typescript. Sadly, much of McClelland & Stewart's early correspondence and other archival material has not survived. However comparison between the published editions and the manuscript shows almost no differences.

2. Kate Waterston (1982–2015) helped decipher Montgomery's handwriting years earlier when the Montgomery Journals were translated from manuscript to type. Her computerized version will be held at the University Guelph, and will be made available on the L.M. Montgomery Research website.

3. L.M. Montgomery loved cats, particularly "Daffy," the cat at the Leaskdale manse. But "Doc" (Dr. Jekyll and Mr. Hyde) is a sinister cat with bi-polar mood swings. Maybe Montgomery introduced him in the opening pages to establish the sense of two worlds: peace and war, Susan gossiping and an archduke assassinated, men and boys marching away, girls and women left behind. We may also wonder why in 1919, the year when Montgomery's husband Ewan Macdonald had his first terrifying episodes of manic mood swings, she created this frightening,

comic picture of a similarly possessed creature.

4. Elizabeth Rollins Epperly first identified Montgomery's method of enumerating notes when she was studying the comparable manuscript of *Emily of New Moon*, at the Centennial Centre in Charlottetown. See "L. M. Montgomery's Manuscript Revisions," *Atlantis*, vol. 20, No. 1, 149–55.

5. A glance at the final page of the auxiliary material that Montgomery titled "Notes" will show the single error she made in her complex system of coding. At the end of her Notes she repeated the indicators "P10," "Q10," and "R10," and ended with "W10." Without this duplication the sequence would have ended with "A11."

6. Montgomery had now experienced eight years of running the "Young People's" group in her husband's church, chivvying them into play productions, enduring their moods and immature crushes and lack of responsibilities. She draws from those young people as she touches up Rilla's first scenes, preparing for the young woman's emergence into genuine anguish and love.

7. Such entries perhaps rise from Montgomery's current obsessive thoughts of her dearest friend, Frederica Campbell. Frede died of influenza in late January, 1919, just five weeks before Montgomery began writing Rilla, leaving her with ravaged nerves. She began the manuscript with a moving dedication to Frederica.

8. Pages iv, ix, and xi of the *Rilla of Ingleside* manuscript are reproduced here with the kind permission of the McLaughlin Library of the University of Guelph. The help and encouragement of Chief Librarian Rebecca Graham is gratefully acknowledged.

Sources

Rilla of Ingleside Manuscript, Archives & Special Collections, University of Guelph.

"Rilla of Ingleside," annotated computer file, accessible on the L.M. Montgomery Research website.

Mary Rubio and Elizabeth Waterston, eds., *The Selected Journals of L.M. Montgomery*, volume II: *1910–1921*. Toronto: Oxford University Press, 1987.

Mary Rubio and Elizabeth Waterston, eds., *The Selected Journals of L.M. Montgomery*, volume III: *1921–1929*. Toronto: Oxford University Press, 1992.

Elizabeth Epperly, "L. M. Montgomery's Manuscript Revisions," *Atlantis*, vol. 20, No. 1, 149–55.

[*In the following version of Montgomery's text and of the set of notes that accompany it, all editorial notes appear in square brackets and italics. Some such notes draw attention to unusual features, including the appearance of several alternative chapter endings, the presence of a tear at the corner of a page resulting in the loss of some words, or the fact that some notes have other notes embedded in them. At the points where Montgomery indicated that a note should be inserted when she typed up a final version, she sometimes used an indicator in the form of a phrase such as "^Note A10^". At other times, however, she simply used a capital letter and number, as in "^B2^". For clarity, I have added the word "[Note]" in italics whenever the short form occurs – EW.*]

An Interpretive Transcription of Montgomery's Manuscript of

Rilla of Ingleside

Alternative Titles

Rilla Blythe

Rilla-my-Rilla

Rilla of Ingleside

By

L.M. Montgomery

"Now they remain to us for ever young
Who with such splendor gave their youth away."

To The Memory
of
Frederica Campbell MacFarlane
who went away from me when the
dawn broke on January 25th, 1919 – a
true friend, a ~~wonderful~~ rare personality,
a loyal and ~~courageious~~ ^**courageous**^ soul.

Contents

[*No page numbers of chapters appear in the manuscript. The following numbers refer to pages in this transcript.*]

~~Rilla Blythe~~

Chapter 1

Glen "Notes" and Other Matters

It was a warm, golden-cloudy, lovable ~~morning~~ afternoon. ~~The~~ ^**In the**^ big living room at Ingleside ~~opening on the vine-hung veranda~~ Susan Baker sat down with a certain grim satisfaction ~~about her~~ hovering about her like an aura; it was ~~four 4~~ ^**four**^ o'clock and Susan, who had been working incessantly since six that morning, felt that she had ^**fairly**^ earned an~~d~~ hour of ~~ease~~ ^**repose**^ and gossip. Susan just then was perfectly happy; everything had gone almost uncannily well in the kitchen that day; Dr. Jekyll had ^**not**^ been Mr. Hyde and so had not ~~got upon~~ ^**grated on**^ her nerves; ^**Note A10**^ ~~a cool, delicious wind was blowing in through the open door that led to the veranda, bringing whiffs of phantom perfume from the garden, outside Susan saw from where she sat she could see the pride of her heart –~~ the bed of peonies, of her own planting and culture, blooming as no other peony plot in Glen St. Mary ever did or could bloom, with peonies ~~as~~ crimson ~~as heart's blood~~, peonies ~~as~~ silvery pink ~~as the sky of morning~~, ^**and**^ peonies ~~as~~ white as drifts of winter snow.

Susan had on a new black silk blouse, quite as elaborate as anything Mrs. Marshall Elliott ever wore, and a white, starched apron, trimmed with complicated crocheted lace fully five inches wide, not to mention insertion to match. Therefore Susan had all ^**the**^ comfortable consciousness of a well-dressed woman ~~and~~ ^**as**^ she opened ~~the~~ ^**her**^ copy of the <u>Daily Enterprise</u> and prepared to read the ~~"Glen St. Mary~~ ^**Glen**^ "Notes," which, as Miss Cornelia had just informed her, filled half a column of it and mentioned almost everybody at Ingleside. There was a big, black headline on the front page of the <u>Enterprise</u>, stating that some Archduke Ferdinand or other had been assassinated at ^**some place bearing the weird name of**^ Sarajevo, but Susan tarried not over ~~that~~ uninteresting, immaterial stuff like that; she was in quest of something really vital. Oh, here it was – "Jottings from Glen St. Mary" – Susan settled down keenly, reading each one over aloud to extract all possible ~~delight~~ ~~satisfaction~~ ^**gratification**^ from it.

Mrs. Blythe and her visitor, Miss Cornelia – alias Mrs. Marshall Elliott – were ~~sitting~~ ^**chatting**^ together ~~in the~~ ^**near**^ the open door that led to the veranda, through which a cool, delicious wind was blowing, bringing whiffs of phantom perfume from the garden, and ~~sounds of gay of voices and laughter~~ ^**charming gay echoes**^ from the ^**vine-hung**^ corner where Rilla and Miss Oliver and Walter ~~were foregathered~~ ^**were laughing**^ and talking. Wherever Rilla Blythe was, there was laughter. ^**Note B10**^

~~There was another occupant of the living room, ^**curled up on a lounge**,^ who must not be overlooked, since he was a creature being ^**creature**^ of marked personality ^**individuality**^, and, ^**moreover, had the distinction of being**^ the only living mortal creature ^**thing**^ whom Susan really hated~~.

All cats are mysterious but Dr. Jekyll-and-Mr. Hyde ^**– "Doc" for short –**^ was trebly so. He was a cat of double personality – or else, as Susan vowed, he was possessed by the devil. To begin with, there had been something ~~weird~~ ^**uncanny**^ about ~~his~~ ^**the**^ very dawn of his existence. ~~Two Three~~ ^**Four**^ years previously Rilla Blythe had ^**had**^ a treasured darling of a kitten, white as snow, with a saucy black tip to ~~his~~ ^**its**^ tail, which she called Jack Frost. Susan disliked Jack Frost, though she could not or would not give any ~~good~~ ^**valid**^ reason therefor.

"Take my word for it, Mrs. Dr. dear," she was wont to say ominously, "that cat will come to no good."

"But why do you think so?" Mrs. Blythe would ask.

"I do not think – I know," was all the answer Susan would vouchsafe.

With the rest of the Ingleside folk Jack Frost was a favorite; he was so very clean and well groomed, and never allowed a spot or stain to be seen on his beautiful white suit; he had endearing ways of purring and snuggling; he was scrupulously honest.

And then a domestic tragedy took place at Ingleside. Jack Frost had kittens!

It would be vain to try to picture Susan's triumph. Had she not always insisted that that cat would turn out to be a delusion and a snare? Now they could see for themselves!

Rilla kept one of the kittens, a very pretty one, with ^**peculiarly sleek glossy**^ fur of ~~dark orange~~ ^**dark ~~gold~~ yellow**^ crossed by darker ^**orange**^ stripes, ^**and large, satiny, golden ears.**^ She called it Goldie and the name seemed appropriate enough to the little frolicsome ~~kitten~~ creature which, during its kittenhood, gave no indication of the sinister nature it really possessed. Susan, ^**of course,**^ warned the family that no good could be expected from any offspring of that diabolical Jack Frost; but Susan's Cassandra-like croakings were unheeded.

The Blythes had been so accustomed to regarding Jack Frost as a member of the male sex that they could not get out of the habit. So they continually used the masculine pronoun, although the result was ludicrous. Visitors used to be quite electrified when Rilla referred casually to "Jack and his kitten," or told Goldie sternly, "~~g~~Go to your mother and get him to wash your fur."

"It is not decent, Mrs. Dr. dear," poor Susan would say bitterly. She herself compromised by always referring to Jack as "it" or "the white beast," and one heart at least did not ache when "it" ~~was poisoned died of poisoning~~ ^**was accidentally poisoned**^ the following winter.

In a year's time "Goldie" became so manifestly an inadequate name for the orange kitten that Walter, ^**who was just ^then^ reading Stevenson's story,**^ changed it to Dr. Jekyll-and-Mr. Hyde. In his Dr. Jekyll mood the cat was a drowsy, affectionate, domestic, cushion-loving puss, who liked petting and gloried in being nursed and ~~petted~~ ^**patted**^. Especially did he love to lie on his back and have his sleek, cream-coloured ~~stomach~~ ^**throat**^ stroked gently while he purred in somnolent satisfaction. ^**Note B**^ ~~He~~ ^**Doc**^ was very handsome; his every movement was grace; his poses magnificent. When he folded his long, dusky-ringed tail about his feet and sat him down on the veranda to gaze steadily into space for ~~an hour at a time~~ ^**long intervals**^ the Blythes felt that an Egyptian sphinx could not have made a more fitting Deity of the Portal.

When the ^**Mr.**^ Hyde mood came upon him – which it ~~also generally did in the twilight and always~~ ^**invariably did**^ before rain, ^**or**

wind,^ he was a wild thing with ~~changed altered~~ ^**changed**^ eyes. The ~~change~~ ^**transformation**^ always came suddenly. He would spring fiercely from a reverie with a savage snarl and bite at any restraining or caressing hand. His fur seemed to grow darker and his eyes gleamed ~~like~~ ^**with**^ a diabolical light. There was really an unearthly beauty about him ^**Note A**^ ~~at such times Dr. Jekyll~~ ~~^**If the transformation happened in the twilight all the Ingleside folk felt a certain terror of him, certainly at such times he was a fearsome beast.**^~~

Dr. Jekyll loved new milk; Mr. Hyde would not touch milk and growled over his meat. Dr. Jekyll came down the stairs so silently that no one could hear him. Mr. Hyde made his tread as heavy as a man's. Several evenings, when Susan was alone in the house, he "scared her stiff," as she declared, by doing this. He would sit in the middle of the kitchen floor, with his terrible eyes fixed ^**unwinkingly**^ upon hers for an hour at a time. This played havoc with her nerves, but poor Susan really held him in too much awe to ~~attempt~~ ^**try**^ to drive him out. Once she had dared to throw a stick at him and he had promptly made a savage leap ~~at~~ towards her. ~~R~~Susan rushed out of doors and never attempted to meddle with Mr. Hyde again – though she visited his misdeeds upon the innocent Dr. Jekyll, ~~When the Hyde transformation took place in the twilight even the older other Ingleside folk felt a certain terror of him. Certainly, at such times he was a fearsome beast. On this afternoon he was Dr. Jekyll, blamelessly curled up on the lounge lounge and Susan ignored him.~~ chasing him ignominiously out of her domain whenever he dared to ~~show~~ ^**poke**^ his nose in and denying him certain savoury tidbits ^**for**^ which he yearned ~~for~~.

"'The many friends of Miss Faith Meredith, ~~Mr.~~ Gerald Meredith and ~~Mr.~~ James Blythe,'" read Susan, rolling the names like sweet morsels under ~~the~~ her tongue, "'were very much pleased to welcome them home a few weeks ago from Redmond College. Mr. ^**James**^ Blythe, ~~we underst~~ who ^**was**^ graduated in Arts ~~a year~~ in 1913, has just completed his first year in medicine.'"

"Faith Meredith has really got to be the most handsomest creature I ever saw," commented Miss Cornelia above her filet crochet. "It's amazing how those ~~manse~~ children came on after Rosemary West went to the manse. People have almost forgotten what imps of mischief they

~~used to be~~ ^**were once**^. Anne, dearie, will you ever forget the way they used to carry on? It's really surprising how well Rosemary got on with them. She's more like a chum than a step mother. They all love her and Una adores her. ^**Note F**^ ~~Are Jem and Faith going to make a match of it?"~~

Mrs. Blythe smiled. It was well known that Miss Cornelia, who had been such a virulent man-hater at one time, had ^**actually**^ taken to match-making in her ~~elder days~~ declining years.

"They are only good friends yet, Miss Cornelia." ~~Jem has many years of study before him yet before he~~

"Very good friends, believe me," said Miss Cornelia emphatically. "I hear all about the doings of the young fry."

"I have no doubt that Mary Vance sees that you do, Mrs. Marshall Elliott," said Susan significantly, "but I think it is a shame to talk about children making matches."

"Children! Jem is twenty-one and Faith is nineteen," retorted Miss Cornelia. "You must not forget, Susan, that we old folks are not the only grown-up people in the world."

Outraged Susan, who detested any reference to her age ^**Note L—**^ returned to her "Notes."

"'Carl Meredith and Shirley Blythe ~~returned~~ ^**came**^ home last Friday evening from Queen's Academy. We understand that Carl will be in charge of the school at Harbor Head next year and we are sure he will be a popular and successful teacher.'"

"He will teach the children all there is to know about bugs, anyhow," said Miss Cornelia. ^**Note C**^ "Mr. Meredith and Rosemary wanted him to go right on to Redmond in the fall, but Carl has a very independent streak in him and means to earn part of his own way through college ~~anyhow~~. He'll be all the better for it."

~~"Mr.~~ "'Walter Blythe, who has been teaching for the past two years at Lowbridge, has ~~we understand,~~ resigned,'" read Susan. "'We understand that he intends going to Redmond this fall.'" ~~His sisters, Miss Nan and Miss Diana, will accompany him."~~

"Is Walter quite strong enough for Redmond yet?" queried Miss Cornelia anxiously.

"We hope that he will be by the fall," said Mrs. Blythe. "~~Of course,~~

~~he is far from strong yet but~~ An idle summer in the open air and sunshine will do a great deal for him."

"Typhoid is a hard thing to get over," said Miss Cornelia emphatically, "especially when one has had such a close shave as Walter had.[22] I think he'd do well to stay out of college another year. But then he's so ambitious. ^**Note E**^ ~~I'm glad the girls are going with him. They'll keep an eye on him ^**Walter**^.~~ I suppose," continued Miss ~~Cordelia~~ ^**Cornelia**^, with a side glance at Susan, "that after the snub I got a few minutes ago it will not be safe for me to suggest that Jerry Meredith is making sheep's eyes at Nan."

Susan ignored this and Mrs. Blythe laughed again.

"Dear Miss Cornelia, I have my hands full, haven't I? – with all these boys and girls sweet-hearting around me? If I took it seriously ~~they~~ it would quite crush me. ~~If~~ But I don't – it is too hard yet to realize that they're grown up. When I look at those two tall ~~boys~~ ^**sons**^ of mine I wonder if they can possibly be the fat, sweet, dimpled babies I kissed and cuddled and sang to slumber the other day – only the other day, Miss Cornelia." ^**Note D**^

"We're all growing older," sighed Miss Cornelia.

"The only part of me that feels old," ~~laughed~~ ^**said**^ Mrs. Blythe, "is the ankle I broke when Josie Pye dared me to walk the Barry ridge-pole in the Green Gables days. I have an ache in it when the wind is east. I won't admit that it is rheumatism, but it does ache.[22] As for the children, they ^**and the Merediths**^ are planning a gay summer before they have to go back to studies in the fall. They are such a fun-loving little crowd. They keep this house in a perpetual whirl of merriment."

"Is Rilla going to Queens when Shirley goes back?"

"It isn't decided yet. I rather fancy not. ~~I'm the~~ For one thing, her father thinks she isn't quite strong enough – she has rather outgrown her strength – she's really absurdly tall for a girl not yet fifteen. ~~I'm~~ ^**I am**^ not anxious to have her go – why, it would be terrible not to have a single one of my babies home with me next winter. Susan and I would fall to fighting with each other to break the monotony."

Susan smiled at this pleasantry. The idea of her fighting with "Mrs. Dr. dear!"

"Does Rilla herself want to go?" asked Miss Cornelia.

"No. The truth is, Rilla is the only one of my flock who isn't ambitious. I really wish she ~~were a~~ had a little more ambition ~~^**She**^~~ ~~She seems to have no aspiration beyond having a good time She~~ – she has no serious ideals at all – her ~~one~~ ^**sole**^ aspiration seems to be to have a good time."

"And why should she not have it, Mrs. Dr. dear?" cried Susan, who could not bear to hear a single word against anyone of the family, even from one of themselves. "A young girl should have a good time, ~~especially when she is as pretty as Rilla~~ ^**and that I will maintain.**^ There will be time enough for her to think of Latin and Greek."

"I should like to see a little sense of responsibility in her, Susan. And you know yourself that she is abominably vain."

"She has something to be vain about," retorted Susan. "She is the prettiest girl in Glen St. Mary. ^**Note H**^ No, Mrs. Dr. dear, I know my place but I cannot allow you to run down Rilla. Listen to this, Mrs. Marshall Elliott."

Susan ~~saw a~~ ^**had found a**^ chance to get square with Miss Cornelia for her ~~hurts~~ digs at the children's love affairs. She read the item with gusto.

"'Miller Douglas ~~will~~ has decided not to go West. He says old P.E.I. is good enough for him and he will continue to farm for his aunt, Mrs. Alec ~~Douglas~~ ^**Davis**^.'" ~~for~~

Susan looked keenly at Miss Cornelia.

"I have heard, Mrs. Marshall Elliott, that Miller is courting Mary Vance."

This shot pierced Miss Cornelia's armour. Her sonsy face flushed.

"I won't have Miller Douglas hanging round Mary," she said crisply. "He comes of a low family. His father was a sort of outcast from the Douglases – they never really counted him in – and his mother was one of those terrible Dillons from the Harbor Head."

"I think I have heard, Mrs. Marshall Elliott, that Mary Vance's own parents were not what you could call ~~respectable~~ aristocratic."

"Mary Vance has had a good bringing up and she is a smart, clever ^**capable**^ girl," retorted Miss Cornelia. "She is not going to throw herself away on ~~a penniless ne'er-do-weel~~ Miller Douglas, believe me! She knows my opinion on the matter and Mary has never disobeyed me yet."

"Well, I do not think you need worry, Mrs. Marshall Elliott, for Mrs. Alec ~~Douglas~~ ^**Davis**^ is as much against it as you could be, and says no nephew of hers is ever going to marry a nameless nobody like Mary Vance."

Susan returned to her mutton, feeling that she had got the best ^**of it**^ in this passage of arms, and read another "note."

"'We are ~~glad~~ ^**pleased**^ to hear that Miss Oliver has been engaged as teacher for another year. Miss Oliver will spend her well-earned vacation at her home in Lowbridge.'"

"I'm so glad Gertrude is going to stay ~~for another year~~," said Mrs. Blythe. "We would miss her horribly. And she has an excellent influence over Rilla who ~~adores~~ ^**worships**^ her. They are chums, in spite of the difference in their ages."

"I thought I heard she was going to be married?"

"I believe it was talked of but I understand ~~that~~ ^**it**^ is postponed for a year ~~^Note E^~~ ~~owing to certain complication in the settlement of~~"

"Who is the young man?"

"Robert ~~Glenn~~ ^**Grant**^. He is a ~~young~~ lawyer in Charlottetown. I hope Gertrude will be happy. She has had a sad life, with much ~~bitterness~~ ^**bitterness**^ in it, and she feels things with a terrible keenness. Her first youth is gone and she is practically alone in the world. This new love that has come into her life seems such a wonderful thing to her that I think she hardly dares believe in its permanence. When her marriage had to be put off she was quite in despair – though it ^**certainly**^ wasn't ~~the~~ Mr. = Grant's fault ~~certainly~~. ~~His father~~ There were complications in the settlement of his father's estate – his father died last winter – and he could not marry till the tangles were unravelled. But I think Gertrude felt it was a bad omen and that her happiness would somehow elude her yet."

"It does not do, Mrs. Dr. dear, to set your affections too much on a man," remarked Susan solemnly.

"Mr. Grant is quite as much in love with Gertrude as she ^**is**^ with him, Susan. ~~She~~ It is not he whom she distrusts – it is fate. She has a little mystic streak in her – I suppose some people would call her superstitious. She has an odd belief in dreams and we have not been able to laugh it out of her. I must own, too, that some of her dreams – but there, it would not do to let the ~~Gilbert~~ Gilbert hear me hinting such heresy. What have you found of much interest, Susan?"

Susan had given an exclamation.

"Listen to this, Mrs. Dr. dear. 'Mrs. ~~Caroline~~ ^**Sophia**^ Crawford has given up her house at Lowbridge and will make her home in future with her niece, Mrs. Albert Crawford.' Why that is my own cousin ~~Caroline~~ ^**Sophia**^, Mrs. Dr. dear. We quarrelled when we were children over who should get a Sunday-school card with ~~the~~ the words ~~"~~'God is Love,' wreathed in rosebuds, on it, and have never spoken to each other since. And now she is coming to live right across the road from us."

"You will have to make up the old quarrel, Susan. It will never do to be at outs with your neighbors."

"Cousin ~~Caroline~~ ^**Sophia**^ began the quarrel, so she can begin the making up also, Mrs. Dr. dear," said Susan loftily. "If she does I hope I am a good enough Christian to meet her half-way. She is not a cheerful person and has been a wet blanket all her life. The last time I saw her her face ~~^**it**^ was so wrinkled with worrying~~ had a thousand wrinkles – maybe more, maybe less – from worrying and foreboding. ^**Note I**^ The next note, I see, describes the special service in our church last Sunday night and says the decorations were very beautiful."

"Speaking of that reminds me that Mr. Pryor strongly disapproves of flowers in church," said Miss ~~Susan~~ ^**Cornelia**^. "I ~~always~~ said there would be trouble ~~not~~ when that man moved here from Lowbridge. He should never have been put in as elder – it was a mistake and we shall live to rue it, ^**believe me!**^ I have heard that he has said that if the girls continue ~~to decorate the~~ to 'mess up the pulpit with weeds' that he will not go to church."

"The church got on very well before ~~to~~ old Whiskers-on-the-Moon came to the Glen and it is my opinion it will get on without him after he is gone," said Susan.

"Who in the world ever gave him that ridiculous nickname?" asked Mrs. Blythe.

"Why, ~~he has been~~ the Lowbridge boys have called him that ever since I can remember, Mrs. Dr. dear – ^**I suppose because his**^ ~~His~~

face is so round and red, ~~and~~ with that fringe of ~~whisker~~ sandy whisker ~~round~~ ^**about**^ it. It does not do for anyone to call him that in his hearing, though, and that you may tie to. ^**But worse than his whiskers, Mrs. Dr. dear,**^ ~~H~~he is a very unreasonable man and has a great many queer ideas. ^**Note K**^ ~~^**Note J – H**^~~ Well, that is all the notes and there is not much else in the paper of any ~~interest~~ ^**importance**^. ^**Note G**^ Who is this Archduke man who has been murdered?"

"What does it matter to us?" asked Miss Cornelia, unaware of the hideous answer ^**to her question which**^ destiny was even then preparing. ~~to let~~. "Somebody is always murdering or being murdered in those Balkan States. It's their normal condition and I don't really think that our papers ought to print such shocking things. The Enterprise is ~~really~~ getting ^**far**^ too sensational with its big headlines. ~~It's just cop~~ Well, I must be getting home. No, Anne dearie, it's no use asking me to stay to supper. Marshall has got to thinking that if I'm not home for a meal it's not worth eating – just like a man.~~" So off I go.~~

[*Montgomery puts a line across the page here to indicate the original chapter end*]

So off I go. Merciful goodness, Anne dearie, what is the matter with that cat? Is he having a fit?" – this, as Doc suddenly bounded to the rug at Miss Cornelia's feet, laid back his ears, swore at her, and then disappeared with one fierce leap through the window.

"Oh, no. He's merely turning into Mr. Hyde – which means that we shall have rain or high wind before morning. Doc is as good as a barometer."

"Well, I am thankful he has gone on the rampage outside this time and not into my kitchen," said Susan. "And I am going out to see about ^(over)^ [*Chapter conclusion is written on back of current page of manuscript*] supper. With such a crowd as we have at Ingleside now it behooves us to think about ^**our**^ meals betimes."

Chap. 2

Dew of Morning

Outside, ~~in the golden~~ the Ingleside lawn was full of golden pools of sunshine and plots of alluring shadows. Rilla Blythe was swinging in the hammock under the big Scotch pine, Gertrude Oliver sat at its roots beside her, and Walter was stretched at full length on the grass, lost in a romance of chivalry wherein ~~all the~~ old heroes and beauties of dead and gone centuries lived vividly again for him.

Rilla was the "baby" of the Blythe family and was in a chronic state of secret indignation ~~what~~ ^**because**^ nobody believed she was grown up. She was so nearly fifteen that she called herself that, and she was quite as tall as Di and Nan; also, she was nearly as pretty as Susan believed her to be. She had great, dreamy, hazel eyes, a milky skin dappled with little golden freckles, and delicately arched eyebrows, ~~that gave ^**which**^~~ ^**giving**^ her a ~~denure~~ demure, questioning look ~~and~~ ^**which**^ made people, especially lads in their teens, want to answer it. Her hair was ripely, ruddily brown and ~~her chin was~~ a little dent in her upper lip looked as if some good fairy had pressed it in with her finger at Rilla's christening. Rilla, whose best friends could not deny her share of vanity, thought her face would do very well, but worried over her figure, and wished her mother could be prevailed upon to let her wear longer dresses. She, who had been so plump and roly-poly in the old Rainbow Valley days, was incredibly slim now, in the arms-and-legs period. Jem and Shirley harrowed her soul by calling her "Spider." Yet she ^**somehow**^ escaped awkwardness ~~somehow~~. There was something in her movements that made you think she never walked but always danced. She had been much petted and was a wee bit spoiled, but still the general opinion was that Rilla Blythe was a very sweet girl, even if she were not so clever as ~~the~~ Nan and Di.

~~Gertrude~~ ^**Miss Oliver** ^**Note M**^ had boarded for a year at ~~Inlge~~ Ingleside. ~~Rilla had D~~ The ~~doctor and Mrs. Blythe~~ ^**Blythes**^ had taken her to please Rilla who was fathoms deep in love with her teacher and was even willing to share her room, since no other was available. Gertrude Oliver was twenty-eight and life had been a struggle for her. She was a ~~clever handsome~~ striking-looking ~~woman~~ girl, with ~~deep-set, rather sad~~ ^**rather sad, almond-shaped**^ brown eyes, ^**a ~~crooked~~ clever ~~mouth~~, rather mocking mouth**^, and enormous masses of black hair twisted about her head. ~~^**and a crooked, clever mouth**^~~ She was not pretty but there was a certain ~~lure~~ ^**charm**^ of interest and mystery in her face, and Rilla found her fascinating. ~~Her very~~ ^**Even her occasional**^ moods of gloom and cynicism had allurement for Rilla. These moods came only when Miss Oliver was tired. At all other times she was a stimulating companion, and the gay set at Ingleside never remembered that she was so much older than themselves. Walter and Rilla were her favourites and she was the ~~coni~~ confidante of the secret wishes and aspirations of both. She knew that Rilla longed to be "out" – to go to parties as ~~D~~Nan and Di did, and ~~wear~~ ^**to have dainty**^ evening dresses and – yes, there is no mincing matters – beaux! In the plural, at that! As for Walter, Miss ~~Elliott~~ Oliver knew that he had written a sequence of sonnets "~~t~~To Rosamond" – i.e., Faith Meredith – and that he ~~aimed~~ ^**aimed**^ at a Professorship of English literature in some big college. She knew his ^**passionate**^ love of beauty and his ^**equally passionate**^ hatred of ugliness;~~. S~~she knew his strength and his weakness. ~~And she knew what Rilla only suspected – that Walter was in love with Faith Meredith, who had eyes and thoughts only for Jem. She was afraid that it might breed bitterness between the brothers ye, but so far nothing had broken their affection and comradeship.~~

Walter was, as ever, the handsomest of the Ingleside boys. Miss Oliver found pleasure in looking at him for his good looks – he was so exactly like what she would have liked her own son to be. Glossy black hair, ~~dreamy~~ ^**brilliant dark**^ gray eyes, faultless features. And a poet to his fingertips! That sonnet sequence was really a remarkable thing for a lad of ~~19~~ ^**twenty**^ to write. Miss Oliver was no partial critic and she knew that Walter Blythe had a wonderful gift. ~~Someday the world would know it.~~

Rilla loved Walter with all her heart. He never teased her as Jem and Shirley did. He never called her "Spider." His pet name for her was "Rilla-my-Rilla" – a little pun on her real name, Marilla~~, which she detested, as being so horribly old fashioned~~. She had been ~~called~~ ^**named**^ ~~after Aunt Marilla of Green Gables~~ ^[*Note*] **X9** ~~**for**~~^ ^**after Aunt Marilla of Green Gables**^, but Aunt Marilla had died before Rilla ~~could~~ was old enough to know her very well, and Rilla detested the name as being horribly old-fashioned and prim ^**Note Y9**^. She did not mind Walter's version, but nobody else was allowed to call her that, ^**except Miss Oliver now and then**^. "Rilla-my-Rilla" in Walter's musical voice sounded very beautiful to her ^**– like the lilt and ripple of some silvery brook**^. She would have died for Walter if it would have done him any good, so she told Miss Oliver ^**Note V**^ and the bitterest drop in her cup was her suspicion that he told Di more of his secrets than he told her.

"He thinks I'm not grown up enough to understand," ^**Note R**^ but I am – I am! And I would never tell them to a single soul – not even to you, Miss Oliver. I tell you all my own – I just couldn't be happy if I had any secret from you, dearest – but I would never betray his. ^**Note N**^ And it ~~hurts~~ hurts me dreadfully when he doesn't tell me things ~~^**Note N**^~~. He shows me all his poems, though – they are marvellous, Miss Oliver. Oh, I just live in the hope that some day I shall be to Walter what Wordsworth's sister Dorothy was to him. Wordsworth never wrote anything like Walter's poems[22] – nor Tennyson, either."

"I wouldn't say just that. Both of them wrote a great deal of trash," said Miss Oliver dryly. Then, repenting, as she saw a hurt look in Rilla's eye, she added hastily,

"But I believe Walter will be a great poet, too – some day – perhaps the first really great poet Canada has ever had – and you will have more of his confidence as you grow older." ~~^Note S^~~ ^**Note S**^

~~"Sometimes," siad Rilla bitterly – she liked to speak bitterly now and then in imitation of Miss Oliver – "sometimes I think Walter cares more for Dog Monday than he does for me."~~

~~Jink~~ ~~^**Rags**^~~ ^**Dog Monday**^ was the Ingleside dog ^**Note C10**^. He really belonged to Jem but was much attached to Walter also. He was lying beside Walter now with ~~his~~ nose snuggled against his arm, ~~Jack was not a collie~~ thumping his tail rapturously whenever Walter gave him an absent pat. ~~Jack~~ ^~~**Rags**~~ **Monday**^ was not a collie or a setter or a hound or a Newfoundland – He was just, as Jem said, "plain dog" – very plain dog, uncharitable people added. ~~Jack's~~ ^~~**Rag's Rag's**~~^ ^**Certainly, Monday's**^ looks were not his strong point. ~~But he possessed one talisman. He knew that not all dogs could be beautiful.~~ Black spots were scattered at random over his yellow ~~hide~~ ^**carcass**^ ~~and~~ one ^**of them,**^ apparently ~~blotted~~ ^**blotting**^ out an eye. His ears were ~~Ra rags~~ ^**in tatters**^, for ~~Jack~~ ^~~**Rags**~~ **Monday**^ was never successful in affairs of honor. But he possessed one talisman. He knew that not all dogs could be handsome or eloquent or victorious, but that every dog could love. Inside his homely hide beat the most affectionate, loyal, faithful heart of any dog since dogs were; and something looked out of his brown eyes that was nearer akin to a soul than any theologian would allow. ~~Everybody at Ingleside~~ ^**Note O**^

"Hasn't June been a ~~perfect~~ ^**delightful**^ month? ~~– perfect in every way,~~" she asked ~~Rilla~~, looking dreamily afar at the little ^**quiet**^ silvery clouds hanging so peacefully over Rainbow Valley. "We've had such lovely times – and such lovely weather. It has just been perfect every way."

"I don't half like that," said Miss Oliver, with a sigh. "It's ominous – somehow. A perfect thing is a gift of the gods – a sort of compensation for what is coming afterwards. I've ~~known~~ ^**seen**^ that so ~~many times~~ ^**often**^ that I don't care to hear people say they've had a perfect time. June <u>has</u> been delightful, though. ~~^**Note U**^~~ ~~What a nice summer all you gay creatures will have! And me moping at Lowbridge!~~" ^**Note U**^

"You'll be over often, won't you? I think there's going to be lots of fun this summer, though I'll just be on the fringe of things as usual, I suppose. Isn't it horrid when people thinking you ^**are**^ a little girl when you're not?"

"There's plenty of time for you to be grown up, Rilla~~-my-Rilla~~. Don't wish your youth away. It goes too quickly. You'll begin to taste life soon enough."

"<u>Taste</u> life! I want to <u>eat</u> it," ~~lau~~ cried Rilla, laughing. "I want everything – everything a girl can have. I'll be ~~15~~ ^**fifteen**^ in another month, and then nobody can say I'm a child any longer. I heard someone say once that the years from fifteen to nineteen are the best years in a girl's life. I'm going to make them perfectly splendid – just fill them with fun." ^**Note P**^ [*Note Q is embedded in this Note.*]

"Have you any notion of going to college this fall?"

"No – nor any other fall. ~~I've no~~ I don't want to. I never cared for all those ologies and isms Nan and Di are so crazy about. And there's five ~~in our f~~ of us going to college already. Surely that's enough. There's bound to be one dunce in every family. I'm quite willing to be a dunce if I can be a pretty, popular, delightful one. I can't be clever ^**Note C2**^ – And I can't be a housewifely, cookly creature, either. I hate sewing and dusting, and when Susan couldn't teach me to make biscuits nobody could. Father says I toil not neither do I spin. ~~I was born~~ ^**Therefore, I must**^ to be a lily of the field," concluded Rilla, with another laugh.

"You are too young to ~~stop learning, Rilla~~ ^**give up your studies altogether, Rilla.**^"

"Oh, mother will put me through a course of reading next winter. It will polish up her B.A. degree. Luckily I like reading. Don't look at me so sorrowfully and so disapprovingly, dearest. I can't be sober and serious – everything looks so rosy ~~to me~~ and rainbowy to me. Next month I'll be fifteen – and next year sixteen – and the year after that, seventeen. ~~Isn't that~~ Could anything be more enchanting?"

"Rap wood," said Gertrude Oliver, half laughingly, ~~if~~ half seriously. "Rap wood, Rilla-my-Rilla."

Chapter 3

Moonlit Mirth

Rilla, who still buttoned up her eyes when she went to sleep, so that she always looked as if she were laughing in her slumber, yawned, stretched, and ~~laughed~~ ^**smiled**^ at ~~Miss~~ ^**Gertrude**^ Oliver~~, who had come over one August morning~~. The latter had come over ~~the night~~ from Lowbridge the ^**previous**^ evening ~~before~~ and had been prevailed upon to remain for the ~~party~~ ^**dance**^ at the Four Winds Lighthouse the next night.

"The new day is knocking at the window. What will it bring us, I wonder."

Miss Oliver shivered a little. She never greeted the days with Rilla's enthusiasm. She had lived long enough to know that a day may bring a terrible thing. ~~She had been lying awake since dawn, thinking.~~

"I think the nicest thing about days is their unexpectedness," went on Rilla. "It's jolly to wake up like this on a ~~fine~~ ^**golden-fine**^ morning and wonder what surprise packet the day will ~~bring~~ ^**hand**^ you. I always ~~day-dream~~ ^**day-dream**^ for ten minutes before I get up, imagining the heaps of splendid things that may happen before night."

"I hope ~~to-days news~~ something very unexpected will happen today," said ~~Miss Oliver~~ ^**Gertrude**^. "I hope the mail will bring us news that war has been averted between Germany and France."

"Oh – yes," said Rilla vaguely. "It ~~would~~ ^**will**^ be dreadful if it isn't, I suppose. But it won't really matter much to us, ^**will it?**^ I think a war would be so exciting. The Boer war was, they say, but I don't remember anything about it, of course. Miss Oliver, shall I wear my white dress to-night or my ~~pale~~ ^**new**^ green one? The green one is by far the ~~prettiest~~ ^**prettier**^, of course, but I'm almost afraid to ~~put it on~~ ^**wear it**^ to a shore dance for fear something will happen to it. And will you ~~fix~~ ^**do**^ my hair ~~for me~~ the new way? None of the other girls in the Glen ~~wear have~~ wear it ~~^**that**^~~ yet and it will make such a sensation."

"How did you induce your mother to let you go to the dance?"

"Oh, Walter coaxed her over. He knew I would be heart-broken if I didn't go. It's my first really-truly grown-up party, Miss Oliver, and I've just lain awake at nights for a week thinking it over. When I saw the sun shining this morning I wanted to ~~sing~~ ^**whoop**^ for joy. It would ~~have been~~ ^be^ simply terrible if it rained tonight. I think I'll wear the green dress and risk it. I want to look my nicest at my first ~~real~~ party. Besides, it's an inch longer than my white one. And I'll wear my silver slippers ~~with them.~~ too. ~~^**I've never had**^~~ ^**Note E2**^ Oh, Miss Oliver, I do hope some of the boys will ask me to dance. I shall die of mortification – truly I will – if ~~nb~~ nobody does and I have to sit stuck up against the wall all the evening. Of course Carl and Jerry ~~will but they're just like my brothers and I'll feel they're only doing it out of charity.~~ ^**can't dance, because they're the minister's sons, or else I could depend on them to save me from utter disgrace."**^

"You'll have plenty of partners – all the over-harbor boys are coming~~." and~~ – ^**there'll be far more boys than girls."**^

"I'm glad I'm not a minister's daughter," laughed Rilla. "Poor Faith is so furious because she ~~can't danc~~ won't dare to dance to-night. Una doesn't care, of course. She ^**has**^ never ~~wanted~~ ^**hankered after**^ ~~to~~ danceing. Somebody told Faith there would be a taffy pull in the kitchen for those who didn't dance and you should have seen the face she made. She and Jem will sit out on the rocks most of the evening, I suppose. ~~They're~~ Did you know that we are all to walk down as far as that little creek below the old House of Dreams and then sail to the lighthouse? Won't it just be absolutely divine?"

"When I was fifteen I talked in italics and superlatives too," said Miss Oliver ^**sarcastically**^. "I think the party promises to be pleasant ^~~**for young fry**~~ **for young fry.**^ I expect to be bored. None of those ~~young lads~~ ^**boys**^ will bother dancing with an old maid like me. Jem and ~~Jerry~~ ^**Walter**^ will take me out once out of charity. There will be nobody for me even to talk to.[22] So you can't expect me to look forward to it with your touching young rapture."

"Didn't you have a good time at your first party, though, Miss Oliver?"

"No. I had a hateful time. I was shabby and homely and nobody asked me to dance except one boy, homelier and shabbier than myself.

He was so awkward I hated him – and even he didn’t ask me again. I had no real girlhood, Rilla. It’s a sad loss. That’s why I want you to have a splendid, happy girlhood. And I hope your first party will be one you’ll remember all your life with pleasure.” ^**Note W.**^

There had been an undercurrent of tension in the Ingleside ~~life~~ ^**existence**^ for several days. Only Rilla ~~^**and Susan**^~~, absorbed in her own ~~hopes and dreams~~ ^**budding life**^, was unaware of it. Dr. Blythe had taken to looking grave and saying little over the daily paper. Jem and Walter were keenly interested in the news it brought. ~~To-day~~ Jem sought Walter out in excitement that evening.

^**“Oh, boy,**^ Germany has declared war on France!~~,” boy.~~ This means that England will fight too, probably – and if she does – well, the Piper of your old fancy will ^**have**^ come at last.”

“It wasn’t a fancy,” said Walter slowly. “It was a presentiment – a vision – Jem, I really <u>saw</u> him for a moment that evening long-ago.~~”~~ Suppose England does fight?”

“Why, we’ll all have to ~~go to her again~~ ^**turn in and help her**^,” cried Jem gaily. “We couldn’t let the ‘old gray mother of the northern sea’ fight it out alone, could we? But ~~you’ll be out of the ^**you can’t go could can’t go**^~~ ^**you can’t go –**^ the typhoid has done you out of that. Sort of a shame, eh?”

Walter did not say whether it was a shame or not. He looked ~~gravely~~ silently over the Glen to the dimpling blue harbor beyond.

“We’re the cubs – we’ve got to ~~join~~ pitch in tooth and claw if it comes to a family row,” Jem went on cheerfully, rumpling up his red curls with a ~~long~~ ^**strong**^, lean, ^**sensitive**^ brown hand – the hand of the born surgeon, his father often thought. “What an adventure it would be! But I suppose ~~Grey~~ ^**Grey**^ or some of those wary old chaps will patch matters up at the eleventh hour. It’ll be a rotten shame if they leave France in the lurch, though. If they don’t, we’ll see some fun.” ^**Well, I suppose it’s time to get ready for the ~~light house spree~~ ^^spree at the light.”**^^^

Jem departed whistling “Wi’ a hundred pipers and a’ and a’,” and Walter stood for a long time where he was. There was a little ~~for~~ frown on his forehead. This ~~thing had come ^**had all**^~~ ^**had all come**^ up with the blackness and suddenness of a thundercloud. A few days ago nobody had even thought of such a thing. It was absurd to think of it now. Some way out would be found. War was a hellish, horrible, hideous thing – too horrible and hideous to happen in the ~~20th~~ ^**twentieth**^ century ~~between~~ ^**between**^ civilized nations. The ~~very~~ ^~~**mere**~~ **mere**^ thought of it was hideous, and made Walter unhappy in its threat to the ~~loveliness~~ beauty of life. He would <u>not</u> think of it – he would resolutely put it out of his mind. ~~Nobody would expect him to go, anyhow the typhoid had seen to that. Through the open window~~ How beautiful the old Glen was, in its August ripeness. ^**Note X**^1 The western sky was ~~^**yel**^~~ like a great golden pearl. Far down the harbor was ~~silvered~~ ^**frosted**^ with a ~~rising~~ dawning moonlight. The air was full of exquisite sounds – sleepy robin whistles, wonderful, mournful, soft ~~sounds~~ ^**murmurs**^ of wind in the twilit trees, ^**Note Y**^ ~~be such~~ lilting ^**young**^ laughter from the windows of rooms were the girls were making ready for the dance. ^**The world was steeped in maddening loveliness of sound and color.** ^ ^**Note D10**^

"Anyhow, no one will expect me to go," ^**he**^ thought ~~Walter~~. "^**As Jem says,**^ ~~The~~ typhoid has seen to that."

Rilla ~~leaned~~ ^**was leaning**^ out of her room window, ~~all~~ dressed for the dance. A yellow pansy slipped from her hair and fell out over the sill like a falling star of gold. She caught at it vainly – but there ~~was~~ ^**were**^ enough left. Miss Oliver had woven a little wreath of them for her pet's hair.

~~"It's clam.~~ "It's so beautifully calm – isn't that splendid? We'll have a perfect night. Listen, Miss Oliver – I can hear those old bells in Rainbow Valley quite clearly. They've been hanging there for over ten years."

~~"It always~~ "Their ~~chime~~ wind chime always makes me think of the aerial, ~~cel~~ celestial music Adam and Eve ~~used to hear~~ ^**heard**^ in ~~the Garden of~~ ^**Milton's**^ Eden ~~– according to Milton~~," ~~said~~ ^**responded**^ Miss Oliver.

"We used to have such fun in Rainbow Valley when we were children," said Rilla dreamily.

Nobody ever played in Rainbow Valley now. It was very silent on summer evenings. Walter liked to go there to read. ~~Jerry~~ Jem and Faith trysted there considerably; Jerry and Nan went there to ~~carry on~~ ^**pur-**

sue^ uninterruptedly the ceaseless wrangles and arguments on profound subjects that seemed to be their ^~~**preferred**~~ **preferred**^ method of sweethearting. And Rilla had a ^**beloved**^ little ~~nook~~ ^**sylvan dell**^ of her own there where she liked to sit and dream. ~~^**Alone or hold**^ She had always gone there to read the sentimental notes Tom Howard used to write her in schooldays when they were both twelve~~

long conversations with too over for

“I must run down to the kitchen before I go and show myself off to Susan. She would never forgive me if I didn’t.”

Rilla whirled into the shadowy kitchen at Ingleside, where Susan was prosaically darning socks, and lighted it up with her beauty. She wore her green dress with its little ~~pink~~ ^**pink daisy**^ garlands, her silk stockings and silver slippers. She had golden pansies in her hair and at her creamy throat. She was so pretty and young and glowing that even Cousin ~~Caroline~~ ^**Sophia**^ Crawford was compelled to admire her ^**– and Cousin** ~~Caroline~~ ^**Sophia**^ ^**Crawford admired few transient earthly things.**^ Cousin ~~Caroline and~~ ~~Caroline~~ ^**Sophia**^ and Susan had made up, or ignored, their old feud since the former had come to live in the Glen, and Cousin ~~Caroline~~ ^**Sophia**^ often came across in the evenings to ~~talk a w~~ make a neighborly call. Susan did not always welcome her rapturously for Cousin ~~Caroline~~ ^**Sophia**^ was not what could be called ~~a cheerful companion~~ ^**an exhilarating companion**^.

“Some ~~things~~ calls are visits and some are visitations, Mrs. Dr. dear,” Susan said once, and left it to be inferred that Cousin ~~Caroline’s~~ ^**Sophia’s**^ were the latter.

Cousin ~~Caroline Caroline~~ ^**Sophia**^ had a long, pale, wrinkled face ^[*Note*] **Y1**^ ~~and ^**very**^ long pale black hands, generally folded ^**resignedly on**^ across her cal black calico lap.~~ She looked mournfully ~~on~~ ^**upon**^ Rilla Blythe and said sadly,

“Is your hair all your own?”

“Of course it is,” cried Rilla indignantly.

“~~O~~Ah, well!” Cousin Sophia sighed. “It might be better for you if it wasn’t! Such a lot of hair takes from a person’s strength. It’s a sign of consumption, I’ve heard, but I hope it won’t turn out like that in your case. ^[*Note*] **B2**^ You ain’t a-going off like that with nothing on your bare neck, are you?”

"It's a hot evening," protested Rilla. "But I ~~have~~ ^**'ll put on**^ a scarf when we go on the water."

"I knew of a boat load of young folks who went sailing on that harbour forty years ago just such a night as this ^**Note ~~C1~~ C1**^" said Cousin Sophia lugubriously, "and they were upset and drowned – every last one of them. I hope nothing like that'll happen to you to-night. Do you ever try anything for the freckles?~~"~~ I used to find plantain juice real good."

"You ^**certainly**^ should be a judge of freckles, Cousin Sophia," said Susan, rushing to Rilla's defence. "You were more speckled than any toad when you was a girl. Rilla's only come in summer but yours stayed put, season in and season out; and you had not a ground colour like hers behind them neither. You look real nice, Rilla, and that way of fixing your hair is ~~real~~ becoming. But you are not going to walk to the harbor in those slippers, are you?"

"Oh, no. We'll all wear our old shoes to the harbor and carry our slippers. Do you like my dress, Susan?"

"It minds me of a dress I wore when I was a girl," sighed Cousin Sophia ^**before Susan could reply**^. "It was green with pink posies on it ^**, too.**^ ^**Note U**^ I tore a big hole in it that night and someone spilled a cup of tea all over it. ~~Ah well,~~ ^**Ruined it completely.**^ ^**But**^ I hope nothing will happen to your dress. It orter to be a bit longer I'm thinking – your legs are so terrible ~~thin."~~ ^**long and thin**^."

"Mrs. Dr. Blythe does not approve of little girls dressing like grown-up ones," said Susan stiffly, intending ^**merely**^ a snub to Cousin Sophia. But Rilla felt insulted. A little girl indeed! She whisked out of the kitchen in high dudgeon. Another time she wouldn't go down to show herself off to Susan – Susan, who thought nobody was grown up until she was sixty! And that horrid ~~old~~ Cousin Sophia with her ~~freckles~~ digs about freckles and legs! ~~^Z1^~~ ^**Note Z1**^ Rilla felt all her pleasure in herself and her evening clouded and spoiled. ^**The very teeth of her ~~soul spirit~~ soul were set on edge and**^ ~~S~~she could have sat down and cried.

But later on her spirits rose again, when she found herself one of ~~a~~ ^**the**^ gay crowd ~~walking down the old habor road. The Blythes picked up~~ ^**bound for the Four Winds light.**^ ^**Note A1**^– the Merediths in the village, and others joined ~~their~~ them as they walked down the old harbor road. Mary Vance ^**Note D1**^ came out of Miss Cornelia's gate and attached herself to Rilla and Miss Oliver who were walking together and who did not welcome her over warmly. Rilla was not very fond of Mary Vance. She had never forgotten the humiliating day when Mary had chased her through the village with a dried codfish. Mary Vance, to tell the truth, was not exactly popular with any of her set. Still, ~~the most of them~~ ^**they**^ enjoyed her society – she had such a biting ~~voracious~~ tongue that it was stimulating. "Mary Vance is a habit of ours – we can't do without her even when we are furious with her," Di Blythe had once said. ~~Most of Most of the~~

Most of the little crowd were paired off after a fashion. Jem walked with Faith Meredith, of course, and Jerry Meredith with Nan Blythe. Di and Walter were together, deep in confidential conversation which Rilla envied. ^**Note Z.**^ [*Note D2 is embedded in this Note.*]

Shirley Blythe was with Una Meredith and both were rather silent because such was their nature. Shirley ~~Blythe~~ was a lad of sixteen, sedate, sensible, ~~full of humor and quiet fun~~ ^**thoughtful, full of a quiet humor.**^ He was ~~always~~ Susan's "little brown boy" yet, with his brown hair, brown eyes, and clear brown skin. He liked to walk with Una Meredith because she ~~did not try~~ ^**never tried**^ to make him talk or badgered him with chatter. Una was as sweet and shy as she had been in the Rainbow Valley days, and her large, dark-blue eyes were as dreamy and wistful. She
[*Comment written on the back of page 37, then crossed out:*] ~~7. now with a lot of "repetitions" in it like this. I shall be contented if I can make~~ had a secret, carefully-hidden fancy for Walter Blythe which nobody but Rilla ever suspected. Rilla sympathized with it and wished Walter would return it. She liked Una ~~much~~ better than Faith, whose beauty and aplomb rather overshadowed other girls – and Rilla ~~hated to be~~ ^**did not enjoy being**^ overshadowed.

But just now she was very happy. It was so delightful to be tripping ~~down the habor road with the others.~~ with her friends down that dark, gleaming road sprinkled with its little ~~firs and spruces,~~ ^**spruces and firs, whose balsam made all the air resinous around them.**^ Meadows of sunset afterlight were behind the westerning hills. Before them was the shining harbor. A bell was ringing in the little church over harbor and the lingering ^**dream-**^ notes died around ^**the**^ dim, ~~amethystine~~ amethystine points. The gulf beyond was still silvery blue in the afterlight. Oh, it was all glorious – the clear air with its salt tang, the balsam of the firs, the laughter of her friends. ~~She was~~ Rilla loved life – its bloom and brilliance; she loved the ripple of music, the ~~hum~~ hum of merry conversation; she wanted to walk on forever over this road of silver and shadow. It was her ~~very~~ first ~~real~~ party and she was going to have a splendid time. There was nothing in the world to worry about – not even freckles and over-long legs – nothing except one little haunting fear that nobody would ask her to dance. ~~But that was too dreadful to happen.~~ It was ~~just~~ beautiful and satisfying ^**just**^ to be alive – to be fifteen – to be pretty. Rilla drew a long breath of rapture – and caught ~~what was Jem saying? He was~~ it midway rather sharply. Jem was telling some story to Faith – something that had happened in the Balkan War.

"The doctor lost both his legs – they were smashed to pulp – and he was left on the field to die. And he crawled about from man to man, to all the wounded men round him, ^**as long as he could,**^ and did everything ~~he could~~ ^**possible**^ to relieve their sufferings – never thinking of himself – he was tying a bit of bandage round another man's ~~arm~~ ^**leg**^ when he ~~died himself. What~~ ^**went under.** ^ ~~– and t~~They found them there ~~and~~ – the doctor's dead hands still held the bandage tight – ~~and~~ the bleeding was stopped and the other man's life was saved. Some ~~hero~~ ^**hero**^, wasn't he, Faith? I tell you when I read that –"

Jem and Faith moved on out of hearing. Gertrude Oliver suddenly shivered. Rilla pressed her arm sympathetically.

"Wasn't it dreadful, Miss Oliver? I don't wonder it made you shiver. I don't know why Jem tells such gruesome things at a time like this when we're all out for ~~a joll~~ fun."

~~"Did you~~ "Do you think it dreadful, Rilla? I thought it wonderful – beautiful. Such a ~~thing~~ story makes one ashamed of ever doubting human nature. That man's action was god-like. And how humanity responds to the ideal of self-sacrifice! As for my shiver, I don't know what caused it. ~~I'm cert~~ The evening is certainly warm enough. Perhaps someone is walking over the dark, starshiny spot that is to be my grave. That is the explanation the old superstition would give. ^**Note B1**^ ~~Here we are at the old House of Dreams! It seems lonely this summer. The Fords didn’t come?~~

“No – at least Mr. and Mrs. Ford and Persis didn’t. ~~Selwyn~~ ^**Kenneth**^ did – but he stayed with his mother’s people over-harbor. We ~~didn’t~~ ^**haven’t**^ ~~see a~~ ^**seen**^ great deal of him this summer. He’s a little lame and so didn’t go about very much.”

“Lame? What happened to him?”

“He broke his ankle in a football game last fall and was laid up most of the winter. He has limped a little ever since but it is getting better all the time and he expects it will be ~~perfectly~~ all right before long. He has been up to Ingleside only twice.”

~~“They say he’s going with Ethel Reese,” said Mary Vance.~~

“Ethel Reese is ^**simply**^ crazy about him,” said Mary Vance. “^**Note F1**^ He walked home with her from the over-harbor church last prayer meeting night and the airs she has put on since would really ~~give you~~ make you weary of life.~~”~~ ^[*Note*] **G1**^

Rilla flushed. It did not matter to her if ~~Selwyn~~ ^**Kenneth**^ Ford walked home with Ethel Reese a dozen times – it did not! ^**Note E1**^ she ~~hated~~ ^**detested**^ Ethel Reese and Ethel Reese hated her ^[*Note*] **H1**^ ~~always had hated her since Walter had and Dan had fought Rainbow Valley days ^[*Note*] **H1**^~~ As for Mary Vance, she was getting to be an out-and-out gossip and thought of nothing but who walked home with people!

There was a little pier ~~below~~ on the harbor shore below the House of Dreams, and two boats were ~~anchored~~ ^**moored**^ there. ~~The gay party got on b… . Jem Blythe skippered one and Joe Milgrave the other.~~ One boat was skippered by Jem Blythe, the other by Joe Milgrave, who knew all about boats and was nothing loth to let ~~Jennie~~ ^**Miranda**^ Pryor ~~know~~ ^**see**^ it. They raced down the harbor and Joe’s boat won. More boats were coming ^**down from the Harbor Head and**^ across the harbor from the ~~other~~ ^**western**^ side. Everywhere there was laughter. The ~~high~~ big ~~light house~~ ^**white**^ tower on Four Winds Point was overflowing with light, while its revolving beacon flashed overhead. A family from Charlottetown, ^**relatives of the ~~light~~ light’s keeper,**^ were ~~summering~~ ^**summering**^ at the light, ~~and~~ and they were giving the party to which all the young people of Four Winds and Glen St. Mary and over-harbor had been invited. As ~~the~~ Jem's boat swung in below the light house Rilla desperately ~~sn~~ snatched off her shoes and donned her silver slippers ^**behind Miss Oliver's screening back**^. A glance had told her that the rock-cut steps climbing up to the light were lined with boys, ^**and lighted by Chinese lanterns,**^ and she was determined she would not walk up those steps ~~without~~ in the heavy shoes her mother had insisted on her wearing for the road. The slippers pinched ~~terribly~~ ^**abominably**^, but nobody would have suspected it as Rilla tripped smilingly up the steps, ~~How lovely everything was! The lanterns the~~, her soft dark eyes glowing and questioning, her colour deepening ^**richly**^ on her round, creamy cheeks. The very minute she reached the top of the steps an over-harbor boy asked her to dance and the next moment they were in the pavilion that had been built seaward of the light house ^**for the dancers**^. It was a ~~fairy~~ ^**delightful**^ spot, roofed over with ~~maple~~ fir boughs and hung with lanterns. Beyond was the ~~great glimmering radiant sea, and the moonlit crests and hall~~ ^**sea in a radiance that glowed and shimmered,**^ to the left the moonlit crests and hollows of the sand-dunes, to the right the rock shore with its inky shadows and its ~~shining~~ ^**crystalline**^ coves. Rilla and her partner swung in among the dancers; she drew a long breath of delight; what witching music ~~Jed~~ Ned Burr of the Upper Glen was coaxing from his fiddle ^[*Note*] **Y4**^ How cool and fresh the ~~sea-br~~ gulf breeze blew; how white and wonderful the moonlight was over everything. This was life – enchanting life. Rilla felt – as if her feet and her soul both had wings.

Chapter 4

The Piper Pipes

Rilla's first party was a triumph. ^[*Note*] **F2**^ She had so many partners that she had to split her dances. Her silver slippers seemed verily to dance of themselves and though they continued to pinch her toes and blister her heels that did not interfere with her enjoyment in the least. Ethel Reese gave her a bad ten minutes by beckoning her mysteriously out of the pavilion and whispering, ^**with a Reese-like smirk,**^ that her dress gaped behind and that there was a stain on the flounce. Rilla rushed miserably to the room in the light house which was fitted up for a ^**temporary**^ ladies' dressing ^**room,**^ and discovered that the stain was merely a tiny grass smear and that the gap was equally tiny where a hook had pulled loose. Irene Howard ~~pinned~~ ^**fastened**^ it up for her and ~~paid her~~ gave her some ~~sweet~~ ^**over-sweet**^, condescending compliments. Rilla felt flattered by Irene's condescension ~~for she thought Irene very wonderful~~. She was an Upper Glen girl of nineteen who seemed to like the society of the younger girls – spiteful friends said because she could ~~pose and~~ queen it over them without ~~let or hindrance~~ ^**rivalry**^. But Rilla thought Irene quite wonderful and loved her for her ~~condes~~ patronage. Irene was pretty ^**and**^ stylish; ~~and as b~~ she sang divinely and spent every winter in Charlottetown taking music lessons. She had an aunt in Montreal who sent her wonderful things to wear; she was reported to have had a sad love affair – nobody knew just what, but its very mystery allured. Rilla felt that Irene's compliments crowned her evening. She ran ^**gaily**^ back to the pavilion~~; and as she went up the ^**its**^ steps~~ and lingered for a moment in the glow of the lanterns at the entrance ~~A~~ looking at the dancers. A momentary ~~space~~ ^**break**^ in the whirling throng gave her a glimpse of ~~Selwyn~~ ^**Kenneth**^ Ford standing at the other side.

Rilla's heart skipped a beat ^**Note G2**^ So he was here, after all. She had concluded he was not coming – not that it mattered ~~at all~~ ^**in the least**^. Would he see her? Would he take any notice of her? Of course, he wouldn't ask her to dance – ~~the~~ that couldn't be hoped for.

He thought her just a mere child. He had called her "Spider" not three weeks ago when he had ~~called one evening at~~ ^**been at**^ Ingleside ^**one evening**^. She had cried about it afterwards upstairs and hated him. But her heart skipped a beat when she saw that he was edging his way round the side of the pavilion towards her. Was he coming to her – was he? – was he? – yes, he was! He was looking for her – he was here beside her – he was gazing down at her with something in his ^**dark-gray**^ eyes that Rilla had never ^**seen**^ in them~~ before~~. Oh, it was almost too much to bear! And everything was going on as before – the dancers were spinning around, the boys who couldn't get partners were hanging ~~around~~ ^**about**^ the pavilion, canoodling couples were sitting out on the rocks – nobody seemed to realize what a stupendous thing had happened.

~~Selwyn~~ ^**Kenneth**^ was a tall lad, very good-looking, ^[*Note*] **J1**^ ~~and supposed to know reported ^**reported**^ to be awesomely clearer ^**Note J1**^ ^[*Note*] **J1**^~~ He had ^**also**^ the reputation of being a bit of a lady-killer. ~~Ethel Reese had said publicly that he was "so dashing and citified."~~ But that probably accrued to him from his possession of a laughing, velvety voice which no girl could hear without a heartbeat, and a dangerous way of listening as if she were saying something that he had longed all his life to hear. ~~There was a careless grace of bearing about him that made all the other boys seem awkward and stiff by contrast. Rilla suddenly wondered.~~

"Is this Rilla-my-Rilla?" he asked in a low tone.

"Yeth," said Rilla – and immediately wished she could throw herself headlong down the light house rock or otherwise vanish from a jeering world.

Rilla had lisped in early childhood; but she had grown out of it pretty thoroughly. Only on occasions of stress and strain did the tendency re-assert itself. She hadn't lisped for a year; and now at this very moment, when she was so especially desirous of appearing grown-up and sophisticated, she must go and lisp like a baby! It was too mortifying; she felt as if tears were going to come into her eyes; the next minute she would be – blubbering – yes, just blubbering. She wished ~~Selwyn~~ ^**Kenneth**^ would go away – she wished he had never come. ~~Everything seemed to turn to dust and ashes. Selwyn would laugh at her.~~ The party was spoiled. Everything had turned to dust and ashes.

And he had called her ~~by Walter's pet-name~~ ^**"Rilla-my-Rilla"**^ – not "Spider" ^**Note T1**^ [*Note H2 is embedded in this Note.*] – ~~or "Miss Rilla," or anything formal or mocking!~~ It would have been so nice if she had not made a fool of herself. She dared not look up lest she should see laughter in his eyes. So she looked down; and as her lashes were very long and dark and her lids very ^**thick and**^ creamy, the effect was quite charming and provocative, and ~~Selwyn~~ ^**Kenneth**^ reflected that Rilla Blythe was going to be the beauty of the Ingleside girls after all. ~~She had been a little girl the other~~ He wanted to make her look up – to catch again that little, demure, questioning glance. She was the prettiest thing at the ~~dance~~ ^**party**^, there was no doubt of that.

What was he saying? Rilla could hardly believe her ears.

"Can we have a dance? ~~I think this game ankle of mine will stand for one hop now.~~"

"Yes," said Rilla. She said it with such a fierce determination not to lisp ~~again~~ that she fairly ~~snapped~~ ^**blurted**^ the word out. Then she writhed in spirit again. It sounded so bold – so eager– as if she were fairly jumping at him! What would he think of her? Oh, why did dreadful things like this happen, just when a girl wanted to appear at her best?

~~Selwyn~~ ^**Kenneth**^ drew her in among the dancers. "I think this game ankle of mine is good for one hop round,~~" he said, "though I have~~ at least," he said.

"How is your ankle?" said Rilla. Oh, why couldn't she think of something ^**else**^ to say? She knew he was sick of inquiries about his ankle. She had heard him say so at Ingleside – heard him tell Di he was going to wear a placard ~~round his neck~~ on his breast announcing to all and sundry that the ankle was improving, ^**etc. etc.**^ And now she must go and ~~make~~ ^**ask**^ this ~~banal~~ ^**stale**^ question again.

~~Selwyn~~ ^**Kenneth**^ was tired of inquiries about his ankle. But then he had not often been asked about it by ~~a m~~ lips with such an adorable ^**kissable**^ dent just above them. Perhaps that was why he answered very ~~pait~~ patiently that it was getting on well and didn't trouble him much, ~~as long as~~ ^**if**^ he didn't walk or stand too long at a time.

"They tell me it will be as strong as ever in time, but I'll have to cut football out this fall."

They danced together ~~and then they went down the rock steps and~~ and Rilla knew every girl in sight envied her. After the dance they went down the rock steps and ~~Selwyn~~ ^**Kenneth**^ found a little flat and they rowed across the moonlit channel to the sandshore; they walked on the sand till ~~Selwyn's~~ ^**Kenneth's**^ ankle made protest and then they sat down among the dunes. ~~Selwyn~~ ^**Kenneth**^ talked to her as he ^**had**^ talked to Nan and Di. Rilla, ~~was~~ overcome with a shyness she did not understand, ~~and~~ could not talk much, and thought he would think her frightfully stupid; but in spite of this it was all very wonderful – the exquisite moonlit night, the shining sea, the tiny little wavelets swishing on the sand ^**Note Q1**^, the music sounding faintly and sweetly over the channel. ^**Note L1**^

And just he and she alone together in the glamour of sound and sight! ^[*Note*] **K1**^ ~~I~~if she could ~~only~~ talk cleverly like Miss Oliver – nay, if she could only talk as she did herself to other boys! But ~~no~~ words would not come; she could only listen and murmur little ~~sentences~~ commonplace sentences now and again. But perhaps her dreamy eyes and her dented lip and her slender throat talked eloquently for her. At any rate ~~Selwyn~~ ^**Kenneth**^ seemed in no hurry to suggest going back; and when they did go back supper was in progress. He found a seat for her near the window of the light house kitchen and sat on the sill beside her while she ate her ~~^**salad and**^~~ ices and cake. Rilla looked about her and thought how perfectly lovely her first party had been. She would <u>never</u> forget it. The room re-echoed to laughter and jest. ^**Note J2**^ From the pavilion outside came the lilt of the fiddle and the rhythmic ~~foot steps of the~~ steps of the dancers. ~~Tro Through the window they~~

There was a little disturbance among a group of boys crowded about the door; a young fellow pushed through and halted on the threshold, looking about him rather ~~sombrely~~ ^**sombrely**^. It was Jack ~~Mr.~~ Elliott from over harbor~~, a McGill the medical student home for vacation was a McGill medical student and~~ – a McGill medical student, a quiet chap not much addicted to ~~society~~ social doings. He had been invited to the party but had not been expected to come, since ~~it was necessary that he should~~ ^**he had to**^ go to Charlottetown that day and could not be back until late. Yet here he was – and he carried a folded paper in his hand.

Gertrude Oliver looked at him from her corner and shivered again. She had ~~my~~ enjoyed the party herself, after all, for she had foregathered with a Charlottetown acquaintance who, being a stranger and much older than most of the guests, felt himself rather out of it, and had been glad to fall in with this clever girl who could talk of world doings and outside events with the zest and vigour of a man. In the pleasure of his society she had forgotten some of her ~~subs~~ misgivings of the day. Now they suddenly returned to her. What news did Jack Elliott bring? ~~Verses of~~ ^**Lines from**^ an old poem ~~crowded~~ ^**flashed**^ unbidden into her mind – "there was a sound of revelry by night" – ^**Note M1**^ why should she think of that ~~no~~ now? Why didn't Jack Elliott speak – if he had anything to tell? ^**Why did he just stand there, glowering importantly?**^

"Ask him – ask him," she said feverishly to ~~her companion~~ ^**Allan Daly**^. But somebody else had already asked him. The room grew very silent all at once. ~~– only the dancing and the music still went on without~~ Outside the fiddler had stopped for a rest and there was silence there, too. Afar off they heard the low moan of the gulf – the presage of a storm already on its way ^**up the Atlantic.**^ A girl's laugh drifted up from the rocks and died away as if frightened ^**out of existence**^ by the sudden stillness.

"England declared war on Germany to-day," said Jack Elliott slowly. "The news came by wire just as I left town."

"God help us," whispered Gertrude Oliver under her breath. ^**Note N1**^

A chorus of exclamations ~~arose~~ ^**had arisen round them –**^ light surprise or ^**idle**^ interest for the most part. Few there realized the import of the message – fewer still realized that it meant anything to them. ~~In a few minutes~~ ^**Before long**^ the dancing was on again and the ~~buzz~~ ^**hum**^ of ~~talk~~ ^**pleasure**^ was as loud as ever. Gertrude and Allan Daly talked the news over in low, troubled tones. Walter Blythe had turned pale and left the room. Outside he met Jem, hurrying up the rock steps.

~~"The~~ "Have you heard the news, Jem?"

"Yes. The Piper has come. Hurrah! I knew England wouldn't leave France in the lurch. ^**Note O1**^ ~~I'm going to get Captain McAlister to~~

~~hoist the flag.~~ Jack says they'll be calling for volunteers to-morrow."

"What a fuss to make over nothing," said Mary Vance disdainfully as Jem dashed off. She was sitting out with Miller Douglas on a lobster trap which was ~~both an uncomfortable and unromantic seat.~~ ^**not only an unromantic but an uncomfortable seat.**^ But Mary and Miller were both ~~very~~ ^**supremely**^ happy on it, which was the main thing. Miller Douglas was a big, strapping, uncouth lad, who thought Mary Vance's tongue uncommonly gifted and Mary Vance's white eyes stars of the first magnitude; and neither of them had the least inkling why Jem Meredith wanted to hoist the light house flag. "What does it matter if there's going to be a war over there in Europe? I'm sure it doesn't concern us."

Walter looked at her and had one of his odd visitations of prophecy.

"Before this war is over," he said – or something said through his lips – "every man and woman and child ^**in Canada**^ will feel it – you, Mary, will feel it – feel it to your heart's core. You will weep tears of blood over it. ~~Some of us will~~ The Piper has come – and he will pipe until every corner of the world has heard his awful ^**and irresistible music.**^ It will be years before the dance of death is over – years, Mary. And in those years ~~millions of lives will go out~~ millions of hearts will break."

"Fancy now!" said Mary ^**Note P1**^. She didn't know what Walter meant but she felt ~~very~~ uncomfortable. Walter Blythe was always saying odd things. That old Piper of his – she hadn't heard anything about him since their play-days in Rainbow Valley – and now ~~Walter was bringing him up~~ ^**here he was bobbing up**^ again. She didn't like it, that was the long and short of it, and she wasn't going to listen to such nonsense.

"Aren't you painting it rather strong, Walter?" asked ~~Laurie~~ ^**Harvey Crawford**^; coming up just then. "This war won't last for years – it'll be over ~~in a before Christmas~~ ^**in a month or two**^. England will ~~just~~ wipe Germany off the map in no time."

"Do you think a war for which Germany has been preparing for twenty years will be over in a few weeks?" said Walter passionately. "This isn't a ~~petty~~ paltry struggle in a Balkan corner, Harvey. It is a death grapple. Germany comes to conquer or to die. And do you know what will happen if she conquers? ~~Canda~~ Canada will be a German colony."

"Well, I guess a few things will happen before that," said Harvey shrugging his shoulders. ~~"Miller ^here, now^ and I here and I, we'd raise a dust, wouldn't we.~~ "The British navy would have to be licked ^**for one ~~thing~~;**^ and ^**for another,**^ Miller here, now, and I, we'd raise a dust, wouldn't we, Miller? No Germans need apply for this old country, eh?"

Harvey ran down the steps laughing.

"I declare, I think all you boys talk the craziest stuff," said Mary Vance ~~angrily~~ in disgust. She got up and dragged Miller off to the rock shore. It didn't happen ~~so~~ often that they had a chance for a talk together; Mary was determined that this one shouldn't be spoiled by Walter Blythe's silly ~~talk~~ ^**blather**^ about Pipers and Germans and ^**such like**^ ~~other unthink~~ absurd things. They left Walter standing alone on the rock steps, ~~^**The best of the**^~~ looking out over the beauty of Four Winds with ^**brooding**^ eyes that saw it not.

The best of the evening was over for Rilla, too. Ever since Jack Elliott's announcement, she had sensed that ~~Selwyn~~ ^**Kenneth**^ was no longer thinking about her. She felt ^**suddenly**^ lonely and unhappy. It was worse than if he had never noticed her at all. Was life like this – something delightful happening and then, just as you were revelling in it, ~~being snatched~~ ^**slipping**^ away from you? Rilla told herself pathetically that she felt ~~ages~~ ^**years**^ older than when she had left home that evening. Perhaps she did – perhaps she was. Who knows? It does not do to laugh at the pangs of youth. They are very terrible because ~~we have~~ ^**youth has**^ not ^**yet**^ learned ~~how to endure pain~~, ^**that "this, too, will pass away."**^ Rilla sighed and wished she were home, in bed, crying into her pillow.

"Tired?" said ~~Selwyn~~ ^**Kenneth**^, ~~sympa~~ gently but absently – oh, so absently. He really didn't care a bit if she were tired or not, she thought.

"~~Selwyn~~ ^**Kenneth,**^" she ventured timidly, "you don't think this war will matter much to us in Canada, do you?"

"Matter? Of course it will matter to the lucky fellows who will be able to take a hand. I won't – thanks to this confounded ankle. Rotten luck, I call it."

"I don't see why we should fight England's battles," cried Rilla.

"She's quite able to fight them herself."

"That isn't the point. We are part of the British Empire. It's a family affair. ~~If somebody attacked a fellow's mother do you think he'd~~ We've got to stand by each other. The worst ~~is it~~ ^**of it is, it**^ will be over before I can be of any use." ~~And I was worrying about being out of football this fall!"~~

"Do you mean that you would really volunteer to go if it wasn't for your ankle?" asked Rilla incredulously. The idea seemed so – so ~~s ri-due~~ ridiculous. ~~This slim lad a soldier!~~

"Sure I would. You see they'll go by thousands. Jem'll be off, I'll bet a cent – Walter won't be strong enough yet I suppose. And Jerry Meredith – he'll go! Oh, boys! And I was worrying ~~because~~ about being out of football this year!"

Rilla was too startled to say anything. Jem – and Jerry! Nonsense! Why father and Mr. Meredith wouldn't allow it. They weren't through college. Oh, why hadn't Jack Elliott kept his horrid news to ~~himself~~ ^**himself**^?

~~Kent~~ ^**Mark**^ Warren came up and asked her to dance. Rilla went, ~~because she knew~~ ^**knowing**^ ~~Selwyn~~ ^**Kenneth**^ didn't care whether she went or stayed. An hour ago on the sand shore he had been looking at her as if she were the only being of any importance in the world. And now she was nobody. His thoughts were full of this Great Game which was to be played out on blood-stained fields with empires for stakes – a Game in which womenkind could have no part. ~~Rilla~~ Women, thought ^**Rilla**^ miserably, ~~They ^**Women**^~~ just had to sit and cry at home. But all this was foolishness. ~~Selwyn~~ ^**Kenneth**^ couldn't go – he admitted that himself – and Walter couldn't – thank goodness for that – and Jem and Jerry would have more sense. She wouldn't worry – she would enjoy herself. But how awkward ~~Kent~~ ^**Mark**^ Warren was! How he bungled his steps! Why, for mercy's sake, did boys try to dance who didn't know the first thing about dancing; ^**and who had feet as big as boats?**^ There, he had bumped her into somebody! She would never dance with him again!

But she danced with others ~~until the party ended~~, ^**though**^ the zest was gone out of the performance and she ~~had began~~ ^**had begun**^ to realize that her slippers hurt her badly. ~~Selwyn~~ ^**Kenneth**^ seemed to have gone – at least nothing was to be seen of him. ~~She sat out the last dance with two dunces down on the rock shore with. During the, She sat out a dance down on the rock shore with~~ ^**After all, her ~~first~~ party was spoiled, though it had seemed so beautiful at one time. Her head ached – her toes burned. And worse was yet to come.**^ She had gone down with some over-harbor friends to the rock shore where they all lingered as dance after dance went on above them. It was cool and pleasant and they were ~~all~~ tired. Rilla sat silent, taking no part in the gay conversation. ~~The wind was blowing up and the gulf was beginning to rim in white-caps.~~ She was glad when someone called down that the over-harbor boats were leaving. A laughing scramble up the light house rock followed. ~~The dancing was. The crowd had thinned out.~~ A few couples still whirled about in the pavilion but the ~~criw~~ crowd had thinned out. Rilla looked about her for ~~some~~ the Glen group. She could not see one of them. She ran into the light house. Still, no sign of anybody. In dismay she ran to the rock steps, down which the over harbor guests were hurrying. She could see the boats below – where was Jem's – where was Joe's?

"Why, Rilla Blythe, I thought you'd gone home long ago," said Mary Vance, who was waving her scarf at a boat ~~for~~ skimming ~~across~~ ^**up**^ the channel, skippered by Miller Douglas.

"Where are the rest?" gasped Rilla.

"Why, they're gone – Jem went an hour ago ~~– Faith was tired of the doing thing~~ – Una had a headache. And the rest went with Joe about fifteen minutes ago. See – they're just going around Birch Point. ^**Note S1**^ [*Note E3 is embedded in this Note.*] ~~I thought you'd gone with them.~~ Where were you?"

"Down on the rocks with Jen and Mollie Crawford. Oh, why didn't they look for me?"

~~"I suppose each crowd thought you were in the other boat.~~ ^**"They did – but you couldn't be found. Then they concluded you must have gone in the other boat.**^ Don't worry. You can stay all night with me and we'll phone up to Ingleside where you are."

Rilla realized ~~in dismay~~ that there was nothing else to do. Her lips trembled and tears came into her eyes. She blinked savagely – she would not let Mary Vance see her crying. But to be forgotten like this!

To think nobody had thought it worth while to make sure where she was – not even Walter. Then she had a sudden ^**dismayed**^ recollection.

“My shoes,” she ~~gasped, in dismay~~ ^**exclaimed.**^ “I left them in the boat. ~~I can’t walk up Four Winds in these slip~~”

“Well, I never,” said Mary. “You’re the most thoughtless kid I ever saw. You’ll have to ask ~~some~~ ~~some of the Lumsons Lewisons~~ ^~~**Nora**~~ **Hazel Lewison**^ to lend ^**you**^ a pair of shoes.”

“I won’t,” cried Rilla, ^**who didn’t like the said Hazel,**^ “I’ll go barefoot first.”

Mary shrugged her shoulders.

“Just as you like. Pride must suffer pain. It’ll teach you to be more careful. Well, ^**let’s hike.”**^ ~~come along, I’m all ready.” I just waited to see Miller off.”~~

~~They slipped away~~ ~~and crossed the~~ ~~and Rilla managed to limp~~ ~~across the~~ ~~up the lane to the harbour road. She could go no further in those ^**detestable**^ slippers.~~ ^**Note V1**^ The pain simply could not be borne. She took them and her ^**dear**^ silk stockings off, and started barefoot. That was not pleasant either; her feet were very tender and the pebbles and ruts of the road hurt them. Her blistered heels smarted. But physical pain was almost forgotten in the sting ~~and smart~~ of her humiliation. This was a nice predicament! If ~~Selwyn~~ ^**Kenneth**^ Ford could see her now, limping along like ~~like one of the for over-harbor fishing village girls.~~ ^**a little girl with a stone bruise!**^ Oh, what a horrid way for her ^**lovely**^ party to end! She just had to cry – it was too terrible. Nobody cared for her – nobody bothered about her at all. ^**Note X1**^ She furtively wiped ~~cry~~ her tears away with her scarf – handkerchiefs seemed to have vanished like shoes! – but she could not help sniffling. Worse and worse!

“You’ve got a cold, I see,” said Mary. “You ought to have known you would, sitting down in the wind on ~~them~~ ^**those**^ rocks. ~~You’re not old are~~ ^**Your mother won’t let you go out again in a hurry I can tell you.**^ It’s certainly been something of a party. The Lewisons know how to do things, I’ll say that for them, though ~~Nora~~ ^**Hazel**^ Lewison is no choice of mine. ~~I saw you dancing once with Selwyn Ford.~~ My, how black she looked when she saw you dancing with ~~Selwyn~~ ^**Ken**^

Ford. ^**Note A32**^ What a flirt he is!”

“I don’t think he’s a flirt,” said Rilla, ~~between into desperate sniffs~~ as defiantly as two desperate sniffs would let her.

“Ah well, you’ll know more about men when you’re as old as I am,” said Mary patronizingly. “Mind you, it doesn’t do to believe all they tell you. Don’t let ~~Selwyn~~ ^**Ken**^ Ford think that all he has to do ^**to get you on a string**^ is to drop his handkerchief. ^**Have more spirit than that, child.**^”

To be thus hectored ^**and patronized**^ by Mary Vance was unendurable! And it was unendurable to walk on stony roads with blistered heels ^**and bare feet!**^ And it was unendurable to be crying and have no handkerchief and not to be able to stop crying!

“I’m not thinking” – sniff – “about ~~Selwyn~~ ^**Kenneth**^” – sniff – “Ford” ~~at all,” cried tortured Rilla – two sniffs –~~ ^– “ **two sniffs –at all,”**^ cried tortured Rilla.

~~“Well, don’t fly off the handle now,~~ ^**“There’s no need to fly off the handle,**^ child. ~~I just thought you might a word of warning~~ You ought to be willing to take advice from older people. I saw how you slipped over to the sands with ~~Selwyn~~ ^**Ken**^ and stayed there ~~an hour~~ ^**ever so long**^ with him. Your mother wouldn’t like it if she knew.” ~~You should wait till you’re grown.~~ ^**Note W1**^

~~“You sat” – sniff – “for hours” – sniff – “with Miller Douglas” – sniff – “on that lobster trap~~

~~“You sat for hours with Miller Douglas, on that lobster trap,” Rilla gasped between sniffs. “What would Miss Cornelia say if she knew?”~~

“Oh, I’m not going to quarrel with you,” said Mary, suddenly retreating to high and lofty ground. “All I say is, you should wait until you’re grown up before you do things like that.”

Rilla gave up trying to hide the fact that she was crying. Everything was spoiled – even that beautiful, dreamy, romantic, moonlit hour with ~~Selwyn~~ ^**Kenneth**^ on the sands was vulgarized ^**and cheapened.**^ She loathed Mary Vance.

“Why, whatever’s wrong?” cried ~~Mary~~ mystified Mary. “What are you crying for?”

“My feet – hurt so –” sobbed Rilla, clinging to the last shred of her pride. It was less humiliating to ~~be~~ ^**admit**^ crying because of your feet than because – because somebody had been amusing himself with you, ^**and your friends had forgotten you,**^ and other people patronized you.

"I daresay they are," said Mary, not unkindly. "Never mind. I know where there's a pot of goose-grease in Cornelia's tidy pantry and it beats all the fancy cold creams in the world. I'll put some on your heels before you go to bed."

Goose-grease on your heels! So this was what your first party and your first beau and ^**your first**^ moonlit romance ended in! ~~Rilla gave up crying and went to sleep in Mary Vance's bed in the calm of despair.~~ [*Montgomery puts a line across the page here to indicate the original chapter end.*]

Rilla gave over crying in sheer disgust at the futility of tears and went to sleep in Mary Vance's bed in the calm of despair. Outside, the dawn came grayly in on wings of storm; Captain Josiah, true to his word, ran up the Union Jack at the Four Winds Light and it streamed ~~up~~ on the ~~fierce~~ ^**fierce**^ wind against the ~~black~~ clouded sky like a gallant unquenchable beacon.

Chap. 5

"The Sound of a Going"

~~Rilla sat was sitting among the fern in her favorite Rainbow Valley nook, with her hands clasped on her lap and her eyes fixed dreamily~~ Rilla ~~Blythe~~ ran down through the sunlit glory of the maple grove behind Ingleside, to her favourite nook in Rainbow Valley. She sat down on a green-mossed stone among the fern, ~~dropped her~~ propped her chin on her hands and stared unseeingly at the dazzling blue sky of the August afternoon – so blue, so peaceful, so unchanged, just as it had arched over the valley ^**in the mellow days of late summer**^ ever since she could remember.

She wanted to be alone – to think things out – to adjust herself, if it were possible, ~~in~~ to the new world into which she seemed to have been transplanted with a suddenness and completeness that left her half bewildered as to her own identity. Was she – could she be – the same Rilla Blythe who had danced at Four Winds Light six days ago – only six days ago? ~~It was more like an year.~~ ^**Note J2**^ That evening, with its hopes and fears and triumphs and humiliations, seemed like ancient history now. Could she really ever have cried ^**just**^ because she had been forgotten and had to walk home with Mary Vance ~~who~~? ~~Ah, thought Rilla, sadly, how trivial and foolish such cause of tears seemed.~~ Ah, thought Rilla sadly, how trivial and absurd such cause of tears now appeared to her ~~who could cry now~~. She could cry now with a right good will – but she would not – she must not. What was it mother had said, ^**looking,**^ with her white lips and stricken eyes, ^**as Rilla had never seen her mother look before,**^

> "When our women fail in courage,
> Shall our men be fearless still?"

Yes, that was it. She must be brave – like mother – and ~~Faith~~ ^**Nan**^ – and ~~Nan~~ ^**Faith**^ ^**Note K2**^ Only, when her eyes ached and her throat burned like this she had to hide herself in Rainbow Valley for a little while, just to think things out and remember that she wasn't a child any longer – she was grown-up and women had to face things like this.

^[*Note*] **M2**^

How sweet and woodsy the ferns smelled! How softly the great feathery boughs of the firs waved and murmured over her! How elfinly rang the bells of the "Tree Lovers" ^**Note L2**^ How purple and elusive the haze where incense was being offered on many ~~a woodland~~ ^**an**^ altar of the hills! How the maple leaves whitened in the wind until the grove seemed covered with pale silvery blossoms! Everything was just the same as she had seen it hundreds of times; and yet the whole face of the world seemed changed.

"How wicked I was to wish that something dramatic would happen!" ~~thought Rilla~~ ^**she thought**^. "Oh, if we could only have those dear, monotonous, pleasant days back! ~~again!~~ I would never, never grumble about them again."

Rilla's world had tumbled to pieces the very day after the party. ~~When the Charlottetown pat~~ As they ~~sat~~ ^**lingered**^ around the dinner table at Ingleside, talking of the war, the telephone had rung. It was a long-distance call from Charlottetown for Jem. When he had finished talking he hung up the receiver and turned around, ~~to face them,~~ with a flushed face and glowing eyes. Before he had said a word his mother ^**and Nan and Di**^ had turned pale. As for Rilla, for the first time in her life she felt that everyone must hear her heart beating and that something had clutched at her throat.

"They are calling for volunteers in town, father," said Jem. ^[*Note*] **N2**^ I'm going in to-night to enlist."

"Oh – Little Jem," cried Mrs. Blythe brokenly. She had not called him that for many years – not since the day he had rebelled against it. "Oh – no – no – Little Jem."

"I must, mother. I'm right – am I not, father?" said Jem.

Dr. Blythe had risen. He was very pale, too, and his voice was husky. But he did not hesitate.

"Yes, Jem, yes – if you feel that way, yes –"

Mrs. Blythe ~~dropped her face in her hands~~ ^**covered her face**^. Walter stared moodily at his plate. Nan and Di ~~looked ^**gazed**^ at each other~~ ^**clasped each others' hands**^. Shirley tried to look unconcerned. Susan sat as if paralysed, her piece of pie half-eaten on her plate. Susan never did finish that piece of pie – a fact which bore eloquent testimony to the upheaval in her inner woman, for Susan considered it a cardinal offence against ~~cev~~ civilized society to begin to eat anything and not finish it. That was wilful waste, ~~heirs~~ hens to the contrary notwithstanding.

Jem turned to the phone again. "I must ring the manse. Jerry will want to go, too."

At this Nan had cried out ^[*Note*] **O2**^ and rushed from the room. Di followed her. Rilla turned to Walter for comfort but Walter was lost to her in some reverie she could not share.

"All right," Jem was saying, as coolly as if he were arranging the details of a picnic. "I thought you would – yes, to-night – the seven o'clock – meet me at the station. So long."

"Mrs. Dr. dear," said poor Susan, pushing away her pie. "I wish you would wake me up. Am I dreaming – ~~or is that~~ or am I awake? Does that blessed boy realize what he is saying? Does he mean that he is going to enlist as a soldier? You do not mean to tell me that they want children like him! It is an outrage. Surely you and the doctor will not permit it."

"We can't stop him," said Mrs. Blythe, chokingly. "Oh, Gilbert!"

Dr. Blythe came up behind his wife and took her hand gently, looking down into the sweet gray eyes that he had only once before seen filled with such imploring anguish as now. They both thought of that other time – the day years ago in the House of Dreams when little Joyce had died.

"Would you have him stay, Anne – when the others are going – when he thinks it his duty – would you have him so selfish and small-souled?"

"No – no! But – oh – our first-born son – he's only a lad – Gilbert – I'll try to be brave after awhile – just now I can't. ~~Give me time."~~ ^**It's all come so suddenly. Give me time."**^

The doctor and his wife went out of the room. Jem had gone – Walter had gone – Shirley got up to go. Rilla and Susan remained staring at each other across the deserted table. Rilla had not yet cried – she was too stunned for tears. Then she saw that Susan was crying – Susan, whom she had never seen shed a tear before. ~~The old world had come to an end.~~

"Oh, Susan, will he really go?" she asked. "It – it – it is just ridiculous, that is what it is," said Susan.

She ~~gu~~ wiped away her tears, gulped resolutely and got up.

"I am going to wash the dishes. That has to be done, even if everybody has gone crazy. There now, dearie, do not you cry. Jem will go, most likely – but the war will be over long before he gets anywhere near it. Let us take a brace and not worry your poor mother."

~~Rilla felt comforted – of course the war would be over before Jem would be ready for it.~~

"In the Enterprise today it ~~says that~~ ^**was reported that**^ Lord Kitchener says the war will last three years," said Rilla dubiously.

"I am not acquainted with Lord Kitchener," said Susan, ^~~**calmly**~~ **composedly,**^ "but I dare say he makes mistakes as often as ~~anybody else~~ ^**other people**^. Your father says it will be over ~~by Christmas~~ ^**in a few months**^ and I have as much faith in his opinion as I have in Lord Anybody's. So just let us be calm and trust in the Almighty and get this place tidied up. I am done with crying which is a waste of time and discourages everybody."

Jem and Jerry went to Charlottetown that night and two days later they came back in khaki. The Glen hummed with excitement over it. ~~Three other boys followed their example.~~ Life at Ingleside had suddenly become a tense, strained, thrilling thing. Mrs. Blythe and Nan ^~~**and Faith**~~^ were brave and smiling ~~Rilla, after the first shock, reacted to the romance of it all. Jem looked magnificent in his uniform~~ and wonderful. Already Mrs. Blythe and ~~Mrs.~~ Miss Cornelia were organizing a Red Cross. The doctor and Mr. Meredith were rounding up the men for a Patriotic Society. Rilla, after the first shock, reacted to the romance of it all, in spite of her heartache. Jem ^**certainly**^ looked magnificent in his uniform. It was splendid to think of the lads of Canada answering so speedily and fearlessly and uncalculatingly to the call of their country. Rilla ~~was proud of Jem; she~~ carried her head high among the girls whose brothers had not so responded. In her diary she wrote:

> "'He goes to do what I had done
> Had Douglas's daughter been his son,'"

and was sure she meant it. If she ~~had been~~ ^**were**^ a boy of course she would go, too! She hadn't the least doubt of that.

She wondered if it was very dreadful of her to feel glad that Walter hadn’t got strong as soon as they had wished after the ~~typhoid~~ fever.

“I couldn’t bear to have Walter go,” she wrote ~~in her diary~~. “I love Jem ever so much ~~and I feel as if~~ but Walter means more to me than anyone in the world and I would die if he had to go. He seems so changed these ~~If only her mother and Nan and Faith~~ days. He hardly ever talks to me. I suppose he wants to go, too, and feels badly because he can’t. He doesn’t go about with Jem and Jerry at all. I shall never forget Susan’s face when Jem came home in his khaki. It worked and twisted as if she were going to cry, but all she said was, ‘You look ~~just~~ ^**almost**^ like a man in that, Jem.’ Jem laughed. He never minds because Susan thinks him just a child still. Everybody seems busy but me. I wish there was something I could do but there doesn’t seem to be anything. Mother and Nan and Di are busy all the time and I just wander about like a lonely ghost. What hurts me terribly, though, is that mother’s smiles, and Nan’s, ~~and Faith Meredith’s~~ just seem put on from the outside. Mother’s eyes never laugh now. ~~It’s just as if they had all made up their minds to be cheerful.~~ It makes me feel that I shouldn’t laugh either – that it’s wicked to ~~want~~ feel laughy. And it’s so hard for me to keep from laughing, even if Jem is going to be a soldier. But when I laugh I don’t enjoy it either, ^**as I used to do**^. There’s something behind it all that keeps hurting me – especially when I wake up in the night. Then I cry, because I am afraid that Kitchener of Khartoum is right and the war will last for years and Jem may be – but no, I won’t write it. It would make me feel as if it ~~was~~ ^**were**^ really going to happen. The other day Nan said, ‘Nothing can ever be quite the same for any of us again.’ It made me feel rebellious. Why shouldn’t things be the same again – when everything is over and Jem ~~is back~~ and Jerry are back? We’ll all be happy and jolly again and these days will seem just like a bad dream.[22]

“The coming of the mail is the most exciting event of every day now. Father just snatches the paper ^– **I never saw father snatch before** –^ and the rest of us crowd around and look at the headlines over his shoulder. Susan vows she ~~will not~~ does not and will not believe a word the papers say but she always comes to the kitchen door, and listens and then goes back, shaking her head. She is terribly indignant all the time, but she ~~makes~~ ^**cooks up**^ all the things Jem likes especially ~~to eat~~, and she did not make a single bit of fuss when she found Rags asleep on the spare-room bed yesterday. ^**Note E10**^ 'The Almighty only knows where your master will be having to sleep before long, you poor ^**dumb**^ beast,' she said as she put him quite gently out. ^[*Note*] **P2**^

"Faith Meredith is wonderful. I think she and Jem are really engaged now. She goes about with a shining light in her eyes, but her smiles are a little stiff ^**and starched,**^ just like mother's. I wonder if I could be as brave as she is if I had a lover and he was going to the war. It is bad enough when it is your brother. Bruce Meredith cried all night, Mrs. Meredith says, when he heard Jem ~~was~~ ^**and Jerry were**^ going ~~to the war~~. And he wanted to know if the 'K of K.' his father talked about was the King of Kings. He is the dearest kiddy. ~~I don't really care much for children – why,~~ I just love him – though I don't really care much for children. ~~I do abominate babies – I'm really.~~ I don't like babies one bit – though when I say so people look at me as if I had said something perfectly shocking. Well, I don't, and I've got to be honest about it. I don't mind looking at a nice clean baby if somebody else holds it – but I wouldn't touch it for anything and I don't feel a single ~~bit interested~~ ^**real spark of interest**^ in it. Gertrude Oliver says she just feels the same. (She is the ~~only person who really understands me)~~ ^**most honest person I know. She never pretends anything.)**^ She says babies bore her until they are old enough to talk and then she likes them – but ^**still**^ a good ways off. Mother and Nan and Di all all ~~so fond of~~ ^**adore**^ babies ~~that they~~ ^**and**^ seem to think I'm ~~really~~ unnatural because ~~I'm not~~ ^**I don't**^.

"I haven't seen ~~Selwyn~~ ^**Kenneth**^ since the night of the party. He was here one evening after Jem came back but I happened to be ~~over at the manse~~ ^**away**^. I don't think he ~~asked for me~~ mentioned me at all – at least nobody told me he did and I was determined I wouldn't ask – but I don't care in the least. All that matters absolutely nothing to me now. ~~All that matters~~ ^**The only thing that does matter**^ is that Jem has volunteered for active service and will be going to Valcartier in a few more days – my big, splendid brother Jem. Oh, I'm so proud of him!

"I suppose ~~Selwyn~~ ^**Kenneth**^ would enlist too if it ~~wasn't~~ ^**weren't**^ for his ankle. I think that is quite providential. He is his mother's only son and how dreadful she would feel if he went. Only sons should never think of going!"

Walter came wandering through the valley as Rilla sat there, with his head bent and his hands clasped behind him. When he saw Rilla he turned abruptly away; then as abruptly he turned and came back to her.

"Rilla-my-Rilla, what are you thinking of?"

"Everything is so changed, Walter," said Rilla ~~piteously~~ ^**wistfully**^. "Even you – you're changed. A week ago we were all so happy – and – and – now I just can't find myself at all. I'm lost."

Walter sat down on a neighbouring stone and took Rilla's little appealing hand.

"I'm afraid our old world has come to an end, Rilla. We've got to face that fact."

"It's so terrible to think of Jem," pleaded Rilla. "Sometimes I forget ^**for**^ for a little ^**while**^ what it really means and feel excited and proud – and then it comes over me again like a cold wind."

"I envy Jem!" said Walter moodily.

"Envy Jem! Oh, Walter ^**you –**^ you don't want to go too."

"No," said Walter, gazing straight before him down the emerald vistas of the valley, "no, I don't want to go. That's just the trouble. Rilla, I'm afraid to go. I'm a – a coward."

"You're not!" Rilla burst out angrily. "Why, anybody would be afraid to go. You might be – why, you might be killed."

"I wouldn't mind that if it didn't hurt," muttered Walter. "I don't think I'm afraid of death itself – ^**it's of the pain that might come before death –**^ it wouldn't be so bad to die and have it over – but to keep on dying! Rilla, I've always been afraid of pain – you know that. I can't help it – I shudder

~~"You always bore it bravely when it came," said Rilla.~~

~~"Yes – but the anticipation of it has always~~

when I think of the possibility of being mangled or – or blinded. Rilla, I ~~could~~ cannot face that thought. To be blind – never to see the beauty of the world again – ~~to be helpless~~ ^[*Note*] **S3**^ I ought to go – I ought to want to go – but I don't – I hate the thought of it – and I'm ashamed – ashamed."

"But, Walter, you couldn't go anyhow," said Rilla piteously. She was sick with a new terror that Walter would go~~, too~~ ^**after all**^. "You're not strong enough."

"I am. I've felt as fit as ever I did this last month. I'd pass any examination – I know it. Everybody thinks I'm not strong yet – and I'm skulking behind that belief. I – I should have been a girl," Walter concluded in a burst of passionate bitterness.

"Even if you were strong enough, you oughtn't to go," sobbed Rilla. "What would mother do? She's breaking her heart over Jem. It would kill her to see you both go."

"Oh, I'm not going – don't worry. I tell you I'm afraid to go – afraid. I don't mince the matter to myself. It's a relief to own up even to you, Rilla. I wouldn't confess it to anybody else – Jem and Di would despise me ~~even mother would be disappointed~~. But I hate the whole thing – the horror, the pain, the ugliness. War isn't a khaki uniform or a drill parade – everything I've read in old histories haunts me.~~" No, don't worry – I'm not going – I've no wish to go."~~ I lie awake at night and see things that have happened – see the blood and filth and misery ~~and~~ of it all. ~~And I can't face it.~~ ^[*Note*] **Q2**^ But it maddens me to see ~~Jem and Jerry~~ ^**them**^ in the khaki. And they think I'm grumpy because I'm not fit to go."

Walter laughed bitterly. It is not a nice thing to feel yourself a coward. But Rilla got her arms about him and cuddled her head on his shoulder. She was so glad he didn't ~~mean~~ want to go – for just one minute she had been horribly frightened. And it was so nice to have Walter confiding his troubles to her – to her, not Di. She didn't feel so lonely and superfluous any longer.

"Don't you despise me, Rilla-my-Rilla?" asked Walter wistfully. Somehow, it hurt him to think Rilla might despise him – hurt him as much as if it had been Di. He realized suddenly how very fond he was of this ~~little~~ ^**adoring**^ kid sister with her ~~adoring insightful appealing~~ ^**appealing**^ eyes and troubled, girlish face.

"No, I don't. Why, Walter, hundreds of people feel just as you do. You know what that verse of Shakespeare in the ^**old**^ Fifth Reader says – 'the brave man is not he who feels no fear.'"

"No – but it is 'he whose noble soul ^**its**^ fear subdues.' I don't do that. We can't gloss it over, Rilla. I'm a coward."

"You're not. Think of how you fought Dan Reese long ago."

"One spurt of courage isn't enough for a lifetime."

"Walter, one time I heard father say that the trouble with you was a sensitive nature and a vivid imagination. I think I know now what he meant. You ~~supp~~ feel things before they really come – ~~when there~~ feel them all alone when there isn't anything to help you bear them ^**– to take away from them.**^ I don't express that very well – but I know that's the trouble. It isn't anything to be ashamed of. When you and Jem got ~~burnt~~ your hands burned when the grass was fired on the sand-hills two years ago Jem made twice the fuss over the pain that you did. As for this horrid old war, there'll be plenty to go ~~witho~~ without you. It won't last long."

"I wish I could believe it. Well, it's supper time, Rilla. You'd better run. I don't want anything."

"Neither do I. I couldn't eat a mouthful. Let me stay here with you, Walter. It's such a comfort to talk things over with someone. The rest all think that I'm too much of a baby to understand."

So they ^**two**^ sat there in the old valley until the evening star shone through a pale-gray, gauzy cloud over the maple grove ^[*Note*] **T3**^ It was one of the evenings Rilla ~~treasured~~ ^**was to treasure**^ in remembrance all her life – the first one on which Walter had ever talked to her as if she were a woman and not a child. They comforted ~~each other~~ and strengthened each other. Walter felt, for the time being at least, that it was not such a despicable thing after all to dread the horror of war; and Rilla was glad to be made the confidant of his struggles – to sympathize with and encourage him. She was of importance to somebody.

When they went back to Ingleside they found callers sitting on the veranda. ^[*Note*] **R2**^ [*Note S2 is embedded in this Note.*] Walter slipped away, not caring to see ~~them~~ ^**or be seen,**^ but Rilla sat down on the steps, where the garden mint was dewy and pungent. ^[*Note*] **U2**^ She felt happier than at any time in the dreadful week that had passed. She was no longer haunted by the fear that Walter would go.

"I'd go myself if I was twenty years younger," Norman Douglas was shouting. Norman always shouted when he was excited. "I'd show the

Kaiser a thing or two! Did I ever say there wasn't a hell? Of course there's a hell – dozens of hells – ^**hundreds of hells –**^ where the Kaiser and all his brood are bound for."

"I knew this war was coming," said Mrs. Norman ~~triumphanty~~ triumphantly. "I saw it coming right along. I could have told all those stupid Englishman what was ahead of them. I told you, John Meredith, years ago what the Kaiser was up to but you wouldn't believe it. You said he would never plunge the world in war. Who was right about the Kaiser, John? You – or I? Tell me that."

"You were, I admit," said Mr. Meredith.

"It's too late to admit it now," said Mrs. Norman, shaking her head, as if to intimate that if John Meredith had admitted it sooner there might have been no war. ^[*Note*] **Y2**^ ~~"But thank God, England's navy is ready. But blind as most of them were somebody had foresight enough to see to that."~~

~~"I am of the opinion that the British navy will settle~~

"Maybe England'll manage not to get into trouble over it," said Cousin Sophia plaintively. "I dunno. But I'm much afraid."

"~~Seeing~~ One would ~~think~~ ^**suppose**^ that England was in trouble over it already, up to her neck, Sophia Crawford," said Susan. "But your ways of thinking are beyond me ^**and always were**^. It is my opinion that the British Navy will settle Germany in a jiffy and that we are all getting worked up over nothing."

Susan spat out the words as if she wanted to convince herself more than anybody else. She had her little store of homely philosophies to guide her through life, but she had nothing to buckler her against the thunderbolts of the week that had just passed. What had an honest, hard-working, ^**Presbyterian**^ old maid of Glen St. Mary to do with a war thousands of miles away? Susan felt that it was indecent that she should have to be disturbed by it.

"The British army will settle Germany," shouted Norman. "Just wait till it gets into line and the Kaiser will find that ^**real**^ war is a different thing from parading round Berlin with your moustaches cocked up."

"Britain hasn't got an army," said Mrs. Norman emphatically. "You needn't glare at me, Norman. Glaring ~~doesn't~~ ^**won't**^ make soldiers out of ~~hay stalks~~ timothy stalks. A hundred thousand men will just be a mouthful for Germany's millions."

"There'll be some tough chewing in the mouthful, I reckon," persisted Norman valiantly. "Germany'll break her teeth on it. Don't you tell me one Britisher ~~one~~ isn't a match for ten foreigners. I could polish off a dozen of 'em myself ^**with both hands tied behind my back!"**^

"I am told," said Susan, "that old Mr. ~~Pyiyr~~ Pryor does not believe in this war. I am told that he says England went into it just because she was jealous of Germany and that she did not ^**really**^ care in the least what happened to Belgium." ~~Is it true?"~~

"I believe ~~he has~~ ^**he's**^ been talking some such rot," said Norman. "I haven't heard him. When I do, Whiskers-on-the-Moon won't know what happened to him. That precious relative of mine, Kitty Alec, holds forth to the same effect, I understand. Not before me though – somehow, folks don't indulge in that kind of conversation in my presence. ~~I reckon~~ ^**Lord love you,**^ they've a kind of presentiment, so to speak, that it wouldn't be healthy for their complaint."

"I am much afraid that this war has been sent as a punishment for our sins," said Cousin Sophia, unclasping her pale hands from her lap and reclasping them solemnly over her stomach. "'The world is very evil – the times are waxing late.'"

"Parson here's got something of the same idea," chuckled Norman. "Haven't you, Parson? That's why you preached 'tother night on the text 'Without shedding of ~~sins~~ ^**blood**^ there is no remission of ~~blood~~ sins.' I didn't agree with you – wanted to get up in the pew and shout out that there wasn't a word of sense in what you were saying, but Ellen, here, she held me down. I never have any fun sassing parsons since I got married."

"Without shedding of blood there is no anything," said ~~Mrs.~~ Mr. Meredith, in the gentle dreamy way which had an unexpected trick of convincing his hearers. "Everything, it seems to me, has to be purchased by self-sacrifice. ~~The~~ Our race has marked every step of its painful ascent with blood. And now torrents of it must flow again. No, Mrs. Crawford, I don't think the war has been sent as a punishment for sin. I think it is the price humanity must pay for some ~~great~~ blessing – some advance great enough to be worth the price – which we may not live to ~~attain~~ ^**see**^ but which our children's children will inherit."

"If Jerry is killed will you feel so fine about it?" demanded Norman, who had been saying things like that all his life ^**and never could be**

made to see any reason why he shouldn't.^ "Now, never mind kicking me in the shins, Ellen. I want to see if Parson meant what he said or if it was just a pulpit frill."

Mr. Meredith's face quivered. He had had a terrible hour alone in his study on the night Jem and Jerry had gone to town. But he answered quietly.

"Whatever I felt, it could not alter my ~~belief – my conviction~~ belief – my assurance that a country whose sons are ~~willing~~ ready to lay down their lives in her defence will ~~rise to the height of~~ win a new vision because of their sacrifice."

"You do mean it, Parson. I can always tell ~~what~~ when people mean what they say. It's a gift that was born in me. Makes me a terror to most parsons, that! But I've never caught you yet saying anything you didn't mean. I'm always hoping I will – that's what reconciles me to going to church. It'd be such a comfort to me – such a weapon to batter Ellen here with when she tries to civilize me. Well, I'm off over the road to see Ab. Crawford a minute. The gods be good to you all."

"~~You~~ The old pagan!" muttered Susan, as Norman strode away. She did not care if Ellen Douglas did hear her. Susan could never understand why fire did not descend from heaven upon Norman Douglas when he insulted ministers the way he did. ~~And yet Mr. Meredith it really seemed to her that~~ ^**But the astonishing thing was**^ Mr. Meredith ~~liked~~ ^**seemed really to like**^ his brother-in-law.

[*Montgomery put a line across the page again here to indicate the original chapter ending.*]

Rilla wished ~~people~~ ^**they**^ would talk of something besides war. ~~She had heard nothing else for six days and she was really a little tired of it. Now that~~ She had heard nothing else for ~~six days~~ a week and she was really a little tired of it. Now that she was relieved from her haunting fear that Walter would want to go it made her quite impatient. But she supposed – with a sigh – that there would be three or four months of it yet.

Chapter 6

Susan, Rilla, and Dog Monday Make a Resolution

The ~~big~~ living room at Ingleside was snowed over with drifts of white cotton. Word had come from Red Cross headquarters that sheets and bandages would be required. Nan and Di and Rilla were hard at work. ~~^**Put in here AA – AA p. 94**^~~ Mrs. Blythe and Susan were upstairs in the boys' room, engaged in a more personal task. With dry, anguished eyes they were packing up Jem's belongings. ~~Word had come that ^**the previous**^ day that~~ He must leave for Valcartier the next morning. They had been expecting ~~it~~ ^**the word**^ but it was none the less dreadful when it came. ^**Put in here AA – AA page 94–97**^ [*Montgomery inserted this note to remind herself about moving a block of material.*]

"Susan," ^**Mrs. Blythe was saying upstairs,**^ "do you remember that first day ~~he~~ ^**Jem**^ lifted up his little arms to me and called me 'mo'er' – the very first word he ever tried to say?" ~~said Mrs. Blythe, folding Jem's hankerchiefs.~~

"You could not mention anything about that blessed baby that I do not ^**and will not**^ remember,~~ Mrs. Dr. dear," said Susan drearily~~ ^**till my dying day,"**^ said Susan drearily.

"Susan, I keep thinking to-day of one night when he cried for me in the night. He was just a few months old. Gilbert didn't want me to go to him – he said the child was well and warm and that it would be fostering bad habits in him. But I went – and took him up – I can feel that tight clinging of his little arms round my neck yet. Susan, if I hadn't gone that night, twenty-one years ago, and taken my baby up when he cried for me I couldn't face tomorrow morning."

"I do not know how we are going to face it anyhow, Mrs. Dr. dear. But do not tell me that it will be the final ~~good-bye~~ ^**farewell**^. He will be back on leave before he goes overseas, will he not?"

"We hope so but we are not very sure. I am making up my mind that he will not, so that there will be no disappointment to bear. Susan, I am determined that I will send my boy off tomorrow with a smile. He shall not carry away with him ~~a~~ ^**the**^ remembrance of a weak mother who had not the courage to send when he had the courage to go. ^**I hope none of us will cry.**^"

"I am not going to cry, Mrs. Dr. dear, ^**and that you may tie to,**^ but whether I shall manage to smile or not will be as Providence ordains ^**and as the pit of my stomach feels.**^ Have you room there for this ~~batch of shortbread? shortbread~~ fruit-cake? And the shortbread? And the mince-pie? ~~Oh, Mrs. Dr. That~~ That blessed boy shall not starve, whether they have anything to eat in that Quebec place or not. Everything seems to be changing all at once, does it not? Even the old cat at the manse has passed away. He ~~died last night~~ ^**breathed his last**^ at a quarter to ten ^**last night**^ and Bruce is quite heart-broken, ^**they tell me**^."

"It's time that pussy went ~~were~~ ^**where**^ good cats go. He must be at least fifteen years old. He has seemed so lonely since ~~old~~ Aunt Martha died."

"I should not ^**have**^ lament^**ed,**^ Mrs. Dr. dear, if ~~it had been~~ that Hyde-beast had died also. He has been Mr. Hyde most of the time since Jem came home in khaki, and that has a meaning ~~I'll~~ ^**I will**^ maintain. I do not know what ~~Rags~~ ^**Monday**^ will do when Jem is gone. The creature just goes about with a human look in his eyes that takes all the good out of me when I see it. ~~We~~ Ellen West used to be always railing at the Kaiser and we thought her crazy, but now I see that there was a method in her madness. This tray is packed, Mrs. Dr. dear, and I will go down and ~~prepare summer~~ ^**put in my best licks preparing supper.**^ I wish I knew when I would cook ~~amo~~ another supper for Jem but such things are hidden from our eyes."

^**----- AA**^ [*Montgomery's note to remind herself about moving a bloc of material*] ~~Rilla was sewing feverishly~~ Rilla was basting the hem of a sheet for the first time in her life. When the word had come that Jem must go she had her cry out ~~in~~ ^**among the ferns in**^ Rainbow Valley and then she had gone to her mother.

"Mother, I want to do something. I'm only a girl – I can't do anything to win the war – but I must do something to help at home."

"The cotton has come up for the sheets, ~~and have~~" said Mrs. Blythe.

"You can help ~~the girls to~~ ^~~**Una**~~ **Nan and Di**^ make them up. And, Rilla, don't you think you could organize a Junior Red Cross among the young girls? I think they would like it better and do better work by themselves than ~~mixed-up~~ if mixed up with the older people."

"But – mother – I've never done anything like that."

~~"A great~~ "We will all have to do a great many things in the months ahead of us that we have never done before, Rilla."

"Well" – Rilla took the plunge – "I'll try, mother – if you'll tell me how to begin. I have ~~decided that I must be ^**as**^ brave and heroic~~ been thinking it all over and I have decided that I must be as brave and heroic ^**and unselfish**^ as I can possibly be."

Mrs. Blythe did not smile at Rilla's italics. Perhaps she did not feel like smiling. Or perhaps she ~~real felt~~ ^**detected**^ a real grain of serious purpose behind Rilla's romantic pose. So here was Rilla hemming sheets and organizing a Junior Red Cross in her thoughts as she hemmed; ~~m~~ moreover, ^**she was**^ enjoying it – the organizing that is, not the hemming. It was interesting and Rilla discovered a certain aptitude ~~for it~~ in herself ^**for it**^ that surprised her. Who would be president? Not she. The older girls would not like that. Irene Howard? No, ^**somehow**^ Irene was not quite as popular as she deserved ^**to be**^. Marjorie ~~W~~ Drew? No, Marjorie hadn't enough backbone. She was too prone to agree with the last speaker. Betty Meade – calm, capable, tactful Betty – the very one! And ~~Jen Vickers~~ ^**Una Meredith**^ for treasurer; and, if they were very insistent, they might make her, Rilla, secretary. ~~Now for the committ~~ As for the various committees, they must be chosen after the Juniors were organized, but Rilla knew just who should be put on which. They would meet around – and there must be no eats – Rilla knew she would have a pitched battle with Olive Kirk over that – and everything should be strictly business like and constitutional. Her minute book should be covered in white with a Red Cross on the cover – and wouldn't it be nice to have some kind of uniform which they could all wear at ^**the**^ concerts they would have to get up to raise money – something simple but smart?

"You have ~~hemm bus~~ basted the top hem of that sheet on one side and the bottom hem on the other," said Di.

Rilla picked out her stitches and reflected that she hated sewing. Running the Junior Reds would be much more interesting. [*Montgomery's note to indicate end of AA.*]

Jem ~~Mer~~ Blythe and Jerry Meredith ~~and the other three volunteers~~ left next morning. ^[*Note*] **Y2**^ Almost everybody in the Glen and Four Winds and Harbor Head and Upper Glen and over-harbor ^**– except Whiskers-on-the-Moon –**^ was there to see them off. The Blythe family and the Meredith family were all smiling. Even Susan, as Providence did ordain, wore a smile, though the effect was somewhat more painful than tears would have been. Faith and Nan were very pale and very gallant. Rilla thought she would get on very well if something in her throat didn't choke her ^**and if her lips didn't take such spells of trembling**^. ~~Rags~~ ^**Dog Monday**^ was there, too. Jem had tried to say good-bye to ~~Rags~~ ^**him**^ at Ingleside but ~~Rags~~ ^**Monday**^ implored so eloquently that Jem relented and let him go to the station. ~~Rags~~ ^**He**^ kept close to Jem's legs and watched every movement of his beloved master.

"I can't bear that dog's eyes," said Mrs. Meredith.

"The beast has ~~sense~~ ^**more sense than most humans,**^" said Mary Vance. "Well, did we any of us ever think we'd live to see this day? I bawled all night to think of Jem and Jerry going like this. I think they're plumb ~~foolish deranged~~ ^**deranged**^. Miller got a maggot in his head about going but I soon talked him out of it – likewise his aunt said a few ^**touching**^ things. For once in our lives Kitty Alec and I agree. It's a miracle that isn't likely to happen again. There's ~~Selwyn Kenneth~~ ^**Ken**^, Rilla."

Rilla knew ~~Selwyn~~ ^**Kenneth**^ was there. She had been acutely conscious of it from the moment he had sprung from Leo West's buggy. ~~Ne~~ Now he came up to her smiling. ^[*Note*] **W2**^

~~"I'm off, too, Rilla-my-Rilla."~~

A queer little wind of desolation, that even Jem's going had not caused blew over Rilla's spirit.

"Why? ~~Your vacation isn't over.~~ ^**You have another month of vacation.**^"

"~~No~~ ^**Yes**^ – but I can't hang around Four Winds and ~~do nothing~~ ^**enjoy myself**^ when the world's on fire like this. It's me for little old Toronto where I'll find some way of helping in spite of this ~~blooming~~ ^**bally**^ ankle. I'm not looking at Jem and Jerry – makes me ^**too**^

sick with envy. You girls are great – no crying, no grim endurance. The boys'll go off with a good taste in their mouths. I hope Persis and mother will be as game when my turn comes."

"^**Oh, Kenneth –**^ ~~T~~the war will be over before your turn come~~s~~th." ~~Thelwyn."~~

There! She had lisped again. Another great moment of life spoiled! Well, it was her fate. And anyhow, nothing mattered. ~~Selwyn~~ ^**Kenneth**^ was off ^**already –**^ he was talking to Ethel Reese, who was dressed, ^**at seven in the morning,**^ in the gown she had ~~wore~~ ^**worn**^ to the dance, and was crying. What on earth had ~~Elthel~~ Ethel to ~~criy~~ cry about? None of the Reeses were in khaki. Rilla wanted to cry, too – but she would not. What was that horrid old Mrs. Drew saying to mother~~?~~, in that melancholy ~~voice~~ ^**whine**^ of hers? "I don't know how you can stand this, Mrs. Blythe. I couldn't if it was my pore boy." And mother – oh, mother ~~was splendid~~ ^**could always be depended on!**^ How her gray eyes flashed in her pale face. ~~"It might~~ "It might have been worse, Mrs. Drew. I might have had to urge him to go." Mrs. Drew did not understand but Rilla did. She flung up her head. ~~Her~~ ^**Her**^ brother did not have to be urged to go. ^**Note B3 ~~B3 B3~~**^

"I told Mark to wait and see if they asked for a second lot of men. If they did I'd let him go – but they won't," said Mrs. Palmer Burr ~~as she walked by~~. ^[*Note*] **C3**^

"I'm frightened to look at my husband's face for fear I'll see in it that he wants to go too," said a little over-harbour ~~boy~~ ^**bride**^.

"I'm scared stiff," ^**said**^ whimsical Mrs. ~~Windy~~ ^**Jim**^ Howard ~~was saying~~. "I'm scared ~~Hilary~~ ^**Tom**^ will enlist – and I'm scared he won't."

"The war will be over by Christmas," said Joe Vickers.

"Let them European nations fight it out between them," said Abner Reese.

"When he was a boy I gave him ^**many**^ a good trouncing," shouted Norman Douglas, who seemed to be referring to some one high in military circles in Charlottetown. "Yes, sir, I ~~lambasted~~ ^**walloped**^ him well, big gun as he is now."

"The existence of the British Empire is at stake," said the Methodist minister ~~as he went by~~.

"There's ^**certainly**^ something about a uniform," sighed Irene

Howard. ^[*Note*] **Z2**^

"The Blythe family are taking it easy," said Kate Drew.

"Them young fools are just going for adventure," ~~They think~~ growled Nathan Crawford. ^[*Note*] **X2**^

~~There disconnected scraps of conversation flowed to Rilla's ears and~~ In ^**these**^ ten minutes ~~she~~ ^**Rilla**^ passed through a dizzying succession of anger, laughter, ^**contempt,**^ depression and inspiration. ~~She wanted to scratch Nathan's eyes out.~~ Oh, people were – funny! How little they understood! "Taking it easy," indeed – when even Susan hadn't slept a wink all night! Kate Drew always was a ~~minx~~ minx. ^[*Note*] **A3**^

There – the train was coming – mother was ~~shaking~~ holding Jem's hand – ~~Rags~~ ^**Dog Monday**^ was licking it – everybody was saying good-bye ~~– every~~ – the train was in! Jem kissed Faith before everybody – ~~Mrs.~~ old Mrs. Drew whooped hysterically – the ~~men~~ men, ^**led by ~~Selwyn~~**^ ^**Kenneth,**^ cheered – Rilla felt Jem seize her hand – "Good-bye, Spider" – ^**Note D3**^ ~~somebody kissed her ^**cheek**^ – she believed it was Jerry~~ – ~~thuy~~ they were off – the train was pulling out – Jem and Jerry ~~and Selwyn~~ were waving to everybody – everybody was waving back – mother and Nan were smiling ^**still, but**^ as if they had ^**just**^ forgotten to take the smile off – ~~Rags~~ ^**Monday**^ was howling dismally and being forcibly ~~keep kept back from~~ ^**restrained**^ by the Methodist minister from tearing after the train – Susan was waving her best bonnet and hurrahing like a man – had she gone crazy? – the train rounded a curve. They had gone.

Rilla came to herself with a ~~sigh~~ ^**gasp**^. There was a sudden quiet. Nothing to do now but go home – and wait. The doctor and Mrs. Blythe walked off together – so did Nan and Faith – ~~the rest stalked of the Blythes~~ so did John Meredith and Rosemary. ~~The rest~~ Walter and Una and Shirley ^**and Di**^ and Carl and Rilla went in a group. Susan had put her bonnet back on her head, ~~wrongside~~ hindside foremost, and stalked grimly off alone. Nobody ~~muss~~ missed ~~Rags~~ ^**Dog Monday**^ at first. When they did ~~Walter~~ ^**Shirley**^ went back for him. He found ~~Rags~~ ^**Dog Monday**^ curled up ~~under~~ ^**in**^ one of the shipping sheds near the station and tried to coax him home. ~~Rags~~ ^**Dog Monday**^ would not ~~move budge~~ ^**move**^. He wagged his tail to show he had no hard feelings but no blandishments availed to ~~stir~~ ^**budge**^ him.

"Guess ~~Rags~~ ^**Monday**^ has made up his mind to wait there till Jem comes back," said ~~Walter~~ ^**Shirley**^, trying to laugh as he rejoined the rest.

Which was exactly what ~~Rags~~ ^**Dog Monday**^ had ~~made up his mind to do. His~~ ^**done.**^ His dear master had gone – he, ~~Rags~~ ^**Monday**^, had been deliberately and of malice aforethought prevented from going with him by a ~~demon garbed~~ ^**demon disguised**^ in the garb of a Methodist minister. Wherefore, he, ~~Rags~~ ^**Monday**^, would wait ~~whe~~ there until the smoking, snorting monster, which had carried ~~Jem~~ ^**his hero**^ off, ~~bro~~ carried him back.

~~Wait,~~ ^**Ay, wait**^ there, little faithful dog with the soft, wistful, puzzled ~~brown~~ eyes. But it will be many a long ^**bitter**^ day before your boyish comrade comes back to you.

The doctor was away on a case that night and Susan stalked into Mrs. Blythe's room on her way to bed to see if her adored "Mrs. Dr. dear" ~~were well~~ ~~was comfortable~~ ^**were "comfortable and composed."**^ She paused solemnly at the foot of the bed and solemnly declared,

"Mrs. Dr. dear, I have made up my mind to be a heroine."

"Mrs. Dr. dear" found herself violently inclined to laugh – which was manifestly unfair, since she had not laughed when Rilla had announced a similar heroic determination. ~~It did not – or should not – make any vital difference that~~ To be sure, Rilla was a slim, ~~flower-like~~ ^**white-robed**^ thing, with a ~~beautiful~~ ^**flower-like**^ face and starry young eyes aglow with feeling; whereas Susan ~~wore~~ was arrayed in a gray flannel nightgown of strait simplicity, and had a ~~red woollen~~ strip of red woollen ~~flounce~~ ^**worsted**^ ~~tide~~ tied around her ~~head~~ ^**gray hair**^ as a charm against neuralgia. ~~Yet~~ ^**But**^ that should not make any vital difference. ^**Note V2**^ Yet Mrs. Blythe was hard put to it not to laugh.

"I am not," proceeded Susan firmly, "going to lament or whine or question the wisdom of the Almighty any more as I have been doing lately. ^[*Note*] **N4**^ ~~Our~~ ^**Those**^ blessed boys ~~has~~ ^**have**^ gone to war; and <u>we women</u>, Mrs. Dr. dear, must tarry by the stuff and keep a stiff upper lip."

Chapter 7

A War Baby and a Soup Tureen

"Liege and Namur – and now Brussels!" The doctor shook his head~~,~~ ~~gravely~~. "I don't like it – I don't like it."

"Do not you lose heart, Dr. dear~~," said~~; they were just defended by foreigners," said Susan superbly. "Wait you till the Germans come against the British; ~~and~~ there will be a very different story to tell and that you may tie to."

The doctor shook his head again ^**, but a little less gravely**^; ~~but~~ perhaps they all shared subconsciously in Susan's belief that "the ~~Brit~~ thin ~~red~~ gray line" was unbreakable, even by the victorious rush of Germany's ready millions. At any rate, when the terrible day came – the first of many terrible days – with the news that the British army was ~~beaten~~ driven back they stared at each other in blank dismay.

"It – it can't be true," gasped Nan, taking a brief refuge in temporary incredulity. ^[*Note*] **F3**^

"'A broken, a beaten, but not a demoralized, army,'" muttered the doctor, from a London dispatch. "Can it be England's army of which such a thing is said?"

~~"The road to Paris is open now," said Walter.~~

"It will be a long time now before the war is ended," said Mrs. Blythe despairingly.

Susan's faith, which had for a moment been temporarily submerged, now ~~emerged~~ ^**reappeared**^ triumphantly.

"Remember, Mrs. Dr. dear, that the British army is not the British navy. Never forget *that*. And the Russians are on their way, too, though Russians are people I do not know much about and consequently will not tie to."

"The Russians will not be in time to save Paris," said Walter gloomily. "Paris is the heart of France – and the road to it is open. Oh, I wish" – he stopped abruptly and went out.

After a paralyzed day ~~the Bly~~ Ingleside folk found it was possible to "carry on" even in the face of ever-~~worsening~~ ^**darkening**^ bad news.

Susan worked fiercely in her kitchen, the doctor went out on his round of visits, Nan and Di ~~and Mrs. Blythe returned~~ ^**returned**^ to ^**their**^ Red Cross activities; ^[*Note*] **G3**^ Rilla, after relieving her feelings by ^**a stormy fit of tears in Rainbow Valley and**^ an outburst in her diary, ~~^**and**^~~ remembered that she had elected to be brave and heroic. And, she thought, it really was heroic to volunteer to drive about the Glen and Four Winds one day, collecting promised Red Cross supplies with Abner Crawford's old gray ~~nag~~ ^**horse**^. One of the Ingleside horses was lame and the doctor needed the other, so there was nothing for it but the Crawford nag, a placid, unhasting, ^**thick-skinned**^ creature with an amiable habit of stopping every few yards to ~~scratch a~~ ^**kick**^ a fly off one leg with the foot of the other. Rilla felt that this, coupled with the fact that the Germans were only ~~a~~ fifty miles from Paris, was hardly to be endured. But she started off gallantly ~~one ^**late**^ August afternoon ^**day**^ of~~ on an errand fraught with amazing results.

Late in the afternoon she found herself, with a buggy full of parcels, ~~wondering whether it was worth~~ at the entrance to ^**a**^ grassy, deep-rutted lane leading ~~down~~ to the harbor shore, wondering ~~wet~~ whether it was worth while to call down at the Anderson house. ~~They were~~ The Andersons were desperately poor and it was not likely Mrs. Anderson had anything to give. On the other hand, her husband, who was an Englishman by birth and who had been working in Kingsport when the war broke out, had promptly ~~enlisted~~ sailed for England to enlist there, without, it may be said, ~~the for~~ coming home or sending much hard cash to represent him. So possibly Mrs. Anderson might feel hurt if she were overlooked. Rilla decided to call. There were times afterwards when she wished she hadn't, but in the long run she was very thankful that she did.

The Anderson house was a ~~very~~ small and ~~vere ^**very**^~~ tumble down affair, crouching in a grove of battered spruces near the shore as if rather ashamed of itself and anxious to hide. Rilla tied her gray nag to the rickety fence and went to the door. It was open; and the sight she saw bereft her temporarily of the power of speech or motion. ~~Through the op~~

Through the open door of the small bedroom opposite ~~it~~ her, Rilla saw Mrs. Anderson lying on the untidy bed; and Mrs. Anderson was dead. There was no doubt of that; neither was there any doubt that the big, ^**frowzy,**^ red-headed, red-faced, ~~frowzy-haired,~~ over-fat woman sitting near the door-way, smoking a pipe quite comfortably, was very much alive. She rocked idly back and forth amid her surroundings of squalid disorder, and paid no attention whatever to the ~~pier~~ piercing wails proceeding from a cradle in the middle of the ~~fron~~ room.

Rilla knew the woman by sight and reputation. Her name was Mrs. Conover; she lived down at the fishing village; she was a great-aunt of Mrs. Anderson; and she drank as well as smoked.

Rilla's first impulse was to turn and flee. But that would not do. Perhaps this woman, repulsive as she was, needed help – though she certainly did not look as if she were worrying over the lack of it.

"Come in," said Mrs. Conover, removing her pipe and staring at Rilla ^**with her little, rat-like eyes**^.

"Is – is Mrs. Anderson really ^ – ^ dead?" asked Rilla timidly, as she stepped over the sill.

"Dead as a door nail," ~~reli~~ responded Mrs. Conover cheerfully. "~~Died~~ ^**Kicked the bucket**^ half an hour ago. I've sent ~~my darter Jen~~ ^**Jen Conover**^ to phone for the undertaker and git some help up from the shore. ~~You~~ ^**Ye**^'re the doctor's miss, ain't ~~you~~ ^**ye?**^ Have a cheer?"

Rilla did not see any chair which was not cluttered with something. She remained standing.

"Wasn't it – very sudden?"

"Well, she's been a pining ever since that worthless Jim lit out for England – which I say it's a pity ^**as**^ he ever left. ~~I say~~ ^**It's my belief**^ she was took for death when she heard the news. That young ~~one~~ ^**'un**^ there was born ~~a week~~ ^**a fortnight**^ ago and since then she's just gone down and to-day ~~finished it."~~ she up and died ^[*Note*] **U3**^

"Is there anything I can do to – to help?" hesitated Rilla.

"Bless ~~you~~ ^**yez**^, no – unless ~~you~~ ^**ye**^'ve a knack with kids. I haven't. That young-un there never lets up squalling, day or night. I've just got that I take no notice of it."

Rilla tiptoed gingerly over to the cradle and more gingerly still pulled down the dirty blanket. She had no intention of touching the baby – she had no "knack with kids" either. She saw ~~a tiny~~ ^**an**^ ugly midget with a red, distorted little face, rolled up in a piece of dingy old flannel. She had never seen an uglier ~~babay~~ baby. Yet a feeling of pity for the desolate, orphaned mite ^[*Note*] ~~**U3**~~ **V3**^ took sudden possession of ~~it~~ her.

"What is going to become of the baby?" she asked.

"Lord knows," said Mrs. Conover candidly. "Min worried awful over that before she died. ^[*Note*] **W3**^ I ain't a-going to trouble myself with it, I can tell ~~you~~ ^**yez**^! I brung up ~~eight of my own ungrateful a and there ain't a one of them to keep me in~~ ^**a boy that my sister left and he skinned out ~~years ago~~**^ ^^**as soon as he got to be some good**^^ **and won't give me a mite o' help in**^ my old age, ungrateful whelps as ~~they were ^are^~~ ^**he is.**^ I told Min it'd have to be sent to an orphan asylum till we'd see if Jim ever came back to look after it. ^[*Note*] **Q3**^ she didn't relish the ~~idea~~ idee. But that's the long and short of it."

"But who will look after it until it can be taken to the asylum?" persisted Rilla. Somehow the baby's fate worried her ~~– why she couldn't tell. The thought of the poor mother, dying worrying ^**fretting**^ over the her baby in the valley of the shadow hurt her terribly. How dreadful it was that the poor woman should have died.~~

~~"A~~ "S'pose I'll have to," grunted Mrs. Conover. She put away her pipe and took an unblushing swig from a black bottle she produced from a shelf near her. "It's my opinion the kid won't live long. It's sickly. Min never had no ~~smeddum~~ ^**gimp**^ and I guess it hain't either. Likely it won't trouble anyone long and good riddance, sez I."

Rilla drew the blanket down a little farther.

"Why, the baby isn't dressed!" she exclaimed, in a shocked tone.

"Who was to dress ~~it~~ ^**him**^ I'd like to know," demanded Mrs. Conover truculently. "I hadn't time – took me all the time there was looking after Min. 'Sides, as I told yez, I don't know nothing of kids. Old Mrs. Billy Crawford, she was here when it was born and she washed it and rolled it up in that flannel, and Jen she's tended it a bit since.[22] ~~I wouldn't touch it with a ten foot pole – a yelling, squirming thing like that.~~ ^**The critter is warm enough. This weather would melt a brass monkey."**^

Rilla was silent, looking down at the crying baby. She had never encountered any of the tragedies of life before and this one smote her to the core of her heart. The thought of the poor mother going down into the valley of the shadow alone, fretting about her baby, with no one near but this abominable old woman, hurt her terribly. ~~Rilla~~ If she had only come a little sooner! Yet what could she have done – what could she do now? She didn't know, but she must do something. She hated babies ^ – ^ but she simply could not go away and leave that poor little creature with Mrs. Conover – who was applying herself again to her black bottle and would probably be helplessly drunk before ~~the undertaker~~ any body came.

"I can't stay," thought Rilla. "Mr. Crawford said I must be home by supper time because he wanted the pony this evening himself. Oh, what can I do?"

~~She couldn't leave the baby. Well, then, she must take it with her.~~ ~~Rilla~~ ^**She**^ made a sudden, desperate, impulsive resolution.

"I'll take the baby home with me," she said. "Can I?"

"Sure, if ~~you~~ ^**yez**^ wants to," said Mrs. Conover amiably. "I ~~haven't~~ ^**hain't**^ any objection. Take it and ~~Rilla looked~~ welcome.^"

~~Rilla looked helplessly around. Oh, for mother – or Susan!~~

"I – I can't carry it," ~~she said~~ ^**said Rilla**^. "I have to drive the horse and I'd be afraid I'd drop it. Is there ~~a~~ ^**a – a**^ basket ~~any~~ anywhere that I could put it in?"

"Not as I knows on. There ain't much here of anything, I kin tell ~~you~~ ^**yez**^. Min was pore and as shiftless ^**as Jim**^. Ef ~~you yez~~ ^**ye**^ opens that drawer over there ~~you~~ yez'll find a few baby clo'es. Best take them along."

Rilla got the clothes – the ~~poor~~ cheap, ^**sleazy**^ little garments the poor mother had made ready as best she could. But this did not solve the pressing problem of the baby's transportation. Rilla looked helplessly round. Oh, for mother – or Susan! Her eyes fell on ~~a large deep platter~~ ^**an enormous** ^^**blue**^^ **soup tureen**^ at the back of the dresser.

"Can I have this to – to lay him ~~on~~ ^**in**^?" she asked.

"Well, 'tain't mine but I guess ~~you~~ ^**yez**^ kin take it. Don't smash it if ~~you~~ ^**yez**^ can help – Jim might make a fuss about it if he comes back alive – ^**Note F10**^ ^[*Note*] **H3**^ He was mighty particler about some things but didn't worry him none that there weren't much in the way o' eatables to put in the ~~platter."~~ dishes."

For the first time in her life Rilla Blythe touched a baby – lifted it

– rolled it in ~~the~~ ^**a**^ blanket, ~~and tattered little quilt~~ trembling with nervousness lest she drop it or – or ~~– or~~ break it. Then she ~~laid it on the platter~~ put it in the soup tureen.

"Is there any fear of it smothering?" she asked anxiously.

"Not much ~~matter~~ ^**odds**^ if it do," said Mrs. Conover. ~~"Don't~~

Horrified Rilla loosened the blanket round the baby's face a little. The mite had stopped crying and was blinking up at her. It had big dark eyes in its ugly little face.

"Better not let the wind blow on it," admonished Mrs. ~~Connor~~ Conover. "Take it's breath if it ~~does~~ ^**do**^."

Rilla wrapped the tattered little quilt around the soup tureen.

"Will you hand this to me after I get into the buggy, please?"

"Sure I will," said Mrs. Conover, getting up with a grunt.

And so it was that Rilla Blythe, who had driven to the Anderson house a self-confessed hater of babies, drove away from it carrying one in a soup tureen on her lap!

Rilla thought she would never get to Ingleside. That miserable pony fairly crawled. ~~In one~~ In the soup tureen there was an uncanny silence. In one way she was thankful the baby did not cry but she wished it would give an occasional squeak to prove that it was alive. Suppose it were smothered! Rilla dared not unwrap it to see, lest the wind, which was now blowing a hurricane, should "take its breath," whatever dreadful thing that might be. She was a thankful girl when at last she reached harbor at Ingleside.

~~Susan's feelings when Rilla entered the kitchen carrying an enormous soup tureen which she~~ Rilla carried the soup tureen to the kitchen, set it on the table under Susan's eyes, and removed the quilt. Susan looked into the tureen and for once in her life was so completely ~~flabbergasted~~ ^**floored**^ that she had not a ~~world~~ word to say.

"What in the world is this?" asked the doctor, coming in.

Rilla poured out her story. ~~"And~~ "I just had to bring it, father," she concluded. "I couldn't leave it there."

~~"No, of course you couldn't," agreed the doctor. "From what I know of old Meg Conover it was out of the question. But~~ "What are you going to do with it?" asked the doctor coolly.

Rilla hadn't exactly expected this kind of question.

"We – we can keep it here for awhile – can't we – until thomething can be arranged?" she stammered confusedly.

Dr. Blythe walked up and down the kitchen for a moment or two while the baby stared at the white walls of the soup tureen and Susan showed signs of returning animation.

Presently the doctor confronted Rilla.

"A young baby means a great deal of additional work and trouble in a household, Rilla. Nan and Di are leaving for ~~college~~ Redmond next week and neither your mother nor Susan is able to assume so much extra care under present conditions. If you want to keep that baby here you must attend to it yourself."

"Me!" Rilla was dismayed into being ungrammatical. "Why – father – I – I couldn't!"

~~"Then the baby must go back to Meg Conover~~ "Younger girls than you have had to look after babies. My advice and Susan's is at your disposal. If you cannot, then the baby must go back to Meg Conover. Its lease of life will be short if it does, for it is evident that it is a ~~very~~ delicate child ~~but~~ ^**and requires particular care.** ~~**I thin**~~^ ^[*Note*]**K3**^ I cannot have your mother or Susan ~~over~~ over-taxed."

The doctor walked out of the kitchen, looking very stern and immovable. In his heart he knew quite well that the ~~baby too~~ small inhabitant of the ^**big**^ soup tureen would remain at Ingleside, but he meant to see if Rilla could not be induced to rise to the occasion.

Rilla sat looking blankly at the baby. It was absurd to think she could take care of it. But – that poor little, frail, dead mother who had worried about it – that dreadful old Meg Conover!

"Susan, what must be done for a baby?" she asked ~~piteously~~ dolefully.

"You must keep it warm and dry and wash it every day, ^[*Note*] **Y3**^ and feed it every ~~too~~ two hours. If it has colic, you put hot things on its stomach," said Susan, rather feebly ^**and flatly**^ for her.

The baby began to cry again.

"It must be hungry – it has to be fed anyhow," said Rilla desperately. "Tell me what to get for it, Susan, and I'll get it."

Under Susan's directions a ration of milk and water was prepared, ~~an old~~ ^**and**^ a bottle obtained from the doctor's office. Then Rilla lifted the baby out of the soup tureen and fed it. She brought down the old basket of her own infancy from the attic and laid the now sleeping baby in it. ^**She put the soup tureen away in the pantry.**^ Then she ~~thought~~ sat down to think things over.

The result of her thinking things over was that she went to Susan when the baby woke.

"I'm going to see what I can do, Susan. I can't let that poor little thing go back to Mrs. Conover. Tell me how to wash and dress it."

Under Susan's supervision Rilla bathed the baby ~~while with perspiration oozing from every pore~~. Susan dared not help, other than by suggestion, for the doctor was in the living room and might pop out at any moment. ^[*Note*] **M3**^ Rilla set her teeth and went ahead. ^**In the name of goodness,**^ how many wrinkles ^**and kinks**^ did a baby have? How absurdly small the creature was! Why, there wasn't enough of it to take hold of. Oh, suppose she let it slip into the water – it was so ~~slippery~~ ^**wobbly**^! If it would only stop howling like that! ^**How could such a tiny morsel make such an enormous noise. ~~Its shrieks~~**^ ^[*Note*] **I3**^

"Am I really hurting it much, Susan, do you suppose?" she asked piteously.

"No, dearie. Most new babies hate like poison to be washed. You are real knacky for a beginner. Keep your hand under its back, whatever you do, and keep cool."

Keep cool! Rilla was oozing perspiration at every ~~poor~~ ^**pore**^. When the baby was ~~dr~~ dried and dressed and temporarily quieted with another bottle she was as limp as a rag.

"What must I do with it to-night, Susan?"

A baby by day was dreadful enough; a baby by night was unthinkable.

"Set the basket on a chair by your bed and keep it covered. You~~'ll~~ ^**will**^ have to feed it once ^**or twice**^ in the night, so you would better take the oil heater upstairs. ^**If you cannot manage it call me and I will go, doctor or no doctor.**^"

"But, Susan, if it cries?"

~~"Most let likely it will. It seems to be good at that.~~

The baby, however, did not cry. ~~Perhaps~~ It was surprisingly good –

perhaps because its poor little stomach was filled with proper food. It slept most of the night but Rilla did not. She was afraid to go to sleep for fear something would happen to the baby. ^[*Note*] **J3**^ She reflected rather bitterly that father was very considerate of mother's and Susan's health, but what about hers? Did he think she could continue to exist if she never got any sleep? But she was not going to back down now – not she. She would look after this ~~baby~~ ^**detestable little ~~imp~~ animal**^ if it killed her. She would get a book on baby hygiene and be beholden to nobody. ~~She~~ ^[*Note*] **L3**^ Thus it came about that Mrs. Blythe, when she returned ^**home**^ two nights later and asked Susan where Rilla was, was electrified by Susan's composed reply.

"She's upstairs, Mrs. Dr. dear, putting her baby to bed."

Chapter 8

Rilla Decides

Families and individuals alike soon become used to new conditions and accept them unquestioningly. By the time ~~two weeks~~ ^**a week**^ had elapsed it seemed as if the Anderson baby had always been at Ingleside; ~~Rilla~~ ^**it was simply part of the routine of daily life**^. After the first three distracted nights Rilla began to sleep again, waking automatically to attend to her charge on schedule time. She ~~wash~~ bathed and fed and dressed it as skilfully as if she had been doing it all her life ~~but~~. She liked neither her job nor the baby any the better; she still handled it as gingerly as if it were some kind of a small lizard, and a breakable lizard at that; but she did her work thoroughly and there was not a cleaner, ~~or~~ better-cared-for infant in Glen St. Mary. She even took to weighing the creature every day and jotting ~~its~~ the result down in her diary; but sometimes she asked herself pathetically why unkind ~~fate~~ ^**destiny**^ had ever led her down the Anderson lane on that fatal day. ~~Mother and~~ Shirley, Nan, and Di did not tease her as much as she had expected. They all seemed rather stunned by the mere fact of Rilla adopting a war-baby; perhaps, too, the doctor had issued instructions. Walter, of course, never had teased her over anything; one day he told her she was a brick ~~and he was proud of her pluck~~.

"It took more courage for you to ~~face~~ ^**tackle**^ that five pounds of new infant, Rilla-my-Rilla, than it would be for Jem to face a mile of Germans. I wish I had half your pluck," he said ruefully. ^[*Note*] **N3**^

~~^**Rilla was very proud of Walter's approval but she sighed**^~~ "I wish I could like ~~it~~ ^**the baby**^ a little bit," ~~sighed Rilla~~. "It would make things easier. But I don't. ~~I detest~~ I've heard people say that when you took care of a baby you got fond of it – but you don't – I don't, anyway. ~~I detest~~ And it's a nuisance – it interferes with everything. It just ties me down – and now of all times when I'm trying to get the Junior Reds started. And I couldn't go to ~~Adella~~ ^**Alice**^ Clow's ~~party dance~~ ^**party**^ last night and I was just dying to. Of course father isn't really unreasonable and I can always get an hour or two off in the evening when it's necessary; but I knew he wouldn't stand for my being out half the night and leaving Susan or mother to see to the baby. I suppose it was just as well, because the thing did take colic – or something – about one o'clock. ^[*Note*] **B4**^ It screamed till it was black in the face; I got up and heated water and put the hot-water bottle on its stomach, and it howled worse than ever and drew up its poor wee ^**thin**^ legs. I was afraid I had burnt it but I don't believe I did. Then I walked the floor with it although '~~Holt~~ ^**Morgan**^ on Infants' says that should never be done. I walked miles, and oh, I was so tired and discouraged and mad – yes, I was. I could have ~~shook~~ ^**shaken**^ the creature if it had been big enough to shake, but it wasn't. Father was out on a case, and mother had had a headache and Susan is squiffy because ^**when she and ~~Holt~~ Morgan**^ ^**differ**^ I insist upon going by what ~~Holt~~ ^**Morgan**^ says, so I was determined I wouldn't call her unless I had to.

"Finally, Miss Oliver came in. She rooms with Nan now, not me, all because of the baby, and I am broken-hearted about it. I miss our long talks after we went to bed, so much. It was the only time I ever had her to myself. I hated to think the baby's yells had wakened her up, for she has so much to bear now. Mr. Grant is at Valcartier, too, and Miss Oliver feels it dreadfully, though she is splendid about it. She thinks he will never come back and her eyes just break my heart ^**– they are too tragic.**^ She said it wasn't the baby that woke her – she hadn't been able to sleep because the Germans are ~~only twenty ^30^ miles from~~ ^**so near**^ Paris; she took ~~it~~ ^**the little wretch**^ and laid it flat on ~~her~~ ^**its**^ stomach across her knee and thumped its back gently a few times ^ – ^ and it stopped shrieking and went right off to sleep and slept like a lamb the rest of the night. I didn't – I was too worn out. ~~^[*Note*] **Q2**^~~ I have just felt all day like something the cats had brought in, as Susan says.

"I'm having a perfectly dreadful time getting the Junior Reds started. I succeeded in ~~having~~ getting Betty Mead as president, ^**and I am secretary,**^ but they put ~~Olive Kirk Ida Crawford~~ Jen Vickers in as treasurer and I despise her. ^[*Note*] **X3**^ ~~I am secretary.~~

"Just as I expected, Olive was determined we should have lunch served ~~when~~ at our meetings ~~and I was just as determined we shouldn't~~.

We had a battle royal over it. ~~but t~~ ^**T**^he majority was against eats and now the minority is sulking. Irene Howard was on the eats side and she has been very cool to me ever since and it makes me feel miserable. I wonder if mother and Mrs. Elliott have ~~the same~~ problems in the Senior Society too. I suppose they have, but they just go on calmly in spite of everything. I go on – but not calmly – I rage and cry – but I do it all in private ^**and blow off steam in this diary;**^ and when it's over I vow I'll show them. I never sulk ~~anyhow~~. I detest people who sulk. Anyhow, we've got the society started ~~and we are all learning to knit. Everybody is knitting now – even Susan's old Cousin Sophia who knits like a streak and forebodes the worst as she knits. I picked it up quite easily and~~ and we're to meet once a ~~fortnight~~ week, ^**and we're all going to learn to ~~knit~~ knit.**^ So much is accomplished.

"Shirley and I went down to the station again ~~to-day~~ ^**yesterday**^ to try to induce ~~Rags~~ ^**Dog Monday**^ to come home but we failed. All the family have tried and failed. Three days after Jem had gone Walter went down and brought ~~Rags~~ ^**Monday**^ home by main force in the buggy and shut him up for ten days; and ^[*Note*] **Z9**^ ~~Rags ^**wouldn't eat a thing but**^ tore off a board on the wall of the stable and got out~~.

"So we have decided to let him alone and father has arranged with the butcher near the station to feed ~~Rags~~ ^**him**^ with bones and scraps ~~every day~~. Besides, one of us ~~wa~~ goes down nearly every day to take him something. He just lies curled up in the shipping-shed, and every time a train comes in he will rush over to the platform, wagging his tail expectantly, and tear around to everyone who comes off the train. And then, when ~~everyone is off~~ ^**the train goes**^ and he realizes that Jem has not come, he creeps dejectedly back to his shed, with his disappointed eyes, and lies down patiently ^**to wait for the next train**^. Mr. Gray, the station master, says there are times when he ~~can't keep the~~ can hardly help crying from sheer sympathy. One day some boys threw stones at ~~Rags~~ ^**Monday**^ and old Johnny Meade, who never was known to take notice of anything before, snatched up a meat axe in the butcher's shop and chased them through the village. Nobody has ~~ever~~ molested ~~Rags~~ ^**Monday**^ since.

"Kenneth Ford has gone back to Toronto. He ~~called tw~~ came up two evenings ago to say good-bye. I wasn't home – some clothes had to be made for the baby and Mrs. Meredith offered to help me, so I was over at the manse, and I didn't see Kenneth. Not that it matters; he told Nan to say good-bye to Spider for him and tell me not to forget him ^**wholly**^ in my ^**absorbing**^ maternal duties. If he could ~~send~~ ^**leave**^ such a frivolous, insulting message as that ~~to~~ for me it shows plainly that our beautiful hour on the sandshore meant nothing to him and I am not going to think about him ^**or it**^ again." ^[*Note*] **C4**^

About the first of September there was an exodus from Ingleside and the manse. Faith, Nan, Di and Walter left for Redmond; Carl betook himself to his ^**Harbor Head**^ school and Shirley was off to Queen's. Rilla was left alone at Ingleside and would have been very lonely if ~~the baby had given her~~ ^**she had had**^ time to be. She missed Walter ~~very much~~ ^**keenly**^; since their talk in Rainbow Valley they had grown very near together and Rilla ~~talked over~~ ^**discussed**^ problems with Walter which she never mentioned to others. But she was so busy with the Junior Reds and her baby that there was rarely a spare minute for loneliness; sometimes, for a ~~few minutes~~ ^**tiny ~~time~~ space**^, after she went to bed, she cried a little in her pillow over Walter's absence and Jem at Valcartier and Kenneth's unromantic farewell message, ~~^**Note Z3**^ and~~ but she was generally asleep before the tears got fairly started.

"Shall I make arrangements to have the baby sent to Hopetown?" the doctor asked one day

For a moment Rilla was tempted to say "yes." The baby could be sent to Hopetown – it would be decently looked after – she could have her free days and untrammelled nights back again. But – but – that poor young mother who hadn't wanted it to go to the asylum! Rilla couldn't get that out of her thoughts. And that very morning she discovered that the baby had gained ~~a pound~~ ^**~~six ozce~~ 8 ounces**^ since its coming to Ingleside. Rilla had felt such a thrill of pride over this.

~~"Hadn't you better wait until you hear from its father?" she said. "He has been written to – he might not want to have it sent to Hopetown. If he is fighting for his country And~~

"You – you said it mightn't live if it went to Hopetown," she said.

"It mightn't. Somehow, institutional care, no matter how good it may be, doesn't always succeed with delicate babies. But you know what it means if you want it kept here, Rilla."

"I've taken care of it for a fortnight – and it has gained ~~a~~ ^**half a**^ pound," cried Rilla. "I think we'd better wait until we hear from its father anyhow. He mightn't want to have it sent to an orphan asylum,[22] ^**when he is fighting the battles of his country.**^"

The doctor and Mrs. Blythe exchanged amused, satisfied smiles behind Rilla's back; and nothing more was said about ~~the orphan asylum~~ Hopetown.

Then the smile faded from the doctor's face; the Germans were twenty miles from Paris. ~~Life was very tense at Ingleside for the older people.~~

~~"We eat up the news," said Miss Oliver ^**told Mrs. Meredith**^ feverishly. "We study the maps and nip the whole~~ Horrible tales were beginning to appear in the papers ~~regarding~~ of deeds done ~~to~~ in martyred Belgium. Life was very tense at Ingleside for the older people.

"We eat up the war news," Gertrude Oliver told Mrs. Meredith, trying to laugh and failing. "We study the maps and nip the whole Hun army in a few well-directed strategic ~~moves~~ ^**moves**^. But ^**Papa**^ Joffre hasn't the benefit of our advice – and ~~the~~ ^**so**^ Paris – must – fall."

"Will they reach it – will not some mighty hand yet intervene?" ~~muttered~~ ^**murmured**^ ~~Mr.~~ John Meredith.

"I teach school like one in a dream," ~~said~~ ^**continued**^ Gertrude; "then I come home and shut myself in my room and walk the floor. I am wearing a path right across Nan's carpet. We are so horribly near this war. It means so much to us all."

~~^**"Them German ^^men^^ are at Senlis.**^~~ ^**Note G10**^

"Nothing nor nobody can save Paris now," wailed Cousin Sophia ~~lugubriously~~. Cousin Sophia ~~in her 71st year~~ had taken to reading the newspapers and had learned more about the ~~geog~~ geography of northern France, ^**if not about the pronunciation of French names,**^ in her seventy-first year than she had ever known in her schooldays.

"I ~~haven't~~ ^**have**^ not such a poor opinion of the Almighty, ^**or of Kitchener,**^" said Susan stubbornly. "^**I see**^ ~~T~~there is a Bernstoff man in the States who says that the war is over and Germany has won ^[*Note*] **O3**^ but I could tell ~~him~~ ^**them both**^ that it is ~~poor~~ ^**chancy**^ work counting chickens even the day before they are hatched,[22] ^**and bears have been known to live long after their skins were sold.**^"

"Why ain't the British navy doing more?" persisted Cousin Sophia.

"Even the British navy cannot sail on dry land, Sophia Crawford. I have not given up hope, and I shall not, Tomascow and Mobbage and all such barbarous names to the contrary notwithstanding. Mrs. Dr. dear, can you tell me if ~~it~~ R-h-e-i-m-s is Rimes or Reems or Rames or Rems?"

"I believe it's really more like 'Rhangs,' Susan." ^[*Note*] **P3**^

"They tell me the Germans has ~~run~~ about ruined the church there," sighed Cousin Sophia. "I always thought the Germans was ~~c~~Christians."

"A church is bad enough but their doings in Belgium are far worse," said Susan grimly. "When I heard the doctor reading about them bayonetting the babies, Mrs. Dr. dear, I just thought, 'Oh, what if it were our little Jem!' I was stirring the soup ^**at the time**^, as you know, when that thought came to me and I just felt that if I could have lifted that saucepan full of that boiling soup and ~~turned it over~~ ^**thrown it at**^ the Kaiser~~'s head~~ I would not have lived in vain."

"To-morrow – to-morrow – will ~~come~~ ^**bring**^ the news that ~~Paris~~ the Germans are in Paris," said ~~Miss Oliver~~ ^**Gertrude Oliver**^, ^[*Note*] **R3**^

But on the morrow ^**and the next morrow**^ came the news of the miracle of the Marne. Rilla ~~came rushing~~ ^**rushed madly**^ home from the office waving the Enterprise with its big red headlines. Susan ran out with trembling hands to hoist the flag. ~~Mr. Meredith came over Mrs. Blythe cried and laughed and cried again~~ The doctor stalked about muttering "Thank God." ~~Mr. Meredith came over and said,~~ ^**Mrs. Blythe cried and laughed and cried again.**^

"God just put out His hand and touched them – 'thus far – no farther'," said Mr. Meredith ~~who had hastened over.~~ that evening.

Rilla ~~sang~~ ^**was singing upstairs**^ as she put the baby to bed ~~that night ^**upstairs**^~~. ^**Paris was saved –**^ the war was over – ~~but not as the German Ambassador had~~ but Germany had lost – there would soon be an end now –Jem and Jerry would be back. The black clouds had rolled by.

[*Montgomery puts a line across the page here to indicate the original chapter end.*]

"Don't you dare have colic this joyful night," she told the baby. "If you do I'll clap you back into your soup tureen and ship you off to Hopetown ^– **by freight** –^ on the early train. You have got beautiful eyes – and you're not quite as red ^**and wrinkled**^ as you were – but you haven't a speck of hair – and your hands are like little claws – and I don't like you a bit better than I ever did. But I hope your poor little white mother knows that you're tucked in a soft basket with a bottle of milk as rich as ~~Holt~~ ^**Morgan**^ allows instead of perishing by inches with old Meg Conover.[22]
[*Montgomery places a second line across the page again here to indicate the second choice of a chapter ending.*]

And I hope she doesn't know that I nearly drowned you ~~that~~ ^**that**^ first morning when Susan wasn't there ~~because~~ ^**and**^ I let you slip right out of my hands into the water. Why will you be so slippery?[22]
[*Montgomery places a third line across the page here to indicate the third choice of a chapter end.*]

No, I don't like you and I never will but for all that I'm going to make a decent, upstanding infant of you. You are going to get
^**Over**^ [*Montgomery's note to remind herself that the rest of the ending is on the back of this page.*]
as fat as a self-respecting infant ^**child**^ should be, for one thing. I am not going to have people saying 'what a puny little thing that baby of Rilla Blythe's is' as old Mrs. Drew said at the senior Red Cross yesterday. If I can't love you I mean to be proud of you[22] at least."

Chapter 9

Doc Has a Misadventure

"The war will not be over before next spring now," said Dr. Blythe, when it became ~~evident~~ ^**apparent**^ that the ^**long**^ battle of the Aisne had resulted in a stalemate. ~~So the Ingleside folk "girded up their loins and pitched in" as Susan expressed it. Ril~~

Rilla was murmuring "knit four, purl one" under her breath, and rocking ~~Jim's~~ ^**the baby's**^ cradle with one foot. ~~Holt~~ ^**Morgan**^ disapproved of cradles for babies but Susan did not, and it was worth while to make some ^**slight**^ sacrifice of principle to keep Susan in good humour. ^**So a cradle had been substituted for Rilla's old basket.**^ ~~Miss Oliver sighed~~ She laid down her knitting for a moment and said, "Oh, how can we bear it so long?" – then picked up her sock and went on. The Rilla of two months before would have rushed ~~upstairs~~ ^**off to Rainbow Valley**^ and cried.

Miss Oliver sighed and Mrs. Blythe clasped her hands for a moment. Then Susan said briskly, "Well, we must just gird up our ~~loies~~ ^**loins**^ and pitch in. Business as usual is England's motto, they tell me, ~~and~~ Mrs. Dr. dear, and I have taken it for mine, ^**not thinking I could easily find a better.**^ I shall make ~~a pudding to-day~~ the same kind of pudding to-day I always make on Saturday. It ~~was Little Jem's favorite~~ is a good deal of trouble to make, and that is well, for it will ~~take up~~ ^**employ**^ my thoughts. I will remember that Kitchener is at the helm and ~~Joffre may be a good general~~ ^**Joffer is doing ~~do~~ very well**^ for a Frenchman.[22] ^**I shall**^ ~~And everywhere the lads of the world, sick and poor, high and low, white and brown, and red, followed the Pipers call.~~ ^**get that box of cake off to ^^little^^ Jem and**^ finish that pair of socks to-day likewise. A sock a day is my allowance. ^[*Note*] **A4**^ Even Cousin Sophia has taken to knitting, Mrs. Dr. dear, and it is a good thing, for she cannot think of quite so many doleful ~~things to say~~ ^**speeches to make**^ when her hands are busy with her needles instead of being ~~clasped~~ ^**folded**^ ~~over~~ ^**on**^ her stomach. She thinks we will all be Germans this time next year but I tell her it will take more than a year to make a German out of me.~~" As long as I can handle a pitchfork~~ Do you know that Rick MacAllister has enlisted, Mrs. Dr. dear? And they say Joe Milgrave would ^**too,**^ only he is afraid that if he does that Whiskers-on-the-Moon will not let him have Miranda. Whiskers says that he will believe the stories of German atrocities when he sees them, and that it ~~was~~ ^**is**^ a good thing that Rangs Cathedral has been destroyed because it was a Roman Catholic church. Now, I am not a Roman Catholic, Mrs. Dr. dear, being born and bred a good Presbyterian and meaning to live and die one, but I maintain that the Catholics have as good a right to their churches as we have to ours and that the Huns had no kind of business to destroy them. Just think, Mrs. Dr. dear," concluded Susan pathetically, "how we would feel if a German shell knocked down the spire of our church here in the glen, and I'm sure it is ~~just~~ ^**every bit**^ as bad to think of Rangs cathedral being ~~knocked~~ ^**hammered**^ to pieces."

And, meanwhile, everywhere, ~~all over the world,~~ the lads of the world rich and poor, low and high, white and brown, were following the Piper's call.

"Even Billy Andrews' boy is going – and Jane's only son – and Diana's little ~~laddy~~ ^**Jack**^," said ~~Anne~~ Mrs. Blythe~~, over her letters~~. "Priscilla's son has gone from Japan and Stella's from Vancouver – and both the Rev. Jo's boys. Philippa writes that her boys 'went right away, not being afflicted with her indecision.'"

"Jem ~~writes~~ says that he thinks they will be leaving very soon now, and that he will not be able to get leave to come so far before they go, as they will have to start at a few hours' notice," said the doctor ~~as he folded up his letter, handed~~, ^~~**hand**~~ **passing**^ the letter to his wife.

"That is not fair," said Susan indignantly. "Has Sir Sam Hughes no regard for our feelings? The idea of whisking that blessed boy away to Europe without letting us even have ~~another~~ ^**a last**^ glimpse of him! If I were you, doctor dear, I would write to the papers about it, that I would."

"Perhaps it is as well," said the disappointed mother. "I don't believe I could bear another parting from him – now that I know the war will not be over as soon as we hoped when he left first. Oh, if only – but no, I won't say it! Like ~~you~~ Susan and Rilla," concluded Mrs. Blythe,

~~determined to~~ achieving a laugh, "I am determined to be a heroine."

"You're all good stuff," said the doctor, "I'm proud of my women folks. Even Rilla here, my 'lily of the field,' is running a Red Cross Society full blast and saving ~~the~~ ^**a**^ little life ~~of a future Canadian~~ for Canada. That's a good piece of work. Rilla, daughter of Anne, what are you going to call your war baby?"

"I'm waiting to hear from Jim Anderson," said Rilla. "He may want to name his own child."

But as the autumn weeks went by no word came from Jim Anderson, who had never been heard from since he sailed from Halifax, and to whom the fate of wife and child seemed a matter of indifference. Eventually Rilla decided to call the baby James, ~~Anders~~ and Susan opined that "Kitchener" should be added thereto. So James Kitchener Anderson became the possessor of a name somewhat more imposing than himself. The Ingleside family promptly shortened it to "Jims," but Susan obstinately called him "Little Kitchener" and nothing else.

"Jims is no name for a Christian child, Mrs. Dr. dear," she said disapprovingly. "Cousin Sophia says it is too flippant, and for once I consider she utters sense, though I would not please her by openly agreeing with her. As for the child, he is beginning to look something like a baby, and I must ~~say~~ ^**admit**^ that Rilla is wonderful with him, though I would not pamper pride by saying so to her face. Mrs. Dr. dear, I shall never, no never, forget the first sight I had of that infant, lying in that big soup tureen, rolled up in dirty flannel. It is not often that Susan Baker is flabbergasted, but flabbergasted I was ~~that moment~~ ~~^**minute**^~~ ^**then**^, and that you may tie to. For one awful moment I thought my ~~brain~~ ^**mind**^ had given way and that I was seeing visions. Then thinks I, 'No, I never heard of anyone having a vision of a soup tureen, so it must be real at least,' and I plucked up confidence. When I heard the doctor tell Rilla that she must take care of the baby I thought he was joking, for I did not believe for a minute she would or could do it. But you see what has happened and it is making a woman of her. When we have to do a thing, Mrs. Dr. dear, we can do it."

Susan added another proof to this concluding dictum of hers one day ~~late~~ in October. ~~The doct Dr. Blythe was away.~~ The doctor and his wife were away. Rilla was presiding over Jims' afternoon siesta upstairs,

~~and~~ purling four and knitting one with ceaseless vim. Susan was seated on the back veranda, shelling beans, and Cousin Sophia was helping her. Peace and tranquility brooded over the Glen ^[*Note*]**O4**^ Rainbow Valley lay in a soft, autumnal haze of fairy purple. The maple grove was a burning ~~splendor~~ ^**bush**^ of color and the hedge of sweet-briar around the kitchen yard was a thing of ~~beauty beauty~~ ^**wonder**^ in its subtle tintings. It did not seem that strife could be in the world, and Susan's faithful heart was ~~momentarily~~ lulled into a brief forgetfulness, although she had lain awake most of the preceding night thinking of Little Jem ^**far**^ out on the ~~ocean~~ ^**Atlantic**^, where the great fleet was carrying Canada's first ~~army~~ army across the ocean. Even Cousin Sophia looked less melancholy than usual and admitted that there was not much fault to be found in the day, although there was no doubt it was a weather-breeder and there would be an awful storm on ~~his~~ ^**its**^ heels.

^**"Things is too calm ~~too~~ ^^to^^ last," she said.**^

~~Suddenly, amid all this longer~~

As if in confirmation of ~~Cousin Sophia's prediction~~ ^**her assertion,**^ a most unearthly din suddenly arose ~~in the kitchen~~ behind them. It was quite impossible to describe the confused medley of bangs and rattles and ~~sup half~~ muffled shrieks and yowls that proceeded from the kitchen, accompanied by occasional ~~smashes~~ ^**crashes**^. Susan and Cousin Sophia stared at each other in dismay.

"What upon airth has bruk loose in there?" gasped Cousin Sophia. ~~"You "Can it be~~

"It must be that Hyde-cat gone clean mad at last," muttered Susan. "I have always expected it."

Rilla came flying out of the side door of the living room.

"What has happened?" she ~~gas~~ demanded.

"It is beyond me to say, but that possessed beast of yours is evidently at the bottom of it," said Susan. "Do not go near him, at least, I will open the door and peep in. There goes some more of the crockery. I have always said that the devil was in him and that I will tie to."

"It is my opinion that the cat has hydrophob~~ia~~ ^**y**^," said Cousin Sophia solemnly. "I ~~knew have~~ ^**once**^ **heerd of**^ a cat ^**that**^ went mad ~~once~~ and bit three people – and they all died a most terrible death, and turned black as ~~stones~~ ^**ink**^."

Undismayed by this, Susan opened the door and looked in. ^~~**AA**~~ **Put in here AA-AA**^ [*Montgomery's note to remind herself about moving a bloc of material.*] Around and around the kitchen tore a frantic cat, with his head wedged tightly in an old salmon can. Blindly he careered about with shrieks and profanity commingled, now banging the can madly against anything he encountered, now trying vainly to wrench it off with his paws. ^**AA**^ The floor was littered with fragments of broken dishes, for it seemed that the fatal tragedy had taken place on the long dresser where Susan's array of cooking bowls had been marshalled in shining state. ^**AA**^

~~"My big blue bowl~~

The sight was so funny that Rilla doubled up with laughter. Susan looked at her reproachfully.

"I see nothing to laugh at. That beast has broken your ma's big blue mixing bowl that she ~~has had ever since she was married and~~ brought from Green Gables ~~ever~~ when she was married. That is no small calamity, in my opinion. But the thing to consider now is how to get that can off ~~the~~ Hyde's head."

"Don't you dast go touching it," exclaimed Cousin Sophia, galvanized into animation. "It might be your death. Shut the kitchen up and send for Albert."

"I am not in the habit of sending for Albert during family difficulties," said Susan loftily. "That beast is in torment, and whatever my opinion of him may be, I cannot endure to see him suffering pain. He is not mad – at least not any madder than he frequently is. But you keep away, Rilla, for little Kitchener's sake, and I will see what I can do."

Susan stalked undauntedly into the kitchen, seized an old storm coat of the doctor's and ^[*Note*] **D4**^ ~~threw it~~ ^**managed to throw it**^ over cat and can. ~~Then she seized the squirming animal and~~ ^**Then she**^ proceeded to saw the can loose with a can-opener, ~~whill~~ ^**while**^ Rilla held the squirming animal, rolled in the coat. Anything like Doc's shrieks while the process was going on was never heard at Ingleside. Susan was in mortal dread that the Albert Crawfords would hear it and conclude she was torturing the creature to death. Doc was a wrathful and indignant cat when he was freed. Evidently he thought the whole thing was a put-up job to bring him low. He gave Susan a baleful glance by way of gratitude and rushed out of the kitchen to take ~~refuge~~ ^**sanctuary**^ in the ^**jungle of the**^ sweet briar hedge, where he sulked ~~n~~ for the rest of the day. Susan swept up her broken ~~bowls~~ ^**dishes**^ ~~in~~ grimly.

"The Huns themselves couldn't have worked more havoc ~~here~~ ^**here**^," she said bitterly. "But when people will keep ~~a cat~~ ^**a Satanic animal**^ like that, in spite of all warnings, they cannot complain when their wedding bowls get broken.

[*Montgomery places a line across the page here to indicate the original chapter end.*]

Things have come to a pretty pass when an honest woman cannot leave her kitchen for a few minutes without a fiend of a cat rampaging through it with his head in a salmon can."

Chapter 10

~~Dark and Bright~~
The Troubles of Rilla

~~The dreary days of November and December went by. To Antwerp fell~~
October passed out and the dreary days of November and December dragged by. The world shook with the thunder of contending armies; Antwerp fell – Turkey declared war – gallant little Serbia gathered herself together and struck a deadly blow at her oppressor; and in quiet, hill-girdled Glen St. Mary, thousands of miles away, hearts beat with hope and fear over the varying dispatches from day to day. ^**Note G4**^

There was just one great event every day – the coming of the mail. ~~For the rest existence went on, busy and tense~~ Even Susan admitted that from the time the mail-courier's buggy rumbled over the little bridge between the station and the village until the papers were brought home and read, she could not work properly.

~~"When I see~~ "I just take up my knitting then and knit hard till the papers come, Mrs. Dr. dear. Knitting is something you can do, even when your heart is going like a trip-hammer and the pit of your stomach feels all gone and your thoughts are catawampus. Then when I see the headlines, be they good or be they bad, I calm down and am able to go about my business again. It is an unfortunate thing that the mail comes in just when ~~the~~ ^**our**^ dinner rush is on, and I think the Government could arrange things better. But the drive on ~~Callais~~ ^**Calais**^ has failed, as I felt perfectly sure it would, and the Kaiser will not eat his Christmas dinner in London this year. Do you know, Mrs. Dr. dear," – Susan's voice lowered as a token ^**that**^ she was going to impart a very shocking piece of information, – "~~they tell~~ I have been told on good authority – or else you may be sure I would not be repeating it when it concerns a minster – that the Rev. Mr. Arnold goes to Charlottetown every week and takes a Turkish bath for his rheumatism. The idea of him doing that when we ~~were~~ ^**are**^ at war with Turkey? One of his own deacons has always insisted that Mr. Arnold's theology was not sound and I am beginning to believe that there is some reason to fear it.

Well, I must bestir myself this afternoon and get ^**Little**^ Jem's Christmas cake packed up for him. He will enjoy it, if the blessed boy is not drowned in mud before that time."

Jem was in camp on Salisbury Plain and was writing gay, cheery letters home in spite of the mud. Walter was at Redmond and his letters to Rilla were anything but cheerful. She never opened one without a dread tugging at her heart that it would tell her he had enlisted. His unhappiness made her unhappy. She wanted to put her arm round him and comfort him, as she had done that day in Rainbow Valley. She hated ~~the Kaiser and ev~~ everybody ~~and everything that~~ who was responsible for Walter's unhappiness.

"He will go yet," she murmured miserably to herself one afternoon, as she sat alone in Rainbow Valley, reading a letter from him, "he will go yet – and if he does I just can't bear it."

Walter wrote that someone had sent him an envelope containing a white feather.

~~"It was just," her~~

"I deserved it, Rilla. I felt that I ought to put it on and wear it – proclaiming ^**myself**^ to all Redmond the coward I know I am. The boys of my year are going – going. Every day ~~a few more~~ ~~^**one or two**^~~ ^**two or three**^ of them join up. Some days I almost make ^**up**^ my mind ~~up~~ to do it – and then I see myself thrusting a bayonet through another man ^[*Note*] **P4**^ – I see myself lying ^**alone**^ torn and mangled, burning with thirst on a cold, wet field, surrounded by dead and dying men – and I know I never can. I can't face even the thought of it. How could I face the reality? There are times ^**when**^ I wish I had never been born. Life has always seemed such a beautiful thing to me – I wanted to make it more beautiful – and now it is a hideous thing. Rilla-my-Rilla, if it weren't for your letters – your dear, bright, merry, funny, comical, believing letters – I think I'd give up. And Una's! Una is really a little brick, isn't she? ~~She hasn't~~ There's a wonderful fineness and firmness under all that shy, wistful girlishness of her. She hasn't your knack of writing laugh-provoking epistles, but there's something in her letters – I don't know what – that makes me feel, at least while I'm reading them – that I could even go to the front. Not that she ever says a word about my going – or hints that I ought to go – she isn't that kind. It's just the spirit of them – the personality that is in them. Well, I can't go. You have a brother and Una has a friend who is a coward."

"Oh, I wish Walter wouldn't write such things," sighed Rilla. "It hurts me. He isn't a coward – he isn't – he isn't!"

She looked wistfully about her ^[*Note*] **L4**^ How everything ~~in Rainbow Valley~~ reminded her of Walter! The red leaves ^~~**that**~~ **still clung to**^ ~~on~~ the wild sweet briars that overhung a curve of the brook; their stems were gemmed with the pearls of the gentle rain that had fallen a little while before. Walter had once written a poem describing them. The wind was ~~breathing softly~~ ^**sighing and rustling**^ among the frosted brown bracken ferns ^[*Note*] **F4**^ Walter had said once that he loved the melancholy of the autumn wind on a ~~gray~~ ^**November**^ day ~~better than briskness~~. The old Tree Lovers still clasped each other in a faithful embrace, ~~Walter had~~ and the White Lady, now a great white-branched tree, stood out ^**beautifully fine,**^ against the gray velvet sky. Walter had named them long ago; and ~~a year ago~~ ^**last November**^, when ~~she and~~ he had walked with her and Miss Oliver in the Valley he had said, ~~speaking~~ looking at the leafless Lady ^[*Note*] **K4**^ "A white birch is a beautiful Pagan maiden who has never lost the Eden secret of being naked and unashamed." Miss Oliver had said, "Put that into a poem, Walter," and he had ^**done so**^, and read it to them the next day – ~~a~~ just a ~~few lines~~ short thing with goblin imagination in every line of it. Oh, how happy they had been then!

Well – Rilla scrambled to her feet – time was up Jims would soon be awake – his lunch had to be prepared – his little slips had to be ironed – there was a committee meeting of the Junior Reds that night – there was her new knitting bag to finish – it would be the handsomest bag in the Junior Society – handsomer even than Irene Howard's – she must get home and get to work. She was busy these days from morning till night. That little monkey of a Jims took so much time. But he was growing ^ – ^ he was certainly growing. And there were times when Rilla felt sure that it was not merely a pious hope but an absolute fact that he was getting ~~a trifle~~ ^**decidedly**^ better looking. Sometimes she felt quite proud of him; and sometimes she yearned to spank him. ~~Susan and Mrs. Blythe made much of him and talked to him, but. However, he was not quite~~ But she never kissed him or wanted to kiss him.

~~"The G~~ "The Germans captured Lodz to-day," said Miss Oliver, one December evening, when ~~they~~ ^**she or Mrs. Blythe, and Susan**^ were ~~all~~ busy sewing or knitting in the cosy living-room. "This war is at least extending my knowledge of geography. Schoolma'am though I am, ~~six was~~ three months ago I didn't know there was such a place in the world as Lodz. Had I heard it mentioned I would have known nothing about it and cared as little. ~~To-day the n~~ I know all about it now – its size, its standing, its military significance. ~~To-day~~ ^**Yesterday**^ the news that the Germans have captured it in their second rush to Warsaw made my heart sink into ~~bo~~ my boots. I woke up ^**in the night and worried over it.**^ ~~at three o'clock last night and worried over it."~~

~~Three o'clock at night is an abominable hour. I don't wonder babies always cry.~~

~~"Three o'clock at night is an abominable hour," said Mrs. Blythe. "I always see Germany victorious then – I never see her so at any other time.~~ I don't wonder babies always cry when they wake up in the night. Everything presses on my soul then and no cloud has a silver lining." ^[*Note*] **E4**^

~~^**Note K4**^ "How do you pronou "Mrs. Dr. dear," said Susan, who was knitting and reading at the same time, "how do you pronounce P-r-s-y-m-y-s-l?"~~

"That last is a conundrum which nobody seems to have solved yet, Susan. And I can make only a guess at the others."

"These foreign names are far from being decent, in my opinion," said disgusted Susan.

"I dare say the Austrians and Russians would think Saskatchewan and Musquodoboit about as bad, Susan," said Miss Oliver. ~~Rilla was upstairs relieving her over-charged feelings by writing in her diary.~~ "The Serbians have done wonderfully of late. They have captured Belgrade ~~and sent the Austrians packing across the Danube~~."

"And sent the Austrian creatures packing across the Danube with a flea in their ear," said Susan with a relish, as she settled down to examine a map of Eastern Europe, prodding each locality with the knitting needle to brand it on her memory. ^[*Note*] **J4**^

Rilla was upstairs relieving her over-charged feelings by writing in her diary.

~~“I am desperately~~

“Things have all ‘gone catawampus,’ as Susan says, with me this week. Part of it was my own fault and part of it wasn’t, and I seem to be equally unhappy over both parts.

“I went to town the other day to buy a new winter hat. It was the first time nobody insisted on coming with me to help me select it, and I felt that mother had really given up thinking of me as a child. ~~I looked over hundreds of~~ And I found the dearest hat – it was simply bewitching. It was ~~of velvet of the and~~ a velvet hat, of the very shade of ^**rich**^ green that was made for me. It ~~just~~ goes with my hair and complexion beautifully, bringing out the red-brown shades and ~~the cream~~ what Miss Oliver calls my “‘creaminess’” so well. Only once before in my life have I come across that precise shade of green. When I was twelve I had a little ~~felt~~ ^**beaver**^ hat of ~~that shade~~ ^**it**^, and all the girls in school were wild over it. Well, as soon as I saw this hat I felt that I simply must have it – and have it I did. The price was dreadful. I will not put it down here because I don’t want my descendants to know I was guilty of paying so much for a hat in war time when everybody is – or should be – trying to be economical.

“When I got home and tried on the hat again in my room I was assailed by qualms. Of course, it was very becoming; but ~~it~~ somehow it seemed too elaborate and fussy for church going and our quiet little doings in the Glen – too conspicuous, in short. It hadn’t seemed so ~~in~~ at the milliner’s but here in my little white room it did. ~~But the worst was~~ And that dreadful price tag! ^[*Note*] **H4**^

“When mother saw the hat and the tag she just looked at me. Mother is some expert at looking. Father says she looked him into love with her years ago in Avonlea school and I can well believe it – though I have heard a weird tale of her banging him over the head with a slate ^**at the very beginning of their acquaintance.**^ Mother was a limb when she was a little girl, I understand, and even up to the time when Jem went away she was full of ginger. But let me return to my ~~mitt~~ mutton – that is to say, my new green velvet hat.

“‘Do you think, Rilla,’” mother said quietly – far too quietly – ‘that it was right to spend so much for a hat, especially just now when the need of the world is so great?’

“‘I ~~go~~ paid for it out of my own allowance, mother,’ I ~~cried~~ exclaimed.

“‘That is not the point. Your allowance is based on the principle of a ~~fair~~ reasonable amount for each thing you need. If you pay too much for one thing you must cut off somewhere else and that is not satisfactory. But if you think you did right, Rilla, I have no more to say. I leave it to your conscience.’”

“I wish mother would not leave things to my conscience! And anyway, what was I to do? I couldn’t take that hat back – I had worn it to a concert in town – I had to keep it! I was so uncomfortable that I flew into a temper – a cold, calm, deadly temper.

“‘Mother,’ I said haughtily, ‘I am sorry you disapprove of my hat –’

“‘Not of the hat exactly,’ said mother, “‘though I consider it in doubtful taste for so young a girl – but of the price you paid for it.’”

“Being interrupted didn’t improve my temper, so I went on, colder and calmer and deadlier than ever, just as if mother had not spoken, – but I have to keep it now. However, I promise you that I will not get another hat for three years or for the duration of the war, if it lasts longer than that. Even you’ – oh, the sarcasm I put into the ‘you’ – cannot say that what I paid was too much when spread over at least three years.’

“‘You will be very tired of that hat before three years, Rilla,’ said mother, with a provoking grin, ^**which, being interpreted, meant that I wouldn’t stick it out.**^

‘Tired or not, I will wear it that long,’ I said: and then I marched upstairs and cried to think that I had been sarcastic to mother.

“I hate that hat already. But three years ^**or the duration of the war**^, I said, and three years ^**or the duration of the war**^ it shall be. I vowed and I shall keep my vow, cost what it will.

“That is one of the ‘catawampus’ things. The other is that I have quarrelled with Irene Howard – or she quarrelled with me – or, no, we both quarrelled.

“The Junior Red Cross met here yesterday. The hour ~~was~~ of meeting was half-past two but Irene came at half-past one, because she got the chance of a drive down from the Upper Glen. Irene ~~has been~~ hasn’t been a bit nice to me since the fuss about the eats; and besides I feel sure she resents not being president. But I have been determined that things should go smoothly, so I have never taken any notice, and when she came yesterday she seemed so sweet and nice again that I hoped she had got over her huffiness and we could be the chums we ~~were before~~ ^**used to be**^.

"But as soon as we sat down Irene began to rub me the wrong way. I saw her cast a look at my new knitting bag. All the girls have always said Irene was jealous-minded ~~but~~ ^**and**^ I would never believe them before. But now I feel that perhaps she is.

"The first thing she did was to pounce on Jims ^– **Irene pretends to adore babies** –^ pick him out of his cradle and kiss him all over his face. Now, Irene knows perfectly well that I don't like to have Jims kissed like that. It is not hygienic. After she had worried him till he began to fuss, she looked at me and gave quite a nasty little laugh but she said, oh, so sweetly,

"'Why, Rilla, ~~dear~~ ^**darling**^, you look as if you thought I was poisoning the baby.'

"'Oh, no, I don't, ^**Irene,**^' I said – every bit as sweetly, 'but you know ~~Holt~~ ^**Morgan**^ says that the only place a baby should be kissed is on its forehead, ^**for fear of germs,**^ and that is ~~our~~ ^**my**^ rule with Jims.'

"'Dear me, am I so full of germs?' said Irene ~~plant~~ plaintively. I knew she was making fun of me and I began to boil inside – but outside, no sign of a simmer. I was determined I would not scrap with Irene.

"Then she began to bounce Jims. Now, Morgan says bouncing is almost the worst thing that can be done to a baby. ~~It~~ I never allow Jims to be bounced. But Irene bounced him and that ~~ungrateful~~ ^**exasperating**^ child ~~actually~~ liked it. He smiled – for the very first time. He is four months old and he has never smiled once ^**before**^. Not even mother ~~and~~ ^**or**^ **Susan have been able to coax that** ^~~**my**~~^ thing to smile, try as they would. And here he was smiling because Irene Howard bounced him! ^**Talk of gratitude!**^

"I admit that smile made a big difference in him. Two of the dearest dimples came out in his cheeks and his big brown eyes seemed full of laughter. The way Irene raved over those dimples was silly, I ~~thin~~ consider. You would have ~~thought~~ ^**supposed**^ she thought she had really brought them into existence. But I sewed steadily and did not enthuse, and soon Irene got tired of ~~playing with~~ ^**bouncing**^ Jims and put him back in his cradle. He did not like that after being played with, and he ^**began to cry and**^ was fussy the rest of the afternoon, whereas if Irene had only left him alone he would not have been a bit of trouble. Irene looked at him ^[*Note*] **M4**^ ~~and said he didn't have much hair – she had never seen a baby as bald at four months.~~

"Of course, I knew Jims hadn't much hair – yet; but ~~the~~ Irene said it in a tone that seemed to imply it was my fault that he hadn't any hair. I said I had seen ~~lots of dozens dozens~~ ^**dozens**^ of babies every bit as bald as Jims, and Irene said, oh, very well, she hadn't meant to offend me – when I wasn't offended.

"It went on like that the rest of the hour; ~~or~~ Irene kept ~~saying things I didn't like in a tone I didn't like~~ giving me little digs all the time. The girls have always said she was revengeful like that if she were peeved about anything; but I never believed it before. I used to think Irene just perfect, and it hurt me dreadfully to find she could stoop to this. But I ~~kept~~ corked up my feelings and sewed away for dear life on a Belgian child's nightgown.

~~"Then, just before the other girls began to come~~

"Then Irene told me the ~~most~~ meanest, most contemptible thing that someone had said about Walter. I won't write it down – I can't ~~– it was too~~. Of course, she said it ~~wasn't true~~ made her furious to hear it and all that – but there was no need for her to tell me such a thing even if she did hear it. She ~~just~~ ^**simply**^ did it to hurt me.

^**"I just exploded.**^ 'How dare you come here and repeat such a thing to me, ~~Irene Howard?'~~ about my brother, Irene Howard?' I exclaimed. 'I shall never forgive you – never. ~~Don't you ever speak to me again~~ ^~~**"Why Rilla**~~ **Your brother hasn't enlisted**^ ~~^**again**^~~ – hasn't any idea of enlisting.'[22]

"'Why Rilla, dear, I didn't say it,' said Irene. 'I told you it was Mrs. ~~Nat~~ ^**George**^ Burr. ~~Of course~~ ^**And**^ I told her' –

"'I don't want to hear what you told her. Don't you ever speak to me again, Irene Howard.'

"Of course, I shouldn't have said that. But it just seemed to say itself. Then the other girls all came in a bunch and I had to calm down and act the hostess' part as well as I could. Irene paired off with Olive Kirk all the rest of the afternoon and went away without so much as a look.

So I suppose she means to take me at my word and I don't care, for I ~~shall never forgive~~ do not want to be friends with a girl who could repeat such a falsehood about Walter. But I feel unhappy over it for all that. We've always been ^**such**^ good ~~friends~~ ^**chums**^ and until lately Irene was lovely to me; and now ~~we are out and~~ another illusion has been stripped from my eyes and I feel as if there wasn't such a thing as real true friendship in the world.

~~"Shirley went down to the station to-day and built~~ ^**"Father got old Joe Mead to build**^ a little ~~knn~~ kennel for ~~Rags~~ ^**Dog Monday**^ in the corner of the shipping shed ^**to-day**^. We thought perhaps ~~Rags~~ ^**Monday**^ would come home when the cold weather came but he wouldn't. No earthly influence can coax ~~Rags~~ ^**Monday**^ away from that shed even for a few minutes. There he ~~sits~~ stays and meets every train. So ~~he had~~ we had to do something to make him comfortable. ~~Shirley~~ ^**Joe**^ built the kennel so that ~~Rags~~ ^**Monday**^ could lie in it and still see the platform, so we hope he will occupy it.

"~~Rags~~ ^**Monday**^ has become quite famous. A reporter of the Enterprise came out from town and photographed him and wrote ^**up**^ the whole story of ~~Rags'~~ ^**his**^ faithful vigil ~~an~~. It was published in the Enterprise and copied all over Canada. But that doesn't matter to poor little ~~Rags~~ ^**Monday**^, Jem has gone away – ~~Rags~~ ^**Monday**^ doesn't know where or why – but he will wait until he comes back. Somehow it comforts me: it's foolish, I suppose, but it gives me a feeling that Jem will come back or else ~~Rags~~ ^**Monday**^ wouldn't ~~wait~~ ^~~**be keep on**~~ **keep on waiting**^ for him.

"Jims is snoring beside me in his cradle. It is just a cold that makes him snore – not adenoids. Irene had a cold yesterday and I know she gave it to him, kissing him. He ~~has~~ is not quite such a nuisance as he was; he has got some backbone and can sit up quite nicely, and he loves his bath now and splashes unsmilingly in the water instead of twisting and shrieking. Oh, shall I ever forget those first two months! I don't know how I lived through them. But here I am and here is Jims and we both are going to "'carry on.'" I tickled him a little bit tonight when I undressed him – I wouldn't bounce him but Morgan doesn't mention tickling – just to see if he would smile for me as well as Irene. And he did – and out popped the dimples. What a pity his mother

couldn't have seen them!
[*Montgomery places a line across the page here to indicate the original chapter end.*]

"I finished my sixth pair of socks to-day. With the first three I got Susan to set the heel for me. Then I thought that was a bit of shirking, so I learned to do it myself. I hate it – but I have done so many things I hate since the fourth of August that one more or less doesn't matter. I just think of Jem joking about the mud on Salisbury Plain and I ~~get~~ go at them."

Chapter 11

Dark and Bright

At Christmas the college boys and girls came home and for a little while Ingleside was gay again. But ~~one was~~ ^**all were**^ not there – for the first time ~~there was a~~ one was missing from the ^**circle around the**^ Christmas table. Jem, of the steady lips and fearless eyes, was far away, and Rilla felt that the sight of ~~Jem's~~ ^**his**^ vacant chair was more than she could endure. Susan had taken a stubborn freak and insisted on setting out Jem's place for him as usual, with the twisted little napkin ring he had always had since a boy, and the odd, high Green Gables ~~tumbler glass~~ ^**goblet**^ that Aunt Marilla had once given him and ^**from**^ which he always insisted on drinking.

"That blessed boy shall have his place, Mrs. Dr. dear," ~~she~~ ^**Susan**^ said firmly, "and do not you feel over it, for you may be sure he is here in spirit and next ~~year~~ Christmas he will be here in the body. ~~Just you wait.~~ Wait you till the Big Push comes in the spring and the war will be over in a jiffy."

They tried to think so, but a shadow stalked in the background of their determined merrymaking. Walter, too, was quiet and dull, all through the holidays. He showed Rilla a cruel, anonymous letter he had received at Redmond – a letter ^**far**^ more conspicuous for malice than for patriotic indignation.

"Nevertheless, all it says is true, Rilla." ~~he said.~~

Rilla had caught it from him and thrown it into the fire.

"There isn't one word of truth in it," she declared hotly. "Walter, you've got morbid – as Miss Oliver says she gets when she broods too long over one thing."

"I can't get away from it at Redmond, Rilla. ~~Even it~~ ^**The whole college**^ is aflame over the war. A perfectly fit fellow, of ~~proper~~ military age, who doesn't join up is looked upon as a shirker and treated accordingly. ~~My Engli~~ Dr. Milne, the English professor, who has always made a special pet of me, has two sons in khaki; and I can feel the change in his manner towards me."

"It's not fair – you're not fit."

"Physically I am. Sound as a bell. The unfitness is in the soul and it's a taint and a disgrace. There, don't cry, Rilla. I'm not going – if that's what you're afraid of. ^[*Note*] **Z5**^

"You would break mother's heart and mine if you did," sobbed Rilla. "Oh, Walter, one is enough for any family."

The holidays were an unhappy time for ~~her. She almost felt relieved when they~~ ^**her**^. Still, having Nan and Di and Walter and Shirley home helped in the enduring of things. A letter and book came for her from Kenneth Ford, too; some sentences in the letter made her cheeks burn and her heart beat – until the last paragraph, which ~~threw~~ ^**sent**^ an icy chill over everything.

"My ankle is about as good as new. I'll be fit to join up in a couple of months more, Rilla-my-Rilla. It will be some feeling to get into khaki all right. Little Ken will ~~feel~~ be able to look the whole world in the face then ^**and owe not any man**^. It's been rotten lately, since I've been able to walk without limping. People who don't know look at me as much as to say "'Slacker!'" Well, they won't have ~~a~~ ^**the**^ chance to look it much longer."

"I hate this war," said Rilla bitterly, as she ~~looked~~ ^**gazed**^ out into the maple grove that was a chill glory of pink and gold in the winter sunset. The red splashes on the of its floor make her think of blood-stained trenches – trenches where Jem and Jerry would soon be – where Kenneth would be later on – yes, and Walter, too.

"I know he'll go yet," thought poor Rilla. "And I can't be brave about it – I can't. ^**I can face anything but that.**^ The very thought of it makes me useless." Oh, if the war would only end soon!"

"Nineteen-fourteen has gone," ~~sea~~ said Dr. Blythe on New Year's Day. "~~It's~~ ^**Its**^ sun, which rose fairly, has set in blood. What will nineteen-fifteen bring?"

"Victory!" said Susan, for once laconic.

"Do you really believe we'll win the war, Susan?" said Miss Oliver drearily. She had come over from Lowbridge to spend the day and see ~~her~~ Walter and the girls before they went back to Redmond. She was in a rather blue and cynical mood and inclined to look on the dark side.

"'Believe' we'll win the war!" exclaimed Susan. "No, Miss Oliver, dear, I do not believe – I know. That does not worry me. What does worry me is the trouble and expense of it all. But then you cannot make omelets without breaking eggs, so we must just trust in God and make big guns.”

“Sometimes I think the big guns are better to trust in than God,” said Miss Oliver defiantly.

“No, no, dear, you do not. The Germans had the big guns at the Marne, had they not? But ~~God settled the Almighty~~ Providence settled them. Do not ever forget that. Just hold on to that when you feel inclined to doubt. Clutch hold of the sides of ~~the~~ ^**your**^ chair and sit tight and keep saying, ‘Big guns are good but the Almighty is better, and He is on our side, no matter what the Kaiser says about it.’ I would have gone crazy many a day lately, Miss Oliver, dear, if I had not sat tight and repeated that to myself. My cousin Sophia is, like you, somewhat inclined to despond. ‘Oh, dear me, what will we do if the Germans ever get here,’ she wailed to me yesterday. ‘Bury them,’ said I, just as ~~cheer-ful~~ ^**off-hand**^ as that. ‘There is plenty of room for the graves.’ Cousin Sophia said that I was flippant but I was not flippant, Miss Oliver, dear, only calm and confident in the British navy and our Canadian boys.” I am like old Mr. William Pollock of the Harbour Head. He is very old and has been ill for a long time, and one night last week he was so low ~~they~~ that his daughter-in-law whispered to someone that she thought he was dead. ‘Darn it, I ain’t,’ he called right out – only, Miss Oliver, dear, he did not use so mild a word as ‘darn’ – ‘darn it, I ain’t, and I don’t mean to die until the Kaiser is well licked.’ Now, that, ~~Mrs. O~~ Miss Oliver, dear,” concluded Susan, “is the kind of spirit I admire.”

“I ~~ardmire~~ admire it but I can’t emulate it,” sighed Gertrude. ~~“I’ve alw~~ “Before this, I have always been able to escape from the hard things of life for a little while by going into dreamland ^[*Note*] **R4**^ But I can’t escape from this.”

“Nor I,” said Mrs. Blythe. “I hate going to bed now. All my life I’ve liked going to bed, to have a gay, mad, ~~time~~ ^**splendid half-hour**^ of imagining things ^**before sleeping**^. Now I imagine them still. But such different things – I see trenches – and blood-stained snow – and dead men – and Little Jem!” And when I hear the wind wailing round the coves I think of all the souls going out on the western front.”

^[*Note*] ~~**Q4**~~ **Q4**^

“I am very thankful that I never had any imagination to speak of,” said Susan. “I have been spared that. I see by this paper that the Crown

Prince is killed again. ~~I wonder if~~ ^**Do you suppose**^ there is any hope of his staying dead this time? And I also see that Woodrow Wilson is going to write another note. I wonder," concluded Susan, with the bitter ~~contempt~~ irony she had of late begun to use when referring to the ^**poor**^ President, "if that man's schoolmaster is alive."

In January Jims was five months old and Rilla celebrated ~~his~~ the anniversary by shortening him ~~and an~~.

"He weighs ~~sixteen~~ ^**fourteen**^ pounds," she announced jubilantly. "Just exactly what he should weigh at five months, according to Morgan."

There was no longer any doubt in anybody's mind that Jims was getting ~~posti~~ positively pretty. His little cheeks were ~~as~~ round and firm and faintly pink, his eyes were big and bright, ^**his tiny paws had dimples at the root of every finger.**^ ~~Even his ha~~ He had even ~~started in~~ ^**begun**^ to grow hair, much to Rilla's unspoken relief. There was a ~~little~~ ^**pale**^ golden fuzz all over his head which was distinctly visible in some lights. He was a good infant, generally sleeping and digesting as Morgan decreed. ~~Occas~~ Occasionally, he smiled but he had never laughed, in spite of all efforts to make him. This worried Rilla also, because Morgan said that babies usually laughed aloud from the third to the fifth month. Jims was five and had no notion of laughing. Why hadn't he? Wasn't he normal?

One night Rilla came home late from a recruiting meeting at the Glen where she had been giving patriotic recitations. Rilla had never been willing to recite in public before. She was afraid of her tendency to lisp, which had a habit of reviving if she were doing anything that made her nervous. When she had first been asked to recite at the Upper Glen meeting she had refused. Then she began to worry over her refusal. Was it cowardly? What would Jem think if he knew? After two days of worry Rilla 'phoned to the ~~chairman~~ ^**president**^ of the Patriotic Society that she would recite. She did, and lisped several times, and lay awake ~~all~~ ^**most of the**^ night in an agony of wounded vanity. Then two nights after she recited again at Harbour Head. She had been at Lowbridge and over-harbour since then and had become resigned to ~~to lisping~~ ^**an occasional lisp**^. Nobody except herself seemed to mind it. And she was so earnest and appealing and shining-eyed! More than one recruit joined up because Rilla's eyes seemed to look right at him when she passionately demanded how could men die better than fighting for the ashes of their fathers and the temples of their gods, or assured her audience with thrilling intensity that one crowded hour of glorious life was worth an age without a name. Even stolid Miller Douglas was so ~~inflamed~~ fired one night that it took Mary Vance a good hour to talk him back to sense. Mary Vance said bitterly that if Rilla Blythe felt as bad as she had pretended to feel over Jem's going to the front she ~~mustn't~~ wouldn't be urging other girls' brothers and friends to go.

On this particular night Rilla was tired and cold and very thankful to creep into her warm nest and cuddle down between her blankets, though as usual with a sorrowful wonder ~~how~~ how Jem and Jerry were faring. She was just getting warm and drowsy when Jims suddenly began to cry – and kept on crying.

Rilla curled herself up in her bed and determined she would let him cry. She had Morgan behind her for justification. Jims was warm, physically comfortable – his cry wasn't the cry of pain – and had his little tummy as full as was good for him. Under such circumstances it would be simply spoiling him to fuss over him, and she wasn't going to do it. He could cry until he got good and tired and ready to go to sleep again.

Then Rilla's imagination began to torment her. Suppose, she thought, I was a ~~tiny~~ tiny, helpless creature only five months old, with my father somewhere in France and my poor little mother, who had been so worried about me, in the graveyard. Suppose I was lying in a basket in a big, black room, without one speck of light, and nobody ~~near me for~~ within miles of me, for all I could see or know. Suppose there wasn't a human being anywhere who loved me – for a father who had never seen me couldn't love me very much, especially when he had never written a word to or about me. Wouldn't I cry, too? Wouldn't I feel just so lonely and forsaken and frightened that I'd have to cry?

Rilla hopped out ~~of bed~~. She picked Jims out of his basket and took him into ~~bed with her~~ her own bed. His hands were cold, poor mite. ^**But he had promptly ceased to cry.**^ And then, as she ~~cuddled~~ ^**held**^ him ~~down beside~~ close to her in the darkness, suddenly Jims laughed – a real, ~~little~~ ^**gurgly**^, chuckly, delighted, delightful laugh.

"Oh, you dear little thing!" exclaimed Rilla. "Are you so pleased at finding you're not all alone, lost in a huge, big, black room?"

Then she knew she wanted to kiss him and she did. She kissed his silky, scented little head, she kissed his chubby little cheek, she kissed his little cold hands. She wanted to squeeze him – to cuddle him, just as she used to squeeze and cuddle her kittens. Something ~~all~~ delightful and yearning ^**and brooding**^ seemed to have taken possession of her. She had never felt like this before.

In a few minutes Jims was sound asleep; and, as Rilla listened to his soft, regular breathing and felt the little body warm and ~~cuddly~~ ^**contented**^ against her, she realized that – at last – she loved her war-baby.

"He ~~is~~ ^**has got to be**^ – such – a – darling," she thought drowsily, as she drifted off to slumberland herself.

In February Jem and Jerry ^**and Robert Grant**^ were in the trenches and a little more ~~tensity~~ ^**tension**^ and dread was added to the Ingleside life. In March "Yiprez," as Susan called it, had ~~begun~~ ^**come**^ to have a bitter significance. The daily list of casualties had begun to appear in the papers and no one at Ingleside ever answered the telephone without a horrible ^**cold**^ shrinking ~~and dread. It~~ ^**– for it**^ might be the station master phoning up to say a telegram had come from overseas. No one at Ingleside ever got up in the morning without a sudden piercing wonder over what the day might bring.

^Note S4^

Mrs. Blythe never saw the full moon shining splendidly over white Rainbow Valley without wondering if ~~Jem were~~ it was looking down on Jem, hurt or dying. ~~Yet life went on as of old in the Glen.~~ Yet the daily busy round of life and duty went steadily on and every week or so someone else went into khaki from the ~~boys~~ ^**Glen lads**^ who had just the other day been rollicking schoolboys.

~~"It's~~ "It is ~~a~~ bitter cold out tonight, Mrs. Dr. dear," said Susan, coming in out of the clear ^**starlit**^ crispness of the Canadian winter ^**twilight**^. "I wonder if the boys in the trenches are warm."

"How everything comes back to this war," cried Gertrude Oliver. "We can't get away from it – not even when we talk of the weather. I never go out these dark cold nights myself without thinking of the men in the trenches – not only our men but everybody's men. I would feel the same if there were nobody I knew at the front. When I snuggle down in my comfortable bed I am ashamed of being comfortable. It seems as if it were wicked of me to be so when ~~many~~ many are not."

"I saw Mrs. Meredith down at the store," said Susan, "and she tells me that they are really troubled over Bruce, he takes things so much to heart. He has cried himself to sleep for a week, over the starving Belgians. 'Oh, mother,' he will say to her, so beseeching-like, 'surely the babies are never hungry – oh, not the babies, mother! Just say the babies are not hungry, mother.' And she cannot say it because it would not be true, and she is at her wits' end. They try to keep such things from him but he finds them out and then they cannot comfort him. And it is dreadful to think of a little child starving, Mrs. Dr. dear."

Mrs. Blythe looked over her knitting at the ~~firl~~ firelight that was no longer reflected in her laughing children's eyes and shivered. It was horrible, indeed. Yet even this had to be borne.

^[*Note*] **X4**^

~~"Jack Crawford is tired of farming, they tell us," Susan went on, "and says he is going to the~~

~~"Jack Crawford~~ Jack Crawford says he is going to the war because he is tired of farming~~," Susan went on~~. I hope he will find it a pleasant change.

^[*Note*] **U4**^

~~And~~ You know Josiah Cooper and William Daley, Mrs. Dr. dear. They ~~quarrelled ten years a~~ used to be fast friends but they quarrelled twenty years ago and have never spoken since. Well, the other day Josiah went to William and said right out, 'Let us be friends. 'Tain't any time to be holding grudges.' William was real glad and held out his hand, and they sat down for a good talk. And in less than half an hour they had quarrelled again, over how the war ought to be ~~run~~ fought, Josiah holding that the Dardanelles expedition was rank folly and William maintaining that it was the one sensible thing the Allies had done. And ~~no~~ now they are madder at each other than ever and ~~J~~William says Josiah is as bad a pro-German as Whiskers-on-the-Moon. Whiskers-on-the-moon vows he is no pro-German but calls himself a pacifist, whatever that may be, Mrs. Dr. dear. It is nothing proper or Whiskers would not be it and that you may tie to. He says that the big British victory at New Chapelle cost more than it was worth and ~~that~~ he has forbid Joe Milgrave to come near the house because Joe ran up his father's flag when the news came. Have you noticed, Mrs. Dr. dear, that the Czar has changed that ~~fortress's~~ ^**Prish~~am~~**^ name to Premysl, ~~and~~

~~It is plain that man has good sense~~ which proves that the man had good sense, Russian though he is?

^[*Note*] **W4**^

Now I shall just look over the papers a minute before going to write a letter to Little Jem. Two things I never did, Mrs. Dr. dear, ~~was~~ ^**were**^ write letters and read politics. Yet here I am doing both regular and I find there is something in politics after all. Whatever Woodrow Wilson means I cannot fathom but I am hoping I will puzzle ~~him~~ ^**it**^ out yet."

Susan, in her pursuit of Wilson and politics, presently came upon something that disturbed her and exclaimed in a tone of bitter disappointment,

"That devilish Kaiser has only a boil after all."

"Don't swear, Susan," said Dr. Blythe, pulling a long face.

"'Devilish' is not swearing, doctor, dear. I have always understood that swearing was taking the name of the Almighty in vain. Can you take the devil's name in vain?"

"Well, it isn't – ahem – refined," said the doctor, winking at Miss Oliver.

"No, doctor, dear, the devil and the Kaiser – if so be that they are really two different people – are not refined~~. So~~ –^ **and**^ you cannot refer to them in a refined way. So I abide by what I said, although you may notice that I am careful not to use such expressions when young Rilla is about. And I maintain that the papers have ~~to~~ ^**no**^ right to say that the Kaiser has pneumonia and raise people's hopes, and then come out and say he has nothing but a boil. A boil, indeed! I wish he was covered with them."

Susan stalked out to the kitchen and settled down to write to Jem; deeming him in need of some ~~inspiration~~ ^**home comfort**^ from certain passages in his letter that day.

"We're ~~lying~~ in an old wine cellar to-night,^ **dad**^," he wrote, "in water to our knees. Rats everywhere – no fire – a ~~diz~~ drizzling rain coming down – rather dismal. But it might be worse. I got Susan's box to-day and everything was in tip-top order and we had a feast. Jerry is up the line ~~on a~~ somewhere and he says the rations are rather worse than Aunt Martha's 'ditto' used to be. But here they're not bad – only monotonous. Tell Susan I'd give a year's pay for a good batch of her monkey-faces; but don't let that inspire her to send any for they wouldn't keep.

"We have been under fire since the last week in February. One boy – he was a Nova Scotian – was ~~blown to pieces~~ ^**killed**^ right beside me yesterday. ^[*Note*] **T4**^ It was the first time I'd been close to anything like that and it was a nasty sensation, but one soon gets used to horrors ~~there~~ here. We're in an absolutely different world. The only things that are the same are the stars – and they are never in their right places, somehow.

"Tell mother not to worry – I'm all right – fit as a fiddle – ^**and**^ glad I came. There's something across from us here that has got to be wiped out of the world, that's all – ~~a spirit for~~ an emanation of evil that would otherwise poison life for ever. It's got to be done, dad, however long it takes, ^**and whatever it costs,**^ and you tell the Glen people this for me. They don't realize yet what it is that has broken loose – I didn't when I first joined up. I thought it was fun. Well, it isn't! But I'm in the right

~~Tell Rilla I'm glad~~

place ~~and that you~~ all right – make no mistake about that. ^**Note Z4**^ [*Note A5 is embedded in this Note.*] ~~^[*Note*] **V4**^~~ ^**Note V4**^

"Tell Rilla I'm glad her war-baby is turning out so well, and tell Susan that I'm ~~waging~~ fighting a good fight against both ~~Hines~~ ^**Huns**^ and cooties."

"Mrs. Dr. dear," whispered Susan solemnly, "what are cooties?"

Mrs. Blythe whispered back and then said in reply to Susan's horrified ejaculations, "It's always like that in the trenches, Susan."

Susan shook her head and went away in grim silence to re-open a parcel she had sewed up for Jem and slip in a fine ~~tee~~ tooth comb.

Chapter 12

In the Days of Langemarck

"How can spring come and be beautiful in such a horror?" wrote Rilla in her diary. "When the sun shines and the fluffy yellow catkins are coming out on the willow trees down by the brook, and the garden is beginning to be beautiful I can't realize that such ~~terrible~~ ^**dreadful**^ things are happening in Flanders. But they are!

"This past week has been terrible for us all, since the news came of the fighting around Ypres and the battles of Langemarck and St. Julien. Our Canadian boys have done splendidly – General French says they 'saved the situation,' when the Germans had all but broken through. But I can't feel pride or ^**exultation or**^ anything but a ~~dreadful~~ ^**gnawing**^ anxiety over Jem and Jerry and Mr. Grant. ~~We ^**Gertrude's eyes just haunt me**^~~ The casualty lists are coming out in the papers every day – oh, there are so many of them. I can't bear to read them ~~beca~~ for fear I'd find Jem's name – for there have been cases where people have seen their boys' names in the casualty lists before ~~they~~ the official telegram came. ~~Mother and Susan read them every day and~~ As for the ~~teel~~ telephone, for a day or two I ~~sim-ply~~ ^**just**^ refused to answer it, because I thought I could not endure the horrible ~~minute~~ ^**moment**^ that came between saying 'Hello' and hearing the response. That moment seemed a hundred years long, for I was always dreading to hear 'There is a telegram for Dr. Blythe.' Then, when I had shirked for a day, I was ashamed of leaving it all for mother ~~o~~ or Susan, and now I make myself go. But it never gets any easier. Gertrude teaches school and reads compositions and sets examination papers just as she always ~~does~~ has done, but I know her thoughts are over in Flanders all the time. Her eyes ~~just~~ haunt me.

"And Kenneth ~~has~~ is in khaki now, too. He has got a lieutenant's commission and expects to go overseas in midsummer, so he wrote me. There wasn't much else in the letter – he seemed to be thinking of nothing but going overseas. I shall not see him again before he goes – perhaps I will never see him again. Sometimes I ask myself if that evening at Four Winds was all a dream. It might as well be – it seems as if it happened in another life lived ages ago – and everybody has forgotten it but me.

"Walter and Nan and Di came home last night from Redmond. When Walter stepped off the train ~~Rags~~ ^**Dog Monday**^ rushed to meet him, frantic with joy. I suppose he thought Jem would be there, too. After the first moment, he paid no more attention to Walter and his pats, but just stood there, wagging his tail nervously and looking past Walter at the other people coming out, with eyes that made me choke up, = ~~when, for any~~ for I couldn't help thinking that, for all we knew, ~~Rags~~ ^**Monday**^ might never see Jem come off that train again. Then, when ~~it~~ all the people were out, ~~Rags~~ ^**Monday**^ looked up at Walter, gave his hand a little lick as if to say, '~~It~~ ^**I know It**^ isn't your fault he didn't come – excuse me for feeling disappointed,' and then he trotted back to his shed ^[*Note*] **Z6**^

"We tried to coax him home with us – Di even got down and kissed him between the eyes and said, '~~Rags~~ ^**Monday**^, ~~darling~~ ^**old duck,**^ won't you come up with us just for the evening?' and ~~Rags~~ ^**Monday**^ said – he did! – ~~"~~'I am very sorry but I can't. I've ~~^I'm^~~ got ~~to be here when~~ ^**a date to meet**^ Jem ~~comes home~~ ^**here**^, ^**you know, and there's a train goes through at ~~8~~ eight.** ^

"It's lovely to have Walter back again ^**though he**^ ~~He~~ seems quiet and sad, just ~~like~~ ^**as**^ he was at Christmas. But I'm going to love him hard and ~~comfort~~ cheer him up and make him laugh as he used to. It seems to me that every day of my life Walter means more to me.

"The other evening ~~someone~~ ^**Susan**^ happened to say that the mayflowers were out in Rainbow Valley. I chanced to be looking at mother when Susan spoke. Her face changed and she gave a queer little choked cry. Most of the time mother is so ~~brave~~ ^**spunky**^ and ~~merry~~ ^**gay**^ you would never guess what she feels inside; but now and then some little thing is too much for her and we see under the surface. 'Mayflowers!' she said. 'Jem brought me ~~the~~ mayflowers last year!' and she got up and went out of the room. I would have rushed off to Rainbow Valley and brought her an armful of mayflowers, but I knew that wasn't what she wanted. And after Walter got home last night he slipped away to the valley and brought mother home all the mayflowers he could find. Nobody had said a word to him about it =

~~it w~~ – he just remembered himself that Jem used to bring mother the first mayflowers and so he brought them in Jem's place. It shows how tender and thoughtful he is. And yet there are people who send him cruel letters!

"It seems strange that we can go in with ordinary life just as if nothing ~~was~~ ^**were**^ happening overseas that concerned us ~~as~~ – just as if any day might not bring us awful news. But we can and do. Susan is putting in the garden, and mother and she are housecleaning, and ~~I am getting up a concert~~ we Junior Reds are getting up a concert in aid of ~~our friends~~ ^**the Belgians**^. We have been practising for a month and having no end of trouble and bother with cranky ~~pople~~ people. Miranda Pryor promised to ~~take part in~~ ^**help with**^ a dialogue and when she had her part all learned ~~off~~ her father put his foot down and refused to allow her to ~~take part~~ ^**help at all**^. ~~^[*Note*] **C5**^~~ ^^**Note C5**^^

"I couldn't get anyone else to take the part, because ~~nobody every other girl~~ nobody liked it, so I finally had to take it myself. Olive Kirk is on the concert committee and goes against me in every single thing. But I got my way in asking Mrs. Channing to come out from town and sing for us, anyhow. She is a beautiful singer and will draw such a crowd that we will make more than we will have to pay her. Olive Kirk thought our 'local talent' good enough and Minnie Clow won't sing at all now ~~wel~~ in the choruses because she would be 'so nervous' before Mrs. Channing. And Minnie is the only good alto we have! There are times when I am so exasperated that I feel tempted to ~~throw up the whole~~ wash my hands of the whole affair; but after I dance around my room a few times in sheer rage I cool down and have another whack at it. Just at present I am racked with worry for fear the Isaac Reeses are taking whooping cough. They have all got a dreadful cold and there are five of them who have important parts in the programme and if they go and develop whooping cough what shall I do? Dick Reese's violin solo is to be one of our tid-bits and Kit Reese is in every tableau and the three small girls have the cutest flag drill. I've been toiling for weeks to train them in it, and now it seems likely that all my trouble will go for nothing.

"Jims cut his first tooth to-day. I am very glad, for he is nearly nine months old and Mary Vance has been insinuating that he is awfully backward about cutting his teeth. He has begun to creep but doesn't crawl ~~on his hands~~ as most babies do. He trots about on all fours ~~like a little dog~~ and carries things in his mouth like a little dog. Nobody can say he isn't up to schedule time in the matter of creeping anyway ^[*Note*] **F5**^ – He is so ~~cuit~~ cute, it will be a shame if his dad never sees him. His hair is coming on nicely, too, and I am not without hope that it will be curly.

"Just for a few minutes, while I've been writing of Jims and the concert, I've forgotten Ypres and the poison gas and the casualty lists. Now it all rushes back, worse than ever. Oh, if we could just know that Jem is all right! ^[*Note*] **D5**^ ~~That he isn't hurt or taken prisoner; so many were taken prisoners~~

Rilla put away her diary and went out to the garden. The spring evening was very lovely. The long, ^**green, seaward-looking**^ glen was filled with dusk, and beyond it were meadows of sunset. The harbor was radiant, purple here, azure there, opal elsewhere. ~~There was an emerald mist on the maple grove.~~ ^**The maple grove was beginning to be misty green.**^ Rilla looked about her with wistful eyes. Who said that spring was the joy of the year? It was the heart-break of the year. And all the pale-purply mornings and the daffodil stars and the wind in the old pine were so many separate pangs of the heart-break. Would life ever be free from dread again?

"It's good to see P.E.I. twilight ~~again~~ ^**once more**^," said Walter, joining her. "I didn't really remember that the sea was so blue and the roads so red and the wood nooks so wild and fairy haunted. Yes, the fairies still abide here. I vow I could find scores of them ~~in the~~ ^**under the**^ ~~viol~~ violets in Rainbow Valley."

Rilla was momentarily happy. This sounded like the ~~way~~ Walter ~~used to talk~~ ^**of yore**^. She hoped he was forgetting certain things that had troubled him. ^[*Note*] **B5**^ Susan wandered by, her head tied up with a shawl, her hands full of garden implements. Doc, stealthy and wild-eyed, was shadowing her steps among the spirea bushes.

~~"That cat has been Hyde all day," said Susan,"~~ ^[*Note*] **C5**^ so we will likely have rain tonight and by the same token I have rheumatism in my shoulder."

~~"Don't~~ "It may rain – but don't think rheumatism, Susan – think violets," said Walter gaily – rather too gaily, Rilla thought.

Susan ~~thought~~ ^**considered**^ him unsympathetic.

"Indeed, Walter dear, I do not know what you mean by thinking violets," she ~~said~~ ^**responded**^ stiffly, "and rheumatism is not a thing to be joked about, as you may some day realize for yourself. I hope I am not of the kind that is always complaining of their aches and pains, ~~B~~ especially now when the news is so terrible. Rheumatism is bad enough but I realize and none better, that it ~~cannot as bad as~~ ^**is not to be compared to**^ being gassed by the Huns."

"Oh, my God, no!" exclaimed Walter passionately. He turned and went back to the house.

Susan shook her head. She disapproved ^**entirely**^ of such ejaculations. "I hope he will not let his mother hear him talking like that," she thought as she stacked the hoes and rake away.

Rilla was standing among the budding daffodils with tear-filled eyes. Her evening was spoiled; she detested Susan, who had somehow hurt Walter; and Jem – had Jem been gassed? Had he died in torture?

"I can't ~~bear~~ ^**endure**^ this suspense any longer," said Rilla desperately.

But she ~~bore~~ ^**endured**^ it as the others did for another week. Then a letter came from Jem. He was all right.

"I've come through ~~the~~ without a scratch, dad. Don't know how I or any of us did it. You'll have seen all about it in the papers – I can't write of it. But the Huns haven't got through – they won't get through. Jerry was knocked ~~out~~ ^**stiff**^ by a shell one ~~day~~ ^**time**^, but it was only the shock. He was all right in a few days. Grant is safe, too."

Nan had a letter from Jerry ^**Meredith**^. "I came back to consciousness at dawn," he wrote. "Couldn't tell what had happened to me ^**but thought I was done for**^. I was all alone – and afraid – terribly afraid. Dead men were all around me, lying on the horrible gray, slimy fields. I was ~~thirsty –~~ woefully thirsty – and I thought of David and the Bethlehem water – and of the old spring in Rainbow Valley under the maples. I seemed to see it just before me – and you standing laughing on the other side of it – and I thought it was all over with me. And I didn't care. Honestly, I didn't care. I just felt a ^**dreadful**^ childish fear of the loneliness and of those dead men around me, and a sort of wonder ~~of~~

how this could have happened to me. Then they found me and carted me off and before long I discovered that there wasn't really anything wrong with me. I'm going back to the trenches to-morrow. Every man is needed there that can be got."

"Laughter is gone out of the world," said Faith Meredith, who had come over to report on her letters. "I remember telling old Mrs. Taylor long ago that the world ~~h~~ was a world of laughter. But it isn't so any longer."

"It's a shriek of anguish," said Gertrude Oliver.

"We must keep a little laughter, girls," said Mrs. Blythe. "A laugh is as good as a prayer sometimes – only sometimes," she added under her breath. She had found it very hard to laugh during the three weeks she had just lived through – she, Anne Blythe, to whom laughter had always come so easily and freshly. And what hurt her ^~~**worst**~~ **most**^ was that Rilla's laughter had grown so rare – Rilla whom she used to think laughed over much. Was all the child's girlhood to be so clouded? Yet how strong and clever and womanly ~~^**and patient**^~~ she was growing! How patiently she knitted and sewed and manipulated ~~the~~ ^**those** ~~**turbulent**~~ **uncertain**^ Junior Reds! And how wonderful she was with Jims.

"She really could not do better for that child than if she had raised a baker's dozen, Mrs. Dr. dear," Susan had ~~said~~ ^**avowed**^ solemnly. "Little did I ever expect it of her ~~that~~ ^**on the**^ day she landed in here with that soup tureen."

Chapter 13

A Slice of Humble Pie

"I am very much afraid, Mrs. Dr. dear," said Susan, who had been ~~down~~ ^**on a pilgrimage**^ to the station with some choice bones for ~~Rags~~ ^**Dog Monday**^, "that something terrible has happened. Whiskers-on-the-Moon came off the train from Charlottetown and he was looking pleased. I do not remember that I ever saw him with a smile on in public before. ~~He may, of course,~~ ^**Of course, he may**^ have just been getting the better of somebody in a ~~butcher's~~ ^**cattle**^ deal but I have an awful presentiment that the Huns have broken through somewhere."

Perhaps Susan was unjust in connecting Mr. Pryor's smile with the sinking of the Lusitania, news of which ~~came~~ ^**circulated**^ an hour later when the mail was distributed. But the Glen boys turned out that night in a body and broke all his windows in a fine frenzy of indignation over the Kaiser's doings.

~~"I tell you, Mrs. Dr. dear~~

"I do not say they did right and I do not say they did wrong," said Susan, when she heard of it. "But I ^**will say that I**^ wouldn't have minded throwing a few stones myself. One thing is certain – Whiskers-on-the-Moon said in the post office ~~yesterday~~ ^**the day the news came,**^ in the presence of witnesses, that folks who ~~must couldn't~~ ^**could not**^ stay home after they had been warned deserved no better fate. ~~And~~ That man, Mrs. Dr. dear,~~" concluded Susan in profound disgust~~ ^**may be and is**^ ~~is~~ a member of our session.~~"~~ ^[*Note*] **C6**^ Norman Douglas is fairly foaming at the mouth over it all. 'If the devil doesn't get those men who sunk the Lusitania then ~~there's~~ ^**there is**^ no use in ~~then~~ ^**there**^ being a devil,' he was shouting in Carter's store last night. ^[*Note*] **D6**^ ~~I never saw anybody so worked up.~~ Bruce Meredith is worrying over the babies who were drowned.~~' Mother,~~ And it seems he prayed for something very special ~~one~~ ^**last ~~Friday Tuesday(?)~~ Friday**^ night and didn't get it, and was feeling quite ~~bad~~ ^**disgruntled**^ over it. But when he heard about the Lusitania he told his mother that he understood now why God didn't answer his prayer – He was too busy attending to the souls of all the people who went down on the Lusitania. That child's brain is a hundred years older than his body, Mrs. Dr. dear. ^[*Note*] **G5**^

Mary Vance dropped in one evening to tell the Ingleside folks that she had withdrawn all opposition to Miller Douglas's enlisting.

"This Lusitania business was too much for me," said Mary brusquely. "When the Kaiser takes to drowning innocent~~s~~ babies it's high time somebody told him where he gets off at. ^**Note H10**^ So I up and told Miller he could go as far as I was concerned. I knew he'd be hankering after it for months. Old Kitty Alec won't be converted though. If every ship in the world was submarined and every baby drowned, ~~old~~ Kitty wouldn't turn a hair. But I flatter myself that it was me kept Miller back all along and not the fair Kitty. I may have deceived myself – but we shall see."

They did see. The next Sunday Miller Douglas walked into the Glen Church beside Mary Vance in khaki. And Mary was so proud of him that her white eyes fairly ~~glowed~~ ^**blazed**^. Joe Milgrave, back under the gallery, looked at Miller and Mary and then at Miranda Pryor, and sighed so heavily that everyone within a radius of three pews heard him and knew what his trouble was. Walter Blythe did not sigh. But Rilla, scanning his face anxiously, saw a look that cut her to the ~~soul~~ ^**heart**^. It haunted her for the next week and made an undercurrent of soreness in her soul, which was externally being harrowed up by the near approach of the Red Cross concert and the worries connected therewith. The Reese cold had not developed into whooping cough, so that tangle was straightened out. But other things were hanging in the balance; and ^**on**^ the very day before the concert came a regretful letter from Mrs. Channing saying that she could not come to sing. Her son, who was in ~~Halifax~~ ^**Kingsport**^ with his regiment, was seriously ill with pneumonia, and she must go to him at once.

The ^**members of the**^ concert committee looked at each other in blank dismay. What was to be done?

"This comes of ~~asking st~~ depending on outside help," said Olive Kirk, disagreeably.

"We must do something," said Rilla, too ~~desperately~~ desperate to care for Olive's ~~tone~~ ^**manner**^. "We've advertised the concert everywhere – and crowds are coming ^[*Note*] **L5**^ – and ~~we're~~ ^**we were**^ short enough of music as it was. We must get some one to sing in Mrs. Channing's place."

"I don't know who you ~~could~~ ^**can**^ get at this late date," said Olive. "Irene Howard could do it; but ~~I will not ask her,~~ ^**it is not likely she will**^ after the way she was insulted by our society."

~~"Wh~~ "How did our society insult her?" asked Rilla, in what she called her "cold, pale tone." Its coldness and pallor did not daunt Olive.

"You insulted her," she answered sharply. ~~"You told her never to spe~~ "Irene told me all about it – she was ~~simply~~ ^**literally**^ heart-broken. You told her never to speak to you again – and Irene told me she simply could not imagine what she had said or done to deserve such treatment. That was why she never came to our meetings again but joined in with the Lowbridge Red Cross. I do not blame her in the least, and I, for one, will not ask her to lower herself by ~~coming to our help now.~~ ^**helping us out of**^ this scrape."

"You don't expect me to ask her?" giggled Amy MacAllister, the other member of the committee. "Irene and I haven't spoken for ^**a hundred**^ years. Irene is always getting 'insulted' by somebody. But she is a lovely singer, I'll admit that, and people would just as soon hear her as Mrs. Channing."

~~"When we sta talked about this concert back in April," said Olive.~~

"It wouldn't do any good if you did ask her," ~~ad~~ said Olive significantly. "Soon after we began planning this concert, back in April, I ~~asked~~ met Irene in town one day and asked her if she wouldn't help us out. She said she'd love to but she really didn't see how she could~~, after the way Rilla Blythe had acted ^**behaved**^ to her. and she said she could not~~ when Rilla ^**Blythe**^ was running the ~~concert~~ ^**programme**^, after the ^**strange**^ way Rilla had behaved to her. So there it is and here we are, and a nice failure our concert will be."

Rilla went home and shut herself up in her room, her soul in a turmoil. She would not humiliate herself by apologizing to Irene Howard! Irene had been as much in the wrong as she had been; and she had told such mean, distorted versions of their quarrel everywhere, posing as a puzzled, injured martyr. ^[*Note*] **H5**^

And yet – the concert over which she had worked so hard was going to be a failure. Mrs. Channing's four solos were the feature of the whole programme.

"Miss Oliver, what ~~y~~ do you think ~~I should do~~ ^**about it?"**^ she asked in ~~despration~~ desperation.

"I think Irene is the one who should apologize," said Miss Oliver. "But ~~will that~~ ^**unfortunately my**^ opinion ^**will not**^ fill the blanks in your programme."

"If I went and apologized meekly to Irene she would sing, I'm sure," sighed Rilla. "She really loves to sing in public ~~–she~~. But I know she'll be ~~so tasteful~~ ^**nasty**^ about it – I feel I'd rather do anything ~~but~~ than go. ~~But~~ I suppose I should go – if Jem and Jerry can face the Huns surely I can face Irene Howard, and swallow my pride to ask a favor of her ^**for the good of the Belgians**^. Just at present I feel that I cannot do it – but for all that I have a presentiment that after supper you'll see me ^[*Note*] **I5**^ ~~trotting ^**meekly**^ along the road to the Upper Glen."~~

Rilla's presentiment ~~came true~~ ^~~**proved proved correct**~~ **proved correct**^. After supper she dressed herself carefully ^**in her blue, beaded** ~~**crape**~~ **crepe**^ – for vanity ~~persisted longer~~ ^**is harder to quell**^ than pride and Irene always saw any flaw or shortcoming in another girl's appearance. ^[*Note*] **A6**^

Rilla ~~put on her dress~~ ^**did**^ her hair very ~~carefully~~ ^**becomingly**^ ~~and put on her beaded blue crepe~~ and donned a long raincoat ~~for fear of a shower~~ ^**for fear of a shower**^. ^[*Note*] **J5**^ ~~And all the while she ^**mentally**^ rehearsed her part in the coming interview distasteful interview~~ She wished it were over – she wished she had never ~~got~~ tried to get up a Belgian Relief concert – she wished she had not quarreled with Irene. After all, ~~haughty~~ ^**disdainful**^ silence would have been much more effective in meeting the slur upon Walter. It was foolish and childish to fly out as she had done – well, she would be wiser in the future, but meanwhile a large and very unpalatable slice of humble pie had to be eaten, and Rilla Blythe was no fonder of that wholesome article of diet than the rest of us.

~~At~~ ^**By**^ sunset she was at the door of the Howard house – a pretentious abode, with white ~~lace~~ scroll-work round the eaves and an eruption of bay windows on ^**all**^ its sides. Mrs. Howard, a plump, voluble dame, met Rilla ^**gushingly**^ and left her in the parlor while she went to call Irene. Rilla threw off her rain-coat and looked at herself critically in the mirror over the mantel. Hair, hat, and dress were satisfactory – nothing there for Miss Irene to make fun of. Rilla remembered how clever and amusing she used to think Irene's biting little ~~remarks~~ ^**comments**^ about other girls.[2] Well, it had come home to her now.

Presently, Irene skimmed down, elegantly ~~dressed~~ ^**gowned**^, with her ~~hair golden~~ ^**pale, straw-colored**^ hair done in the ~~very~~ latest ~~Charlottetown~~ ^**and most extreme**^ fashion, ^**Note I10**^

"Why how do you do, Miss Blythe?" she said sweetly. "This is a very unexpected pleasure."

Rilla had risen to take Irene's chilly finger tips and now, as she sat down again, she saw something that temporarily stunned her. Irene saw it, too, as she sat down, and a little amused, impertinent smile appeared on her lips and hovered there ^**during**^ the rest of the ~~evening~~ ^**interview**^.

On one of Rilla's feet was ~~an~~ a smart little ^**steel-**^buckled shoe and a filmy ^**blue**^ silk stocking. ~~On the other was~~ ^**The other was clad in**^ a stout ~~boot!~~ and rather shabby boot and black lisle!

Poor Rilla! She had ~~meant~~ changed, or begun to change her boots and stockings after she had put on her dress. This was the result of doing one thing with your hands and another with your brain. Oh, what a ridiculous position to be in – and before Irene Howard of all people – Irene, who was staring at Rilla's feet as if she had never seen feet before! And once she had thought Irene's manner perfection!

Everything that Rilla had prepared to say vanished from her memory. Vainly trying to tuck her unlucky foot under her chair, she blurted out a blunt statement.

"I have come to athk a favour of you, Irene."

There – lisping! Oh, she had been prepared for humiliation but not to this extent! Really, there were limits!

"Yes?" said Irene ~~with a cool~~ in a cool, questioning tone, lifting her ^**shallowly-set, insolent**^ eyes to Rilla's crimson face for a moment and then dropping them again ~~to her feet ^**the**^~~ as if she could not tear them from their fascinated gaze at the ~~black~~ shabby boot and the gallant shoe.

~~"Mrs. Channing~~

Rilla gathered herself together. She would not lisp – she would be calm and composed.

"Mrs. Channing cannot come because her son is ill in ~~Halifax~~ ^**Kingsport**^, and I have come on behalf of the committee to ask you if you will be so kind as to sing for us in her place." Rilla enunciated every word so precisely and carefully that she seemed to be reciting a lesson.

"It's something of a fiddler's invitation, isn't it?" said ~~Irren~~ Irene, with one of her disagreeable ~~little~~ smiles.

"Olive Kirk asked you to help when we first thought of the concert and you refused," said Rilla.

"Why, I could hardly help – then – could I?" ~~said~~ asked Irene plaintively. "After you had ordered me never to speak to you again? It would have been ~~unpleasant~~ ^**very awkward**^ for us both, don't you think?"

Now for the humble pie.

"I want to apologize to you for saying that, Irene," said Rilla steadily. "I should not have said it and I have been very sorry ever since. Will you forgive me?"

"And sing at your concert?" said Irene sweetly and insultingly. ~~She might as well have said added, 'that is just ^**you only**^ why you are apologizing to me' for her tone said it for her. And the worst of it, from Rilla's point of view, was that it was quite true.~~

"If you mean," said Rilla miserably, "that I would not be apologizing to you if it were not for the concert perhaps that is true. But it is ^**also**^ true that I have felt ever since it happened that I should not have said what I did and ^**that**^ I have been sorry for it all winter. That is all I can say.[22] If you feel you can't forgive me I suppose there is nothing more to be said."

"Oh, Rilla dear, don't snap me up like that," pleaded Irene. "Of course I'll forgive you – though I did feel awfully about it – how awfully I hope you'll never know. ^~~**I cried for weeks**~~^ ~~And when I hadn't done or said a thing!~~ I cried for weeks over it. And I hadn't said or done a thing!"

Rilla choked back a retort. After all, there was no use in arguing with Irene, and the Belgians were starving.

"Don't you think you can help us with the concert," she forced herself to say. Oh, if only Irene would stop looking at that boot! ^[*Note*] **P5**^

"I don't see how I really can ~~at this late date~~ ^**at the last moment like this**^," ~~said~~ ^**protested**^ Irene ~~apologetically~~. "There isn't time to learn anything new."

"Oh, you have lots of lovely songs that nobody in the Glen ever heard before," said Rilla, who knew Irene had been ~~taking~~ ^**going to town for**^ lessons ~~in town~~ all winter and that this was ~~simply an excuse~~ ^**only a pretext**^. "They will all be new down there."

"But I have no accompanist," protested Irene.

"~~Millicent Arnold will or is a beautiful~~ ^**Una Meredith** ~~**will play for**~~ ^^**can accompany you**^^^," ~~pianist and can play accompaniment at sight,"~~ said Rilla. ~~"If you went down early to-morrow.~~

"Oh, I couldn't ask her," sighed Irene. ~~"She~~ "We haven't spoken since last fall. She was so hateful to me the time of our Sunday School Concert that I simply had to give her up."

Dear, dear, was Irene at feud with everybody? ^[*Note*] **E6**^

"Miss Oliver ~~can play for you and will if I ask her~~ is a beautiful pianist and can play any accompaniment at sight," said Rilla desperately. "She will play for you if I ask her and you could run over your songs easily to-morrow evening at Ingleside before the concert."

~~"I haven~~ "~~And~~ ^**But**^ I haven't anything to wear. ~~M~~ My new evening dress isn't home from Charlottetown yet, and I simply cannot wear my old one at such a big affair. It is too shabby and old-fashioned."

^[*Note*] **B7**^

Rilla concluded that she had humiliated herself enough. ^[*Note*] **Q5**^ No more coaxing, concert or no concert. She got up, boot and all.

"I am sorry you can't help us, Irene, but ~~if~~ ^**since**^ you cannot ~~there is no more to be said. We~~ ^**we**^ must do the best we can."

Now this did not suit Irene at all. She ~~was dying ^**wanted**^~~ ^^**desired**^^ ^**exceedingly**^ to sing at that concert, and all her hesitations were merely by way of enhancing ~~her~~ the boon of her final consent. Besides, ~~she~~ she really wanted to be friends with Rilla again. Rilla's ^**whole-hearted, ungrudging**^ adoration had been very sweet incense to her. And Ingleside was a very charming house to visit, especially when a handsome college student like Walter was home. ^**She stopped**

looking at Rilla's feet.^

"Rilla, darling, don't be so abrupt. I really want to help you, if I can manage it. Just sit down and let's talk it over."

"I'm sorry, but I can't. I have to be home soon – ~~it~~ Jims has to be settled for the night, you know."

"Oh, yes – the baby you are bringing up by the book. ^[*Note*] **N5**^ How cross you were ^**just**^ because I kissed him! But we'll forget all that and be chums again, ^**won't we?**^ Now, about the concert – I dare-say I can run into town on the morning train ^**after my dress**^, and out again on the afternoon one in plenty of time ~~for the concert~~ ^**for the concert**^, if you'll ask Miss Oliver to play for me. I couldn't – she's so dreadfully haughty and supercilious that she simply paralyses poor little me."

Rilla did not waste time or breath defending Miss Oliver. She ^**coolly**^ thanked Irene, who had suddenly become very ^**amiable and**^ gushing, and got away.

^[*Note*] **K5**^ [*Note O5 is embedded in this note.*]

But not until ~~she found~~ ^**Rilla**^ had traversed the Upper Glen Road and found herself in the moon-dappled solitude of Rainbow Valley did she ^**fully**^ recover her composure of spirit. Then she stopped ^[*Note*] **M5**^ and laughed.

"There is only one thing of importance just now – and that is that the Allies win the war," she said aloud. "Therefore, it follows ~~as a logical deduction~~ without dispute that the fact that I went to see Irene Howard with odd shoes and stockings on is of no importance whatever. Nevertheless, I, ^~~**Bertha Marilla Cuthbert Blythe**~~ **Bertha Marilla Blythe,**^ swear solemnly with the moon as witness" – Rilla lifted her hand dramatically to the ~~said moon~~ ^**said moon**^, "that I will never leave my room again without looking carefully at both my feet."

Chapter Fourteen

Rilla was wildly busy all the next day, helping to decorate the vill Glen hall for the concert and doing a hundred last things. Nan had offered to take care of Jims for the day and so set her free. Susan kept the flag flying at Ingleside all day, in honor of Italy's declaration of war!' And not before

Chap. 14

~~The Valley of Decision~~

The Valley of Decision

Susan kept the flag flying at Ingleside all the next day, in honour of Italy's declaration of war.

"And not before it was time, Mrs. Dr. dear, considering the way things have begun to go on the Russian front. Say what you will, those Russians are kittle cattle ^[*Note*] **H6**^ It is a fortunate thing for Italy that she has come in on the right side, but whether it is as fortunate for the Allies I will not predict until I know more about Italians than I do now. However, she will give that old reprobate of a Francis Joseph something to think ~~of~~ ^**about**^. A pretty Emperor indeed – with one foot in the grave and yet ~~planning~~ ^**plotting**^ wholesale murder" – and Susan thumped and kneaded her bread with ~~such~~ ^**as much**^ vicious energy ~~that~~ as she could have expended in punching Francis Joseph himself ^**if he had been so unlucky as to fall into her clutches**^.

Walter had gone to town on the early train, and Nan offered to look after Jims for the day and so set Rilla free. Rilla was wildly busy all day, helping to decorate the Glen hall and seeing to a hundred last things. The evening was beautiful, in spite of the fact that Mr. Pryor was reported to have said that he "hoped it would rain pitch forks points down," ^[*Note*] **Y5**^ Rilla, rushing home from the hall, ~~at the last minute~~ dressed hurriedly ~~but did not forget to take a final look at her feet before she left the room~~. Everything had gone surprisingly well at the last; Irene was even then downstairs practising her songs with Miss Oliver; Rilla was excited and ~~for the moment~~ happy, forgetful even of the Western front for the moment. It gave her a sense of achievement and victory to have brought her efforts of weeks to such a successful conclusion. ~~Where~~ She knew that there had not lacked people who thought and hinted that ~~pleasure-loving~~ Rilla Blythe had not the tact or patience to engineer a concert programme. She had shown them! Little snatches of song ~~came to her~~ bubbled from her lips as she dressed. She thought she was looking very well. ~~Her hair gleamed with red-brown luster and~~ ~~e~~Excitement brought a faint becoming pink into her round creamy cheeks, ^**quite drowning out her few freckles,**^ and her hair gleamed with red-brown lustre. Should she wear crab-apple blossoms in it, or her little fillet of pearls? After some agonised wavering she decided on the crab-apple blossoms and tucked the white waxen ~~spray~~ cluster behind her left ear. Now for a final look at her feet. Yes, both slippers were on. ~~She hurried down the hill to the hall. Already it was filling. Her concert was going to be a brilliant success.~~ ^**She gave the sleeping Jims a kiss – what a dear little** ^^**warm,**^^ **rosy, satin face he had –**^

~~The hall filled until it was crowded. Even Miranda Pryor had come~~

~~She ran to her mother's room. "Ready, mother darling?"~~

~~Mrs. Blythe was ready, looking very handsome in her dark blue crepe dress and her hat with its floating plume.~~

~~She~~ ^**and**^ hurried down the hill to the hall. Already it was filling – soon it was crowded. Her concert was going to be a brilliant success.

The first three numbers were ^**successfully**^ over. Rilla was in the little dressing-room behind the platform ~~alone~~, looking out on the moonlit harbor and rehearsing her own recitations. ^[*Note*] **T5**^ Suddenly she felt two soft ^**bare**^ arms slipping round her waist, ~~and~~ then Irene Howard dropped a light kiss on her neck.

"Rilla, you sweet thing, you're looking simply angelic to-night. You have spunk – I thought you would feel so badly over Walter's enlisting that you'd hardly be able to bear up at ~~hall~~ all." ^[*Note*] **F6**^

Rilla ~~did~~ stood perfectly still. She felt no emotion whatever – she felt nothing. The world of feeling had just gone blank.

~~"Has~~ "Walter – enlisting" – she heard herself saying – then she heard Irene's ~~silly~~ ^**affected**^ little laugh.

"Why, didn't you know? I thought you did of course, or I wouldn't have mentioned it. ^[*Note*] **U5**^ Yes, that was what he went to town for to-day – he told me coming out on the train to-night. ^**I was the first person he told.**^ He isn't in khaki yet – ~~there is a abe~~ they were out of uniforms – but he will be in a day or two I always said Walter ~~wasn't – what Mrs. Burr said he was."~~ ^**had as much pluck as anybody.**^ I assure

~~Feeling was~~ you I felt proud of him, Rilla, when he told me what he'd done. Oh, there's an end of Rick MacAllister's reading – I must ~~run~~ ^**fly**^. I ~~have to play~~ ^**promised I'd play**^ for the next chorus – ~~Min~~ ^**Alice**^ Clow has such a headache."

She was gone – oh, thank God, she was gone! Rilla was alone again, staring out at the ~~moonlit harbor~~ unchanged, dream-like beauty of moonlit Four Winds. ~~She would hate moonlight forever~~ Feeling was coming back to her – ~~^**in**^~~ a pang of agony so acute as to be almost physical seemed to rend her ~~in two~~ apart.

"I cannot bear it," she said. And then came the awful thought that perhaps she could bear it and that there might be years of this hideous suffering before her.

She must get away – she must rush home – she must be alone. She could not go out there and play for drills and give readings and take part in dialogues now. It would spoil half the concert – but that did not matter – nothing mattered. Was this she, Rilla Blythe – this tortured thing who had been quite happy a few minutes ago? Outside, ~~the cho~~ a quartette was singing "We'll never let the old flag fall" – the music seemed to be coming from ~~niles miles ^**some place**^ away~~ ^**some remote distance**^. Why couldn't she cry, as she had cried when Jem told them he must go? If she could cry perhaps this horrible something that seemed to have seized on her very life might let go. But no tears came! Where were her ~~hat~~ ^**scarf**^ and ~~jacket~~ coat? She must ~~go~~ get away and hide herself like an animal ^**hurt to the death**^.

Was it a coward's part to run away like this? The question came to her suddenly as if someone else had asked it. She thought of the shambles of the Flanders front – she thought of her brother and her playmate ~~holding~~ ^**helping to hold**^ those fire-swept trenches. What would they think of her if she shirked her little duty here – the humble duty of carrying the programme through for her ~~little~~ Red Cross? ~~Oh she couldn't~~ But she couldn't stay – she couldn't – ~~nobody~~ ^**yet**^ what was it mother had said when Jem went – "when our women fail in courage shall our men be fearless still?" But this – this was unbearable.

Still, she ~~did not go for her hat~~ stopped half way to the door and went back to the window. Irene was singing now – her beautiful voice ^**– the only real thing about her –**^ soared clear and ~~true~~ sweet through the building. Rilla knew that the girls' Fairy Drill came next. Could she go out there and play for it? Her head was aching now – her throat was burning? Oh, why had Irene told her just then,~~" She might have waited inti until the concert was over, since~~ ^**when**^ telling now could do no good? Irene ~~was~~ had been very cruel. Rilla remembered now that more than once that day she had caught her mother looking at her with an odd expression. She had been too busy to wonder what it meant. She ~~knew~~ ^**understood**^ now. Mother had known why Walter went to town but ~~would not tell her until the c hadn't wanted her to know~~ ^**wouldn't tell her**^ until the concert was over. What spirit ~~mother had – what endurance – what bravery!~~ ^**and endurance mother had!**^

"I must stay here and see things through," said Rilla, clasping her cold hands together.

The rest of the evening always seemed like ~~a nightmare~~ ^~~**an ugly**~~ ^^**a fevered**^^ **dream**^ to her. Her body was crowded by people but her soul was alone in a torture chamber of its own. Yet she played ^**steadily**^ for the drills ~~and gave her acted in the dialogues and~~ ^**and**^ gave her readings without faltering; ^[*Note*] **R5**^ As she stood before the audience she saw one face only – that of the ~~pale~~ handsome, ^**dark-haired**^ ~~boy with the dark, thick hair,~~ ^**lad**^ sitting beside her mother – and she saw that same face in the trenches – saw it lying cold and dead under the stars – saw it pining in prison – saw the light of its eyes blotted out – saw a hundred horrible things as she stood there on the beflagged platform of the Glen hall with her ~~white face and her cold hands. Would the concert never end.~~ ^**own face whiter than the milky crab blossoms in her hair.**^ Between ~~the~~ ^**her**^ numbers she walked restlessly up and down the little dressing-room. Would the concert <u>never</u> end!

It ended at last. Olive Kirk rushed up and told her exultantly that they had made a hundred dollars. "That's good," Rilla said mechanically. Then she was away from them all – oh, thank God, she was away from them all – Walter was waiting for her at the door. He put ~~her~~ ^**his**^ arm through hers silently and they went together down the ~~white ro~~ moonlit road. The frogs were singing in the marshes, ^**the**^ dim, ensilvered fields of home lay all around them. The spring night was lovely and appealing. Rilla felt that its beauty was an insult to her pain. She would hate moonlight for ever. △~~**The eyes of youth could not see how she was to go on living.**~~△

“You know?” said Walter.

“Yes. Irene told me,” answered Rilla chokingly.

“We didn’t want you to know till the evening was over. I knew when you came out for the drill that you had heard. Little sister, I had to do it. I couldn’t live any longer on such terms with myself as I have been ~~since Langemarck.”~~ since the Lusitania was sunk.~~” When I – I’ve got to go~~ When I pictured those

~~“There are plenty – without you,” said Rilla.~~

~~“That isn’t the point, Rilla-my-Rilla.~~

dead women and children floating about in that pitiless, ice-cold water – well, at first I just felt a sort of nausea with life. I wanted to get out of the world where such a thing could happen – shake its accursed dust from my feet for ever. Then I knew I had to go.”

“There are – plenty – without you.”

“That isn’t the point, Rilla-my-Rilla. I’m going for my own sake – to save my soul alive. It will shrink to something small and mean and lifeless if I don’t go. That ~~will~~ would be worse than ~~death~~ blindness or mutilation or any of the things I’ve feared.”

“You may – be – killed,” Rilla hated herself for saying it – she knew it was a weak and cowardly thing to say – but she had rather gone to pieces after the tension of the evening.

“‘Comes he slow or comes he fast
It is but death who comes at last.’”

quoted Walter. “It’s not death I fear – I told you that long ago. One can pay too high a price for ~~life~~ mere life, little sister. There’s so much hideousness in this war – I’ve got to go and help wipe it out of the world. I’m going to fight for the beauty of life, Rilla-my-Rilla –that is my duty. There may be a higher duty, perhaps – but that is mine. ^[*Note*] **S5**^ Rilla, tonight for the first time since Jem left I’ve got back my self-respect. I could write poetry,” Walter laughed. “I’ve never been able to write a line since ~~the~~ last August. To-night I’m full of it.~~”~~ Little sister, be brave – you were so plucky when Jem went.”

“This – is – different,” Rilla had to stop after every word to fight down a wild outburst of sobs. "I loved – Jem – of course – but ^[*Note*] **V5**^ – you are – everything to me, Walter."

"You must be brave to help me, Rilla-my-Rilla. I'm ~~exallted~~ exalted to-night – drunk with the excitement of victory over myself – but there will be other times when it won't be like this – I'll need your help then."

"When – do – you – go?" She must know the worst at once.

"Not for a week – then we go to Kingsport for training. I suppose we'll go overseas about the middle of July – we don't know."

One week – only one week more with Walter! The eyes of youth did not see how she was to go on living.

When they turned in at the Ingleside gate Walter stopped ~~under~~ ^**in**^ the shadows of the old pines and drew Rilla close to him.

"Rilla-my-Rilla, there were girls as sweet and pure as you in Belgium and Flanders. You – even you – know what their fate was. We must make it impossible for such things to happen again while the world lasts. You'll help me, won't you?"

"I'll – try, Walter," ~~said~~ she said. "Oh, I will try."

~~She knew that it had~~

As she clung to him with her face ~~buried~~ pressed against his shoulder she knew that it had to be. She accepted the fact then and there. He must go – her beautiful Walter ^**with his beautiful soul and dreams and ideals**^. And she had known all along that it would come sooner or later. ^[*Note*] **B6**^ Amid all her pain she was conscious of an odd feeling of relief in some hidden part of her soul, where a little dull, ~~ar~~ unacknowledged soreness had been lurking all winter. No one – no one – could ever call Walter a slacker now.

Rilla did not sleep that night. Perhaps no one at Ingleside did except Jims. The body grows slowly and steadily, but the soul grows by leaps and bounds. It may come to its full stature in an hour. From that night Rilla Blythe's soul was the soul of a woman in its capacity for suffering, for strength, for endurance.

When the bitter dawn came she rose and went to her window. Below her was a big apple tree, a great swelling cone of rosy blossom. Walter had planted it years ago when he was a little boy. Beyond Rainbow Valley there was a cloudy shore of morning with little ripples of sunrise breaking over it. The far, cold beauty of a lingering star shone above it. Why, in this world of springtime loveliness, must hearts break?

Rilla felt arms go about her, lovingly, protectingly. It was mother – pale, large-eyed mother.

"Oh, mother, how can you bear it?" she cried wildly.

"Rilla, dear, I've known for several days that Walter meant to go. I've had time to – to rebel and grow reconciled. We must give him up. There is a Call greater and more insistent than the call of our love – he has listened to it. ~~The Piper Pied Piper of his old fancy has piped him away at last.~~ We must not ~~make~~ add to the bitterness of his sacrifice."

"Our sacrifice is greater than his," cried Rilla passionately. "Our boys give only themselves. We give them."

~~"Yes, that is true.~~

Before Mrs. Blythe could reply Susan stuck her head in at the door, never troubling over such frills of etiquette as knocking. Her eyes were suspiciously red but all she said was,

"Will I bring up your breakfast, Mrs. Dr. dear."

"No, no, Susan. We will all be down presently. Do you know – that Walter has joined up."

"Yes, Mrs. Dr. dear. The doctor told me last night. I suppose the Almighty has His own reasons for allowing such things. We must submit and endeavour to look on the bright side. It may cure him of being a poet, at least" – ^**Susan still persisted**^ ~~Susan persisted~~ in thinking that poets and tramps were ~~equally disreputable disreputable members one of another~~ ^**tarred with the same brush** –^ "and that would be something. But thank God," she muttered in a lower tone, ~~as she~~ "that Shirley ~~isn't~~ ^**is not**^ old enough to go."

"Isn't that the same thing as thanking Him that some other woman's son has to go in Shirley's place?" asked the doctor, pausing on the threshold.

"No, it is not, doctor dear," said Susan defiantly, as she picked up Jims, who was opening his big dark eyes and stretching up his ~~chubby arms~~ ^**dimpled paws**^. "Do not you put words in ~~ny~~ my mouth that I would never dream of uttering. I am a plain woman and cannot argue with you, but I do not thank God that anybody has to go. I only know that it seems they ^**do**^ have to go, unless ~~they~~ ^**we**^ all want to be

Kaiserised ^[*Note*] **W5**^ ~~^**The Huns Dr.**^ As for me, Dr. dear, if I were given my choice," concluded Susan darkly, "I would rather die in the trenches then live under German rule.~~

~~"The Huns~~

dear,"~~ concluded Susan darkly, "will <u>never</u> be brought to books by notes."~~

[*Montgomery places a line across the page here to indicate the original chapter end.*]

---

^**The Huns, Dr. dear,**^ will never be brought to book by notes. And now," concluded Susan, ~~packing~~ tucking Jims in the crook of her ^**gaunt**^ arm and marching downstairs, "having cried my cry and said my say I shall take a brace, and if I cannot look pleasant I will look as pleasant as I can."

Chapter 15

"Until The Day Break"

"The Germans have ~~got~~ ^**recaptured**^ ~~Preniysl~~ Premysl ~~again~~," said Susan despairingly, looking up from her newspaper, "and now I suppose we will have to begin calling it by that ~~unearthly~~ uncivilised name again. Cousin Sophia was in when the mail came and when she heard the news she hove a sigh up from the depths of her stomach, Mrs. Dr. dear, and said, 'Ah yes, and they~~'ll~~ ^**will**^ get Petrograd ~~^**tomorrow**^~~ next I have no doubt.' <u>I</u> said to her, 'My knowledge of geography is not so profound as I wish it was but I have an idea that it is quite a walk from ~~Warsaw~~ ^~~**Premysll**~~ **Premysl**^ to Petrograd.' ^[*Note*] **I6**^ But you cannot cheer Cousin Sophia up, no matter how sarcastic you are, Mrs. Dr. dear. She sighed ~~again and said, 'The~~ ^**for the third time and groaned out, 'But the**^ Russians are retreating fast,' and <u>I</u> said, 'Well, what of it? They have plenty of room for retreating, have they not?' But all the same, Mrs. Dr. dear, ^[*Note*] **G6**^ I do <u>not</u> like the situation on the Eastern front."

Nobody else liked it either; but all summer the Russian retreat went on – ^**a long-drawn-out agony**^.

"I wonder if I shall ever again be able to await the coming of the mail with feelings of composure – never to speak of pleasure," said Gertrude Oliver. "The thought that haunts me night and day is – will the Germans smash Russia completely and then hurl their Eastern army, flushed with victory, against the ~~E~~Western front?"

"They will <u>not</u>, Miss Oliver dear," said Susan, assuming the role of prophetess. "In the first place, the Almighty will not allow it, in the second, Grand Duke Nicholas, though he may have been a disappointment to us in some respects, knows how to run away decently and in order, and that is a very useful knowledge when Germans are chasing you. Norman Douglas declares he is just luring them on and killing ten of them to one he loses. But I am of the opinion he cannot help himself and is just doing the best he can under the circumstances, the same as the rest of us. So do not go so far afield to borrow trouble, Miss Oliver, dear, when there is plenty of it already camping on our very doorstep."

Walter had gone to Kingsport the first of June. ^[*Note*] **J6**^ In mid-July ~~he~~ ^**Walter**^ came home for a week's leave before going overseas. Rilla had lived through the days of his absence on the hope of that week, and now that it had come she drank every minute of it thirstily, hating even the hours she had to spend in sleep, they seemed such a waste of precious moments. In spite of its sadness, it was a beautiful week, full of poignant, ~~trea~~ unforgettable hours, when she and Walter had long walks and talks ~~together~~ and silences together. He was all her own and she knew that he found strength and comfort in her sympathy and understanding. It was very wonderful to know she meant so much to him – the knowledge helped her through moments that would otherwise have been unendurable, and gave her power to smile – and even to laugh a little by times. ~~After~~ When Walter had gone she might indulge in the comfort of tears, but not while he was here. She would not even let herself cry at night, lest her eyes should betray her to him in the morning.

~~TOn~~ ^**On**^ his last evening at home they went together to Rainbow Valley and sat down on the bank of the brook, under the White Lady, where the gay revels of olden days had been held in the cloudless years. Rainbow Valley was roofed over with a ~~sun~~ sunset of unusual splendor that night; a wonderful gray dusk just touched with starlight followed it; and then came moonshine, hinting, hiding, revealing, lighting up little ~~glens an~~ dells and hollows here, leaving others in dark, ~~whispering~~ ^**velvet**^ shadow~~s~~.

"When I am 'somewhere in France,'" said Walter, looking around him with ~~greedy~~ eager eyes on all the beauty his soul loved, "I shall remember these still, dewy, moon- drenched places. The balsam of the fir trees – the peace of those white pools of moonshine – the 'strength of the hills' – what a beautiful old Biblical phrase that is. Rilla! Look at those old hills around us – the hills we looked up at as children, wondering what lay for us in the great world beyond them. How calm and strong they are – how patient and changeless – like the heart of a good woman. Rilla-my-Rilla, do you know what you have been to me this past year? I want to tell you before I go. I could not have lived through it if it had not been for you, little loving, believing heart."

Rilla ~~could not s~~ dared not try to speak. She slipped her hand into Walter's and pressed it hard.

"And when I'm over there, Rilla, in that hell upon earth ~~that~~ ^**which**^ men ~~have made~~ who have forgotten God, have made, it will be the thought of you that will ~~com~~ help me most. I know you'll be as plucky and patient as you have shown yourself to be this past year – I'm not afraid for you. I know that no matter what happens, you'll be Rilla-my-Rilla – no matter what happens."

Rilla repressed tear and sigh, but she could not repress a little shiver, and Walter knew that he had said enough. After a moment of silence, in which each made an unworded promise to each other, he said,

"Now we won't be sober any more. We'll look beyond the years – to the time when the war will be over and Jem and Jerry and I will come marching home and we'll all be happy again."

"We won't be – happy – in ~~qu~~ the same way," said Rilla.

"No, not in the same way. Nobody whom this war has touched will ever be happy again in quite the same way. But it will be a better happiness, I think, little sister – a happiness we've earned. We were very happy before the war, weren't we? With a home like Ingleside, and a father and mother like ours we couldn't help being happy. But that happiness was a gift from life and love; it wasn't really ours – life could take it back at any time. It ~~will~~ ^**can**^ never take away the happiness we win for ourselves in the way of duty. I've realised that since I went into khaki. In spite of my occasional funks, when I fall to living over things beforehand, I've been ~~happier~~ ^**happy**^ since that night in May~~, than I~~. Rilla, be awfully good to mother while I'm away. It must be a horrible thing to be a mother in this war – the mothers and sisters and ^**wives and**^ sweethearts have the hardest times. Rilla, you beautiful little thing, are you anybody's sweetheart? ~~Tell~~ If you are, tell me before I go."

"No," said Rilla. Then, impelled by a wish to be ~~perfectly~~ ^**absolutely**^ frank with Walter in this talk that might be the last they would ever have, she added, blushing wildly in the moonlight, "but – but if – Kenneth Ford – wanted me to be –"

"I see," said Walter. "And Ken's in khaki, too. Poor little girlie, it's ~~has~~ a bit hard for you all round. Well, I'm not leaving any girl to break her heart about me – thank God for that."

Rilla glanced up at the Manse on the hill. She could see a light shining in Una Meredith's window. She felt tempted to say something – then she knew she must not. It was not her secret: and, anyway, she did not know – she only suspected.

Walter looked about him lingeringly and lovingly. This spot had always been so dear to him. What fun they ~~ha~~ all had had here lang syne. Phantoms of memory ~~pa~~ seemed to pace the dappled paths and peep merrily through the swinging boughs – Jem and Jerry, bare-legged, ~~sunbeamed~~ sunburned schoolboys, fishing in the brook and frying trout over the old stone fireplace, Nan and Di and Faith, in their dimpled, fresh-eyed ~~cut~~ childish beauty, Una the sweet and shy, Carl, ~~und~~ poring over ants and bugs, little slangy, sharp-tongued, ^**good-hearted**^ Mary Vance – the old Walter that had been himself lying on the grass reading poetry ^[*Note*] **Y6**^ ~~^**or dreaming dreams**^~~ They were all there around him – he could see them almost as plainly as he saw Rilla – as plainly as he had once seen the Pied Piper piping down the valley in a vanished twilight. And they said to him, those gay little ghosts of other days, ~~"Figh~~ "We were the children of yesterday, Walter – ~~fight for~~ fight a good fight for the children of to-day and to-morrow."

"Where are you, Walter," cried Rilla, laughing a ~~litter~~ ^**little**^. "Come back – come back."

Walter came back with a ~~sigh~~ ^**long**^ breath. He stood up and looked about him at the beautiful valley of moonlight, as if to ~~carry away with him~~ impress on his mind and heart ~~every~~ every ~~lovel~~ charm it possessed – ^**Note X6**^ ~~^**the great firs branching out like**^~~ – the ~~sharp pointed firs~~ against the silvery sky, the stately White Lady, the ^**old magic of the**^ dancing brook, the ~~old~~ ^**faithful**^ Tree Lovers, the beckoning, tricksy paths.

~~"I shall see it so in my dreams amid the hor horror that is waiting for me," he thought. "But will I ever see it again in reality?"~~

"I shall see it so in my dreams," he said, as he turned away.

They went back to Ingleside. Mr. and Mrs. Meredith were there, ~~and~~ ^**with**^ Gertrude Oliver, who had come ~~over to say~~ from Lowbridge to say good-bye. Everybody was quite cheerful and bright, but nobody said much about the war being soon over, as they had said when Jem went away. They did not talk about the war at all – and they thought of nothing else. At last they gathered around the piano and sang the grand old ~~home "Oh, God our help in ages past~~ hymn,

> 'Oh God, our help in ages past
> Our hope for years to come.
> Our shelter from the stormy blast
> And our eternal home.'

"We all come back to God in these days of soul-sifting," said Gertrude to ~~Mr.~~ ^**John**^ Meredith. "There have been many days in the past when I didn't believe in God – not <u>as</u> God – only as ~~some~~ ^**the**^ impersonal Great First Cause of the scientists. I believe in Him now – I <u>have</u> to – there's nothing else to fall back on but God – humbly, starkly, unconditionally."

"'Our help in ages past' – 'the same yesterday, to-day and forever,'" said the minister gently. "When we forget God – He remembers us."

There was no crowd at the Glen Station the next morning to see Walter off. It was becoming a commonplace for a khaki clad boy to board that early morning train after his last leave. ~~His own people and Only the manse people were there besides his own.~~ ^**Besides his own, only the Manse folk were there, and Mary Vance.**^ ^[*Note*] **L6**^ Mrs. Blythe, who had sent Jem off with a smile, could not quite manage one for Walter. But at least no one cried. ~~Rags~~ ^**Dog Monday**^ came out of his lair in the shipping shed and sat down close to Walter, thumping his tail vigorously on the boards of the platform ^**whenever Walter spoke to him**^, and looking ~~at Walter~~ ^**~~up~~ up**^ with confident eyes, as if to say, "I know you'll find Jem and bring him back to me."

"So long, old fellow," said Carl Meredith cheerfully, when the ~~last moment~~ good-byes had to be said. "Tell them over there to keep their spirits up – ~~I am~~ ^**~~I'm~~ <u>I</u> am**^ coming ~~next year."~~ ^**along presently**^."

"Me too," said Shirley laconically, proffering a brown paw. Susan heard him and her face turned very gray.

Una shook hands quietly, looking at him with wistful, sorrowful, dark-blue eyes. But then Una's eyes had always been ~~wit~~ wistful. Walter bent his handsome black head in its khaki cap and kissed her ~~as if she had been his sister~~ ^**with the ~~wam~~ warm, comradely kiss of a**

brother^. He had never kissed her before, and for a fleeting moment Una’s face betrayed her, if anyone had noticed. But nobody did; the conductor was shouting “all aboard” ^~~**K6**~~ **Note K6**^ Walter turned to Rilla; she held his hands and looked up at him. ^**Note J10**^ ~~and said “good-bye.”~~ On her lips it lost all the bitterness it had won through the ages of parting and bore instead all the sweetness of ^**the**^ old loves of all the women who had ever loved and prayed for the beloved. ~~^[*Note*] **M6**^ Walter smiled into her gallant eyes; after all, it was not a hard thing to fight for a land that bre bore daughters like this.~~ ^[*Note*] **M6**^

He stood on the rear platform and waved to them as the train pulled out. Rilla ~~stood~~ ^**was standing**^ by herself but Una Meredith came to her and the two girls who loved him most stood together and held each other’s cold hands as the train rounded the curve of the wooded hill.

Rilla spent an hour in Rainbow Valley that morning about which she never said a word to anyone; she did not even write in her diary about it; when it was over she went home and made rompers for Jims during the rest of the day; in the evening she went to a ~~Red Cross~~ Junior Red Cross committee meeting and was severely businesslike.

“You would never suppose,” said Irene Howard to Olive Kirk afterwards, “that Walter had left for the front only this morning. But some people really have no depth of feeling. I suppose it is much the best thing for them. I often wish I ~~didn’t~~ ^**could**^ take things ~~as seriously~~ as lightly as Rilla Blythe.”

Chapter 16

Realism and Romance

"Warsaw has fallen," said Dr. Blythe with a resigned air, ~~coming in with~~ ^**as he brought**^ the mail ^**in**^ one warm August day.

Gertrude and Mrs. Blythe looked dismally at each other, and Rilla, who was feeding Jims a Morganized diet ~~form~~ from a carefully sterilized spoon, laid the said spoon down on ~~a chair~~ ^**his tray**^, utterly regardless of germs, and said, "Oh, dear me," in as tragic a tone as if the news had come as a thunderbolt instead of being a ~~foreg~~ foregone conclusion from the preceding ~~day's~~ ^**week's**^ dispatches. They had thought they were quite resigned to Warsaw's fall but now they knew they had, ^**as always,**^ hoped against hope.

"Now, let us take a brace," said Susan. "It is not the terrible thing we have been thinking. I read a dispatch ~~from~~ three columns long in the Montreal Herald yesterday which proved that Warsaw was not important from a military point of view at all. So let us take the military point of view, Dr. dear."

"I read that dispatch, too, and it has encouraged me immensely," said Gertrude. "I knew then and I know now that it was a lie from beginning to end. ^**But**^ I am in that state ~~where~~ of mind where even a lie is a comfort, providing it is a cheerful lie."

"For that case, Miss Oliver dear, the German official reports ought to be all you need," said Susan ^**sarcastically.**^ "I never read them now because they make me so mad I cannot put my thoughts properly on my work after a dose of them. ~~But~~ Even this news about Warsaw has ~~upset~~ taken the edge off my afternoon's ~~work~~ ^**plans**^. Misfortunes never come singly. I spoiled my baking of bread to-day – and now Warsaw has fallen – and here is little Kitchener bent on choking himself to death."

Jims was evidently trying to swallow his spoon, germs and all. Rilla rescued him mechanically and was about to resume ~~her~~ the operation of feeding him when a casual remark of her father's sent such a ~~thrill~~ shock and thrill over her that for the second time she dropped that doomed spoon~~, conplete with its~~.

"Kenneth Ford is down at ~~his~~ Martin West's over harbour," the doctor was saying. "His regiment ~~has been held up in~~ was on its way to the front but was held up in Kingsport for some reason, and Ken got leave of absence to come over to the Island ~~for a day or two~~."

"I hope he will come up to see us," exclaimed Mrs. Blythe.

"He only has a day or two off, I believe," said the doctor absently.

Nobody noticed Rilla's flushed face and trembling hands. Even the most thoughtful and watchful of parents do not see everything that goes on under their very noses. ~~Rilla gave Jims the rest of his dinner~~ Rilla made a third attempt to give ~~the long-suffering~~ ^**the long-suffering**^ Jims his dinner but all she could think of was the question – Would Ken come to see her before he went away? She had not heard from him for a long while. Had he forgotten her completely? If he did not come she would know that he had. Perhaps there was even – some other girl back there in Toronto. Of course there was. She was a little fool to be thinking about him at all. She would not think about him. If he came, well and good. It would only be courteous of him to make a farewell call at Ingleside where he had often been a guest. If he did not come – well and good, too. It did not matter very much. Nobody was going to fret. That was all settled comfortably – ~~but Jims was fed with mean~~ she was quite indifferent – but meanwhile Jims was being fed with a haste and recklessness that would have filled the soul of Morgan with ~~despair~~ ^**horror**^. Jims himself didn't like it, being a ~~placid, well~~ methodical ~~infant~~ ^**baby**^, accustomed to ~~eating~~ swallowing spoonfuls with a decent interval for breath between ^**each**^. He protested, but his protests availed him nothing. Rilla, as far as the care and feeding of infants was concerned, was utterly demoralized.

Then the ~~telep~~ telephone-bell rang. ~~Rilla~~ There was nothing unusual about the telephone ringing. It rang on an average every ten minutes at ~~Ril~~ Ingleside. But Rilla dropped Jims' spoon again – on the carpet this time – and flew to the 'phone as if life depended on her getting there before anybody else. Jims, his patience exhausted, lifted up his ~~voice~~ voice and wept.

~~"Hello, is that Rilla?" called a voice.~~

"Hello, is this Ingleside?

"Yes."

"~~Is~~ That you, Rilla?"

"Yeth – yeth." Oh, why couldn't Jims stop howling for just one little minute? Why didn't somebody come in and ~~attend to~~ ^**choke**^ him?

"Know who's speaking?"

Oh, didn't she know! Wouldn't she know that voice anywhere – at any time?

"It's Ken – isn't it?"

"Sure thing. I'm here for a look-in. Can I come up to Ingleside to-night and see you?"

"Of ~~course~~ courthe."

~~Did "you~~ Had he used "you" in the singular or plural sense? Presently she would wring Jims' neck – oh, what was Ken saying?

"See here, Rilla, can you arrange that ~~other folks won't be poking about too much. It's you I want to see~~ there won't be more than a few dozen people round? ~~Can't say more over Can~~ Understand? I can't make my meaning clearer over this ~~blessed~~ bally rural line. There are a dozen receivers down."

Did she understand! Yes, she understood.

"I'll – try ," she said tremulously.

"I'll be up about eight then. By-by."

Rilla hung up the 'phone and flew to Jims. But she did not wring that injured infant's neck. Instead she snatched him bodily out of his chair, ~~kissed and~~ crushed him against her face, kissed him rapturously on his milky mouth, and danced wildly around the room with him in her arms. After this Jims was relieved to find that she returned to sanity, ~~and~~ gave him the rest of his dinner properly, and tucked him away for his afternoon nap with the little ~~lul~~ lullaby he loved best of all.

She sewed at Red Cross ~~gingham ^**jean**~~^ shirts for the rest of the afternoon and built a crystal ~~dre~~ castle of dreams, all a-quiver with rainbows. Ken wanted to see her ~~alone~~ ^**– to see her alone**^. That could be easily managed. Shirley wouldn't bother them, father ~~was would be out~~ and mother were going to the manse, Miss Oliver never played gooseberry, and Jims always slept ~~like an angel~~ the ~~evening through~~ clock round from seven to seven. She would entertain Ken on the veranda – it would be moonlight – she would wear her white

^**Georgette**^ dress and do her hair up – yes, she would – at least in a ~~Madonna~~ ^**low**^ knot at the nape of her neck. Mother couldn't object to that, surely. ~~Oh, she did hope it wouldn't rain – Doc was Dr. Jekyll and the barometer was up, so there was practical assurance it wouldn't.~~ Oh, how wonderful and romantic it would be! Would Ken say anything – he must mean to say something or why should he ~~would~~ be so particular about seeing her alone? What if it rained – Susan had been complaining about Mr. Hyde that morning! What if some officious Junior Red ~~dropped in~~ ^**called**^ to discuss Belgians and ~~shrts~~ ^**shirts**^? Or, worst of all, what if Fred Arnold dropped in? He did occasionally.

The evening came at last and was all that could be desired in an evening. The doctor and his wife went to the manse, Shirley and Miss Oliver went they alone knew where, Susan went to the store for household supplies, and Jims went to ~~sleep~~ ^**Dreamland**^. Rilla ~~dressed~~ put on her Georgette gown, knotted up her hair and bound a little ~~pearl fillet~~ ^**double string of pearls**^ around it ~~and~~. ^**Then she**^ tucked a cluster of pale pink baby roses at her belt. Would Ken ask her for a rose for a keepsake? She knew that Jem had carried to the trenches in Flanders a faded rose that Faith Meredith had kissed and given him the night before he left. ~~It would be very romantic.~~

Rilla looked very sweet when she met Ken in the mingled moonlight and ^**vine**^ shadows of the big veranda. ~~She~~ The hand she gave him was cold and she was so desperately anxious not to lisp that her greeting was prim and precise. How handsome tall Kenneth looked in his lieutenant's uniform! It made him seem older, too – ^**so much so that**^ Rilla felt rather foolish. Hadn't it been the height of absurdity for her to suppose that this splendid young officer ~~could~~ had anything special to say to her, little Rilla Blythe of Glen St. Mary? Likely she hadn't understood him after all – he had only meant that he didn't want a mob of folks around making a fuss over him and trying to lionize him, ~~the way~~ ^**as**^ they had ~~likely~~ ^**probably**^ done over-harbor . Yes, of course, that was all he meant – and she, little idiot, had gone and vainly imagined that he didn't want anybody but her. And he would think she had manoeuvred everybody away so that they could be alone together, ~~lau~~ and he would laugh ~~at her~~ to himself at her.

"This is better luck than I hoped for," said Ken, leaning back in his chair and looking at her with very unconcealed admiration in his ~~dark~~ ^**eloquent**^ eyes. "I was sure someone would be hanging about and it was just you I wanted to see, Rilla-my-Rilla."

Rilla's dream castle flashed into the landscape again. This was ~~plain~~ ^**unmistakable**^ enough certainly – not much doubt as to his meaning here.

"There aren't ~~so~~ – so many of us – to poke around as there used to be," she said softly.

"No, that's so," said Ken gently. "Jem and Walter and the girls away – it makes a big blank, doesn't it? ~~But You must be lonely~~ But –" he leaned forward until his dark curls almost brushed ~~hers~~ ^**her hair**^ – "doesn't Fred Arnold try to fill the blank occasionally? I've been told so."

At this moment, before Rilla could make any reply, Jims began to cry at the top of his voice in the room whose open window was just above them – Jims, who hardly ever cried in the evening. Moreover, he was crying, as Rilla knew from experience, with a vim and energy that betokened that he had been already whimpering softly unheard for some time and was thoroughly exasperated. When Jims started in crying like that he made a thorough job of it. Rilla knew that there ~~was~~ ^**it**^ no use to sit still and pretend to ignore him. He wouldn't stop; and conversation of any kind was out of the question when ^**such**^ shrieks and howls ~~like that~~ were floating ~~out of~~ over your head ^**besides, she was afraid Ken would think she was utterly unfeeling if she sat still and let a baby cry like that.** [*Note*] **O6**^

~~Rilla~~ ^**She**^ got up. "~~Excuse~~ Jims has had a nightmare, I think. He sometimes has one and he is always badly frightened by it. Excuse me for a moment."

Rilla flew upstairs, wishing quite frankly that soup tureens had never been invented. But when Jims, at sight of her, lifted his little arms entreatingly and swallowed several sobs, with tears rolling down his cheeks, resentment went out of her heart. After all, the poor darling was frightened. She picked him up gently and rocked him soothingly until his sobs ceased and his ~~eylid~~ eyes closed. Then she essayed to lay him down in his crib. Jims opened his eyes and shrieked a protest. This performance was repeated twice. Rilla grew desperate. She couldn't leave Ken down ~~their~~ there alone any longer – she had been away nearly half an hour already. ~~With~~ ^**With**^ a resigned air she marched downstairs, ~~with Jims in her arms~~ ^**carrying Jims,**^ and sat down on the veranda. It was, no doubt, a ridiculous thing to sit and cuddle a ~~war~~ contrary war baby when ~~your~~ your best young man was making his farewell call, but there was nothing else to be done.

~~"He's a dec~~

Jims was supremely happy. He kicked his little pink-soled feet rapturously out under his white nighty and gave one of his rare laughs. He was beginning to be a very pretty baby; his golden hair curled in ~~adorable~~ ^**silken**^ ringlets all over his little round head and his eyes were beautiful.

"He's a decorative kiddy all right, ~~isn't~~ isn't he?" said Ken.

"His looks are ~~all right~~ ^**very well**^," said Rilla, bitterly, as if to imply that they were much the best of him. Jims, being an astute infant, sensed trouble in the atmosphere and realized that it was up to him to clear it away. He turned his face up to Rilla, smiled ~~bewitchingly~~ ^**adorably**^ and said, clearly ~~and distin~~ and distinctly~~, "Will – Will."~~ and beguilingly, "Will – Will."

It was the <u>very</u> first time he had spoken a word or tried to speak. Rilla was so delighted that she forgot her grudge against him. She ~~hugged him~~ forgave him with a hug and kiss. Jims, understanding that he was restored to favor, cuddled down against her just where a gleam of light from the lamp in the living-room struck across his hair and turned it into ~~a golden halo ^**smudge** ^^**halio**^^ **of gold against her breast**^~~ ^**a halo of gold against her breast**^. Kenneth sat very still and silent, looking at Rilla – at the delicate, girlish silhouette of her, her long lashes, her ~~parted ^**cleft**^ lips, her cleft~~ ^**dented**^ lip, her adorable chin. In the dim moonlight, ~~she~~ as she sat with her head bent a little over Jims, the lamplight glinting on her pearls until they glistened like a ~~min~~ slender nimbus, he thought she looked exactly like the Madonna that hung over his mother's desk at home. He carried that picture of her in his heart to the horror of the battlefields of France. He had had a strong fancy for Rilla Blythe ever since the night of the Four Winds dance; but it was when he saw her there, with little Jims in her arms, that he loved her and ~~knew~~ ^**realized**^ it. And all the while, poor Rilla was sitting, disappointed and humiliated, feeling that her ~~wonderful~~ last evening with Ken was spoiled and wondering why things always had to go so contrarily outside of books. She felt too absurd to try to

~~Hope revived momentarily for~~

try to talk. Evidently Ken was completely disgusted, too, since he was sitting there in such stony silence.

Hope revived momentarily when Jims went so thoroughly asleep that she thought it would be safe to lay him down on the couch in the living-room. But when she came out again Susan was sitting on the veranda, loosening her bonnet strings with the air of one who meant to stay where she was for some time.

"Have you got your baby to sleep?" she asked kindly.

"Your baby." Really, Susan might have more tact. "Yes," said Miss Rilla shortly.

Susan laid her parcels on the reed table, ~~with~~ as one determined to do her duty. She was very tired but she must help Rilla out. Here was Kenneth Ford who had come to call on the family and they were all ^**unfortunately out**^ out, and "the poor child" had had to entertain him alone. But Susan had come to her rescue – Susan would do her ~~duty~~ ^**part**^ no matter how tired she was.

"Dear me, how you ~~children~~ have grown up," she said, looking at Ken's six feet of khaki uniform without the least awe. Susan had grown used to khaki now, and at sixty four even a ~~luit~~ lieutenant's uniform is just clothes and nothing else. ~~"It is~~ ^**"It is**^ an amazing thing how fast children do grow up. Rilla here, now, is almost fifteen."

"I'm going on seventeen, Susan," cried Rilla almost passionately. She was a whole month past sixteen. It was intolerable of Susan.

"It seems just the other day that you were all babies," said Susan, ignoring Rilla's protest. ^[*Note*] **P6**^ ^**"You were really a pretty baby, though your mother had an awful time trying to cure you of sucking your thumb.**^ Do you remember the day I spanked you?~~, Ken?~~"

"No," said Ken.

"Ah well, I suppose you would be too young – you were only about four and you were here with your mother and you insisted on teasing Nan until she cried. I had tried ~~p~~ several ways of stopping you but none availed, ~~so~~ ^**and**^ I ~~soon~~ saw that a spanking was the only thing that would serve. So I picked you up and laid you across my knee and lambasted you well. You howled at the top of your voice but you left Nan alone after that."

Rilla was writhing. ~~Didn~~ Hadn't Susan any realization that she was addressing an officer of the Canadian Army? Apparently she had not. ~~What would Ken think! Would he think she had put Susan~~ Oh, what would Ken think?

"I suppose you ~~don't re~~ do not remember the time your mother spanked you either," ~~went on~~ ^**continued**^ Susan, who seemed to be bent on reviving tender reminiscences that evening. "I shall never, ^**no never,**^ forget it. ~~You were~~ She was up here one ~~evening~~ ^**night**^ with you ~~and you and I~~ when you were about three, and you and Walter were playing ~~on the~~ out in the kitchen yard with a kitten. I had a big ~~hogs-head~~ ^**puncheon**^ of ~~soft water~~ ^**rain**^water by the spout which I was reserving for making soap. And you and Walter began quarrelling over the kitten. Walter was at one side of the ~~hogshead~~ ^puncheon^ standing on a chair, holding the kitten, and you were standing on a chair at the other side. You leaned across that ~~hogshead~~ ^**puncheon**^ and grabbed the kitten and pulled. You were always a great hand for taking what you wanted ^**without too much ceremony**^. Walter held on tight and the poor kitten yelled but you dragged Walter and the kitten half over and then you both lost your balance and tumbled into that puncheon, kitten and all. If I had not been on the spot you would both have been drowned. I flew to the rescue and hauled you all three out before much harm was done, and your mother, ~~came out and picked~~ ^**who had seen it all**^ from the upstairs window, came down and picked ~~up~~ you up, dripping as you were, and gave you a ~~beating~~ beautiful spanking. Ah," said Susan with a sigh, "those were happy old days at Ingleside."

"Must have been," said Ken. His voice sounded ~~ele~~ queer and stiff. Rilla supposed he was hopelessly ~~offended~~ enraged. ^~~**S6**~~ **Note S6**^ ^**The truth was he dare not trust his voice lest it betray his frantic desire to laugh.**^

"Rilla here, now," said Susan, looking affectionately at that unhappy damsel, "never was much spanked. She was a real well-behaved child for the most part. But her father did ~~spark~~ spank her once ~~and he made a thorough job of it~~. She got two bottles of pills out of his office and

~~an~~ dared Alice Clow to see which of them could ~~eat all~~ swallow all the pills first, and if ~~y~~ her father had not happened in the nick of time those two children would have been corpses by night. As it was, they were both sick enough shortly after. But the doctor spanked Rilla then and and there and he made such a thorough job of it that she never meddled with anything in his office afterwards. We hear a great deal ^**nowadays**^ of something that is called 'moral persuasion,' but in my opinion a good spanking and no nagging afterwards is a much better thing."

Rilla wondered viciously whether Susan meant to relate all the family spankings. But Susan had finished with the subject and branched off to another cheerful one.

~~"Little~~ "I remember little Tod MacAllister over harbor killed himself that very way, eating up a whole box of ~~pills~~ fruitatives because he thought they were candy. It was a very sad affair. He was," said Susan earnestly, "the very cutest little corpse I ever laid my eyes on. ^[*Note*]**W6**^ Let me see – would~~n't he~~ ^~~**he**~~ **not Tod**^ be some relation of yours? Your Great-grandmother West was a MacAllister ~~on her mother's side~~. Her brother Amos was a MacDonaldite in religion. ~~My, but~~ ^**I am told**^ he used to take the jerks something fearful. But you look more like your Great-Grandfather West than the MacAllisters. He died of a paralytic stroke quite early in life."

"Did you see anybody at the store?" asked Rilla desperately, in the faint hope of directing Susan's conversation into more agreeable channels.

"Nobody except Mary Vance," said Susan, "^**and she was**^ stepping round as brisk as the Irishman's flea."

What terrible similes Susan used! Would Kenneth think she acquired them from the family!

"To hear Mary talk about Miller Douglas you would think he was the only Glen boy who had enlisted," ~~said~~ Susan went on. "But of course she always did brag and she has some good qualities I am willing to admit, though I did not think so that time she chased Rilla here through the village with a dried codfish till ~~she~~ the poor child fell, heels over head, into the puddle before Carter Flagg's store."

Rilla went cold all over with wrath and shame. Were there any more disgraceful scenes in her past that Susan could rake up? As for Ken, he could have howled ~~with laughter~~ over Susan's speeches, but he would not so insult the ~~duenn a~~ ^**duenna**^ of his lady, so he sat with a preternaturally solemn face which seemed to poor Rilla a ~~disgusted~~ ^**haughty**^ and offended one.

"I paid eleven cents for a bottle of ink to-night," complained Susan. "Ink is twice as high as it was last year. Perhaps it is because Woodrow Wilson has been writing so many notes. It must cost him considerable. My cousin Sophia says Woodrow Wilson is not the man she expected him to be – but then no man ever was. Being an old maid, I do not know much about men and have never pretended to, but my cousin Sophia is very hard on ~~the men~~ ^**them**^, although she married two of them, which you might think was a fair share. Albert Crawford's chimney blew down in that big gale we had last week, and when Sophia heard the bricks clattering on the roof she thought it was a Zeppelin raid and went into hysterics. And Mrs. Albert Crawford says that of the two things she would have preferred the Zeppelin raid."

Rilla sat limply in her chair like one hypnotized. She knew Susan would ~~talk like~~ stop talking when she was ready to stop and that no earthly power could make her stop ~~before~~ any sooner. As a rule, she was very fond of Susan but just now she hated her with a deadly hatred. It was ten o'clock. Ken would soon have to go – the others would soon be home – and she had not even ^**had**^ a chance to explain to Ken that Fred Arnold filled no blank in her life nor ever could. Her rainbow castle lay in ruins round her.

Kenneth got up at last. He realized that Susan was there to stay as long as he did, and it was a ~~long~~ ^~~**3**~~ **three mile**^ walk to Martin MacAllister's over-harbour. He wondered if Rilla had put Susan up to this, not wanting to be left alone with him, lest he say something Fred Arnold's sweetheart did not want to hear. Rilla got up, too, and walked silently the length of the veranda with him. They stood there for a moment, Ken on the lower step ~~looking up at her. The ^**edge of the**^ step was ^**were**^ overgrown with mint and the trodden leaves sent sweet spicy whiffs of fragrance up around them.~~ ^**Note U6**^ Ken looked up at Rilla, whose hair was shining in the moonlight and whose eyes were ~~deep and tender~~ ^**pools of allurement**^ ^**Note K10**^. ~~She seemed em-~~

~~inently~~

"Rilla," he said in a ^**sudden, intense**^ whisper, "you are the sweetest thing."

Rilla flushed and looked at Susan. Ken looked, too, and saw that Susan's back was turned. He put his arm about Rilla and kissed her. It was the first time Rilla had ever been kissed. She thought perhaps she ought to resent it but she didn't. ^**Note N6**^ ~~She trembled and thrilled.~~

"Rilla-my-Rilla," said Ken, "will you promise that you won't let anyone else kiss you until I come back?"

"~~Yeth~~ ^**Yes**^," said Rilla, ~~trembling and thrilling~~ ^**trembling and thrilling**^.

Susan was turning round. Ken loosened his hold and stepped to the walk.

"Good-bye," he said casually. Rilla heard herself saying it just as casually. She stood and watched him down the walk, out of the gate, and down the road. When the fir wood hid him from her sight she suddenly said "Oh," in a choked way and ran down to the gate, sweet blossomy things catching at her skirts as she ran. ~~She leaned~~ ^**Leaning**^ over the gate ~~Lar~~ ^**she saw**^ Kenneth ~~was~~ walking briskly down the road, ^[*Note*] **Q6**^ his tall, erect figure gray in the ~~moonlight~~ ^**white radiance**^. As he reached the turn he stopped and looked back and saw her ^**standing amid the tall white lilies by the gate**^. He waved his hand – she waved hers – he was gone around the turn.

Rilla stood there for a little while, ^**gazing across the fields of mist and silver**^. She had heard her mother say that she loved turns in roads – they were so provocative and alluring. Rilla thought she hated them. She had seen Jem and Jerry vanish from her around a bend in the road – then Walter – and now Ken. Brothers and playmate and sweetheart – they were all gone. ^[*Note*] **T6**^ Yet still the Piper piped and the dance of death went on.

When Rilla ~~went~~ ^**walked**^ slowly back to the house Susan was still sitting by the veranda table and Susan was sniffing suspiciously.

"I have been thinking, Rilla dear, of the old days in the House of Dreams, when ~~Kenen~~ Kenneth's mother and father were courting and Jem was a little baby and you were not born or thought of. It was a very romantic affair and his mother was a great beauty ~~your mother~~

~~an~~ ^**she**^ and your mother were ~~great~~ ^**such**^ chums. To think I should have lived to see her son going to the front. ~~He is such a handsome boy.~~ As if she had not had enough trouble in her early life, without this coming upon her! But we must take a brace and see it through."

^**All**^ Rilla's anger against Susan had ~~all ev~~ evaporated. With Ken's kiss still burning on her lips ^[*Note*] **A7**^ she could not be angry with anyone. She put her slim white hand into Susan's ~~hard~~ brown, work-hardened one ^**and gave it a squeeze**^. Susan was a faithful old dear and would ~~have~~

~~"We just have to work and hope and be patient~~

~~laid~~ ^**lay**^ down her life for any one of ~~the Ingleside folks~~ them.

"You are tired, Rilla dear, and had better go to bed," Susan said, patting her hand. "I noticed you were too tired to talk to-night. I am glad I came home in time to help you out. It is very tiresome trying to entertain young men when you are not ~~used to it."~~ ^**accustomed to it**^."

Rilla ~~went to bed~~ carried Jims upstairs and went to bed, but not before she had sat for a long time at her window ^~~recons~~ [*Note*] **R6**^

"I wonder," she said to herself, "if I am, or am not engaged to Kenneth Ford."

Chapter 17

~~cam~~

The Weeks Wear By

Rilla ~~was sitting in a her~~ ^**read her first love letter in her fir-shadowed**^ Rainbow Valley nook ~~steeped that was steeped in mellow September sunshine reading and re-reading her first love letter – which~~ ^**– and a girl's first love letter**^, whatever blase, older people may think of it, is an event of tremendous importance in the teens. After Kenneth's regiment had left Kingsport there came a fortnight of dully-aching anxiety and when the ~~choir~~ ^**congregation**^ sang in Church on Sunday evenings,

> "Oh, hear us when we ~~pray~~ ^**cry**^ to thee
> For those in peril on the sea,"

Rilla's voice always failed her, for with the words came a horribly vivid mind picture of a submarined ship sinking beneath pitiless waves ~~and~~ amid the struggles and cries of drowning men. Then word came that Kenneth's regiment had arrived safely in England; and now, at last, here was his letter. It began with something that made Rilla supremely happy for the moment and ended with a paragraph that ~~made her cheeks burn~~ ^**crimsoned her cheeks**^ with the wonder and thrill and delight of it. Between beginning and ending the letter was just such a jolly, newsy epistle as Ken might have written to anyone; but for the sake of that beginning and ending Rilla ~~kissed the letter raptu~~ slept with ~~that~~ ^**the**^ letter under her pillow for weeks, sometimes waking in the night to slip her fingers under ~~the pillow~~ and just touch it, and looked with secret pity on other girls whose sweethearts could ~~not~~ never have written them anything half so wonderful and exquisite. Kenneth was not the son of a famous novelist for nothing. He "had a way" of expressing things in a few poignant, significant words that seemed to suggest far more than they uttered, and never ~~left any aftermath for flatness~~ grew stale or flat or foolish with ever so many scores of readings. Rilla went home from Rainbow Valley as if she flew rather than walked.

But such moments of uplift were rare that autumn. To be sure, there was one day in September when great news came of ~~the big~~ ^**~~a~~ a big**^ Allied victory in the west and Susan ran out to hoist the flag ~~– the last time she ^**was to his**^ hoisted it for many months.~~ ^[*Note*] **L7**^

"Likely the Big Push has begun at last, Mrs. Dr. dear," she exclaimed, "and we will soon see the finish of the Huns. Our boys will be home by Christmas now. ~~Cousin Sophia~~ Hurrah!"

Susan was ashamed of herself for hurrahing the minute she had done it, and apologized meekly for ~~just~~ ^**such**^ an outburst of juvenility. "But indeed, Mrs. Dr. dear, this good news has gone to my head after this awful summer ~~for Russian slumps and~~ ~~Dardenelles doings."~~ ~~Gallipoli doings." set-back."~~ ^**of Russian slumps and Gallipoli setbacks**^.

"Good news!" said Miss Oliver ^**rather**^ bitterly. "I wonder if the women whose men have been killed for it will call it good news. Just because our own men are not on that part of the front we are rejoicing as if the victory had cost no lives."

"Now, Miss Oliver, dear, do not take that view of it," deprecated Susan. "We have not had much to rejoice over of late and yet men were being killed just the same. Do not let yourself slump like poor Cousin Sophia. She said, when the word came, 'Ah, it is nothing but a rift in the clouds. We are up this week but we will be down the next.' 'Well, Sophia Crawford,' said I – for I never will give in to her, Mrs. Dr. dear – ~~'I have also~~ 'God Himself cannot make two hills without a hollow between them, as I have heard it said, ~~and~~ but that is no reason why we should not take the good of the hills when we are on them.' But Cousin Sophia ~~is no~~ moaned on. 'Here is the Gallipolly expedition a failure and the Grand Duke Nicholas sent off, and everyone knows the Czar of Rooshia is a pro-German ~~and nothing can prevent the Huns from winning the war.~~ ^**and the Allies have no ammunition and Bulgaria is going in against us**^. And the end is not yet, for England and France must be punished for their deadly sins until they repent in sackcloth and ashes.' 'I think myself,' I said, 'that they will do their repenting in khaki and trench mud, and it also seems to me that the Huns should have a few sins to repent of also.' 'They are instruments in the hand of the Almighty, to purge the garner,' said Sophia. And then I got mad, Mrs. Dr. dear, and told her ~~she was would~~ I did not and never would believe that the Almighty ever took such dirty instruments in hand for any purpose whatever, and that ~~she could~~ I did not consider it decent for her to be ~~quoting texts~~ ^**using the words**^ of Holy Writ as glibly as she was doing in ordinary conversation. She was not, I told her, a ~~minus~~ minister or even an elder. And for the time being I squelched her, Mrs. Dr. dear. "Cousin Sophia has no spirit. She is very different from her niece, Mrs. Dean Crawford over-harbour. You know the Dean Crawfords ~~have~~ ^**had**^ five boys and ~~the other day Mrs. Dean~~ now the new baby is another boy. All the connection and especially Dean Crawford were much disappointed because their hearts had been set on a girl; but Mrs. Dean just laughed and said, 'Everywhere I went this summer I saw the sign 'Men Wanted' staring me in the face. Do you think I could go and have a girl under such circumstances?' There is spirit for you, Mrs. Dr. dear. But Cousin Sophia would say the child was just so much more cannon fodder."

Cousin Sophia had full range for her pessimism that gloomy autumn, and even Susan, incorrigible old optimist, as she was, was hard put to it for cheer. When Bulgaria lined up with Germany Susan only remarked scornfully, "One more nation anxious for a licking," but the ~~behavior of Constantine of Greece~~ ^**Greek tangle**^ worried her beyond her powers of philosophy to endure calmly.

"Constantine of Greece has a German wife, Mrs. Dr. dear, and ~~I can~~ that fact squelches hope. To think that I should have lived to care what kind of a wife Constantine of Greece had! ~~He is mad~~ The miserable creature is under his wife's thumb and that is a bad place for any man to be. I am an old maid and an old maid has to be independent or she will be squashed out. But if I had been a married woman, Mrs. Dr. dear, I would have been meek and humble. ~~But~~ It is my opinion that ~~the Queen~~ ^**this Sophia**^ of Greece is a ~~min muix~~ minx."

Susan was furious when the news came that ~~Greece – th~~ Venizelos had met with defeat.

"I could spank Constantine ~~of Greece~~ and skin him alive afterwards, that I could," she exclaimed bitterly.

"Oh, Susan, ~~I am~~ I'm surprised at you," said the doctor, pulling a long face. "Have you no regard for the proprieties? Skin him alive by all means but omit the spanking."

"If he had been well spanked in his younger days he might have more sense now," retorted Susan. "But I suppose princes are never spanked, more is the pity. I see the Allies have sent him an ultimatum. ~~It~~ ^**I could tell them that it**^ will take more than ultimatums to skin a snake like Constantine. Perhaps the Allied blockade will hammer ~~some~~ sense into his head; but that will take ~~sone~~ ^**some time**^ I am thinking, and in the meantime what is to become of ^**poor**^ Serbia?"

They saw what became of Serbia, and during the process Susan was hardly to be lived with. In her exasperation she abused everything and everybody except Kitchener, and she fell upon poor President Wilson tooth and claw.

"If he had done his duty and gone into the war long ago we should not have seen this mess in Serbia," she avowed.

"It would be a serious thing to plunge a great country like the United States, with its mixed population, into the war, Susan," said the doctor, who ~~see~~ sometimes came to the defence of the President, not because he thought Wilson needed it especially, but from an unholy love of baiting Susan.

"Maybe, doctor dear – maybe! But that makes me think of the old story of the girl who told her grandmother she was going to be married. 'It is a solemn thing to be married,' said the old lady. 'Yes, but it is a solemner thing not to be,' said the girl. And I can testify to that out of my own experience, Dr. dear. And I think it is a solemner thing for the Yankees ~~to have~~ that they have kept out of the war than it would have been if they had gone into it. However, though I do not know much about them, I am of the opinion that we will see them starting something yet, Woodrow Wilson or no Woodrow Wilson, when they get it into their heads that this war is not a correspondence school. They will not," said Susan, energetically waving a saucepan with one hand and a soup ladle with the other, "be too proud to fight then."

On a pale-yellow, windy evening in October Carl Meredith went away ~~in his khaki. His father saw him off with a set face~~. He had enlisted on his eighteenth birthday. John Meredith saw him off with a set face. His two boys were gone – there was only little Bruce left now.

He loved Bruce and Bruce's mother dearly; but Jerry and Carl were the sons of the bride of his youth and Carl was the only one of all his children who had Cecilia's very eyes. As they looked lovingly out at him above Carl's uniform the pale minister suddenly remembered the day when, for the first and last time, he had tried to whip Carl for his prank with the eel. That was the first time ~~it he~~ he had realised how much Carl's eyes were like Cecilia's. Now he realised it ~~again.~~ once more. Would he ever again see his dead wife's eyes looking at him from his son's face? What a bonny, clean, handsome lad he was! It was – hard – to see him go ~~to the~~. John Meredith seemed to be looking at a torn plain strewed with the bodies of "able-bodied men between the ages of eighteen and forty-five." Only the other day Carl had been a little scrap of a boy, hunting bugs in Rainbow Valley, ~~and carrying~~ ^**taking**^ lizards to bed with him, and scandalizing the Glen by carrying frogs to Sunday School. It seemed hardly – right – somehow that he should be an "able-bodied man" in khaki. Yet John Meredith had said no word to dissuade him when Carl had told him he must go.

Rilla felt Carl's going keenly. They had always been cronies and playmates. He was only a little older than she was and they had been children in Rainbow Valley together. She ~~thought~~ recalled all their old pranks and escapades as she walked slowly home alone. The full moon peeped through the scudding clouds with sudden floods of ~~white~~ ^**weird**^ illumination, ^[*Note*] **G7**^ [*Note K7 is embedded n this Note.*] ~~and shadow and silver chased each other in waves over the Glen.~~ On such a night as this, long ago, Carl would come over to Ingleside and whistle her out to the gate. "Let's go on a moon-spree, Rilla," he would say, and the two of them would scamper off to Rainbow Valley. ~~Once when~~ Rilla had never been afraid of his beetles and bugs, though she drew a hard and fast line at snakes. They used to talk together of almost everything and were teased about each other at school; but one evening when they were about ~~nine~~ ^**ten**^ years of age they had solemnly promised, by the old spring in Rainbow Valley, that they would never marry each other. ~~They did not like the idea at all.~~ Alice Clow had "crossed out" their names on her slate in school that day, and it came out that "both married." They did not like the idea at all, ~~and~~ hence the mutual vow in Rainbow Valley. There was nothing like an ounce of prevention. Rilla laughed over the old memory – and then sighed. That very day a dispatch from some London paper had ~~made~~ ^**contained**^ the cheerful announcement that "the present moment is the darkest since the war began." It was dark enough, and Rilla wished desperately that she could do something besides waiting and serving at home, ~~when~~ ^as^ day after day the Glen boys she had known went away. If she ~~could~~ were ^**only**^ a boy, speeding in khaki by Carl's side to the Western front! ^[*Note*] **M7**^

The moon burst triumphantly through an especially dark cloud and shadow and silver chased each other in waves over the Glen. Rilla remembered ~~that it had been moonlight on the evening~~ one moonlit evening of childhood when she had said to her mother, "The moon just looks like a sorry, sorry face." She thought it looked like that still – an agonised, ^**careworn**^ face, ~~careworn~~ as though it looked down on dreadful sights. What did it see on the Western front? In ~~battered~~ ^**broken**^ Serbia? ~~See~~ ^**On**^ shell-swept Gallipoli?

~~"I wonder," thought Rilla, "what it must have been like to be sixteen years old before the war.~~

"I am tired," Miss Oliver had said that day, in a rare outburst of impatience, "of this horrible rack of strained emotions, when every day brings a new horror or the dread of it. No, don't look reproachfully at me, Mrs. Blythe. There's nothing heroic about me to-day. I've slumped. I wish England had ~~let~~ left Belgium to her fate – I wish Canada had never sent a man – I wish we'd tied our ~~men~~ boys to our apron strings and not let one of them go. Oh – I shall be ashamed of myself in half an hour – but at this very minute I mean every word of it.~~"~~ ^**Will the Allies never strike?**^"

"Patience is a tired mare but she jogs on," said Susan ~~profoun~~.

"While the steeds of Armageddon thunder,~~" retorted Miss Oliver~~ trampling over our hearts," retorted Miss Oliver. ^[*Note*] **J7**^ "Susan, tell me – don't you ever – didn't you ever – take spells of feeling that you must scream – or swear – or smash something – just because your torture reaches a point when it becomes unbearable?"

~~"They tell me toothache affects some people like that, Miss Oliver dear, but~~

"I have never sworn or desired to swear, Miss Oliver dear, but I will admit," said Susan, with the air of one determined to make a clean breast of it ^**once and for all,**^ "that I have ~~known~~ ^**experienced**^ occasions when it ~~would have been a relief to~~ was a relief to do considerable banging."

"Don't you think that is a kind of swearing~~?~~, Susan? What is the difference between slamming a door viciously and saying d —"

"Miss Oliver dear," interrupted Susan, desperately determined to save Gertrude from herself, ^**if human power could do it,**^ "you are all tired out and unstrung – and no wonder, teaching those obstreperous youngsters all day and coming home to bad war news. But just you go upstairs and lie down and I will bring you up a cup of hot tea and a bite of toast and very soon you will not want to slam doors or swear."

~~"Susan, you're 'Yon pearl of Susans~~

"Susan, you're a good soul – a very pearl of Susans! ~~I wish I'd half your grit~~ But, Susan, it would be such a relief – to say just one soft, low, little tiny d —"

"I will bring you a hot-water bottle for ^**the soles of**^ your feet, also," interposed Susan resolutely, "and it would not be any relief to say that word you are thinking of, Miss Oliver, and that you may tie to. ~~You have a touch of nerves, Miss Oliver dear~~"

"Well, I'll try the hot water bottle first, ~~Susan,~~" said Miss Oliver, ^[*Note*] **C7**^ vanishing upstairs, to Susan's intense relief. ~~Rilla was within earshot.~~ Susan shook her head ominously as she filled the hot water bottle. The war was certainly relaxing the standards of behaviour ^**woefully**^. Here was Miss Oliver admittedly on the point of profanity.

"We must draw the blood from her brain," said ~~^**to the**^~~ Susan, ~~deciding to resort to a mustard plaster of the hot water bottle~~ "and if this bottle ~~does not do it~~ ^**is not effective**^ I will see what can be done with a mustard plaster."

Gertrude rallied and carried on. Lord Kitchener went to Greece, whereat Susan ~~opined~~ ^**foretold**^ that Constantine would soon experience a change of heart. ^[*Note*] **D7**^ The gallant Anzacs withdrew from Gallipoli and Susan approved the step, ^**with reservations**^. The siege of Kut-El-Amara began and Susan pored over maps of Mesopotamia and abused the Turks. Henry Ford started for Europe and Susan ~~bestowed~~ on ~~him his agony the scornful benediction of "God spread~~

~~all travellers~~ flayed him with sarcasm. Sir John French was superseded by Sir Douglas Haig and Susan dubiously ~~opined~~ ^**opined**^ that it was poor policy to swap horses crossing a stream, ~~“To be sure,” she admitted~~ ^**though, to be sure,**^ ~~“~~Haig ~~is~~ ^**was**^ a good name and French had a foreign sound, say what you ~~will would~~ might. Not a move on the great chess board of king or bishop or pawn ~~got by~~ ^**escaped**^ Susan, who had once read only Glen St. Mary notes. ^**Note L10**^ ~~But it was cold comfort she got from any, and~~

When Christmas came again ~~she~~ ^**Susan**^ did not set any vacant places at the festive board. Two empty chairs were too much even for Susan who had thought in September that there would not be one.

“This is the first Christmas that Walter was not home,” Rilla wrote in her diary that night. “Jem used to be away for Christmases up in Avonlea, ~~when~~ but Walter never was. I had letters from both Ken and him to-day. They are still in England but expect to ~~go to~~ be in the trenches very soon. And then – but I suppose we’ll be able to endure it somehow. ~~The~~ ^**To me,**^ ~~T~~the strangest ~~thing~~ of all the strange things since 1914 is how we have all learned to accept things we never thought we could – to go on with life as a matter of course. ^**I know that**^ Jem and Jerry are in the trenches – ^**that**^ Ken and Walter will be soon – that if one of them does not come back my heart will break – yet I go on and work and plan – yes, and even enjoy life by times. There are ~~hours~~ ^**moments**^ when we have real fun because, just for the moment, we don’t think about things and then – we remember – and the remembering ~~is so bitter we almost wish we hadn’t been able to forget~~ ^**is worse than thinking of it all the time would have been**^. ^**Note E7**^

This hasn’t been a nice Christmas Day in any way. Nan had toothache and Susan had red eyes, and assumed a weird and gruesome flippancy of manner to deceive us into thinking she hadn’t; and Jims had a bad cold all day and I’m afraid of croup. He has had croup twice since October. The first time I was nearly frightened to death, for father and mother were both away – father always is away, ~~anyhow,~~ ^**it seems to me,**^ when any of this household gets sick. But Susan was cool as a fish and knew just what to do, and ~~we~~ by morning Jims was all right. ~~He is a cross between a~~ That child is a cross between a duck and an imp. He’s a year and four months old, trots about everywhere, and says quite a few words. ~~It’s so~~ He has the cutest little way of calling me

“Will – will.” It always brings back that dreadful, ridiculous, delightful night when Ken came to say good-bye, and I was so furious and happy. Jims is pink and white and big-eyed and curly-haired ^**and every now and then I ~~find~~ discover a new dimple in him**^. I can never quite believe he is really the same creature as that scrawny, yellow, ugly little ~~mite~~ ^**changeling**^ I brought home in the soup tureen. Nobody has ever heard a word from Jim Anderson. If he never ~~keeps~~ comes back I shall keep Jims always. Everybody here worships and spoils him – or would spoil him if Morgan and I didn’t stand remorselessly in the way. Susan says Jims is the cleverest child she ever saw and can recognize Old Nick when he sees him – this because Jims threw ~~Doc~~ poor Doc out of an upstairs window one day. Doc turned into Mr. Hyde on his way down and landed in a currant bush, spitting and swearing. I tried to console his inner cat with a saucer of milk but he would have none of it, and remained Mr. Hyde the rest of the day. Jims’ latest exploit was to paint the cushion of the big arm-chair in the sun parlour with molasses; and before anybody found it out Mrs. Fred Clow came in on Red Cross business and sat down on it. Her new silk dress was ruined and ~~she was~~ nobody could blame her for being vexed. But she went into one of her tempers and said nasty things and gave me such slams about “‘spoiling’” Jims that I nearly boiled over, too. But I kept the lid on till she had waddled away and then I exploded.

“The fat, clumsy, horrid old thing,’ I said – and oh, what a satisfaction it was to say it.

“‘She has three sons at the front,’” mother said rebukingly.

“‘I suppose that covers all her shortcomings in manners,’” I retorted. But I <u>was</u> ashamed – for it is true that all her boys have gone and she was very plucky and loyal about it too; and she is a perfect tower of strength in the Red Cross. ^**Note H7**^ ~~All~~ ^**Just**^ the same, ~~that is~~ ^**it was**^ her second new silk dress in one year and that when everybody is – or should be – trying to “‘save and serve.’”

“I had to bring out my green velvet hat again lately and begin wearing it. I hung on to my blue straw sailor as long as I could. How I hate the green velvet hat! It is so elaborate and conspicuous~~, and everybody know me by it~~. I don’t see how I could ever have liked it. But I vowed to wear it and wear it I will.

"~~Susan~~ ^**Shirley**^ and I went down to the station this morning to take ~~Dog~~ Little Dog Monday a bang-up Christmas dinner. Dog Monday waits and watches there still, with just as much hope and confidence as ever. Sometimes he ~~sets~~ ^**hangs**^ around the station house and talks to people ~~but~~ and the rest of the time he sits at his little kennel door and watches the track ^**unwinkingly**^. We never try to coax him home now: we know it is of no use. When Jem comes back ~~Little Dog~~ Monday will come home with him; and if Jem – never comes back – Monday will wait there for him as long as his dear dog heart goes on beating.

"Fred Arnold was here last night. He was eighteen in November and is going to enlist just as soon as his mother is over an operation she has to have. He has been coming here very often lately and though I like him so much it makes me uncomfortable, because I am afraid he is thinking that perhaps I could care something for him. I can't tell him about Ken – because, after all, what is there to tell? And yet I don't like to behave coldly and distantly when he will be going away so soon. It is very perplexing. I remember I used to think it would be such fun to have dozens of beaux – and now I'm worried to death because ~~I have two~~ two are too many.

"I am learning to cook. Susan is teaching me~~, and I am really getting on surprisingly well~~. I tried to learn long ago – but no, let me be honest – Susan tried to teach me, which is a very different thing. I never seemed to succeed with anything and I got discouraged. But since the boys have gone away I wanted to be able to make cake and things for them ^**myself,**^ and so I started in again and this time I'm getting on surprisingly well. Susan says it is all in the way I hold my mouth and ~~Sus~~ father says my subconscious mind is desirous of learning now, and I daresay they're both right. Anyhow, I can make dandy short-bread and fruitcake. I got ambitious last week and attempted cream puffs, but made an awful failure of them. They came out of the oven flat as flukes. I thought maybe the cream would fill them up again and make them plumb but it didn't. I think Susan was secretly pleased. She is past mistress in the art of making cream puffs and it would break her heart if anyone else here could make them as well. I wonder if Susan tampered – but no, I won't suspect her of such a thing.

“Miranda Pryor ~~was here~~ ^**spent an afternoon here**^ a few days ago, helping me cut out certain Red Cross garments known ~~as~~ by the charming name of “‘vermin shirts.’” Susan thinks that name is not quite decent, so I suggested she call them “‘cootie sarks,’” which is old Highland Sandy’s ~~name for them~~ ^**version of it**^. But she shook her head and I heard her telling mother later on that, in her opinion, “‘cooties’ and “‘sarks’” were not proper things ^**subjects**^ for young girls to talk about. ^~~**H7**~~ [*Note*] **I7**^

“Miranda grew confidential over our vermin shirts and told me all her troubles. She is desperately unhappy. She is engaged to Joe Milgrave and Joe joined up in October and has been training in Charlottetown ever since. Her father was furious when he joined and forbade Miranda ever to have any dealing or communication with him again. ~~Now p~~Poor Joe expects to go overseas any day and wants Miranda to marry him before he goes~~. She~~ – which shows that there have been “‘communications’” in spite of Whiskers-On-The-Moon. Miranda wants to marry him ~~b~~ but cannot, and she declares it will break her heart.

“‘Why don’t you run away and marry him?’” I said. It didn’t go against my conscience in the least to give her such advice. Joe Milgrave is a splendid fellow and Mr. Pryor fairly beamed on him until ~~Joe enlisted~~ ^**the war broke out and**^ I know Mr. Pryor would forgive Miranda very quickly, once it was over and he wanted his housekeeper back. But Miranda shook her ~~pale yellow~~ ^**silvery**^ head dolefully.

“‘Joe wants me to but I can’t. Mother’s last words to me, as she lay on her dying bed were, “‘Never, never run away, Miranda,”’ and I promised.’”

~~I thought~~ “Miranda’s ~~was only ten when her mother died and I thought it odd for Mrs. Pryor to exact such a promise of a child~~ ^**mother died two years ago,**^ ~~But~~ ^**and**^ it seems, according to Miranda, that her mother and father actually ran away to be married themselves. To picture Whiskers-on-the-Moon as the hero of an elopement is ~~past~~ ^**beyond**^ my power. But such was the case~~. Mrs. Pryor~~ and Mrs. Pryor at least lived to repent it. She ~~was~~ had a hard life of it with Mr. Pryor, and she thought it was a punishment on her for running away. ~~Hence,~~ So she made Miranda promise she would never, for any reason whatever, do it.

"Of course, you cannot urge a girl to break a promise made to a dying mother, so I did not see what Miranda could do unless she got Joe to come to the house when her father was away and marry her there. But Miranda said that couldn't be managed. Her father seemed to suspect she might be up to something of the sort and he ~~stayed home almost all of the time~~ never went away for long at a time, and, of course Joe couldn't get leave of absence at an hour's notice.

"'No, I shall just have to let Joe go, and he will be killed – I know he will be killed – and my heart will break,'[22] said Miranda, her tears running down ^~~**freely**~~ **copiously**^ and bedewing the ~~verimin~~ vermin shirts!

"I am not writing like this ~~bec~~ for lack of any real sympathy with poor Miranda. I've just got into the habit of giving things a comical twist if I can, when I'm writing to Jem and Walter and Ken, to make them laugh. I really felt very sorry for Miranda ~~and~~ ^[*Note*] **H7**^ I think she understood that I did, for she said she ~~was~~ had wanted to tell me all about her worries because I had grown so sympathetic this past year. I wonder if I have. I know I used to be a selfish, thoughtless creature – how selfish and thoughtless I am ashamed to ~~think~~ ^**remember**^ now, so I ~~must~~ can't be quite so bad as I was.

"I wish I could help Miranda ~~but I don't see how I can, unless I~~. It would be very romantic to contrive a war wedding and I should dearly love to get the better of Whiskers-on-The-Moon. But at present the oracle has not spoken."

Chapter 18

A War Wedding

~~"I tell you, M~~ "I can tell you this Dr. dear," said Susan, pale with wrath, "that Germany is getting to be perfectly ridiculous."

They were all in the big Ingleside kitchen. Susan was ~~mixing~~ ^**mixing**^ biscuits for supper. Mrs. Blythe was making short-bread for Jem, ~~and~~ ^**and**^ Rilla was compounding candy for Ken and Walter – it had once been "Walter and Ken" in her thoughts but somehow, quite unconsciously ~~to herself~~, this had changed until Ken's name came naturally first. Cousin Sophia was also there, knitting ~~faithfully but gloomily~~. All the boys were going ~~to be~~ ^**to be**^ killed in the long run, so Cousin Sophia felt in her bones, but they might ~~as well~~ ^**better**^ die with warm feet than cold ones, so Cousin Sophia knitted faithfully and gloomily.

~~Into this~~ Into this peaceful ~~scene~~ ^**scene**^ erupted the doctor, wrathful and excited over the burning of the Parliament Buildings ~~at~~ ^**in**^ Ottawa. And Susan became automatically quite as wrathful and excited.

"What will those Huns do next?" she demanded. "Coming over here and burning our Parliament buildings! Did anyone ever hear of such an outrage?"

"We don't know that the Germans are responsible for this," said the doctor – much as if he felt quite sure they were, though. "Fires do start without their agency sometimes. And Uncle Mark McAllister's barn was burned last week. You can hardly accuse the Germans of that, Susan."

"Indeed, Dr. dear, I do not know." ^[*Note*] **O7**^ Whiskers-on-the-Moon was there that very day. The fire broke out half an hour after he was gone. So much is a fact – but I shall not accuse a Presbyterian elder of burning anybody's barn until I have proof. ~~But~~ However, everybody knows, Dr. dear, that ~~all~~ ^**both**^ Uncle Mark's boys have enlisted, ~~except~~ and that Uncle Mark himself makes speeches at all the recruiting meetings. So ~~it would be with the German's ^Germany^ while to~~ no doubt Germany is anxious to get square with him."

“I could never speak at a recruiting meeting,” said Cousin Sophia solemnly. “I could never reconcile it to my conscience to ask another woman’s son to go, ~~over there and be murdered.”~~ to murder and be murdered.”

“Could you not?” said Susan. “Well, Sophia Crawford, I felt as if I could ask anyone to go when I read last night that there were no children under eight years of age left alive in Poland. Think of that, Sophia Crawford” – Susan shook a floury finger at ~~the solemn~~ Sophia – “not – one – child – under – eight – years – of – age!”

“I suppose the Germans has et ’em all,” sighed Cousin Sophia.

“Well, no-o-o,” said Susan reluctantly, ~~“~~as if she hated to admit that there was any crime the Huns couldn’t be accused of. “The Germans have not turned cannibal yet – as far as I know. They have died of starvation and exposure, the poor little creatures. ~~And here we are eating our fill every day~~ There is murdering for you, Cousin Sophia Crawford. The thought of it poisons every bite and sup I take.”

“I ~~hear~~ ^**see**^ that Fred Carson of Lowbridge has ~~won~~ been awarded a Distinguished Service medal,” remarked the doctor, over his local paper.

“I heard that last week,” said Susan. ~~“The news~~ ^**Note N7**^ “His letter, telling his folks about it, came when his old Grandmother Carson was on her dying bed. She had only a few minutes more to live and the Episcopal minister, who was there, asked her if she would not like him to pray. ‘Oh yes, ^**yes,**^ you can pray,’ she said impatient-like – she was a Dean, Dr. dear, and the Deans were always high-spirited – ‘you can pray, but for pity’s sake pray low and don’t disturb me. ~~I’m I am thinking this splendid news over~~ I want to think over this splendid news ~~as long as I can think at all,~~ and ~~there is~~ ^**I have**^ not much time left to do it.’~~”~~ That was Almira Carson all over. Fred was the apple of her eye. She was seventy five years of age and had not a gray hair in her head, they tell me.”

“By the way, that reminds me – I found a gray hair this morning – my very first,” said Mrs. Blythe.

“I have noticed that gray hair for some time, Mrs. Dr. dear, but I did not speak of it. Thought I to myself, ‘She has enough to bear.’ But now that you have discovered it let me remind you that gray hairs are honourable.”

"I must be getting old, Gilbert," – Mrs. Blythe laughed a trifle ruefully. "People are beginning to tell me I look so young. They never tell you that when you are young. But I shall not worry over my ~~gray hair~~ silver thread. I never liked red hair. Gilbert, ~~as you~~ did I ever tell you of that time, years ago at Green Gables, when I dyed my hair? ~~I bough~~ Nobody but Marilla and I knew about it."

"Was that the reason you came out once with your hair shingled to the bone?" ~~asked the doctor.~~

"Yes. I bought a bottle of dye from a German Jew peddler. ~~And it turned~~ I fondly expected it would turn my hair black – and it turned it green. So it had to be cut off."

~~"Of cou~~

"You had a narrow escape, Mrs. Dr. dear," exclaimed Susan. "Of course you were too young then to know what a German was. It was a special mercy of Providence that it was only green dye and not poison."

"It seems hundreds of years since those Green Gables days," sighed Mrs. Blythe. "They belonged to another world altogether. Life has been cut in two by the chasm of war. What is ahead I don't know – but it can't be a bit like the ~~old~~ past. I wonder if those of us who have lived half our lives in the old world will ever feel wholly at home in the new."

"Have you noticed," asked Miss Oliver, glancing up from her book, "how everything written before the war seems so far away now, too? One feels as if one was reading something as ancient as the Iliad. This ~~p~~ poem of Wordsworth's ~~now~~ – the Senior class have it in their Entrance work – I've been glancing over it. Its classic calm and repose and the beauty of its lines seem to belong to another planet, and to have as little to do with the present world-welter as the evening star."

"The only thing that I find much comfort in reading nowadays is the Bible," remarked Susan, whisking her biscuits into the oven. "There are so many passages in it that seem to me exactly descriptive of the Huns. Old ~~Uncle~~ Highland Sandy declares that there is no doubt that the Kaiser is the Anti-Christ spoken of in Revelations, but I do not go as far as that. It would, in my humble opinion, Mrs. Dr. dear, be too ~~mu~~ great an honour for him."

~~Ane~~ Early one ~~Monday~~ morning, several days later, Miranda ~~Milgrave~~ ^**Pryor**^ slipped up to Ingleside, ostensibly to get some Red Cross sewing, but in reality to talk over with ~~sypn~~ sympathetic Rilla troubles that were past bearing alone. She brought ~~with~~ her ~~her~~ dog with her – ~~a fat~~ ^**an**^ over-fed, ^**bandy-legged**^ little animal very dear to her heart because Joe Milgrave had given it to her when it was a puppy. Mr. Pryor ~~looked upon~~ ^**regarded**^ all dogs with disfavor; but in those days he had looked kindly upon Joe as a suitor for Miranda's hand and so he had allowed her to keep the puppy. Miranda was so grateful that she endeavoured to please her father by naming her dog after his political idol, the great Liberal chieftain, Sir Wilfrid Laurier – though his title was soon abbreviated to Wilfy. ~~W~~ Sir Wilfrid grew and flourished and waxed fat; but Miranda spoiled him absurdly and nobody else liked him. Rilla especially ~~detested him~~ hated him because of what she thought his detestable ~~habit~~ ^**trick**^ of lying flat on his back and entreating you with waving paws to tickle his sleek stomach. When she saw that Miranda's ~~pale~~ ^**pale**^ eyes bore ~~um~~ unmistakable ~~tendenc~~ testimony of her having cried all night Rilla asked her to come up to her room, knowing Miranda had a tale of woe to tell, but she ordered ~~W~~ Sir Wilfrid to remain below.

"Oh, can't he come, too~~,~~?" said Miranda wistfully. "~~He~~ ^**Poor Wilfy**^ won't be any bother – and I wiped his paws <u>so</u> carefully before I brought him in. He is always so lonesome in a strange place without me – and very soon he'll be – all – I'll have left – to remind me – of Joe."

Rilla yielded, and Sir Wilfrid, ~~wets~~ with his tail curled ~~in~~ ^**at**^ a saucy angle over his brindled back, trotted triumphantly up the stairs before them~~,. bounded into Rilla's room, selected her favorite cushion with an unerring eye, and~~.

"Oh, Rilla," sobbed Miranda, when they had reached sanctuary. "I'm <u>so</u> unhappy.~~"~~ I can't begin to tell you how unhappy I am. Truly, my heart is breaking."

Rilla sat down on the lounge beside her. Sir Wilfrid squatted on his haunches before them, with his impertinent pink tongue ~~so~~ stuck out, and listened.

"What is the trouble, Miranda?" ^**Note U7**^

~~“Joe is ^**coming**^ home ^**tonight**^ – on his last leave. He came Saturday night but I didn’t know it till I saw him in church last night. Of as and I hadn’t a chance to say one single word to him – father was there – but he slipped a letter into my hand in the crowd at the door. ^**I had a letter from him Saturday – he sends his letters to me to Bob Crawford, you know**^ And oh Rilla, he has only ^**will have only**^ four days more – he has to go away Friday morning – and I may never see him alive again.”~~

“Does he still want you to marry him?” asked Rilla ~~– whereat Sir Wilfrid gave a loud but short melancholy yelp~~.

“Oh, yes. He implored me in his letter to run away and be married. But I cannot do that, Rilla, not even for Joe. My only comfort is that I will be able to see him for a little while to-morrow afternoon. Father has to go to Charlottetown on business ~~– he has to go, or I’m sure he wouldn’t when Joe is home~~. At least we will have one good farewell talk. But oh – afterwards – why, Rilla, I know father won’t even let me go to the station Friday morning to see Joe off.”

“Why in the world don’t you and Joe get married tomorrow afternoon at home?” demanded Rilla.

Miranda swallowed a sob in such amazement that she almost choked.

“Why – why – that is impossible, Rilla.”

“Why?” ^**briefly**^ demanded the organizer of the Junior Red Cross and the transporter of babies in soup tureens.

“Why – why – we never thought of such a thing – Joe hasn’t a license – I have no dress – I couldn’t be married in black – I – I – we – we – you – you – “

Miranda lost herself altogether and Sir Wilfrid, seeing that she was in dire distress threw back his head and ~~gave a weird~~ ^**emitted a**^ melancholy yelp.

Rilla Blythe thought hard and rapidly for a few minutes. Then she said,

“Miranda, if you will put yourself into my hands I’ll have you married to Joe before four o’clock to-morrow afternoon.”

“Oh – you couldn’t.”

“I can and I will. But you’ll have to do exactly as I tell you.”

“Oh – I – don’t think – oh, father will kill me –”

“Nonsense. He’ll be very angry I suppose. But ~~do you~~ are you more afraid of your father's anger than you are of Joe's never coming back to you?"

"No," said Miranda, with sudden firmness, "I'm not."

"Will you do as I tell you then?"

"Yes, I will." ^**Note Q7**^

~~"Wait here for a minute then, while I go down and tell telephone to Joe." I want him~~ "^**and meanwhile, you**^ go home ~~then~~ and make what preparations you can. When I phone down to you to come up and help me sew come at once."

As soon as Miranda, ~~pale~~ ^**pallid**^, scared, but desperately resolved, had gone, Rilla flew to the telephone and put in a long-distance call for Charlottetown. She got through with such surprising quickness that she was convinced Providence approved of her undertaking, but it was a good hour before she could get in touch with Joe Milgrave at ^~~**his**~~^ ^~~**headquarters**~~^ his camp. Meanwhile, she paced impatiently about, and prayed that when she did get Joe there would be no listeners ~~at~~ on the line to carry news to Whiskers-on-the-Moon.

"Is that you, Joe? Rilla Blythe is speaking – Rilla – Rilla – oh, never mind. Listen to this. Before you come home to-night get a marriage license ^**– a marriage license – yes, a license –**^ and a wedding ring. Did you get that? – And will you do it?[22] Very well, be sure you do it – it is your only chance."

Flushed with triumph – for her only fear was that she might not be able to locate Joe in time – Rilla p rang the Pryor ring. This time she had not such good-luck for she drew Whiskers-on-the-Moon.

"Is that Miranda? Oh – Mr. Pryor! Well, Mr. Pryor, will you kindly ask Miranda if she can come up this afternoon and help me with some sewing. It is very important, or I would not trouble her. Oh – thank you!"

Mr. Pryor had consented somewhat grumpily, but he had consented – he did not want to offend Dr. Blythe, and he knew that if he refused to allow Miranda to do any Red Cross work public opinion would make the Glen too hot for comfort. Rilla went out to the kitchen, shut all the doors with a mysterious expression which alarmed Susan, and then said solemnly,

"Susan can you make a wedding-cake this afternoon?"

"A wedding-cake!" Susan stared. Rilla had, without any warning,

~~co-opted~~ ^**brought her**^ a war baby once upon a time. Was she now, with equal suddenness, going to ~~be married to someone?~~ produce a husband?

"Yes, a wedding-cake – a scrumptious wedding-cake, Susan ^[*Note*] **R7**^ And we must make other things, too. ^**I'll help you in the morning,**^ But I can't help you this afternoon for I have to make a wedding dress~~. To-morrow morning I'll help you~~ and time is the essence of the contract, Susan."

Susan felt that she was really too old to be subjected to such shocks.

"Who are you going to marry, Rilla?" she asked feebly.

"Susan, darling, ~~I'm~~ ^**I am**^ not the happy bride. Miranda Pryor is going to marry Joe Milgrave tomorrow afternoon while her father is away in town. A war wedding, Susan – isn't that ^**thrilling and**^ romantic? I never was so excited in my life."

The excitement soon spread over Ingleside, infecting even Mrs. Blythe and Susan.

"I'll go to work on that cake at once," vowed Susan, with a glance at the clock. ~~I'll have it ready for the oven by the evening.~~ "Mrs. Dr. dear, will you pick over the fruit and beat up the eggs? If you will I can have that cake ready for the oven by the evening. To-morrow morning we can make salads and other things. I will work all night if necessary to get the better of Whiskers-on-The-Moon."

Miranda arrived, ~~pale~~ ^**tearful**^ and breathless.

"We must fix over my white dress for you to wear," said Rilla. "It will fit you very nicely with a little alteration."

To work went the two girls, ripping, fitting, basting, sewing for dear life. By dint of unceasing effort they got the dress done by seven o'clock and Miranda tried it on in Rilla's room.

"It's very pretty – but oh, if I could just have a veil," sighed Miranda. "I've always dreamed of being married in a lovely white veil."

Some good fairy evidently waits on the wishes of war brides. The door opened and Mrs. Blythe came in, her arms full of a filmy burden.

"Miranda dear," she said, "I want you to wear my wedding veil to-morrow. It is ^**twenty four**^ years since I was a bride ^**at old Green Gables**^ – the happiest bride that ever was ~~^**at old Green Gables**^~~ – and the wedding veil of a happy bride brings good luck, they say."

"Oh, how sweet of you, Mrs. Blythe," said Miranda, the ready tears starting to her eyes.

The veil was tried on and draped. Susan dropped in to approve but dared not linger.

"I've got that cake in the oven," she said ~~with~~, "and I am pursuing a policy of watchful waiting.[22] ^~~**P7**~~ **Note P7**^

Susan disappeared downstairs to the kitchen, whence a dreadful thud and a piercing shriek presently sounded. Everybody rushed to the kitchen – the doctor and Miss Oliver, Mrs. Blythe, Rilla, Miranda in her wedding veil. Susan was sitting flatly in the middle of the kitchen floor with a dazed, bewildered look on her face, while "Doc," evidently in his Hyde incarnation, was standing on the dresser, with his back up, his eyes blazing, and his tail the size of three tails.

"Susan, what has happened?" cried Mrs. Blythe in alarm. "Did you fall? Are you hurt?"

Susan picked herself up.

"No," she said grimly, "I am not hurt, though I am jarred all over. Do not be alarmed. As for what has happened – I tried to kick that darned cat with both feet, that is what happened."

~~The doctor~~ Everybody shrieked with laughter. ~~They could not help it.~~ The doctor was quite helpless.

"Oh, Susan, Susan," he gasped, "that I should live to hear you swear."

"I am sorry," said Susan in real distress, "that I used such an expression before two young girls. But I said that beast was darned, and darned it is. It belongs to Old Nick."

"Do you expect it will vanish some of these days with ~~the~~ ^**a**^ bang and the odor of brimstone, Susan?"

"It will go to its own place in due time and that you may tie to," said Susan dourly, shaking out her raddled bones and going to her oven. "I suppose my ~~plurk plurke~~ plunking down like that has shaken my cake so that it will be as heavy as lead."

But the cake was not heavy. It was all a bride's cake should be, and Susan iced it beautifully. Next ~~forenoon~~ ^**day**^ she and Rilla worked all the forenoon, making delicacies for the wedding feast, and as soon as Miranda 'phoned up that her father was safely off everything was packed in a big hamper and taken down to the Pryor house. Joe soon arrived ~~in a state of~~ in his uniform and a state of violent excitement ^**Note S7** ~~**S7**~~^ There were quite a few guests, for all the manse and Ingleside ~~folks~~ ^**folk**^ were there, and a dozen or so of Joe's relatives, including his mother, "Mrs. Dead Angus Milgrave," so called ~~her~~, cheerfully, to distinguish her from another lady whose Angus was living ~~who cam~~. ^**Mrs. Dead Angus**^ wore a rather disapproving expression, not caring over much for this alliance with the house of Whiskers-on-the-Moon.

So Miranda Pryor was married to ^**Pte.**^ Joseph Milgrave ^**on his last leave**^. It should have been a romantic wedding but it was not. There were too many factors working against romance, ^**as even Rilla had to admit ~~in disappointment~~**^. In the first place, Miranda, in spite of her dress and veil, was such a ~~plain~~ flat-faced, commonplace, ~~unni~~ uninteresting little bride. In the second place, Joe cried bitterly all through the ceremony, and this ~~made~~ ^**vexed**^ Miranda unreasonably. Long afterwards she told Rilla, "I just felt like saying to him then and there, 'If you feel so bad over having to marry me you don't have to.'" ~~Fancy a~~ But it was just because he was thinking all the time of how soon he would have to leave me."

In the third place, Jims, who was usually so well-behaved in public, took a fit of shyness and contrariness ^**combined**^ and began to cry at the top of his voice for "Willa." Nobody wanted to take him out, because everybody wanted to see the marriage, so Rilla ~~was compelled~~ who was ~~standing beside~~ bridesmaid, had to take him and hold him during the ceremony.

In the fourth place, Sir Wilfrid Laurier took a fit.

Sir Wilfrid was ^**entrenched**^ in a corner of the room behind Miranda's piano. During his seizure he made the weirdest, most unearthly noises. He would begin with a series of choking, spasmodic sounds, continuing into a gruesome gurgle, and ending up with a strangled howl. Nobody could hear a word ~~the minister~~ ^**Mr. Meredith**^ was saying, except now and then, when Sir Wilfrid stopped for breath. Nobody looked at the bride except Susan, who never dragged her fascinated eyes from Miranda's face – all the others were gazing at the dog. Miranda had been trembling with nervousness but as soon as Sir Wilfrid began his performance she forgot it. All that she could think of was that her dear dog was dying and she could not go to him. She never remembered a word of the ceremony.

Rilla, who in spite of Jims, had been trying her best to look rapt and romantic, as beseemed a war bridesmaid, gave up the hopeless attempt, and devoted her energies to choking down untimely ~~mirth~~ ^**merriment**^. She dared not look at anybody in the room, especially Mrs. Dead Angus, for fear all her suppressed mirth should suddenly explode in a most un-young-ladylike yell of laughter.

But married they were, and then they had a wedding supper in the dining room which was so lavish and bountiful that you would have thought it was the product of a month's labour. Everybody had brought something. Mrs. Dead Angus had brought a large ~~crus~~ apple pie, which she placed on a chair in the dining room and then absently sat down on it. Neither her temper nor her black silk wedding garment ~~were~~ ^**was**^ improved thereby, but the pie was never missed at the gay bridal feast. Mrs. Dead Angus eventually took it home with her again. Whiskers-on-the-Moon's pacifist pig should not get it, anyhow.

That evening Mr. and Mrs. Joe, ^**accompanied by the recovered Sir Wilfrid,**^ departed for the Four Winds Light house, which was kept by Joe's uncle and ~~where~~ ^**in which**^ they meant to spend their brief honeymoon. ~~The~~ Una ^**Meredith**^ and Rilla and Susan washed the dishes, ~~tudi~~ tidied up, left a cold supper and Miranda's pitiful little note on the table for Mr. Pryor, and walked home, ~~through the beautiful pearls and smokes and grays of the late winter afternoon~~ ^**while the mystic veil of dreamy, haunted winter twilight wrapped itself over the Glen**^.

"I would really not have minded being a war-bride myself," remarked Susan sentimentally.

But Rilla felt rather flat – perhaps as a reaction to all the excitement and rush of the past thirty-six hours. She was disappointed somehow – the whole affair had been so ~~comical~~ ^**ludicrous**^, and Miranda and Joe so lachrymose and commonplace.

"If Miranda hadn't given that wretched dog such an enormous dinner he wouldn't have had that fit," she said crossly. "I warned her – but she said she couldn't starve the poor dog – he ~~was all~~ would soon be all she had left, etc. I could have shaken her."

"The best man was more excited than Joe was," said Susan. "He wished Miranda many happy returns of the day. She did not look very happy, but perhaps you could not expect that under the circumstances." ^**Note N7**^

But if Rilla was rather disappointed in the war wedding she found nothing lacking on Friday morning when Miranda said ~~her~~ good-bye to ~~Joe~~ ^**her bridegroom**^ ~~on~~ ^**at**^ the Glen station. The dawn was white as a pearl, clear as a diamond. Behind the station the balsamy copse of young firs was ~~white-silver~~ frost-misted. The cold moon of dawn hung over the ~~white~~ ^**westering**^ snow fields but the golden fleeces of sunrise shone above the maples up at Ingleside. Joe took his pale little bride in his arms and she lifted her face to his. Rilla choked suddenly. It did not matter that Miranda was ~~little~~ ^**insignificant**^ and common-place and flat-featured. It did not matter that she was the daughter of Whiskers-on-the-Moon. All that mattered was that rapt, sacrificial look in her eyes – that ever-burning, sacred fire of devotion and loyalty and fine courage that she was mutely promising Joc she ^**and thousands of other women**^ would keep alive at home while their men held the ~~fro~~ Western front.

Rilla walked away, realising that she must not spy on such a moment. ^**Note O9**^

When the train had gone ~~she~~ ^**Rilla**^ rejoined the little trembling Miranda.

"Well, he's gone," said Miranda, "and he may never come back – but I'm his wife, and I'm going to be worthy of him. I'm going home."

"Don't you think you had better come with me just now?" asked Rilla doubtfully. Nobody knew yet how Mr. Pryor had taken the matter.

"No. If Joe can face the Huns I guess I can face father," said Miranda daringly. "A soldier's wife can't be a coward. ^**Com on, Wilfy.**^ I'll go straight home and meet the worst."

There was nothing very dreadful to face, however. Perhaps Mr. Pryor had reflected that housekeepers were hard to get and that there were many Milgrave homes open to Miranda~~. At all events, though he told her grumpily that she had made a nice fool of herself and would find herself a~~ – ~~and~~ ^**also**^, that there was such a thing as a separation allowance. At all events, though he told her grumpily that she had made a nice fool of herself, ^**and would live to regret it,**^ he said nothing worse, and Mrs. Joe put on her apron and went to work as usual ^**Note T7**^

Chapter 19

"They Shall Not Pass"

One cold gray morning in February Gertrude Oliver ~~woke~~ ^**wakened**^ with a shiver, slipped into Rilla's room, and crept in beside her.

"Rilla – I'm frightened – frightened as a baby – I've had another of my strange dreams. Something terrible is before us – I know."

"What was it?" ~~asked Rilla, who never laughed at Miss Oliver's dreams.~~ ^**asked Rilla.**^

"I was standing again on the veranda ^**steps**^ – just as I stood in that dream ~~bef~~ on the night before the light house dance; and in the sky a ~~dreadful~~ ^**huge**^ black, menacing thunder cloud rolled up from the east. I could see its shadow racing before it and when it enveloped me I shivered with icy cold. Then the storm broke – and it was a dreadful storm – blinding flash after flash and deafening peal after peal, ^**driving torrents of rain.**^ I turned ^**in panic**^ and tried to run for shelter, and as I did so a man – ~~all~~ a soldier in the uniform of a French army officer – dashed up the steps and stood beside me on the threshold of the door. ~~I can see his white drawn face, Rilla, and his blazing eyes. Blood was flowing over his~~ His clothes ~~seemed~~ ^**were**^ soaked with blood from a wound ~~that seemed to be~~ in his breast; he ~~was~~ seemed spent and exhausted; but his white face was set and his eyes blazed in his hollow face. 'They shall not pass,' he said, in low, passionate tones which I heard distinctly amid all the turmoil of the storm. Then I wakened. Rilla, I'm frightened – the spring ~~from which he hped~~ will not bring the Big Push we've all been hoping for – instead it is going to bring some dreadful blow to France. I am sure of it. The Germans ~~are going~~ ^**will**^ ~~Rilla did not~~ ~~to~~ try to smash through somewhere."

"But he told you that they would not ^**pass,"**^ said Rilla, ^**seriously. She never**^ ~~who never~~ laughed at Gertrude's dreams as the doctor did.

~~"Was that a prediction~~ "I do not know if that was ~~a prediction or~~ prophecy or desperation~~."~~. Rilla, the horror of that dream holds me yet in an ~~cold an~~ ^**icy**^ grip. We shall need all our courage before long."

Dr. Blythe did laugh at the breakfast table – but he never laughed at

Miss Oliver's dreams again; for that day brought news of the opening of the ~~Homeric struggle for Verdun~~ ^**Verdun offensive**^, and thereafter ~~for weeks~~ ^~~**then all weeks of the spring**~~ **through all the beautiful weeks of spring**^ the Ingleside family, one and all, lived in ~~the~~ a trance of ~~daily~~ dread. There were days when they waited in despair for the end as foot by foot the Germans crept nearer and nearer to the grim barrier of desperate France.

~~"If the Ger Huns capture Verdun the spirit of France will be broken,"~~ Susan's deeds were in her spotless kitchen at Ingleside, but her thoughts were on the hills around Verdun. "Mrs. Dr. dear," she would stick her head in at Mrs. Blythe's door the last thing at night to remark, "I do ~~wonder if~~ ^**hope**^ the French have ~~bud~~ ^**hung**^ onto the Crow's Wood to-day," and she woke at dawn to wonder if Dead Man's Hill – ^**surely**^ so-named ~~surely~~ by some ~~propet~~ ^**prophet**^ – was still held by the ~~poili~~ "poyloos." Susan could have drawn a map of the ~~hills and forts~~ ^**country**^ around Verdun that would have satisfied a Chief of Staff.

~~"Was there ever a battle like this in the would before?" asked Mr. Meredith on the fifty first day of the struggle. "France is certainly very wonderful. It seems to me that in her I see the white form of civilization making am ^**an**^ uni un~~

~~"If the Germans capture~~

"If the Germans capture Verdun the spirit of France will be broken," Miss Oliver said bitterly.

"But they will not capture it," staunchly said Susan, who could not eat ^**her dinner that day**^ for ~~wor~~ fear lest they do that very thing. "In the first place, you dreamed they ~~wouldn't~~ ^**would not**^ – you dreamed the very thing the French are saying before they ever said it – 'they shall not pass.' I declare to you, Miss Oliver, dear, when I read that in the paper ~~after you had~~, and remembered your dream, I went cold all over with awe. It seemed to me like Biblical times when people dreamed things like that quite frequently."

"I know – I know," said Gertrude, walking restlessly about. "I ~~hold~~ ^**cling**^ to a ~~stubborn~~ persistent faith in my dream, too – but every time bad news comes it fails me. Then I tell myself '~~mure~~ ^**mere**^ coincidence –' 'subconscious memory' ~~"ate."~~ ^**and so forth."**^

"I do not see how any memory could remember a thing before it was ever said at all," persisted Susan, "though of course I am not educated like you and the doctor. I would rather not be, if it makes anything as simple as that so hard to believe. But in any case we need not worry over Verdun, even if the Huns get it. Joffer says it has no military significance."

"That old sop of comfort has been served up too often already when reverses came," retorted Gertrude. "It has lost its power to charm. These weeks are slowly killing me. I feel as if I were ~~slowly~~ ^**gradually**^ bleeding to death as France is ~~being bled~~ ^**bleeding**^ in the shambles of Verdun."

"Was there ever a battle like this in the world before?" said Mr. Meredith, one evening in mid-April. ^[*Note*] **W7**^ "France is certainly very wonderful. It seems to me that in her I see the white form of civilization making a ~~desperate~~ ^**determined**^ stand against the black powers of barbarism.[22] I think ~~the wo~~ ^**our**^ whole world realizes this[22] and that is why we all await the issue so breathlessly.[22] It ~~isn't~~ isn't merely the question of a few forts changing hands or a few miles of blood-soaked ground lost and won."

"I wonder," said Gertrude dreamily, "if some great blessing, great enough for the price, will be the meed of all our pain? Is the agony in which the world is shuddering the birth-pang of some wondrous new era? Or is it merely a futile

~~"struggle of ants~~
"'struggle of ~~Amts~~ ants
'In the gleam of a million million of suns?'[22]

"~~We~~ ^**We**^ think very lightly, Mr. Meredith, of a calamity which ~~would~~ destroys an ant-hill and half its inhabitants. Does the Power that runs the universe think us of more importance than we think ants?"

~~"Yes,"~~ ^**"You forget,"**^ said Mr. Meredith, with a flash of his dark eyes, ~~"You forget~~ "that ~~your God~~ ^**an infinite Power**^ must be infinitely little as well as infinitely great. We are ~~nether~~ neither, therefore there are things too little as well as too great for us to ~~comprehend or~~ apprehend. To the infinitely little an ant is of as much importance as a mastodon. We ~~are~~ ^**are**^ witnessing the birth-pangs of ~~an~~ a new era

– but it ~~won't be born~~ will be born a feeble, wailing ~~thing like~~ ^**life**^ like everything else. I am not one of those who expect a new heaven and a new earth as the immediate result of this war. That is not the way God works. But work He does, ~~and~~ Miss Oliver, and in the end His ~~last~~ ^**purpose**^ will be fulfilled."

"Sound and orthodox – sound and orthodox," muttered Susan approvingly in the kitchen. Susan liked to see Miss Oliver sat upon by the minister ~~occasionally~~ ^**now and then**^. Susan was very fond of her but she thought Miss Oliver liked saying heretical things to ministers ^**far**^ too well, and deserved ~~a bit of~~ an occasional reminder that these ~~things~~ ^**matters**^ were quite beyond her ~~province~~ province.

~~In late Apr~~ ~~That week~~ ~~^**In late April**^~~ ^^**In May**^^ Walter wrote home that he had been awarded a D.S. Medal. He did not say what for, but the other boys took care that the Glen should know the ~~brave~~ thing Walter had done. "In any war but this," wrote Jerry Meredith, "it would have meant a V.C. But they can't make V.C.'s as common as the brave things done every day here."

"He should have had the V.C.," said Susan, and was ~~quite~~ ^**very**^ indignant over it. She was not quite sure who was to blame for his not getting it, but if it were General ~~Haig~~ she began ^**for the first time**^ to entertain serious doubts as to his fitness for being Commander-in-Chief.

Rilla was beside herself with delight. It was her dear Walter who had done this thing – Walter, to whom someone had sent a white feather at Redmond – it was Walter who had dashed ~~out of the~~ ^**back from the safety of the**^ trench to drag in a wounded comrade who had fallen on No-man's-land. Oh, she could see his white beautiful face and wonderful eyes as he did it! ~~What if a~~ What a thing to be the sister of such a hero! And he hadn't thought it worth while writing about. His letter was full of other things – little intimate things that they two had known and loved together in the dear old cloudless days of a century ago.

"I've been thinking of the daffodils in the garden at Ingleside," he wrote. "By the time you get this they will be out, blowing there under that lovely rosy sky. Are they really as bright ^**and golden**^ as ever, Rilla? It seems to me that they must be dyed red with blood – like our poppies here. ^[*Note*] **H8**^

"'"There is a young moon to-night – a slender, silver, lovely thing hanging over these pits of torment. Will you see it tonight over the ~~firs in Rainbow Valley?~~ maple grove?~~"~~

"'I'm enclosing a little scrap of verse, Rilla. I wrote it one evening in my trench dug-out by the light of a bit of candle – or rather it came to me there – I didn't feel as if I were writing it – something seemed to use me as an instrument. I've had that feeling once or twice before, but very rarely and never so strongly as this time. ~~I sent~~ That was why I sent it over to the London Spectator. It printed it and the copy came to-day. I hope you'll like it. It's the only poem I've written since I came overseas."

~~Rilla though~~

The poem was a short, poignant little thing ~~of only three verses; called "The Piper."~~. In a month it had carried Walter's name to every corner of the globe. Everywhere it was copied ~~and talked~~ – in metropolitan dailies and little village weeklies – in profound reviews and "agony columns."

^[*Note*] **X7**^

"The Piper" by Pte. Walter Blythe, ~~written in the trenches of Flanders~~ was a classic from its first printing ~~and made its writer famous~~.

Rilla copied it in her diary at the beginning of an entry in which she poured out the story of the hard week that had just passed.

"It has been such a dreadful week," she wrote, ~~"and yet such a wonderful one~~ "and ~~now that~~ ^**even though**^ it is over and we know that it was all a mistake that does not seem to do away with the ~~results of all the misery~~ ^**bruises left by it**^. And yet it has in some ways been a very wonderful week and I have had some glimpses of things I never realized before – of how fine and brave people can be even in the midst of horrible suffering. I am sure I could never be as splendid as Miss Oliver ~~was has been~~ was.

"Just a week ago to-day she ~~got~~ ^**had**^ a letter from Mr. Grant's mother in Charlottetown. And it told her that a ~~let~~ cable had just come saying that Major Robert Grant had been killed in action a few days before.

"Oh, poor Gertrude! At first she was crushed. Then ^**after just a day**^ she pulled herself together and went back to her ~~work~~ ^**school**^.

She did not cry – I never saw her shed a tear – but oh, her face and her eyes!

~~“~~‘I must go on with my work,’ she said. ~~“~~‘That is my duty just now.” ~~Canada is very dear to me – my lover has died for her – I must live for her. My – My work is to train~~ ^~~**to train**~~^ ~~her children to be worthy of the land saved at the price of so many beloved lives.”~~ ^**Note Y7**^

“She never spoke bitterly except once, when Susan said something about spring being ~~really~~ here at last, and Gertrude said,

“‘Can the spring ~~co~~ really come this year?~~”~~’

“Then she laughed – such a dreadful little laugh – just as one might laugh in the face of death, I think, and said,

~~Note~~ “^**Observe**^ my egotism. Because I, Gertrude Oliver, have lost a friend, it is incredible that the spring can come as usual. The spring does not fail because of the million agonies of others – but for mine – oh, can the universe go on?~~”~~’

“‘Don’t feel bitter with yourself, dear,” mother said gently. “It is a very natural thing to feel as if things couldn’t go on just the same when some great blow has changed the world for us. We all feel ~~just the same way.”~~ ^**like that**^.’

“Then that horrid old Cousin Sophia of Susan’s piped up. She was sitting there, knitting and ~~fore~~ croaking like ~~the~~ ^**an**^ old ‘raven of bode and woe’ as Walter used to call her.

“‘You ain’t as bad off as some, Miss ~~Olver~~ Oliver,’ she said, ‘and you shouldn’t take it so hard. There’s some as has lost their husbands; that’s a hard blow; and there’s some as has lost their sons. You haven’t lost either husband or son.~~”~~’

“‘No,’ said Gertrude, more bitterly still. ~~“~~‘It’s true I haven’t lost a husband – I have only lost the man who would have been my husband. I have lost no son – only the sons and daughters who might have been born to me – who will never be born to me now.’

“‘It isn’t ladylike to talk like that,’ said Cousin Sophia in a shocked tone; and then Gertrude laughed right out, so wildly that Cousin S. was really frightened. And when poor tortured Gertrude, unable to endure it any longer, hurried out of the room, Cousin Sophia asked mother if the blow hadn’t affected Miss Oliver’s mind.

“‘I suffered the loss of two good kind partners,’ she said, ‘but it did not affect me like that.'

"I should think it wouldn't! Those poor men must have been thankful to die.

"I heard Gertrude walking up and down her room most of the night. ~~I didn't go~~ She walked like that ~~uvery~~ every night. But never so long as that night. And once I heard her give a dreadful sudden little cry as if she had been ~~suddenly~~ stabbed. I couldn't sleep for suffering with her; and I couldn't help her. I thought the night would never end. But it did; and then 'joy came in the morning' as the Bible says. Only it didn't come exactly in the morning but well along in the afternoon. The telephone rang and I answered it. It was old Mrs. Grant speaking from Charlottetown, and her news was that it was all a mistake – Robert wasn't killed at all; he had only been slightly wounded in the arm and was safe in the hospital out of harm's way for a time anyhow. They ~~hadn't didn't know~~ ^**hadn't learned yet**^ how the mistake had happened but supposed there must have been another Robert Grant.

~~It had seemed to me~~

"I hung up the telephone and flew ~~– better~~ to Rainbow Valley. I'm sure I did fly – I can't remember my feet ever touching the ground. I met Gertrude on her way home from school in the glade of spruces where we used to play, and I just gasped out the news to ^**her**^. I ought to have had more sense, of course. ~~But a doctor's daughter to do such a thing!~~ But I was so crazy with joy and excitement that I never stopped to think. Gertrude just dropped there among the golden young ferns as if she had been shot. ^[*Note*] **Z7**^ A pretty time I had! I never saw anybody faint before, and I knew there was nobody up at the house to help, because everybody ^**else**^ had gone to the station to meet Di ^**and Nan**^ coming home from Redmond. But I knew ^**– theoretically –**^ how people in a faint should be treated ^ – ^ and now I know it practically. Luckily the brook was handy, and after ~~what seemed an hour to me~~ ^**I had worked frantically over her for a while**^ Gertrude came back to life. She never said one word about my news and I didn't dare to refer to it again. I helped her walk up through the maple grove and up to her room, and then she said, ~~"He~~ ^**"Rob**^ – is – living," ^**as if the words were torn out of her**^, and flung herself on her bed and cried and cried and cried. I never saw anyone cry so before. All the tears that she hadn't shed all that week came then. She cried most of last night, I think, but her face this morning looked as if she had seen a vision of some kind, and we were all so happy that we were almost afraid.

"Di and Nan are home for a couple of weeks. Then they go back to Red Cross work in ~~Kingsport among~~ the training camp at Kingsport. I envy them. Father says I'm doing just as good work here, with Jims and ~~the~~ my Junior Reds. But it lacks the romance theirs must have.[22]

~~"As for Verdun, the battle goes on and on.~~

"Kut has fallen. It was almost a relief when it did fall, we had been dreading it so long. It ~~flattened~~ ^**crushed**^ us ~~out~~ ^**flat**^ for a day and then we picked up and put it behind us. Cousin Sophia was as gloomy as usual and came over and groaned that the British were losing everywhere.

"'They're good losers,' said Susan grimly. 'When they lose a thing they keep on looking till they find it again! ~~My My~~ Anyhow, my king and country need me now to ~~plant potatoes~~ cut potato sets for the back garden, so get you a knife and help me, Sophia Crawford. It will divert your thoughts and keep you from worrying over a campaign that you are not called upon to run.'

"Susan is an old brick, and the way she flattens out poor Cousin Sophia is beautiful to behold.

"As for Verdun, the battle goes on and on, and ~~now~~ we see-saw between hope and fear. But I know that strange dream of Miss Oliver's foretold the victory of France. 'They shall not pass.'"

~~Chapter 20~~

~~Every village has its own little unwritten history, handed down through the generations from lip to lip, of tragic, comic and dramatic events. In those oral annals the tale of the union prayer-meeting~~

Chapter 20

Norman Douglas Speaks Out In Meeting

~~"What~~ "Where are you wandering, ~~girl~~ ^**Anne**^ o' mine?" asked the doctor, who even yet, after twenty four years of marriage, occasionally addressed his wife thus when nobody was about. ~~Mrs. Blythe~~ ^**Anne**^ was sitting on the veranda steps, gazing ~~dreas~~ absently over the wonderful ~~white~~ bridal world of ~~spring~~ spring blossom ~~^**in its ruby altern**^~~. Beyond the white orchard was a copse of dark young firs and creamy wild cherries, where the robins were whistling madly; for it was evening and the fire of early stars was burning over the maple grove.

Anne came back ~~to~~ with a little sigh.

"I was just taking ~~a~~ relief from ~~almost an unendurable~~ ^**intolerable**^ realities in a dream, Gilbert – a dream that all our children were ~~young~~ ^**home**^ again – and all small again – playing in Rainbow Valley. It is always so silent now – but I was imagining I heard clear voices and ~~laughter~~ ^**gay, childish sounds**^ coming up as I used to ~~hear~~. I could hear Jem's whistle and Walter's yodel, and the twins' laughter, and for just a few blessed minutes I forgot ~~that my two sons are in the tranches of the Western front~~ about the guns ~~^**we**^~~ on the Western front~~."~~, ^**and had a little false, sweet happiness.**^"

The doctor did not answer. Sometimes his work tricked him into forgetting for a few moments the Western front, but not often. There was a good deal of gray now in his still thick curls that had not been there two years ago. Yet he smiled down into the starry ~~gray~~ eyes he loved – the eyes that had once been so full of laughter, and ~~were now~~ ^**now seemed always**^ full of unshed tears.

Susan wandered by with a hoe in her hand and her ^**second**^ best bonnet on her head.

~~"There is half an hour yet before prayer-meeting time," she said, "so I am going around to the kitchen garden to have a little evening hate ^**strafe**^ with the weeds.~~ "I have just finished reading a piece in the <u>Enterprise</u> which told of a couple being married in an aeroplane. Do you think it would be legal, doctor dear?" she inquired anxiously.

"I think so," said the doctor gravely.

"Well," said Susan dubiously, "it seems to me that ~~marriage~~ ^**a wedding**^ is too solemn ~~a thing to~~ for anything so giddy as an aeroplane. But nothing is the same as it used to be. Well, it is half an hour yet before prayer-meeting time, so I am going around to the kitchen garden to have a little evening ~~strafe~~ ^**hate**^ with the weeds. ^**But**^ all the time I am ~~hat~~ strafing them I will be thinking about this new worry in the Trentino. I do not like this Austrian caper, Mrs. Dr. dear."

"Nor I," said Mrs. Blythe ruefully. "All ~~day I've been preserving~~ ^**the forenoon I preserved**^ rhubarb with my hands and ~~waiting~~ waited for the war news with my soul. ^**When it came I shrivelled.**^ Well, I suppose I must go and get ready for the prayer-meeting, too." ~~Going, Gilbert?"~~

~~"Yes, I promised Mr. Meredith I'd drop in~~

Every village has its own little unwritten history, handed down from lip to lip through the generations, of tragic, comic, and dramatic events. They are told at weddings and festivals, and ~~rh~~ rehearsed around winter firesides. And in these ~~anna~~ oral annals of Glen St. Mary the tale of the union prayer-meeting held that night in the Methodist Church ~~in the~~ was destined to fill an imperishable place.

The union prayer-meeting was Mr. Arnold's idea. The county battalion, which had been training all winter in Charlottetown, was to leave shortly for overseas. The Four Winds Harbour boys ^**belonging to it from**^ ~~of~~ the Glen and ~~Over-~~ ^**over-**^harbour and Harbour Head and Upper Glen were all home on their last leave and Mr. Arnold thought, ^**properly enough, that**^ it would be a fitting thing to hold a union prayer-meeting for them before they went away. Mr. Meredith having agreed, the meeting was announced to be held in the Methodist Church. ~~The evening was~~ ^**Glen**^ ~~P~~prayer-meetings were not apt to be too well attended but on this particular evening the Methodist Church was crowded. Everybody who could go was there. Even Miss Cornelia came – and it was the first time in her life that Miss Cornelia had ever set foot inside a Methodist Church. It ~~tok~~ took no less than a world conflict to bring that about.

"I used to hate Methodists," said Miss Cornelia calmly, when her husband expressed surprise over her going, "but I don't hate them now. There is no sense in hating Methodists when there is a Kaiser or a Hindenburg in the world."~~I am sixty nine years old and I have never~~ ~~^**this will be the first time I've ever**^ darkened the door of a Methodist church."~~ ~~^**Though to be sure," added Miss Cornelia with a sigh**^~~

So Miss Cornelia went ~~with a portentous expression~~. ~~Mrs.~~ Norman Douglas and his wife went too. And Whiskers-on-the-Moon ~~walked~~ ^**strutted**^ up the aisle ^**to a front pew,**^ as if he fully realized what a distinction he conferred upon the building. People were somewhat surprised that he should be there, since he usually avoided all assemblages connected ^**in any way**^ with the war. But Mr. Meredith had said that he hoped his session would be well represented, and ~~Whiskers~~ Mr. Pryor had evidently taken the request to heart. ^**He wore his best**^

~~The prayer-meeting opened conventionally and continued quietly.~~

~~broad cloth~~ ^**black**^ suit and white tie, his thick, tight, iron-gray curls were neatlyy arranged, and his broad, red round face looked, as Susan most uncharitably thought, more "sanctimonious" than ever.

"The minute I saw that man coming in to the Church, looking like that, I felt that mischief was brewing, Mrs. Dr. dear," she said afterwards. "What form it would take I could not tell, but I knew from face of him that he had come there for no good."

The prayer-meeting opened conventionally and continued quietly. Mr. Meredith spoke first with his usual eloquence and ~~effect~~ ^**feeling**^. Mr. Arnold followed with an address which even Miss Cornelia had to confess was ~~excellent~~ ^**irreproachable**^ in taste and subject-matter.

And then Mr. Arnold asked Mr. Pryor to lead in prayer.

Miss Cornelia had always averred that Mr. Arnold had no gumption. Miss Cornelia was not apt to err on the side of charity in her judgment of Methodist ministers, but in this case she did not greatly overshoot the mark. The Rev. Mr. Arnold certainly did not have much of that desirable, indefinable quality known as gumption, or he would never have asked Whiskers-on-The-Moon to lead in prayer at a khaki prayer-meeting. He thought he was returning the compliment to Mr. Meredith, who, at the conclusion of his address, had asked a Methodist deacon to lead.

Some people expected Mr. Pryor to refuse grumpily – and that would have made enough scandal. But Mr. Pryor bounded briskly to his feet, unctuously said, "Let us pray," and forthwith ~~began~~ ^**prayed**^. In a sonorous voice which penetrated to every corner of the crowded building Mr. Pryor poured forth a flood of fluent words, and was well on in his prayer before ~~the~~ his ^**dazed and**^ horrified audience ~~realized~~ ^**awakened to the fact**^ that they were listening to a pacifist appeal of the rankest sort. ~~Mr. Pryor~~ ~~^**Mr. Pryor had at least the courage of**^~~ ^[*Note*] **A8**^ He prayed that the ~~war~~ unholy war might cease – that the deluded armies being driven to slaughter on the Western front might have their eyes opened to their iniquity and repent while yet there was time – that the poor young men ^**present in khaki,**^ who had been hounded into a path of murder and militarism, should yet be rescued –

Mr. Pryor had got this far without let or hindrance; and so paralysed ~~wa~~ were his hearers, and so deeply imbued with their born-and-bred conviction that no disturbance must ever be made in a church, ^**no matter what the provocation,**^ that it seemed likely that he would continue unchecked to the end. But one man at least in that ~~church~~ ^**audience**^ was not hampered by inherited or acquired reverence for the sacred edifice. Norman Douglas was, as Susan had often vowed crisply ~~but as she never vowed again~~, nothing more or less than a "Pagan." But he was a ~~very~~ ^**rampantly**^ patriotic pagan, and when ~~it fully dawned upon him~~ ^**the significance of**^ what Mr. Pryor was saying ^**fully dawned on him**^, Norman Douglas suddenly went ~~Buserk~~ ^**Berserk**^. With a positive roar he bounded to his feet ^**in his side pew, facing the audience,**^ and shouted in tones of thunder:

"Stop – stop – stop that abominable prayer! What an abominable prayer!"

Every head in the church flew up. A boy in khaki at the back gave a faint cheer. Mr. Meredith raised a deprecating hand, but Norman was past caring for anything like that. Eluding his wife's restraining ~~hand~~ ^**grasp**^, he ~~rushed up the~~ gave one mad spring over the front of the pew and caught the unfortunate ~~Mr. Pryor~~ Whiskers-on-the-Moon by his coat collar. Mr. Pryor had not "stopped" when so bidden, but he stopped now perforce for Norman, his ~~busy~~ ^**long red**^ beard ^~~**fairly**~~ **literally**^ bristling with fury, was shaking him ~~as a mastiff might shake a rat~~ ^**until his bones fairly rattled,**^ and punctuating his shakes with a lurid assortment of abusive epithets.

"You blatant beast!" – shake – "you ~~ml~~ malignant carrion" – shake – "you pig-headed varmint" – shake – "you putrid pup" – shake – "you – you pestilential parasite" ^– **shake** –^ "you ~~– you~~ – Hunnish ~~worm~~ ^**scum– shake –**^ "you ~~– you –~~ indecent reptile – you – you – "

Norman choked for a moment. Everybody believed that the next thing he would say, church or no church, would be something that would have to be spelled with asterisks; but at that moment Norman encountered his wife's eye and he fell back with a thud on Holy Writ. "You whited sepulchre!" he bellowed, with a final shake, and cast Whiskers-on-the-Moon from him ~~towards the choir door~~ with a vigor ~~that~~ which impelled that unhappy pacifist to the very verge of the choir entrance door. Mr. Pryor's ^**once**^ ruddy face was ashen. But he turned at bay. "I'll have the law on you for this," he gasped.

"Do – do," roared Norman, making another rush. But Mr. Pryor was gone. ^[*Note*] **C8**^ ~~He did not want another ^**Note C8 a second**^ another such shaking~~ Norman turned ~~triumphantly~~ to the ~~audience~~ platform ^**for one graceless, triumphant moment**^.

"Don't look so flabbergasted, parsons," he ~~said ^**boomed**^~~ ^^**boomed**^^. "You couldn't do it – nobody would expect it of the cloth – but somebody had to do it. ^**You know you're glad I threw him out**^ ^**Note M10**^ Sedition and treason – ~~sedition and treason –~~ somebody had to deal with it. I was born for this hour – I've had my innings in church at last. ~~I can That old Hun gave~~ I can sit quiet for another ~~fifty~~ ^**sixty ~~60~~**^ years ^**now**^! Go ahead with your meeting, parsons. I reckon you won't be troubled with any more pacifist prayers."

But the spirit of devotion and reverence had fled. Both ~~Mr.~~ the ministers realized it and realized that the only thing to do was to close the meeting quietly and let the excited people go. Mr. Meredith addressed a few earnest words to the boys in khaki – which probably saved Mr. Pryor's windows from a second onslaught – and Mr. Arnold pronounced an incongruous benediction, at least he felt it was incongruous, ~~Mr. Arnold had a keen sense of humor~~ for he could not at once banish ~~his~~ from his memory the sight of ~~that~~ gigantic Norman Douglas shaking the fat, pompous little Whiskers-on-the-Moon as a huge mastiff might shake an overgrown puppy. ^[*Note*] **B8**^ Altogether the union prayer-meeting could hardly be called an unqualified success. But it was remembered in Glen St. Mary when scores of orthodox and undisturbed assemblies were totally forgotten.

"You will never, no, never, Mrs. Dr. dear, hear me call Norman Douglas a pagan again," said Susan ~~that night~~ when she reached home. "If Ellen Douglas is not a proud woman this night she should be."

[*Montgomery puts a line across the page here to indicate the original chapter end.*]

"Norman Douglas did a wholly indefensible thing," said the doctor. "Pryor should have been let severely alone until the meeting was over. Then, later on, his own minister and session should deal with him. That would have been the proper procedure. Norman's performance was utterly ~~scandalous~~ ^**improper**^ and ~~improper~~ ^**scandalous**^ and ~~indefensible~~ outrageous; ~~but –" the~~ but, by ~~Jove~~ ^**George,**^" – the doctor threw back his head and chuckled, "by ~~Jove~~ ^**George**^, Anne-girl, it was satisfying."

Chapter 21

"Love Affairs Are Horrible."

"Ingleside,
20th June 1916

"We have been so busy, and day after day has brought such exciting news, good and bad, that I haven't had time and composure to write in my diary for weeks. I like to keep it up regularly, for father says a diary of the years of the war should be a very interesting thing to hand down to one's children. The trouble is, I like to write a few personal things in this blessed old book that might not be exactly what I'd ~~like~~ ^**want**^ my children to read. I feel that I shall be a far greater stickler for propriety in regard to them than I am for myself!

"The first week in June was ~~a~~ ^**another**^ dreadful one. The Austrians seemed just on the point of overrunning Italy: and then came the first awful news of the Battle of Jutland, which the Germans claimed as a great victory. I shall never forget that day. We just gave up ~~in despair~~ ^**completely**^. If the British navy had failed in what was there to trust us? ^**Note D8**^ Susan was the only one who carried on. 'You need never tell me that the Kaiser has defeated the British Navy,' she said, with a contemptuous sniff. 'It is all a German lie and that you may tie to.' And when a couple of days later we found out that she was right and that it had been a British victory instead of a British defeat, we had to put up with a great many 'I told you so's,' but we endured them very comfortably.

"It took Kitchener's death to finish Susan. For the first time I saw her down and out. We all felt the ~~sch~~ shock of it but Susan plumbed the depths of despair. The news came at night by 'phone but Susan wouldn't believe it until she saw the Enterprise headline the next day. She did not cry or faint or go into hysterics; but she forgot to put salt in the soup and that is something ~~Susan~~ ^**Susan**^ never did in my recollection. Mother and Miss Oliver and I cried but Susan looked at us in stony sarcasm and said,

'The Kaiser and his six sons are all alive and thriving. So the world is not left wholly desolate. Why cry, Mrs. Dr. dear?' Susan continued in this stony, hopeless condition for ~~two whole days~~ ^**twenty four hours**^, and then Cousin Sophia appeared and began to condole with her.

"This is terrible news, ain't it, Susan? We might as well prepare for the worst for it is bound to come. You said once – and well do I remember the words, Susan Baker – that you had complete confidence in God and Kitchener. Ah well, Susan Baker, there is only God left now.'

"Whereat Cousin Sophia put her handkerchief to her eyes pathetically ^**as if the world were indeed in terrible straits.**^

"As for Susan, Cousin Sophia was the salvation of her. She came to life with a jerk.

~~"I am not~~ "'Sophia Crawford, ^**hold your peace!**^' she said sternly. 'You may be an idiot but you need not be an irreverent idiot. ~~I am of the not going to~~ ^**It is no more than decent to be**^ weeping and wailing because the Almighty is the sole stay of the Allies now. As for Kitchener, his death is a great loss and I do not dispute it. But the outcome of this war does not depend on one man's life and ~~we have Lloyd George~~ now that the Russians are coming on ~~so splendidly~~ again you will soon see ~~the~~ a change for the better."

"Susan said this so energetically that she convinced herself and cheered up immediately. But Cousin Sophia shook her head.

'"Albert's wife wants to call the baby after Brusiloff," she said, 'but I told her to wait and see what becomes of him first. Them Russians ~~have~~ ^**has**^ such a habit of petering out.'

"The Russians are doing splendidly, however, and they have saved Italy. But even when the daily news of their sweeping advance comes we don't feel like running up the flag as we used to do. As ~~Miss Oliver~~ ^**Gertrude**^ says, Verdun has slain all exultation. We would all feel more like rejoicing if the victories were on the Western front. 'When will the British strike?' Gertrude sighed this morning. 'We have waited so long – so long.'

~~The county battalion made a route march through the county before they left for overseas~~

"Our greatest local event in recent weeks was the route march the county battalion made through the county before it left for overseas.

~~They paraded when they marched through the Glen everybo~~ They marched from Charlottetown to Lowbridge, then round ~~through~~ the Harbour Head and through the Upper Glen and so down to the St. Mary station. Everybody turned out to see them, except old Aunt Fannie Clow, who is bedridden and Mr. Pryor, who ~~has never gone anywhere even to church~~ ^**hadn't been seen out even in church**^ since the night of the union prayer meeting ~~a w~~ the previous week.

"It was wonderful and heartbreaking to see that battalion marching past. There were young men and middle-aged men in it. There was Laurie McAllister from over harbour who is only sixteen but swore he was eighteen, so that he could enlist; and there was Angus Mackenzie, from the Upper Glen who is fifty-five if he is a day and swore he was forty-four. There were two South African veterans from Lowbridge, and the three ^**eighteen-year-old**^ ~~Sotherby~~ ^**Baxter**^ triplets from Harbour Head. Everybody cheered as they went by.

^**Note F8**^

"At the station Dog Monday nearly went out of his head. He tore about and sent messages to Jem by them all.

^**Note G8**^

"Fred Arnold was in the battalion and I felt dreadfully about him, ~~because~~ ^**for**^ I realized that it was because of me that he was going away with such a ~~heavy heart~~ ^**sorrowful expression**^. I couldn't help it but I felt as badly as if I could.

"The last evening of his leave Fred came up to Ingleside and told me he loved me and asked me if I ~~couldn't~~ ^**would**^ promise to marry him ~~when he came back~~ ^**some day, if he ever came back**^. He was ~~so~~ desperately in earnest and I felt more wretched than I ever did in my life. I couldn't promise him that – why, even if there was no question of Ken, I don't care for Fred that way and never could – but it seemed so cruel and heartless to send him away to the front without any hope of comfort. I cried like a baby; and yet – oh, I am afraid that there must be something incurably frivolous about me, because, right in the middle of it all, with me crying and Fred looking so wild and tragic, the thought popped into my head that it would be an unendurable thing to see that nose across from me at the breakfast table every morning of my life. There, that is one of the entries I wouldn't want my descendants to read in this journal. But it is the humiliating truth; and perhaps it's just as well that thought did come or I might have been tricked by pity and remorse into giving ^**him**^ some rash assurance. If Fred's nose were as handsome as his eyes and mouth some such thing might have happened. And then what an unthinkable predicament I should have been in!

"When poor Fred became convinced that I couldn't promise him, he behaved beautifully – though that rather made things worse. If he had been nasty about it I wouldn't have felt so heartbroken and remorseful – though why I should feel remorseful I don't know, for I never encouraged Fred to think I cared a bit about him. ~~He~~ Yet feel remorseful I did – and do. If Fred Arnold never comes back from overseas, ~~I shall~~ this will ~~hurt~~ ^**haunt**^ me all my life.

"Then Fred said if he couldn't take my love with him to the trenches at least he wanted to feel that he had my friendship, ~~Of course I assured him he had and I promise said~~ and would I kiss him just once in good-bye before he went – perhaps for ever?

"I don't know how I could ever had imagined that love affairs were delightful, interesting things. They are horrible. I couldn't even give poor heartbroken Fred one little kiss, because of my promise to Ken. It seemed so brutal. I had to tell Fred ~~it was because I had promised why I couldn't~~ ^**that of course he would have my friendship, but that I** ~~**coul**~~ **couldn't** ^^**kiss him**^^ **because I had promised somebody else I wouldn't.**^

"He said,

"'It is – is it – Ken Ford?'

"I nodded. ~~I had~~ It seemed dreadful to have to tell it – it was such a sacred little secret just between me and Ken ~~– and if Ken really hadn't meant anything in particular I would ^**might**^ be in a very humiliating position when he came back~~.

"When Fred went away I came up here to my room and cried ~~and~~ so long and so bitterly that mother came up and insisted on knowing what was the matter. I told her ~~and the~~. ^**Note E8**^ she was so nice and understanding and sympathetic ~~lly ethic~~, oh, just so race-of-Josephy – that I felt ~~in~~ indescribably comforted. Mothers are the dearest things.

"'But oh, mother,' I sobbed, 'he wanted me to kiss him good-bye –

and I couldn't – and that hurt me worse than all the rest.'

"'Well, why didn't you kiss him?' asked mother coolly. "~~In th~~ Considering the circumstances, I think you might have.'

"'But I couldn't, mother – I promised Ken when he went away that I wouldn't kiss anybody else until he came back.'

"This was another high explosive for poor mother. She ~~said~~ ^**exclaimed**^, with the queerest little catch in her voice,

"'Rilla, are you engaged to Kenneth Ford?'

"'I – don't – know,' I sobbed.

"'You – don't – know?' repeated mother.

"Then I had to tell her the whole story, too; and every time I ~~told~~ ^**tell**^ it it ~~seemed~~ ^**seems**^ sillier and sillier to imagine that Ken meant anything serious. I felt idiotic and ashamed by the time I got through.

"Mother sat a little while in silence. Then she came over, sat down beside me, and took me in her arms.

~~"My baby," she said. "My last little baby – and now she is a woman grown the war has made a woman of her."~~

"'Don't cry, dear little ~~woman-child~~ ^**Rilla-my-Rilla**^. You have nothing to reproach yourself ~~for~~ ^**with**^ in regard to Fred; and if Leslie West's son asked you to keep your lips for him, I think you may consider yourself engaged to him. But – oh, my baby – my last little baby – I have lost you – the war has made a woman of you too soon.'

"I shall never be too much of a woman to find comfort in mother's ~~hugs~~ ^**hugs**^. Nevertheless, when I saw Fred marching by ~~that day~~ ^**two days later**^ in the parade, my heart ached unbearably.

"But I'm glad mother thinks I'm really engaged to Ken!"

Chapter 22

Little Dog Monday Knows

"It is two years tonight since the dance at the light, when Jack Elliott brought us news of the war. Do you remember, Miss Oliver?" ~~^**asked Rilla.**^ And we all thought the war would be over in a few months."~~

~~"I see by to-day's Montreal paper ^**Albert read out of a Montreal paper to-day**^ that a war expert gives it as his opinion that it will last five years more," remarked Cousin Sophia. "~~

Cousin Sophia answered for Miss Oliver.

"Oh, indeed, Rilla, I remember that evening ~~very~~ ^**only too**^ well and you a-prancing down here to show off your party clothes. Didn't I warn you that we could not tell what was before us? Little did you think that night what was before you."

"Little did ~~more~~ ^**any**^ of us think that," said Susan sharply, "not being gifted with the power of prophecy. It does not require any great ~~power for fore of~~ foresight, Sophia Crawford, to tell a body that she will have some trouble before her life is over. I could do as much myself."

"We all thought the war would be over in a few months then," said Rilla wistfully. "When I look back it seems so ridiculous that we ever could have ~~thought~~ ^**supposed**^ it."

"And now, two years later, it is no nearer the end than it was then," said Miss Oliver gloomily.

Susan clicked her knitting-needles briskly.

"Now, Miss Oliver, dear, you know that is not a reasonable remark. You know we are ^**just**^ two years nearer the end, whenever the end is appointed to be."

"Albert read in a Montreal paper to-day that a war expert gives it as his opinion that it will last five years more," was Cousin Sophia's cheerful contribution.

"It can't," ~~said~~ ^**cried**^ Rilla; then she added with a sigh. "Two years ago we would have said 'It can't last two years.' But five more years of this!"

~~"I am no war expert," said Susan, "but~~

"If Rumania comes in, as I have strong hopes ^**now**^ of her doing, you will see the end in five months instead of five years," ^ **said Susan**^. "I've no faith in furriners," sighed Cousin Sophia.

"The French are foreigners," retorted Susan, "and look at Verdun. ~~Why. Ane~~ One of your ~~war~~ ^**precious war**^ experts says 'there is not the slightest doubt that Verdun is saved.' Not the slights doubt, Sophia Crawford. And think of all the Somme victories this blessed summer. The Big Push is on and the Russians are still going well. Why, General Haig says that the German officers he has captured admit that they have lost the war."

"You can't believe a word the Germans say," ~~pret~~ protested Cousin Sophia. "There is no sense in believing a thing just because you'd <u>like</u> to believe it, Susan Baker. The British have lost millions of men at the Somme and how far have they got? Look facts in the face, Susan Baker, look facts in the face."

"They are wearing the Germans out and so long as that happens it does not matter whether it is done a few miles east or a few miles west. ~~That is a fact which~~ I am not," admitted Susan in tremendous humility, "I am not a military expert, Sophia Crawford, but even <u>I</u> can see that, and so could you if you were not determined to take a gloomy view of everything. ^**Note O10**^ Well, I am going to leave the war to Haig ~~this afternoon~~ for the rest of the day and make a frosting for my chocolate cake. And when it is made I shall put it on the top shelf. The last one I made I left it on the lower shelf and little Kitchener sneaked in and clawed all the ~~frosting~~ icing off and ate it. We had company for tea that night and ~~wer~~ when I went to get my cake ~~that is~~ what ~~I beheld."~~ a sight did I behold!"

"Has that pore orphan's father never been heerd from yet?" asked Cousin Sophia.

"Yes, I had a letter from him in July," said Rilla. "He said that when he got word of his wife's death and of my taking the baby – Mr. Meredith wrote him, you know – he wrote right away, but as he never got any answer he had begun to think his letter must have been lost."

"It took him two years to begin to think it," said Susan scornfully. "Some people think very slow. Jim Anderson has not got a scratch, for all he has been two years in the trenches. A fool for luck, as the old proverb says."

"He wrote very nicely about Jims and said he'd like to see him," said Rilla. "So I wrote and told him all about the wee man, and sent him snapshots. Jims will be two years old next week and he is a perfect duck."

"You didn't used to be very fond of babies," said Cousin Sophia.

"I'm not a bit fonder of babies in the abstract than ever I was," said Rilla, frankly. "But I do love Jims, and I'm afraid I wasn't really half as glad as I should have been when Jim Anderson's letter ~~turned~~ proved that he was safe and sound."

"You wasn't hoping the man would be killed!" cried Cousin Sophia in horrified accents.

"No – no – no! I just hoped he would go on forgetting about Jims, Mrs. Crawford."

"And then your pa would have the expense of raising him," said Cousin Sophia reprovingly.

"You young ~~creeturs~~ ~~^**critters**^~~ ^^**creeturs**^^ are terrible thoughtless."

Jims himself ran in at this juncture, so rosy and curly and kissable, that he extorted ~~an e~~ ^**a qualified**^ compliment even from Cousin Sophia.

"He^**'s**^ ~~is~~ a reel healthy looking child now, though mebbee his color is a mite too high – sorter consumptive looking, as you ~~neig~~ might say. I never thought you'd raise him when I saw him the day after you brung him home ~~in the soup tureen~~. I ~~really~~ reely did not think it was in you and I told Albert's wife so when I got home. Albert's wife says, says she, 'There's more in Rilla Blythe than you'd think ^**for**^, Aunt Sophia.' Them was her very words. 'More in Rilla Blythe than you'd think for.' Albert's wife always had a good opinion of you."

Cousin Sophia sighed, as if to imply that Albert's wife stood alone ^**in this**^ against the world. But Cousin Sophia really did not mean that. She was quite fond of Rilla in her own melancholy way; but young ~~critters~~ ^**creeturs**^ had to be kept down. If they were not kept down society would be demoralized.

"Do you remember your walk home from the light two years ago to-night?" Gertrude Oliver whispered to Rilla, teasingly.

"I should think I do," smiled Rilla; and then her smile grew dreamy and absent; she was remembering something else – that ~~moonlit~~ hour with Kenneth on the sandshore. Where would Ken be to-night? And Jem and Jerry and Walter and all the other boys who had danced and moonlighted ~~at~~ on the old Four Winds Point that ~~night~~ evening~~?~~ of mirth and laughter – their last joyous unclouded evening. ^**Note J8**^ Two of them were sleeping under ~~a little wh~~ the ~~blood-stained sort of~~ Flanders ^**poppies**^ – Alec Burr from the Upper Glen, and Clark Manley of Lowbridge. Others were wounded in the hospitals. But so far nothing had touched the manse and the Ingleside boys. They seemed to bear charmed lives. Yet the suspense never grew any easier to bear as the weeks and months of war went by.

"It isn't as if it ~~was the~~ ^**were**^ some sort of ~~contagious~~ ^**fever**^ to which you might conclude they were immune when they hadn't taken it for ~~four~~ ^**two**^ years," sighed Rilla. "The danger is just as great and just as real as it was the first day they went into the trenches. I know this, and it tortures me every day. And yet I can't help hoping that since they've come this far unhurt they'll come through. Oh, ~~Miss~~ ^**Miss**^ Oliver, what would it be like not to wake up in the morning feeling afraid of the news the day would bring? I can't picture such a state of things somehow. And two years ago this morning I woke wondering what delightful ~~gf~~ gift the new day would give me. These are the two years I thought would be filled with fun."

"Would you exchange them – now – for two years filled with fun?"

"No," said Rilla slowly. "I wouldn't. It's strange – isn't it? – they have been two terrible years – and yet I have a queer feeling of thankfulness for them – as if they had brought me something very precious, ~~in~~ with all their pain. I wouldn't want to go back and be the girl I was two years ago, not even if I could. Not that ~~I'm~~ I think I've made any wonderful progress – but I'm not quite the selfish, frivolous little doll I was then. ~~Even Susan admits that~~ I suppose I had a soul then, Miss Oliver – but I didn't know it. I know it now – and that is worth a great deal – worth all the suffering of the past two years. And still –" Rilla gave a little apologetic laugh, "I don't want to suffer any more – not even for the sake of more soul growth. At the end of two more years I might look back and be thankful for the development they had brought me, too; but I don't want it now."

"We never do," said Miss Oliver. "That is why we are not left to choose our own means and measure of development, I suppose. No matter how much we value what our lessons have brought us we don't want to go on with the bitter schooling. Well, let us hope for the best, as Susan says; things are really going well now and if Roumania ~~comes in~~ ^**lines up**^, the end may come with a suddenness that will surprise us all."

^**Note I8**^

So the summer passed away. ^~~**Rumania did come in Se**~~^ Early in September word came that the Canadians had been shifted to the Somme front and anxiety grew tenser and deeper. For the first time Mrs. Blythe's spirit failed her a little, and ^**as the days of suspense wore on**^ the doctor began to look gravely at her ~~as the days of suspense wore on~~, and veto this or that special effort in Red Cross work.

"Oh, let me work – let me work, Gilbert," she entreated feverishly. "While I'm working I don't think so much. If I'm idle I imagine everything – rest is only torture for me. My two boys are on the frightful Somme front – and Shirley pores day and night over aviation literature and says nothing. But I see the purpose growing in his eyes. No, I can not rest – don't ask it of me, Gilbert."

But the doctor was inexorable.

"I can't let you kill yourself, Anne-girl," he said. "When the boys come back I want a mother here to welcome them. Why, you're getting transparent. It won't do – ask Susan there if it will do."

"Oh, if Susan and you are both banded together against me!" said Anne helplessly.

One day the glorious news ~~of~~ came that the Canadians had taken Courcellette and Martenpuich, with many prisoners and guns. Susan ran up the flag and said it was plain to be seen that Haig knew what soldiers to pick for a hard job. The others dared not feel exultant. Who knew what price had been paid?

Rilla woke that morning ~~just as~~ ^**when the**^ dawn was beginning to break and went to her window to look out, her thick creamy eyelids heavy with sleep. Just at dawn the world looks as ~~if~~ it never looks at any other time. The air was cold with dew and the orchard and grove and Rainbow Valley were full of mystery and wonder. Over the eastern hill ~~was a soft silvery-pink sky.~~ ^**were golden deeps and silvery-pink shallows.**^ There was no wind, and Rilla heard distinctly a dog howling in a melancholy way down in the direction of the station. Was it ~~Rags~~ Dog Monday? And if it were, why was he howling like that? ~~He had never done so before.~~ Rilla shivered; the sound had something boding and grievous in it. ~~Ri~~ She remembered that Miss Oliver had said once, when they were coming home in the darkness and heard a dog howl, "When a dog ~~howls~~ ^**cries**^ like that the Angel of Death is passing." Rilla listened with a curdling fear at her heart. It was Dog Monday – she felt sure of it. Whose ~~spirit was hovering over him~~ dirge was he howling – ^**to**^ whose ^~~**passing**~~ **hovering**^ spirit was he sending that anguished greeting and farewell?

Rilla went back to bed but she could not sleep. All day she watched and waited in a dread of which she did not speak ^**to anyone**^. ~~But there was no bad news – nor on the next – or the next. Rilla's fear lifted. Dog Monday howled no more at nights – perhaps ^^**he thought he had howled that night**^^ it had not been ^**he**^ who howled at all.~~ She ~~had gone~~ ^**went**^ down to see ~~him and he had greeted her with his usual the station master had spoken of in – spoke of – said,~~ ^**Dog Monday and the station master said,**^

"That dog of yours howled from midnight to sunrise something weird.~~" he told her. "~~I dunno what got into him. He kept the wife awake and I got up once and went out and hollered at him but he paid no 'tention to me. He was sitting all alone in the moonlight out there at the end of the platform, and every few minutes ^**the poor lonely little beggar'd**^ ~~he'd~~ lift his nose and howl as if his heart was breaking. He never did it afore – ~~used to sleep his~~ ^**always slept**^ in his kennel real quiet and canny from train to train. But he sure had something on his mind last night."

Dog Monday was lying in his kennel. He wagged his tail and licked Rilla's hand. But he would not touch the food she brought for him.

"I'm afraid he's sick," she said anxiously. ~~"Oh, I hope nothing will happen to him.~~ She hated to go away and leave him. But no bad news came that day – nor the next – nor the next. Rilla's fear lifted. Dog

Monday howled no more and resumed his routine of train meeting and watching. When five days had passed the Ingleside people began to feel that they might be cheerful again. Rilla dashed about the kitchen helping Susan with the breakfast and singing so sweetly and clearly that Cousin Sophia across the road heard her and croaked out to Mrs. Albert,

"'Sing before eating, cry before sleeping,' I've always heard."

But Rilla Blythe shed no tears before the nightfall. When ~~the tel tele-phone rang that afternoon and the~~ her father, his face gray and drawn and old, came to her that afternoon and told her that Walter had been killed in action at Courcelette she crumpled up in a pitiful little heap ~~on the floor and spent~~ of merciful unconsciousness in his arms. Nor did she waken to her pain for many hours.

Chapter 23

"And So, Good-Night."

The fierce flame of agony had burned itself out and the gray dust of ~~as~~ its ashes was over all the world. Rilla's younger life recovered physically ~~before her mother~~ sooner than her mother. For weeks Mrs. Blythe lay ill from grief and shock. Rilla found it was possible to go on with ~~life~~ ^**existence**^, since ~~life was not~~ ^**existence**^ had still to be reckoned with. She could not die, even though her anguish called for merciful death. There was work to be done, for Susan could not do all. ~~After a few days~~ For her mother's sake she had to ~~be~~ put on calmness and endurance as a garment in the day; but night after night she lay in her bed, ~~shaken with~~ ^**weeping**^ the bitter rebellious tears of youth until at last tears were all wept out and the little ^**patient**^ ache that was to be in her heart until she died took ~~its pl~~ their place.

"Oh," she cried despairingly to Miss Oliver, "how can I ever get used to thinking that Walter isn't anywhere in the world? 'Somewhere in France' was dreadful but 'nowhere in the world' is unthinkable."

Her beautiful Walter ~~in his p~~ – he would never come to her again – never sit with her in Rainbow Valley. The ~~wide~~ womanful gray eyes she had loved were shut forever. She clung to Miss Oliver, who knew what to say and what not to say. So few people did. Kind, well-meaning callers and comforters gave Rilla some terrible moments.

"You'll get over it in time," Mrs. William Reese said, cheerfully. Mrs. Reese had three stalwart sons, not one of whom had gone to the front.

"It's such a blessing it was Walter who was taken and not Jem," said ~~Mrs. Elder~~ Miss Sarah Clow. "Walter was a member of the church, and Jem wasn't. I've told Mr. Meredith many a time that he should have spoken seriously to Jem about it before he went away."

"I hope pore Walter didn't have to suffer much before he died," sighed Mrs. ~~Dave Mead~~ ^**Reese**^. "When Clark Manley was killed he laid for hours in the cold snow, all fevered up and burning for a drink, and died just as they found him. I hope pore Walter didn't have to suffer like that – and it so ~~bu~~ hot there this time of year~~."~~ – pore, ~~poor~~ ^**pore**^ Walter."

"~~Don't~~ ^**Do not**^ you come here calling him poor Walter," said Susan ~~indeed~~ indignantly, appearing in the kitchen door, much ~~to Releas re-lief~~ the relief of Rilla, who felt that she could endure no more just then. "He ~~is~~ ^**was**^ not poor. He ~~is~~ ^**was**^ richer than any of you. ~~He had feelings~~ It is you who stay at home and ~~won't~~ ^**will not**^ let your sons go who are poor – poor and naked and mean and small – pisen poor, and so are your sons, with all their prosperous farms and fat cattle and their souls no bigger than a flea's – if as big."

"I came here to comfort the afflicted and not to be insulted," said Mrs. Reese, taking her departure ~~tp everyones relief~~, ^**unregretted by anyone**^. Then the fire went out of Susan and she ~~li~~ retreated to her kitchen and ~~sat miserably down at her table.~~

~~"It seems as if the sun had gone out," she muttered to herself. "And I do not suppose he would ever get that last cake I sent him, the dear little fellow. I never held with his being a poet but short of that there was no fault in him from the time he was born. ^**Note P10**^ I used to rock him to sleep and toast his little toes before the fire. And now the Huns have gone and murdered him and we can not even have a funeral for a little comfort. And here is Mrs. Dr. dear sick, and Rilla working herself to death and me neither able to help the one or prevent the other. I – I – kind of fell played out."~~

~~Poor Susan~~ laid her faithful old head on her ~~knotted~~ hands and wept bitterly ^**for a time**^. Then she went to work and ironed Jims's little ~~dresses for him~~ rompers. Rilla scolded her gently for it when she herself came in to do it.

"I am not going to have you kill yourself working ^**for any war baby,**^ ~~child~~" Susan said obstinately.

"Oh, I wish I could just keep on working all the time, Susan," cried poor Rilla. "And I wish I didn't have to go to sleep. It is hideous to go to sleep and forget it for a little while, and wake up and have it all rush over me anew the next morning. Do people ever get used to things like ~~that~~ ^**this**^, Susan?~~"~~ And oh, Susan, I can't get away from what Mrs. Reese said. Did Walter suffer much – he was always so sensitive to pain. Oh, Susan, if I knew that he didn't, I think I could gather up a little courage and strength."

This merciful knowledge was given to Rilla. A letter came from Walter's commanding officer, telling them that he had been killed instantly by a ~~gunshot~~ bullet during a charge at Courcellette. The same day ~~a letter came~~ ^**there was a letter for**^ ~~to~~ Rilla from Walter himself.

Rilla carried it unopened to Rainbow Valley and read it there, in the spot where she had had her last talk with ~~Walter~~ ^**him**^. It is a strange thing to read a letter after the writer is dead – a bitter-sweet thing, in which pain and ~~pleasure~~ ^**comfort**^ are strangely mingled. For the first time since the blow had fallen Rilla felt – a different thing from tremulous hope and faith – that Walter, ~~still lived somewhere~~ of the glorious gift and the splendid ideals, ~~lived~~ still lived, with just the same gift and just the same ideals. That could not be destroyed – those could suffer no eclipse. The personality that had expressed itself in that last letter, written ~~the~~ on the eve of Courcellette, could not be snuffed out by a German bullet. It must carry on, though the earthly link with things of earth were broken. ~~Walter's body~~

"We're going over the top to-morrow, Rilla-my-Rilla," wrote Walter. "I wrote ~~most of my letters yesterday but~~ mother ^**and Di**^ yesterday, but somehow I feel as if I must write you to-night ~~– here in my dug-out by the light of a bit of candle.~~ I hadn't intended to do any writing to-night – but I've got to ~~somehow~~. Do you remember ~~Low~~ old Mrs. Tom Crawford over harbour, who was always saying that it was 'laid on her' to do such and such a thing? Well, that is just how I feel. It's 'laid on me' to write you tonight – you, ~~dear faithful little sister and chum~~ ^**sister and chum of mine**^. There are some things I want to say before – well, before to-morrow.

"You and Ingleside seem strangely near me to-night. It's the first time I've felt this since I came. Always home has seemed so far away – so hopelessly far away from this hideous welter of filth and blood. But tonight it is quite close to me – it seems to me I can almost see you – hear you speak ~~– feel the breeze blowing ^**purring**^ from Rainbow Valley~~. ^**Note S8**^

"It must be autumn at home now – the harbour is a-dream and the old Glen hills blue with haze, and Rainbow Valley a haunt of delight~~, I can see it all.~~ with wild asters ^**– blowing all over it**^ – our old "farewell-summers." I always liked that name so much better than 'aster' – it was a poem in itself.

"Rilla, you know I've always had premonitions. You remember the Pied Piper – but no, of course you wouldn't – you were too young. ~~But Nan and Di will.~~ One evening long ago when Nan and Di and Jem and the Merediths and I were together in Rainbow Valley I had a queer vision or presentiment~~, or something~~ ^– **whatever you like to call it**^. Rilla, I saw the Piper coming down the Valley with a shadowy host ~~of lads~~ behind him. The others thought I was only pretending – but I saw him for just one moment. And Rilla, last night I saw him again. I was doing sentry-go and I saw him marching across No-man's-land from our trenches to the German trenches – the same tall shadowy form, piping weirdly ~~– and behind him followed the~~ ^– **and behind him followed boys in khaki.**^ Rilla, I tell you I saw him – it was no fancy – no illusion. I heard his music, ~~and it was all that I could do to prevent myself from rushing after him.~~ ^~~**I wanted to follow him – I felt that I had must follow him.**~~^ and then – he was gone. But I had seen him – and I knew what it meant – ^**I knew that I was ~~one of those~~ among those who followed him.**^

~~To-morrow~~ "Rilla, the Piper will pipe me 'west' to-morrow. I feel sure of this. And, Rilla, I'm not afraid. When you hear the news, remember that. I've won my own freedom here – freedom from all fear. I shall never be afraid of anything again – not of death – nor of life, if after all, I am to go on living. And life, I think, would be ^**the**^ harder of the two to face ^~~**It**~~ **– for it could never be beautiful for me again.**^ There would always be such horrible things to remember – things that would make life ugly and painful always ^**for me**^. I could never forget them. But whether it's life or death, I'm not afraid, Rilla-my-Rilla, and I am not sorry that I came. I'm satisfied. I'll never write the poems I once dreamed of writing – but I've helped to make Canada safe for the poets of the future – for the workers ~~and dreamers~~ of the future ^**Note R8**^ ^– **ay, and the dreamer too, even if no man dream there will be nothing for the workers to fulfil.**^ ~~when the 'red rain' of Langemarck and Verdun state~~ ^– **the future,**^ not of Canada only but of the world – when the 'red rain' of Langemarck and Verdun shall have brought forth a golden harvest – not in a year or two, as some foolishly think, but a generation later, when the seed sown now will have had time to germinate and grow. ~~For we shall win, Rilla – we shall win. Never for~~

~~a moment doubt that.~~ Yes, I'm glad I came, Rilla. It isn't ^**only**^ the fate of the little sea-born island I love that is in the balance – nor of Canada – nor of England. It's the fate of mankind. That is what we're fighting for. And we shall win – never for a moment doubt that, Rilla. For it isn't only the living who are fighting – the dead are fighting too. Such an army cannot be defeated.

"Is there laughter in your face yet, Rilla~~-my-Rilla~~? I hope so. ~~We We~~ ^**The world will**^ need laughter and courage more than ever in the years that will come next. ~~And there's a work for you to do – for all our girls back in the home-land to do.~~ I don't want to preach – this isn't any time for it. But I just want to say something that may help you over the worst when you hear that I've 'gone West.' I've a premonition about you, Rilla, as well as about myself. I think Ken will go back to you – and that there are long years of happiness for you by-and-by. And ~~when~~ you will tell your children of the Idea we fought and died for – teach them it must be lived for as well as died for, else the price paid for it will have been given for nought. This will be part of your work, Rilla~~- my-Rilla~~. And if you ~~and the~~ – all you girls back in the homeland – do it, then we who ~~sleep shall have gone west~~ ^**don't come back**^ will know that you have ~~not "broken faith"~~ ^~~**kept faith**~~ **not "broken faith"**^ with us.

"I meant to write to Una to-night, too, but ~~there isn't~~ I won't have time ^**now**^. Read this letter to her and tell her it's really meant for you both – you two dear, fine loyal girls. To-morrow, when we go over the top, I'll think of you both – of your laughter, Rilla-my-Rilla, and the steadfastness in Una's blue eyes – somehow I see ~~her~~ ^**those eyes**^ very plainly to-night, too. Yes, you'll both keep faith – I'm sure of that – you and Una. And so – good-night. We go over the top at dawn."

Rilla read her letter over many times. There was a new light on her pale young face when she finally stood up, amid the asters Walter had ~~spoken of~~ ^**loved**^, with the sunshine of autumn around her. For the moment, at least, she was lifted above pain and loneliness.

"I will keep faith, Walter," she said steadily. "I will work – and teach – and learn – and laugh, yes, I will even laugh – through all my years, because of you and because of what you gave when you followed the call."

Rilla meant to keep Walter's letter as ~~her~~ a sacred treasure. But, ~~when she saw~~ ^**seeing**^ the look on Una Meredith's ~~faith~~ face when Una had read ~~the letter~~ ^**it**^ and held it back to her, she thought of something. Could she do it? Oh, no, she could not give up Walter's letter – his last letter. ~~But Una had so little.~~ ^**~~A copy would not be the same thing at all a soulless thing~~ Surely it was not selfishness to keep it. ~~But Un~~**^ ^**A copy would be such a soulless thing.**^ But Una – Una had so little – and her eyes were the eyes of a woman stricken to the heart, who ~~could~~ ^**yet must**^ not cry out or ask for sympathy.

"Una, would you like to have this letter – to keep?" she asked slowly.

"Yes – if you can give it to me," Una ~~answered through her white lips.~~ ^**said**^ dully.

"Then – you may have it," said Rilla hurriedly.

~~"I'll keep a copy~~

"Thank you," said Una. ^**It was all she said.**^ ^**Note Q10**^

~~She~~ ^**Una**^ took the letter and when Rilla had gone she pressed it against her ^**~~white~~ lonely**^ lips. Una knew that love would never come into her life now – it was buried for ever under the blood-stained soil "Somewhere in France." No one but herself – and ~~peh~~ perhaps Rilla – knew it – would ever know it. She had no right in the eyes of her world to grieve. She must hide and bear her long pain as best she could ^**– alone**^. But she, too, would keep faith.

Chapter 24

Mary Is Just In Time

The autumn of 1917 was a bitter season for ~~the~~ Ingleside. Mrs. Blythe's ~~slowly struggled back to health and Rilla's~~ return to health was slow, and sorrow and loneliness ~~was~~ ^**were**^ in ~~every~~ ^**all**^ hearts. Every one tried to hide it from the others and "carry on" cheerfully. Rilla laughed a good deal. Nobody at Ingleside was deceived by her laughter; it came from her lips only, never from her heart. But outsiders said some people got over trouble very easily, and Irene Howard ~~had all that she was so glad to see that said~~ ^**remarked**^ that she was surprised to find how shallow Rilla Blythe ^**really**^ was~~; after are. Rilla~~.

"Why," ~~^she confided to Olive Kirk^~~ after all her pose of being so devoted to Walter, she ~~didn't~~ ^**doesn't**^ seem to mind his death at all. Nobody ~~had~~ ^**has**^ ever seen her shed a tear or heard her mention his name. She ~~had~~ ^**has**^ evidently quite forgotten him. Poor fellow~~. She hadn't even put on mourning for him – and he was so splendid and fine and brave~~ – you'd really think his family would feel it more. I spoke of him to Rilla ^**at**^ the last ~~day the~~ Junior Red meeting ^**Note K8**^ and said life could ever be just the same to me again, now that Walter had gone – we were such friends, you ~~kmo~~ know – why I was the very first person he told about having enlisted – and Rilla ~~just went on curring out said,~~ ^**answered,**^ as coolly and indifferently as if she were speaking of an entire stranger, 'He was just one of many fine and splendid boys who have given everything for their country.' Well, I wish I could take things as calmly – but I'm not made like that. I'm so sensitive – things hurt me terribly – I really never get over them. I asked Rilla right out why she didn't put on ~~war~~ mourning for Walter. She said her mother didn't wish it. ~~Well, we all k~~ But every one is talking about it."

"Rilla doesn't wear colours – nothing but white," protested ~~Olive, who thought Irene was~~ Betty ~~Clow~~ Meade.

"White becomes her better than anything else," said Irene significantly. "And we all know black doesn't suit her complexion at all. But of course I'm not saying that is the reason she doesn't wear it. Only, it's funny. If my brother had died I'd have gone into deep mourning. I wouldn't have had the heart for anything else. I confess I'm disappointed in Rilla Blythe."~~" I thought~~

~~Rilla~~ "I am not, then," cried Betty ~~Clow~~ ^**Meade**^, loyally. "I think Rilla is just a wonderful girl. A few years ago ^**I admit**^ I did think she was rather too vain and gigglesome, but now she is nothing of the sort. I don't think there is a girl in the Glen who is so unselfish and plucky as Rilla, or who has 'done her bit' ~~as~~ ^**as**^ thoroughly and patiently. Our Junior Red Cross would have gone on the rocks a dozen times if it hadn't been for her tact and perseverance and enthusiasm – you know that perfectly well, Irene."

"Why, I am not running Rilla down," said Irene, opening her eyes widely. "It was only her lack of feeling I was criticizing. I suppose she can't help ~~that~~ ^**it**^. Of course, she's a born manager – everyone knows that. She's very fond of managing, too – ^**and**^ people like that are very necessary I admit. So don't look at me as if I'd said something perfectly dreadful, Betty, please. I'm quite willing to ~~admit~~ ^**agree**^ that Rilla Blythe is the embodiment of all the virtues, if that will please you. And no doubt it is a virtue to ~~have ^**be able**^ perfect control of be able~~ be quite unmoved by things that would crush most people."

~~Rilla heard some of the things Irene said~~ ^**Some of Irene's remarks were reported to Rilla;**^ but they did not hurt her as they would once have done. They didn't matter, that was all. ~~To help mother and Susan and father – to look after Jims – to~~ Life was too big ~~and~~ to leave room for pettiness. She had a pact to keep and a work to do; and through the long hard days and weeks of that disastrous autumn she was faithful to her task. The war news was consistently bad, for Germany marched from victory to victory over poor Roumania ~~and~~.

~~"Furrine~~ "Foreigners – foreigners," Susan muttered dubiously. "Russians or Roumanians or whatever they may be, they are foreigners and you cannot tie to them. But after Verdun I shall not give up hope. And can you tell me, Mrs. Dr. dear, if the Dobruja is a river or a mountain range, or a condition of the atmosphere?"

The Presidential election in the ~~U.S.~~ ^**United States**^ came off in November, and Susan was red-hot over that – and quite apologetic for her excitement.

"I never thought ~~I'd~~ I would live to see the day when I would be interested in a Yankee election, Mrs. Dr. dear. It only goes to show ~~me~~ ^~~**one**~~ **we**^ can never know what we will come to in this world and therefore we should not be proud."

Susan stayed up late on the evening of the eleventh, ostensibly to finish a pair of socks. But she 'phoned down to Carter Flagg's store at intervals, and when the first report came through that Hughes had been elected she stalked solemnly upstairs to Mrs. Blythe's room and announced it in a thrilling whisper ^**from the foot of the bed**^.

"I thought if you were not asleep you would be interested in knowing it. I believe it is for the best. Perhaps he will just fall to writing notes, too, Mrs. Dr. dear, but I hope for better things. I never was very partial to whiskers, but one cannot have everything."

When news came in the morning that after all Wilson was re-elected, Susan ~~switched about to~~ ^**tacked to catch**^ another breeze of optimism.

"Well, better a fool you know than a fool you ~~don't k~~ do not know, as the old proverb has it," she remarked cheerfully. "Not that I hold Woodrow to be a fool by any means, though by times you would not think he has the sense he was born with. But he is a good letter writer at least, and we do not know if the Hughes man is even that. All things being considered I commend the Yankees. They have shown good sense and I do not mind admitting it. Cousin Sophia wanted them to elect Roosevelt, and is much disgruntled because they would not give him a chance. I had a hankering for him myself, but we must believe that Providence overrules these matters and ~~so we must~~ be satisfied – though what the Almighty means in this ~~matter~~ ^**affair**^ of Roumania I cannot fathom – saying it with all reverence." ~~It keeps me so worked up.~~

~~But~~ Susan fathomed it – or thought she did – when the Asquith ministry went down and Lloyd George became Premier.

"Mrs. Dr. dear, Lloyd George is at the helm at last. ^**I have been praying for this for many a day.**^ Now we shall soon see a blessed change. It took the Roumanian disaster to bring it about, no less, and that is the meaning of it, though I could not see it before. There will be no more shilly-shallying. I consider that the war is as good as won, and that I shall tie to, whether Bucharest falls or not."

Bucharest did fall – and Germany proposed peace negotiations. Whereat Susan scornfully turned a deaf ear and ^**absolutely**^ refused to listen to ~~her~~ ^**such**^ proposals ~~at all~~. ~~She was~~ When President Wilson ~~wrote~~ ^**sent**^ his famous December peace note Susan's ~~was~~ ^~~**became**~~ **waxed**^ violently sarcastic.

"Woodrow Wilson is going to ~~try to~~ make peace, I understand. First Henry Ford had a try at it and now comes Wilson. But peace is not made with ink, Woodrow, and that you may tie to," said Susan, apostrophizing the unlucky President out of the kitchen window nearest the United States. "Lloyd George's speech will tell the Kaiser what is what, and you may keep your peace screeds at home and save postage."

"What a pity President Wilson can't hear you, Susan," said Rilla slyly.

"Indeed, Rilla dear, it is a pity that he has no one near him to give him ~~sensible~~ ^**good**^ advice, as it is clear he has not, in all those Democrats and Republicans," ~~We may well be thankful that we have no such things in Canada. A Conservative I was born and a Conservative I hope to die and my own opinion is that Sir Robert Bordon is~~ retorted Susan ~~scornfully~~. "I do not know the difference between them, for the politics of the Yankees is ~~something I cannot see through~~ ^**a puzzle I cannot solve,**^ study ~~them~~ ^**it**^ as I may. But as far as ~~common sense~~ ^**seeing through a grindstone**^ goes, I am afraid –" Susan shook her head dubiously, "that they are all tarred with the same brush."

"I am thankful Christmas is over," Rilla wrote in her diary during the last week of a stormy December. "We had dreaded it so – the first Christmas since Courcelette. But we had all the Merediths down for dinner and nobody tried to be gay or cheerful~~, but just quiet and~~. We were ^**all**^ just quiet and friendly, and that helped. Then, too, I was so thankful that Jims had got ~~quite well again~~ ^**better**^ – so thankful that I almost felt glad – almost but not quite. I wonder if I shall ever feel really glad over anything again. It seems as if gladness were killed in me – shot down by the same bullet that pierced Walter's heart. Perhaps some day a new kind of gladness will be born in my soul – but the old kind will never live again.

~~Ten days before Ch~~

"Winter set in awfully early this year. Ten days before Christmas we had a big snowstorm – at least we thought it big at the time. As it happened, it was only a prelude to the real performance. It was fine the next day, and Ingleside and Rainbow Valley were wonderful, with the trees all covered with snow, and big drifts everywhere, carved into the most fantastic shapes by the chisel of the northeast wind. Father and mother went up to Avonlea. Father thought the change would do mother good, and they wanted to see poor Aunt Diana, whose ~~son~~ ^**son Jack**^ had been seriously wounded a short time before. They left ~~me~~ Susan and me to keep house, and father expected to be back the next day. But he never got back for a week ~~– and in that week~~. That night it began to storm again, and it stormed unbrokenly for four days. It was the worst and longest storm that P. E. Island has known for years. Everything was disorganized – the roads were completely choked up, the trains blockaded, and the telephone wires put entirely out of commission.

"And ^**then**^ Jims ~~took croup – the real true croup.~~ ^~~**took croup took ill**~~^ took ill.

"He had a little cold when father and mother went away, and he kept getting worse for a couple of days, but it didn't occur to me that there was danger of anything serious. I never even took his temperature, and I can't forgive myself. Because it was ~~just~~ ^**sheer**^ carelessness. The truth is I had slumped just then. Mother was away, so I let myself go. All at once I was tired of keeping up and pretending to be brave and cheerful, and I just gave up for a few days and spent most of the time lying on my face on my bed, crying. I neglected Jims – that is the hateful truth – I was cowardly and false to what I promised Walter – and if Jims had died I could never have forgiven myself.

"Then, the third night after father and mother went away, Jims suddenly got worse – oh, so much worse – ~~just~~ all at once. Susan and I were all alone. ~~Miss Oliver~~ ^**Gertrude**^ had been at Lowbridge when the storm began and had never got back. At first we were not much alarmed. Jims has had several bouts of ~~cr~~ croup and Susan and Morgan and I have always brought him through without much trouble. But it wasn't very long before we were dreadfully ~~scared~~ ^**alarmed**^.

"'I never saw croup like this before,' said Susan.

"As for me, I knew, ~~at last~~ ^**when it was too late,**^ what kind of croup it was. I knew it was not the ^**ordinary croup –**^ 'false croup' as doctors call it – but the 'true' croup – ~~and~~ I knew that it was a deadly and dangerous thing. And father was away and there was no doctor nearer than Lowbridge – and ~~the 'phone was no good~~ ^**we could not 'phone**^ – and neither horse nor man could get through the drifts that night.

^**"Gallant little Jims put up a good fight for his life,**^ – Susan and I tried every remedy we could ^**think of or find in father's books,**^ but ~~Jims~~ ^**he**^ continued to grow worse. It was heart-rending to see and hear him. He gasped so horribly for breath – the poor little soul – and his face turned a dreadful bluish colour and had such an agonized expression ^**Note L8**^ – as if he were appealing to us to help him somehow. ~~It~~ I found myself thinking that the boys who had been gassed at the front must have looked like that, and the thought haunted me amid all my dread and misery over Jims. And all the time the ~~dreadful~~ ^**fatal**^ membrane in his wee throat grew and thickened and he couldn't ~~cough~~ ^**get**^ it up.

"Oh, I was just wild! I never realized ~~just~~ how dear Jims was to me until that moment. And I felt so utterly helpless. It was just as if we were fighting a relentless foe without any real weapons. ~~Poultice and doses did no good.~~ ^**Note P10**^

[*This is the second use of the indicator "P10" in the manuscript of the text*]

"And then Susan gave up ~~and wrung her hands~~.

"'We cannot save him – oh, if your father was here – look at him, the poor little fellow! I know not what to do.[22]'

"I looked at Jims and I thought he was dying. Susan was holding ~~up~~ him up in his crib to give him a better chance for breath, but it didn't seem as if he could breathe at all. My little war baby, with his dear ways and sweet roguish face, was choking to death before my very eyes, and I couldn't ~~save~~ help him. I threw down the hot poultice I had ready in despair. Of what use was it? Jims was dying, and it was my fault – I hadn't been careful enough!

"Just then – at eleven o'clock at night – the door bell rang. Such a ring – it pealed all over the house above the roar of the storm. Susan couldn't go – she dared not lay Jims down – so I rushed downstairs. In the hall I paused just a minute – I was suddenly overcome by an absurd dread. I thought of a weird story ~~Miss Oliver~~ ^**Gertrude**^ had told me once. An aunt of hers was alone in a house one night with her sick husband. She heard a knock at the door. And when she went and opened it – there was nothing there – nothing that could be seen, at least. But when she opened the door a deadly cold wind blew ~~right~~ in and seemed to sweep past her right up the stairs, although it was a calm, warm summer night outside. ~~and~~ Immediately she heard a cry ~~and~~ she ran upstairs – and her husband was dead. And she always believed, so ~~Miss Oliver~~ ^**Gertrude**^ said, that when she opened that door she let Death in.

"It was so ridiculous of me to feel so frightened. But I was distracted and worn out, and I simply felt for a moment that I dared not open the door – that death was waiting outside. Then I remembered that I had no time to waste – must not be so foolish – I sprang forward and opened the door.

"Certainly a cold wind did blow in and filled the hall with a whirl of snow. But there on the threshold stood a form of flesh and blood

^[*Note*] **R10**^ ~~**^– Mary Vance, coated from head to foot with snow ^– ^and she brought Life, and not Death, with her.^** I just stared at her. I didn't know **^that then – I just stared at her –^**~~

~~They did. 'I haven't been turned out," grinned Mary, ^as she stepped in and shut the door^. 'I came got came up to Carter Flagg's two days ago and I've been stormed-stayed there ever since. But I simply couldn't stand old Mrs. Carter somehow all this evening I had a feeling that I ought to come up here.~~ Abbie Flagg got on ~~my nerves~~ and tonight I just made up my mind to come up here. I thought I could wade ~~so~~ this far, but I can tell you it was as much as a bargain. Once I thought I was stuck for keeps. Ain't it an awful night?'

"I ~~resurs~~ came to myself and knew I must hurry upstairs. I explained as quickly as I could to Mary, and left her trying to brush the snow off. Upstairs I found that Jims was over that paroxysm, ~~and~~ but almost as soon as I got back to the room he was in the grip of another. I hung over him and wrung my ands. I was completely 'no good' – I couldn't do anything but moan and cry – oh, how ashamed I am when I think of it; and yet what could I do – we had tried everything we knew – and then all at once I heard Mary Vance saying ^**loudly**^ behind me,

"'Why, that child is dying!'

"I whirled around. Didn't I know he was dying – my little Jims! I could have thrown Mary Vance out of the door or the window – anywhere – at that moment. There she stood, cool and composed, looking down at my baby, ^**with those, weird white eyes of hers,**^ as she might look at a choking kitten. I had always disliked Mary Vance – and just then I hated her.

"'We have tried everything,"' said poor Susan dully. "'It is not ordinary croup."'

"'No, it's the dipthery croup,"' said Mary briskly, snatching up an apron. "'And there's mighty little time to lose – but I know what to do. When I lived over harbour with Mrs. Wiley, years ago, Will Crawford's ~~baby~~ kid died of dipthery croup, in spite of two doctors. And when old Aunt ~~Mary Crawford~~ ^**Christina MacAllister**^ heard of it ^**Note N8**^ she said she could have saved him with her grandmother's remedy if she'd been there. She told Mrs. Riley what it was and I've never forgot it. I've the greatest memory ever – a thing just lies in the back of my head till the time comes to use it. Got any sulphur in the house, Susan?"'

"Yes, we had sulphur. Susan went down with Mary to get it, and I held Jims. I hadn't any hope – not the least. Mary Vance might brag as she liked – she was always bragging – but I didn't believe any grandmother's remedy could save Jims now. Presently Mary came back. She had tied a piece of thick flannel over her mouth and nose, and she carried Susan's old tin chip pan, half full of burning coals.

"'You watch me,"' she said boastfully. "'I've never done this but I know how it's done. It's kill or cure – but that child is dying anyway."'

"She sprinkled a spoonful of sulphur over the coals; and then she picked up Jims, turned him over, and held him face downward, right over those choking, blinding fumes. I don't know why I didn't spring forward and snatch him away. Susan says it was because it was foreordained that I shouldn't, and I think she is right, because it did really seem that I was powerless to move. Susan herself seemed transfixed, watching Mary from the doorway. Jims writhed in those big, firm, capable hands of Mary – oh yes, she is capable all right ~~– and choked and coughed –~~ ~~^**choked and wheezed**^~~ ~~– ^and I felt that he was being tortured to death and I couldn't interfere to prevent it^ – and then all at once he coughed ^**up**^ the membrane that was killing him up.~~ ^**Note R10**^ [*This is the second use of the indicator "R10" in the manuscript of the text.*] Mary turned him over and laid him back on his bed. He was white as marble and the tears were pouring out of his brown eyes – but that awful livid look was gone from his face and he could breathe quite easily.

"'Wasn't that some trick?' said Mary gaily. ~~"Sulphur'll kill any germ it can get at.~~ 'I hadn't any idea how it would work, but I just took a chance. I'll smoke his throat out again once or twice before morning, just to kill all the germs, but you'll see he'll be all right now.”'

"Jims went right to sleep – real sleep, not coma, as I feared at first. Mary 'smoked him,' as she called it, twice ~~time~~ ^**more**^ through the night, and at daylight his throat was perfectly clear and his temperature was almost normal. When I ^**had**^ made sure of that I turned and looked at Mary Vance. She was sitting on the lounge laying down the law to Susan on some subject about which Susan must have known forty times as much as she did. But I didn't mind how much law she laid down or how much she bragged. She had a right to brag – she ^**had dared to do what I would never have dared, and**^ had saved ~~Jims' life~~ Jims from a horrible death. It didn't matter any more that she had once chased me through the Glen with a codfish – it didn't matter that she had smeared goose-grease all over my dream of romance the night of the light house dance – it didn't matter that she thought she knew more than anybody else ^**and always rubbed it in**^ – I would never dislike Mary Vance again. I went over to her and kissed her.

"'What's up now?”' she said.

"'Nothing – only I'm so grateful to you, Mary.'

"'Well, I think you ought to be, that's a fact. You two would have let that baby die on your hands if I hadn't happened along,”' said Mary, just beaming with complacency. She got Susan and me a tip-top breakfast and made us eat it, and 'bossed the life out of us,' as Susan says, for two ~~^**three**^~~ days, ~~when~~ until the roads were opened so that she could get home. Jims was almost well by that time and father turned up. He heard our tale without saying much. Father is rather scornful generally about what he calls ~~"Old Wive's Remedies"~~ 'old wives' remedies.' He laughed a little and said, 'After this, Mary Vance will expect me to call her in for consultation in all my serious cases.' ~~That girl has a nerve.~~

"So ~~Chr I was~~ Christmas was not so hard as I expected it to be; and now the New Year is coming – and we are still hoping for the 'Big Push' that will end the war – and Little Dog Monday is getting stiff and rheumatic from his cold vigils, but still he 'carries on.' ^**Note M8**^ ~~From For~~ ^**~~And Shirley reads all the aviation stuff he can find.~~**^ Oh, nineteen-seventeen, what will you bring?"

Chapter 25

Shirley Goes

"No, Woodrow, there will be no peace without victory," said Susan, sticking her knitting needle viciously through President Wilson's name in the newspaper column. "We Canadians mean to have peace and victory, too. You, if it pleases you, Woodrow, can have the peace without the victory" – and Susan stalked off to bed with the comfortable consciousness of having got the better of the argument with the President. But a ~~week later~~ few ~~days~~ ~~^**evenings**^~~ ^^**days**^^ later she ~~burst into the livin~~ rushed to Mrs. Blythe in red-hot excitement.

"Mrs. Dr. dear, what do you think? A 'phone message has just come through from Charlottetown that Woodrow Wilson has sent that German ambassador man to the right about ^**at last**^. They tell me that means war. So I begin to think that Woodrow's heart is in the right place after all, wherever his head may be, and I am going to commandeer a little sugar and celebrate the occasion with some fudge, despite the howls of the Food Board. I thought that submarine business would bring things to a crisis. ^**I told Cousin Sophia so when she said it was the beginning of the end for the Allies.**^"

"Don't let the doctor hear of the fudge, Susan," said Anne, with a smile. "You know he has laid down very strict rules for us along the lines of economy the government has asked for."

"Yes, Mrs. Dr. dear, and a man should be master in his own household, and his women folk should bow to his decrees. ^**Note Q8**^ ~~B~~but one can exercise a little gumption on the quiet now and then. Shirley was wishing for some of my fudge the other day – the Susan ~~bra~~ brand, as he called it – and I said 'The first victory there is to celebrate I shall make you some.' I consider this news quite equal to a victory, and what the doctor does not know will never ~~hurt~~ ^**grieve**^ him. I take the whole responsibility, Mrs. Dr. dear, so do not you ~~w~~ vex your conscience."

Susan ~~was spoiling~~ ^**spoiled**^ Shirley shamelessly that winter. He came home from Queen's every weekend and Susan had all his favourite dishes for him, in so far as she could evade or wheedle the doctor, and waited on him hand and foot. Though she talked war constantly to everyone else she never mentioned it to him or before him; but she watched him like a cat watching a mouse; and when the German retreat from the Bapaume salient began and continued, Susan's exultation was linked up with something deeper than anything she expressed. Surely the end was in sight – would come now before – anyone else – could go.

"Things are coming our way at last. ~~We have out Kut and~~ We have got ~~them~~ ^**the Germans**^ on the run," ~~The Allies will be in Berlin by May," she said.~~ ^**she ~~said~~ boasted.**^

"The Germans are just luring them on," said Cousin Sophia. "That man Simonds says their retreat has put the allies in a ~~bad mess."~~ hole."

"That man Simonds has said more than he will ever live to ~~mad~~ see made good," retorted Susan. "I do not worry myself about any Yankee's opinion as long as Lloyd George is ~~at the helm~~ ^**Premier of England**^. He will not be bamboozled and that and that you may tie to. We have got Kut and Bagdad back, as I always told you we would, Sophia ~~Aa~~ Crawford, and you will see that the Allies will be in Berlin by ~~Ma~~ June – and the Russians, too, since they have got rid of the Czar. That, in my opinion was a good piece of work."

"Time will show if it is," said Cousin Sophia, who would have been very indignant if anyone had told her that she would rather see Susan put to shame as a seer, than a successful overthrow of tyranny, ^**or even the march of the Allies down Unter den Linden.**^ But then the woes of the Russian people were quite unknown to Cousin Sophia, while this aggravating, optimistic Susan was ~~a constant~~ an ever-present thorn in her side.

Just at that moment Shirley was sitting on the edge of the table in the ~~big~~ living-room, swinging his legs – a brown, ruddy, wholesome lad, from top to toe, every inch of him – and saying coolly,

"Mother and dad, ^**I was eighteen last Monday.**^ Don't you think it's about time I joined up?"

The pale mother looked at him.

"Two of my sons have gone and one will never return. Must I give you too, Shirley?"

The age-old cry – "Joseph is not and Simeon is not; and ye will take Benjamin away." How the mothers of the Great War echoed the old Patriarch's moan of ~~five~~ so many ~~th~~ centuries agone!

"You wouldn't have me a slacker, mother? I can get into the flying corps. What say, dad?"

The doctor's hands ~~trembled a little~~ ^**were not quite steady**^ as he folded up the powders he was concocting for ~~old Mrs.~~ ^**Abbie**^ Flagg's ~~indigestion~~ ^**rheumatism**^. He had known this moment was coming, yet he was not ~~quite~~ ^**altogether**^ prepared for it. ~~But~~ He answered ~~calmly~~ ^**slowly**^,

"I won't try to hold you back from what you believe to be your duty. But you must not go unless your mother says you may." ~~That is for~~

Shirley said nothing more. He ~~sat and waited~~ was not a lad of many words. ~~He sat Jem had gone radiantly, as to high adventure; Walter had gone in a flame of sacrifice; Shirley was going in a cool business like way mood of doing something, rather dirty and disagreeable, that had just got to be done.~~ Anne did not say anything more just then, either. She was thinking of little Joyce's ~~who in~~ grave in the old burying-ground over harbor – little Joyce who would have been a woman now, had she lived – ~~of Walter's gr~~ of the white cross in France and the splendid gray eyes of the little boy who had ~~learned his fir~~ been taught his first lessons of duty ^**and loyalty**^ at her knee –of Jem in the ^**terrible**^ trenches – of Nan and Di and Rilla, ~~waiting~~ ^**Note T8**^ – and she wondered if she could bear any more. She thought not; surely she had given enough.

Yet that night she ~~went~~ told Shirley that he ~~could~~ ^**might**^ go.

They did not tell Susan right away. She did not know it until, a few days later, Shirley presented himself ~~before her~~ in her kitchen in his aviation uniform. Susan didn't make half the fuss she had made when Jem and Walter had gone. She said stonily,

"So they're going to take you, too."

"Take me? No. I'm going, Susan – got to."

Susan sat down by the table, folded her knotted old hands – that had grown warped and twisted working for the Ingleside children – to still their shaking, and said:

"Yes, you must go. I did not see once why such things must be, but

I can see now."

"You're a brick, Susan," said Shirley. He was relieved that she took it so coolly – he had been a little bit afraid, with a boy's ~~horor~~ horror of "a scene." He went out whistling gaily; but half an hour later, when pale Anne Blythe came in, Susan was still sitting there, ~~with~~ ^**with unwashed dishes around her.**^

"Mrs. Dr. dear," said Susan, ~~drear~~ making an admission she would once have died rather than make, "I feel very old.[22] Jem and Walter were yours but Shirley is mine. And I cannot bear to think of him flying – and ~~era~~ his machine crashing down – the life crushed out of his body – the dear little body I nursed and cuddled when he was a wee baby."

"Susan – don't," cried Anne.

"Oh, Mrs. Dr. dear, I beg your pardon. I ought not to have said anything like that out loud. I sometimes forget that I resolved to be a heroine. This – this has shaken me a little. But I will not forget myself again. Only if things do not go as smoothly ^**as usual**^ in the kitchen for a few days ~~as~~ I hope you will make due allowance for me. At least," said poor Susan, forcing a grim smile in a desperate effort to recover lost standing, "at least flying is a clean job. He will not get so dirty and messed up as he would in the trenches, and that is well, for he has always been a tidy ~~lad~~ child."

So Shirley went – not radiantly, as to a high adventure, like Jem, not in a white flame of sacrifice, like Walter, but in a cool, business-like mood, as of one doing something, rather dirty and disagreeable, that had just got to be done. He kissed Susan for the first time since he was five years old, and said, "Good-bye, Susan – Mother Susan."

"My little brown boy – my little brown boy," said Susan ~~smiling gallantly ^**painfully**~~^. "I wonder," she thought bitterly, as she looked at the doctor's sorrowful face, "if you remember how you spanked him once when he was a baby. I am thankful I have nothing like that on my conscience now."

The doctor did not remember the old ~~disapline~~ ^**discipline**^. But before he put on his hat to go out on his round of calls he stood for a moment in the great silent living room that had once been full of children's laughter.

~~"Our house is left unto us desolate," he said aloud.~~ "Our last son – our last son," ^**he said aloud.**^ "– a good, sturdy, sensible lad, too. Always reminded me of my father. ~~'Our house is left unto us desolate.'~~ I suppose I ought to be proud that he wanted to go – I was proud when Jem [*Error in ms: page number "386" appears on two consecutive pages*] went – even when Walter went – but – 'our house is left us desolate.'"

"I have been thinking, doctor," old Highland Sandy of the Upper Glen said to him that afternoon, "that your house will be seeming very big the day."

Highland Sandy's quaint phrase struck the doctor as ~~very~~ ^**perfectly**^ expressive. Ingleside did seem very big and empty that night. Yet Shirley had been away all winter except for week ends, and had always been a quiet fellow even when home. Was it because he ~~was the last day~~ ^**had been the only one left**^ that his going seemed to leave such a huge blank – that every room seemed vacant and deserted – that the very ~~garden~~ trees on the lawn seemed to be ~~conferring with each other~~ trying to comfort each other with caresses of freshly-budding boughs for the loss of the last of the ^**little**^ lads who had ~~played~~ ^**romped**^ under them in childhood?

Susan ~~wo had~~ worked very hard all day and late into the night. When she had wound the kitchen clock and put Dr. Jekyll out, ^**none too gently,**^ she stood for a little while on the doorstep, looking down the Glen, which lay tranced in faint, silvery light from a sinking young moon. But Susan did not see the familiar hills and harbor. She was looking at the aviation camp in Kingsport where Shirley was that night.

"He called me 'Mother Susan,'" she ~~said aloud~~ was thinking. ^**Note O8**^ ~~"Well, all our men folk etc.~~

The moon sank lower into ^**a**^ black cloud in the west, ~~and the~~ the Glen went out in an eclipse of sudden shadow ~~– Susan stood there for quite a long time, a gaunt, unlovely,~~ – and thousands of miles away the Canadian boys in khaki ~~had taken Vim were in possession ^**had come**^ of Vimy Ridge.~~ ^**– the ~~dead~~ living and the dead –**^ were in possession ^**of the Vimy Ridge.**^

Vimy Ridge is a name written in crimson and gold on the Canadian annals of the Great War. "The British couldn't take it and the French couldn't take it," said a German prisoner to his captors, "but you Canadians are such fools that you don't know when a place can't be taken!" ^**So the "fools" took it – and paid the price.**^

Jerry Meredith was seriously wounded at Vimy Ridge – shot in the back, the telegram said.

"Poor Nan," said ~~Anne~~ Mrs. Blythe, when the news came. She thought of her own happy girlhood at old Green Gables. There had been no tragedy like this in it. How the girls of to-day had to suffer! When Nan came home from Redmond ~~three~~ two weeks later her face showed what those weeks had meant to her. ~~But~~ John Meredith, too, seemed to have grown old ~~in~~ suddenly in them. Faith did not come home; she ~~^**had graduated**^~~ was ~~already~~ on her way across the Atlantic as a V.A.D. Di had ~~wrung~~ ^**tried to ~~wring~~ wring**^ from her father consent to her going also, but had been told that for her mother's sake it could not be given. So Di, after a flying visit home, went back to her Red Cross work in Kingsport.

The mayflowers bloomed in the secret ~~nork~~ nooks of Rainbow Valley. Rilla was watching for them~~, near~~. Jem had once taken his mother the earliest mayflowers; Walter brought them to her when Jem was gone; last spring Shirley had sought them out for her; now, Rilla thought she must take the boys' place in this. But before she had discovered any, Bruce Meredith came to Ingleside one twilight with his hands full of delicate pink ~~buds~~ sprays. He ~~came~~ ^**stalked**^ up the steps of the veranda and laid them ~~shlyly~~ on ~~Anne~~ ^**Mrs.**^ Blythe's lap.

~~"I thought~~

"Because ~~Shirley~~ ^~~**Jem**~~ **Shirley**^ isn't here to bring them," he said in his funny, shy, blunt way.

"And you thought of this – you darling," said Anne, her lips quivering, as she looked at the stocky, black-browed little chap, standing before her, with his ~~square paws~~ ^**hands**^ thrust into his pockets.

"I wrote Jem to-day and told him not to worry 'bout you not getting your Mayflowers," said Bruce seriously, ~~"'cause~~ 'cause I'd see to that. ~~This is my birthday~~ And I told him I would be ten pretty soon now, so it won't be very long before I'll be eighteen, and then ~~I'd~~ ^**I'll**^ go to help him fight,[22] and maybe ^**let him**^ come home for a rest while I took his place. ^**Note P8**^ Do you know,

~~You blessed child," said Susan, you won't ^**will never**^ have to go.~~

~~The Kaiser cannot possibly last as long as that."~~

Mrs. Blyth," – Bruce ~~spoke in a low, confidential~~ ^**dropped to a "whispering"**^ tone, edging a little nearer to Anne – "what I would like to do to the Kaiser if I could."

~~"Wo~~ "What would you like to do, laddie?"

"Norman Reese said in school to-day that he would like to tie the Kaiser to a tree and set ~~Mr. John Warren's~~ cross dogs to worrying him," said Bruce gravely. "And Emily ~~Howard~~ Flagg said she would like to put him in a cage and poke sharp things into him. And they all said things like that. But Mrs. Blythe –" Bruce took a little square paw out of his pocket and put it earnestly on Anne's knee – "I would like to ~~make~~ ^**turn**^ the Kaiser into a good man – a very good man – ~~if~~ all at once if I could. That is what I would do. Don't you think, Mrs. Blythe, that would be the very worstest punishment of all?"

"Bless the child," said Susan, "how do you make out that would be any kind of a punishment for that wicked fiend?"

"Don't you see," said Bruce, looking levelly at Susan, out of his blackly blue eyes, "if he was turned into a good man he would understand how dreadful the things he has done are, and he would feel so terrible about it that he would be more unhappy and miserable than he could ever be in any other way. He would feel just awful – and he would go on feeling like that forever. Yes" – Bruce clenched his hands and ~~nodded his head clicked his white teeth together~~ nodded his head emphatically, "yes, I would make the Kaiser a good man – that is what I would do – it would serve him 'zackly right."

Chapter 26

Susan Has a Proposal of Marriage

An aeroplane was flying over Glen St. Mary, like a great bird poised against ~~the~~ a western sky ~~so clear ^**that was**~~ **– a sky so**^ clear and of such a pale, silvery yellow, ~~gav~~ that it gave an impression of a vast, wind-freshened space of freedom. The little group on the Ingleside lawn looked up at it with fascinated eyes, although it was by no means an unusual thing to see ~~a hovering~~ an occasional hovering plane that summer. Susan was always intensely excited. Who knew but that it might be Shirley away up there in the clouds, flying over to the Island from Kingsport? But Shirley had gone overseas ^**now**^, so Susan was not so keenly interested in this particular ~~aeoplane~~ aeroplane and its pilot. Nevertheless, she looked at it with awe.

"I wonder, Mrs. Dr. dear," she said solemnly, "what the old folks down there in the graveyard would think if they could rise out of their graves for one moment and behold that sight. I am sure my father would disapprove of it, for he was a man who did not believe in new-fangled ideas of any sort. He always ~~reaped his harvest~~ ^**cut his grain**^ with a reaping hook to the day of his death. A mower he would not have. What was good enough for his father was good enough for him, he used to say. ~~I hope it is in I do not~~ I hope it is not unfilial to ~~think~~ ^**say**^ that I think he was wrong in that point of view, but I am not sure I ^**go so far as to**^ approve of aeroplanes, though they may be a military necessity. If the Almighty had meant us to fly he would have provided us with wings. Since He did not it is plain He meant us to stick to the solid earth. At any rate, you will never see me, Mrs. Dr. dear, cavorting through the sky in an aeroplane."

"But you won't refuse ~~a dr ride~~ ^**to cavort a bit**^ in father's new automobile when it comes, will you, Susan?" teased Rilla.

"I do not expect to trust my old bones in automobiles, ^**either,**^" retorted Susan. "But I do not look upon them as some narrow-minded people do. Whiskers-on-the-Moon says the Government should be turned out of office for permitting them to run on the Island at all. He foams at the mouth, they tell me, when he sees one. The other day he saw one coming along that narrow side-road by his ~~wheat-field turnip~~ ^~~hay~~ **wheat-**^ field, and Whiskers bounded over the fence and stood right in the middle of the road, with his pitchfork. The man in the machine was an agent of some kind, and Whiskers hates agents as much as he hates automobiles. He made that ~~machine~~ ^**car**^ come to a halt, because there ~~wasn't~~ ^**was not**^ room to pass him on either side, ^**and the agent could not actually run over him**^. Then he raised his pitchfork and ~~said~~ ^**shouted**^, 'Get out of this with your devil-machine or I will run this pitchfork clean through you.[22]' And Mrs. Dr. dear, if you will believe me, that poor agent had to back his car clean out to the Lowbridge road, ^**nearly a mile,**^ Whiskers following him every step, shaking his pitchfork and bellowing insults. Now, Mrs. Dr. dear, I call such conduct unreasonable; but all the same," added Susan, with a sigh, "what with aeroplanes and automobiles and all the rest of it, this ~~world has got to be a changed place~~ Island is not what it used to be."

The aeroplane soared and dipped and circled, and soared again, until it became a mere speck far over the sunset hills.

"'With the majesty of pinion
Which the Theban eagles bear
Sailing with supreme dominion
Through the azure fields of air.'"

quoted Anne Blythe dreamily.

"I wonder," said Miss Oliver, "if humanity will be any happier because of aeroplanes. It seems to me that the sum of human happiness remains much the same from age to age, no matter how it may vary in distribution, and that all the 'many inventions' neither lessen nor increase it."

"After all, the 'kingdom of heaven is within you,'" said Mr. Meredith, gazing after the vanishing speck which symbolized man's latest victory ~~over~~ in a world-old struggle. "It does not depend on material achievements and triumphs."

"Nevertheless, an aeroplane is a fascinating thing," said the doctor. "It has always been one of humanity's favorite dreams – the dream of flying. Dream after dream comes true – or rather is made true by persevering effort ~~and~~. I should like to have a flight in an aeroplane myself."

"Shirley wrote me that he was dreadfully disappointed in his first flight," said Rilla. "He had expected to experience the sensation of ~~flying~~ soaring up from the earth ^**like a bird**^ – and instead he just had the ~~sen~~ feeling that he wasn't moving at all but that the earth was ~~just~~ dropping away under him. And the first time he went up alone he suddenly felt terribly homesick. He had never felt like that before; but all at once, he said, he felt as if he were adrift in space – ~~off the old planet altogether~~ and he had a wild desire to get back home to the old planet and the companionship of fellow creatures. He soon got over that feeling, but he says his first flight alone was a nightmare to him because of that dreadful sensation of ghastly loneliness."

~~"When I~~

The aeroplane disappeared. The doctor threw back his head with a sigh.

"When I ^**have**^ watched one of those bird-men out of sight~~," he said, "I have a feeling that I am a crawling~~ "I come back to earth with an odd feeling of being merely a crawling ~~ins~~ insect. Anne," he said, turning to his wife, "do you remember the first time I took you for a buggy ride in Avonlea – that night we went to the Carmody concert in the first fall you taught in Avonlea? I had our little black mare ^**with the white star on her forehead,**^ and a shining brand-new buggy – and I was the proudest fellow in the world, barring none. I suppose our grandson~~s~~ will be taking ~~their~~ his sweetheart~~s~~ out quite casually for an evening 'fly' in ~~their~~ his aeroplane~~s~~."

"An aeroplane won't be as nice as little Silverspot was," said Anne. "~~Machines have no personality~~ ^**A machine is simply a machine**^ – ~~and~~ ^**but**^ Silverspot, why she ~~had something like a soul,~~ ^**was a personality,**^ Gilbert. A drive behind her had something in it that not even a flight among sunset clouds could have. No, I don't envy my grandson~~'~~s' sweethearts after all. Mr.Meredith is right. 'The Kingdom of heaven' – and of love – and of happiness – doesn't depend on externals." ^[*Note*] **V8**^ [*Note W8 (number 2) is embedded at this point in Note V8, followed by Note W8 (number 1).*]

~~"Father," said Rilla casually,~~ ^**"By the way, father," said Rilla,**^ "I'm going to take Jack Flagg's place in his father's store for a month~~, if you don't object~~. I promised him to-day that I would, if you didn't object. Then he can help the farmers get the harvest in. I don't think I'd be much ~~of~~ use in a harvest myself – though lots of the girls are – but

I can set Jack free while I do his work. Jims isn't much bother in the day-time now, and I'll always be home at night."

"Do you think you'll like weighing out sugar and beans, and trafficking in butter and eggs?" said the doctor, twinkling.

"Probably not. That isn't the question. ~~I can do it.~~ It's just one way of doing my bit."

So Rilla went behind Mr. Flagg's counter for a month; and Susan went into Albert Crawford's oat fields ~~and ^**and**^ "built" loads and stacks~~.

"I am as good as any of them yet," she said proudly. "Not a man of them can beat me when it comes to building a ~~load~~ ^**stack**^."

^**Note U8**^

Susan, standing on a load of grain, her gray hair whipping in the breeze and her skirt kilted up to her knees for safety and convenience – no overalls for Susan, if you please – was neither a romantic nor a beautiful figure; but the spirit that animated her gaunt arms was the self-same one that captured Vimy Ridge and held the German legions back from Verdun.

It is not the least likely, however, that this consideration was the one which appealed most strongly to Mr. Pryor when he drove past one afternoon and saw Susan ~~now~~ pitching sheaves gamely.

"Smart woman that," he reflected. "Worth two of many a younger one yet. I might do worse – I might do worse. If Milgrave comes home alive I'll lose Miranda and hired housekeepers cost more than a wife and are liable to leave a man in the lurch any time. I'll think it over."

~~Mr. Pryor evidently thought it over to some purpose.~~

A week later Mrs. Blythe, coming up from the village ^**late in the afternoon,**^ paused at the gate of Ingleside in an amazement which temporarily bereft her of the power of motion. An extraordinary sight met her eyes. ~~Out of the kitchen door~~ Around the end of the kitchen burst Mr. Pryor, running as stout, pompous Mr. Pryor had not run in years, with terror imprinted on every lineament – a terror quite justifiable, for behind him, ^**like an avenging fate,**^ came Susan, with a huge, smoking iron pot grasped in her hands, and an expression in her eye that boded ill to the object of her indignation, if she should overtake him. Pursuer and pursued tore across the ~~Ingleside~~ lawn. Mr. Pryor reached the gate a few feet ahead of Susan, wrenched it open, and fled down the road, without a glance at the transfixed lady of Ingleside.

"Susan," gasped Anne.

Susan ~~stopped~~ halted in her mad career, set down her pot, and shook her fist after ~~the flying~~ Mr. Pryor, who had not ceased to run, evidently believing that Susan was still full cry after him.

"Susan, what does this mean?" demanded Anne, a little severely.

"You may well ask that, Mrs. Dr, dear," Susan replied wrathfully. "I have not been so upset in years. That – that – that pacifist has actually had the audacity to come up here and, in my own kitchen, to ask me to marry him. Him!"

Anne choked back a laugh.

"But – Susan! Couldn't you have found a – well, a less spectacular method of refusing him? Think what a ~~scandal~~ gossip this would have made if anyone had been going past and had seen such a performance."

"Indeed, Mrs. Dr. dear, you are quite right. I did not think of it because I was quite past thinking rationally. I was just clean mad. Come ~~into~~ in the house and I will tell you all about it."

Susan picked up her pot and marched into the kitchen, still trembling with wrathful excitement. ~~She set her pot~~ ^**She set her pot on the stove with a vicious thud.**^

"Wait a moment until I open all the windows to air this kitchen well, Mrs. Dr. dear~~, and I will~~. There, that is better. And I ~~will~~ ^**must**^ wash my hands, too, because I shook hands with Whiskers-on-the-Moon when he came in – not that I wanted to, but when ~~she~~ he stuck out his fat, oily hand I did not know just what else to do at the moment. I had just finished my afternoon cleaning and thanks be, everything was shining and spotless; and thought I, 'now that dye is boiling and I will get my rug rags and have them nicely out of the way before supper.' Just then a shadow fell over the floor and looking up I saw Whiskers-on-the-Moon, standing in the doorway, dressed up ~~and barbered, smelling as a basket of chips~~ ^**and looking as if he had just been starched and ironed.**^ I shook hands with him, as aforesaid, Mrs. Dr. dear, and told him you and the doctor were both away. But he said, ~~as smooth as cream,~~

"'I have come to see you, Miss Baker.'

"I was dumbfoundered, for not a ~~suspicion~~ ^**notion**^ of his design occurred to me, ~~But I ask~~ and what he wanted of me I could not imagine, ~~unless he was going to try to lure me away from you for a house-keeper.~~ But I asked him to sit down, for the sake of my own manners, and then I stood there right in the middle of the floor and ~~look~~ gazed at him as contemptuously as I could. In spite of his brazen assurance this seemed to rattle him a little; but he began trying to look sentimental at me out of his little piggy eyes, ~~Mrs. Dr. dear,~~ and all at once an awful suspicion flashed into my mind. Something told me, Mrs. Dr. dear, that I was about to receive my first proposal. I have always thought that I would like to have just one offer of marriage to reject, so that I might be able to look other women in the face, but you will not hear me bragging of *this*. I consider it an insult and if I could have thought of any way of preventing it I would. But just then, Mrs. Dr. dear, you will see I was at a disadvantage, being taken so completely by surprise. *Some* men, I am told, ~~cors~~ consider a little preliminary courting the proper thing before a proposal, if only to give fair warning of their intentions; but Whiskers-on-the-Moon probably thought it was any port in a storm for *me* and that I would jump at him. Well, he is undeceived – yes, he is undeceived, Mrs. Dr. dear. I wonder if he has stopped running yet."

"I understand that you don't feel flattered, Susan. But *couldn't* you have refused him a little more delicately~~, Susan,~~ than by chasing him off the premises in such a fashion."

"Well, maybe I might have, Mrs. Dr. dear, and I intended to, but one remark he made aggravated me beyond my powers of endurance. If it had not been for that I would not have chased him with my dye-pot, although of course I would never have dreamed of accepting him. I will tell you the whole interview. Whiskers-on-the-Moon sat down, as I have said, and right beside him on ~~the sofa Dr. Jekyll~~ ^**another chair Doc**^ was lying. The animal was pretending to be asleep but I knew very well he was not, for he ~~had~~ has been Hyde all day and Hyde never sleeps. By the way, Mrs. Dr. dear, have you noticed that that cat is far oftener Hyde than Jekyll now? The more victories Germany wins the *Hyder* he becomes. I leave you to ~~ju~~ draw your own conclusions from that. I suppose Whiskers-on-the-Moon thought he might curry favour with me by praising ~~my cat, as he supposed it to be,~~ ^**the creature, little dreaming what my real sentiments towards it were,**^ ~~S~~so he stuck out his pudgy hand and stroked Mr. Hyde's back. 'What a nice cat,' he said. The nice cat flew at him and bit him. Then it gave a fearful ~~growl~~ ^**yowl**^, and bounded out of the door. Whiskers looked after it quite ~~aghast~~ amazed. 'That is a queer kind of a varmint,' he said. ~~For once~~ I agreed with him on that point, but I was not going to let him see it. Besides, what business had he to call our cat a varmint? 'It may be a varmint or it may not,' I said, 'but it knows the difference between a Canadian and a Hun.' You would have thought, would you not, Mrs. Dr. dear, that a hint like that would have been enough for him? But it went no deeper than his skin. I saw him settling back quite comfortable, as if for a good talk, and thought I, 'If there is anything coming it may as well come soon and be done with, for with all these rags to dye before supper I have no time to waste ^**in flirting**^,' so I spoke right out. 'If you have ~~any particular busin~~ anything particular to discuss with me, Mr. Pryor, I would feel obliged if you would mention it without loss of time, because I am very busy this afternoon.' He fairly beamed at me out of that circle of red whisker, and said, 'You are a business-like woman and I agree with you. There is no use in wasting time beating around the bush. I came up here to-day to ask you to marry me.' So there it was, Mrs. Dr. dear. I had a proposal at last, after waiting sixty-four years for one. ~~^**But I assure you I had no hankering to become Mrs. Whiskers-on-the-Moon.**^~~ I just glared at that presumptuous creature and I said, 'I would not marry you if you were the last man on earth, ~~Mr.~~ ^**Josiah**^ Pryor. So there you have my answer and you can take it away forthwith.' You never saw a man so taken aback as he was, Mrs. Dr. dear. He was so flabbergasted that he just blurted out the truth. 'Why, I thought you'd be only too glad to get a chance to be married,' he said. That was when I lost my head, Mrs. Dr. dear. Do you think I had a good excuse, when a Hun and a pacifist made such an insulting remark to me? 'Go,' I thundered, and I just caught up that iron pot ~~full of boiling dye~~. I could see that he thought I had suddenly gone ~~ns~~ insane, and I suppose he considered an iron pot full of boiling dye ~~is~~ was a dangerous weapon in the hands of a lunatic. At any rate he went, and stood not upon the order of his going, as you saw for yourself. And I do not think we will see him back here proposing to us again in a hurry. No, I think he has learned that there is at least one single woman in Glen St. Mary who has no hankering to become Mrs. Whiskers-on-the-Moon."

Chapter 27

Waiting! ~~*Waiting*~~*!*

Ingleside
Nov. 1, 1917

~~"Sometimes in the dull hopelessness~~

"It is November – and the Glen is all gray and brown, except where the Lombardy poplars stand up here and there like great golden torches in the sombre landscape, although every other tree has shed its leaves. It has been very hard to keep our courage alight ~~these dull, hopeless autu~~ of late. The Caporetto disaster is a dreadful thing and not even Susan can extract much consolation out of the present state of affairs. The rest of us don't try. ~~Miss Oliver~~ ^**Gertrude**^ keeps saying desperately, "They ~~must not~~ ^**must not**^ get Venice – they ~~must not~~ ^**must not**^ get Venice," as if by saying it often enough she can prevent them. But what is to prevent them from getting Venice I cannot see. Yet, as Susan fails not to point out, there was ^**seemingly**^ nothing to prevent them from getting to Paris in 1914, yet they did not get it, and she affirms they shall not get Venice either. Oh, how I hope ~~they won't~~ ^**and pray they will not**^ – Venice the beautiful ~~city of the sea~~ ^**Queen of the Adriatic**^. Although I've never seen it I feel about it just as Byron did – I've always loved it – it has always been to me 'a fairy city of the ~~sea~~ ^heart^.' Perhaps I caught my love of it from Walter, who worshipped it. It was always one of his dreams to ~~visit it~~ ^**see Venice**^. I remember we planned once – ~~it was~~ ^**down in Rainbow Valley one evening**^ just before the war broke out – that ^**sometime**^ we would go together ~~sometime~~ to see it and float in a gondola through its ~~moonlight~~ ^**moon-lit**^ streets.

"Every fall since the war began there has been some terrible blow to our troops – ~~Amt~~ Antwerp in 1914, Serbia in 1915; last fall, Roumania, and now Italy, the worst of all. I think I would give up in despair if it were not for what Walter said in his dear last letter – that 'the dead as well as the living were fighting on our side and such an army cannot be defeated.' No it cannot. We will win in the end ~~– but perhaps even~~

~~our Venice must be part of the price paid for victory~~. I ~~won't let myself~~ ^**will not**^ doubt it for one moment. To let myself doubt would be to 'break faith.'

"We have all been campaigning furiously of late for the new Victory Loan. We Junior Reds canvassed diligently and landed several tough old customers who had at first flatly refused to invest. I – even I – tackled Whiskers-on-the-Moon. I expected a bad time and a refusal. But to my amazement ~~Whiskers~~ ^**he**^ was quite ~~amiable~~ ^**agreeable**^ and ~~agreed~~ ^**promised on the spot**^ to take a thousand dollar bond ~~on the spot~~. He may be a pacifist, but he knows a good investment when it is handed out to him. Five and a half per cent is five and a half per cent, even when a militaristic government pays it.

^"Father^, ~~I don't think~~ to tease Susan, says it was her speech at the Victory Loan Campaign meeting that converted ~~Whiskers-on-the-Moon~~ ^**Mr. Pryor**^. ~~But~~ I don't think that at all likely, since Mr. Pryor has been publicly very bitter against Susan ever since her ~~very~~ ^**quite**^ unmistakable rejection of his lover-like advances. But Susan did make a speech – and the best one made at the meeting, too. It was the first time she ever did such a thing and she vows it will be the last.

"Everybody in the Glen was at the meeting, and quite a number of speeches were made, but somehow things were a little flat and no especial enthusiasm could be worked up. Susan was quite dismayed at the lack of zeal, because she has been burningly anxious that the Island should go over the top in regard to its quota. She kept whispering ^**viciously** ~~**viciously to**~~^ to ~~Miss Oliver~~ ^**Gertrude**^ and me that there was 'no ginger' in the speeches; and when nobody went forward to subscribe to the loan at the close Susan ~~seemed~~ 'lost her head.' At least, that is ~~show~~ how she describes it herself. She ~~got right up on~~ ^**bounded to**^ her feet, her face grim and set under her ~~old~~ bonnet – Susan is the only woman in Glen St. Mary who still wears a bonnet – and said sarcastically and loudly, ^**'No doubt**^ It is much cheaper ~~no doubt~~ to talk patriotism than it is to pay for it. And we are asking charity, of course – we are asking you to lend us your money for nothing! ^**No doubt**^ ~~T~~the Kaiser will feel quite ~~elated~~ ^**downcast**^ when he hears of this meeting!" ~~no doubt.~~

"Susan has ~~or seems to know~~ an unshaken belief that the Kaiser's spies – presumably ^**represented by**^ Mr. Pryor – promptly inform him of every happening in [*Next page wrongly numbered, repeating "411".*] our Glen.

"Norman Douglas shouted out 'Hear! Hear!' and some boy at the back said, ~~'Do you think it will worry Lloyd George?'~~ 'What ~~'I stand~~ about Lloyd George?' in a tone Susan didn't like. Lloyd George is her pet hero, now that Kitchener is gone.

"'I stand behind Lloyd George every time,' retorted Susan.

"'I suppose that will hearten him up greatly,' said Warren Meade, with one of his disagreeable 'haw-haws.'

"Warren's remark was spark to powder. Susan just 'sailed in' as she puts it, and 'said her say.' She said it remarkably well, too. ^**There was no lack of 'ginger' in her speech, anyhow.**^ When Susan is warmed up she has no mean powers of oratory, and the way she trimmed those men down~~, with sarcasm and appeal as~~ was funny and wonderful and effective all at once. She said it was the likes of her, millions of her, ~~standing~~ that did stand behind Lloyd George, and did hearten him up. That was the key-note of her speech. ^**Note X8**^ Susan always vows she is no suffragette, but she gave womanhood its due that night, and she literally made those men cringe. When ~~Susan~~ ^**she**^ finished with them they were ready to eat out of her hand. She wound up by ordering them – yes, ordering them – to march up to the platform forthwith and subscribe for Victory Bonds. ^**And after wild applause,**^ ~~And~~ most of them did it, ~~Norman Douglas led if~~ too, ~~They all said they had meant to do it anyhow~~ even Warren Meade. When the total amount subscribed came out in the Charlottetown dailies the next day we found that the Glen led every district on the Island – and certainly Susan has the credit for it. She, herself, after she came home that night was quite ashamed ^**and**^ ~~of herself and said she feared she had been very unladylike; she has been rather subdued ever since and doesn't like to be teased about her 'maiden speech.'~~ evidently feared that she had been guilty of conduct unbecoming an unmarried woman: she confessed to mother that she had been 'rather unladylike.' ~~Dear old Susan! She is a perfect dynamo for patriotism and loyalty and hope and courage ^**and contempt for slackers of all kinds**^ and when she let it loose on that audience she lack in her one proud outburst she electrified them.~~

“We were all – except Susan – out for a trial ride in father’s new automobile to-night. A very good one we had, too, though we did get ingloriously ditched ~~– in a sandy ditch, two~~ at the end, owing to a certain grim old dame – ^**to wit,**^ Miss Elizabeth Carr of the Upper Glen – who wouldn’t rein her horse out to let us pass, honk as we ~~would~~ ^**might**^. Father was quite furious; but in my heart I believe I sympathized with Miss Elizabeth. If I had been a ~~maiden~~ ^**spinster**^ lady, driving along behind my own old nag, in maiden meditation fancy free, I believe I wouldn’t have lifted a rein when an obstreperous car hooted blatantly behind me. I should just have sat up as ~~dunl~~ dourly as she did and said ‘Take the ditch if you are determined to pass.’

“We did take the ditch – and got up to our axles in sand – and sat foolishly there while Miss Elizabeth clucked up her horse and rattled victoriously away form us.

“Jem will have a laugh when I write him this. He knows Miss Elizabeth of old.

“But – will – Venice – be – saved?”

November 19, 1917

“~~‘~~It is not saved yet – it is still in great danger. But the Italians are making a stand at last on the Piave line. To be sure military critics say they cannot possibly hold it and must retreat to the Adige. But Susan and ~~Miss Oliver~~ ^**Gertrude**^ and I say they must hold it, because Venice must be saved, so what are the military critics to do?

“Oh, if I could only believe that they can hold it!

“Our Canadian troops have won another great victory – they have stormed the Passchendaele Ridge and held it in the face of all counter attacks. None of our boys were in the battle – but oh, the casualty list of other people’s boys! ^[*Note*] **Y8**^

“The Russian news is bad, too – Kerensky’s government has fallen and Lenin is dictator of Russia. ~~But Susan gave up all hope in Russia several months ago.~~ Somehow, it is very hard to keep up courage in the dull hopelessness of these gray autumn days of suspense and ~~^**bod**^~~ boding news. But we are beginning to ‘get in a low,’ as old Highland Sandy says, over the approaching election. ~~Compulsory milit~~

Conscription is the real issue at stake and it will be the most exciting election we ever had. ~~Som~~ All the women ~~of proper~~ 'who have got de age' ~~as little Jo~~ ^– **to quote little Jo ~~Poirier,~~**^ Poirier, ~~says~~ and who have husbands, sons, and brothers at the front, can vote. Oh, if I were only twenty-one! ~~Gertrude~~ ^**~~Miss Oliver~~ Gertrude**^ and Susan are both furious because they can't vote.

"'It is not fair,' ~~Gertrude~~ ^**~~Miss Oliver~~ Gertrude**^ says passionately. ~~'Ma~~ 'There is Agnes Carr who can vote because her husband went. ~~He~~ She did everything she could to prevent him from going, and now she is going to vote against the Union Government. Yet I have no vote, because my man at the front is only my sweetheart and not my husband!

"As for Susan, when she reflects that she cannot vote, while a rank old pacifist like Mr. Pryor can – and will – ~~she is speechless with indignation~~ her comments are sulphurous.

"I really feel sorry for the Elliotts ^**and Crawfords**^ and MacAllisters ~~clans~~ over harbor. They have always ~~live~~ lined up in clearly divided camps of Liberal and Conservative, and now they are torn from their moorings – I know I'm mixing my metaphors dreadfully – and set hopelessly adrift. It will kill some of those old Grits to vote for Sir Robert Borden's side – and yet they have to ~~or be branded as~~ because they believe ~~in cons~~ the time has come when we must have conscription. And some poor Conservatives who are against conscription must vote for Laurier, who always has been anathema to them. ~~I really~~ Some of them are taking it terribly hard. Others seem to be in much the same attitude as Mrs. Marshall Elliott has come to be regarding Church Union.

"She was up here last night. She doesn't come as often as she used to. She is growing too old to walk this far – dear old 'Miss Cornelia.' I hate to think of her growing old – we have always loved her so and she has always been so good to us Ingleside young fry.

"She used to be so bitterly opposed to Church Union. But last night, when father told her it was practically decided, she said in a resigned tone,

"'Well, in a world where everything is being rent and torn what matters one more rending and tearing? Anyhow, compared with Germans even Methodists seem attractive to me.'

~~So I suppose some of the dyed-in-the-wools over habor feel the same regard to politics – compared to the Hums even Sir Robert~~

~~Our Junior~~

[*At the top of the next page in the manuscript (p. 417), the following fragment appears:*]

Notes 59

~~she comes regularly to our Junior Red Cross, and now she is going to vote for and she does – yes, she does – put on funny little 'married woman' airs that are hugely and quite killing. ^But^ She is the only war bride in the Glen and surely nobody can grudge her the satisfaction she gets out of it!~~

[*Apparently Montgomery picked up a sheet of paper on which she had begun to write page 59 of her "Notes" bundle, and had written on it the end of Note J8 (which is about Miranda Pryor as a bride). She then crossed this out, and proceeded with the Rilla's journal entry of November 19, 1917.*]

~~"Our Junior~~

"Our Junior R.C. goes on quite smoothly, in spite of the fact that Irene has come back to it – having ~~falling~~ ^**fallen**^ out with the Lowbridge society, I understand. She gave me a sweet little jab last meeting – about knowing me across the square in Charlottetown 'by my green velvet hat.' Everybody does knows me by that detestable and detested hat. ~~But~~ This will be my fourth season for it. Even mother wanted me to get a new one this ~~year~~ ^**fall**^; but I said, 'No.' As long as the war lasts so long do I wear that velvet hat in winter."

~~December 6,~~ Nov. 23 19~~20~~ 17

"The Piave line still holds – and ~~Russia has begun~~ General Byng has won a splendid victory at Cambrai ~~– 'the greatest victory.'~~. I did run up the flag for that – but Susan only said 'I shall set a kettle of water on the ~~stove~~ kitchen range tonight. I notice little Kitchener always has an attack of croup after any British victory. I do hope he has no pro-German blood in his veins. Nobody knows much about his father's people.'

"Jims has had a few attacks of croup this fall – just the ordinary croup – not that terrible thing he had last year. But ~~I~~ whatever blood runs in his little veins it is good, healthy blood. He is rosy and plump and curly and cute; and he ~~^**asks**^~~ ~~keeps us all in gives us all a bit of~~ says such funny ~~things~~ things and asks such comical questions. ~~Susan~~ He likes very much to sit in a special chair in the kitchen; but that is Susan's favourite chair, too, and when she wants it, out Jims must go. The last time she put him out of it he turned around and asked solemnly, 'When you are dead, Susan, can I sit in that chair?' Susan thought it quite dreadful, and I think that was when she began to feel anxiety about his possible ancestry. The other night I ~~I was bringing~~ took Jims with me for a walk down to the store. It was the first time he had ever been out ~~in a starl~~ so late at night, and ~~the first thing he said was,~~ ^**when he saw the stars ~~was~~ he exclaimed,**^ 'Oh, Willa, see the big moon and all the little moons.' ~~Another~~ And last Wednesday morning, when he woke up, my little alarm clock had stopped because I had forgotten to wind it up. Jims bounded out of his crib and ran across to me, his face quite aghast above his little blue flannel ~~pyja~~ pyjamas. ~~'Oh, Willa,' he~~ 'The clock is dead,' he gasped, 'oh Willa, the clock is dead.'

~~I don't~~ "One night he was quite angry with both Susan and me because we would not give him something he wanted very much. When he ~~plump~~ said his prayers he plumped down ~~quite~~ wrathfully, and when he came to the petition "'make me a good boy"' he tacked on ~~quite savagely~~ emphatically, 'and please make Willa and Susan good, 'cause they're not.'

"I don't go about ~~talking~~ quoting Jims's speeches to all I meet. That always bores me when other people do it! I just enshrine them in this old hotch-potch of a journal!

~~Una~~ "This very evening as I put Jims to bed he looked up and asked me gravely, 'Why can't yesterday come back, Willa?'

"Oh, why can't it, Jims? That beautiful 'yesterday' ^**of dreams and laughter**^ ~~when there was no war~~ – when ~~Jem and Jerry and Carl and Ken were home~~ ^**our boys were home**^ – when Walter and I read and rambled ~~in~~ ^**and watched new moons and sunsets together in**^ Rainbow Valley. If it could just come back! But yesterdays never come back, little Jims – and the to-days are dark with clouds – and we dare not think about the to-morrows."

~~It is a year w~~

December 11, 1917

“Wonderful news came to-day. The ~~Birtish~~ British troops ~~have~~ captured Jerusalem ^**yesterday**^. We ran up the flag and some of Gertrude’s old sparkle came back to her for a moment.

“‘After all,’ she said, ‘it is worth while to live in the days which see the object of the ~~old Crusaders~~ ^**Crusades**^ attained. The ghosts of all the old Crusaders must have crowded the walls of Jerusalem last night, with Coeur-de-lion at their head.’

Susan ~~was elated also~~ ^**had cause for satisfaction also**^.

“‘I am so thankful I can pronounce Jerusalem and Hebron,’ she said. ‘They give me a real comfortable feeling after ~~Pres Pres Prshymysl~~ ^**Prshymsl**^ and Brest-Litovsk! Well, we have got the Turks on the run, at least, and Venice is safe and Lord Lansdowne is not to be taken seriously; and I see no reason why we should be downhearted.’

“Jerusalem! The ‘meteor flag of England!’ floats over you – the Crescent is gone. How Walter would have thrilled over that!” ~~if he had~~

December 18, 1917

“Yesterday the election came off. In the evening ~~M~~ mother and Susan and ~~Miss Oliver~~ ^**Gertrude**^ and I forgathered in the living room and waited in breathless suspense, father having gone down to the village. We had no way of hearing the news; ~~for~~ Carter Flagg’s store is not on our line, ~~so there was no use in listening in on the phone~~ and when we tried to get it Central always answered that the line “‘was busy”’ – as no doubt it was, for everybody for miles around was trying to get Carter’s store for the same reason we were.

“About ten o’clock ~~Sus Gertrude~~ ^~~**Miss Oliver**~~ **Gertrude**^ went to the ’phone and happened to catch someone from over-harbor talking to Carter Flagg. Gertrude shamelessly listened in and got for her comforting what eavesdroppers are proverbially supposed to get – to wit, ~~the news that~~ ^**unpleasant hearing;**^ the Union Government had “‘done nothing”’ in the West.

“We looked at each other in dismay. If the Government had failed to carry the West, it was defeated.

“‘Canada is disgraced in the eyes of the world,’ said ~~Gertrude~~ ~~**^Miss**~~

~~**Oliver**~~△ ~~bitterly.~~ Gertrude bitterly.

"'If ~~all the~~ everybody was like the Mark Crawfords over harbor this would not have happened,' groaned Susan. ~~"~~'They locked their Uncle up in the barn this morning and would not let him out until he promised to vote Union. That is what I call effective ~~persuasion~~ argument, Mrs. Dr. dear.~~"~~'

~~Gertrude~~ ~~△**Miss Oliver**△~~ "Gertrude and I couldn't rest ^**at all**^ after that. We walked the floor until our legs gave out and we had to sit down perforce. Mother knitted away as steadily as clock work and pretended to be calm and serene – pretended so well that we were all deceived and envious ~~unitl~~ until the next day, ^**when**^ I caught her ravelling out four inches of her sock. She had knit that far past where the heel should have begun!

"It was twelve before father came home. He stood in the door^**way**^ and looked at us and we looked at him. We did not dare ask him what the news was. Then he said that it was Laurier who had ~~"~~'done nothing~~"~~' in the west, and that the Union Government was in with a big majority. ~~Gertrude~~ ^~~**Miss Oliver**~~ **Gertrude**^ ~~gave a queer sound between a whoop and a gasp.~~ ^**clapped her hands.**^ I wanted to laugh and cry, mother's eyes flashed ~~like great gray stars~~ ^**with their old-time starriness**^, and Susan emitted ~~an unearthly~~ a queer sound between a gasp and a whoop. ~~Then we all felt limp.~~ ^[*Note*] **Z8**^

"Then we went to bed, but were too excited to sleep. Really, as Susan said solemnly this morning, 'Mrs. Dr. dear, I think politics are too strenuous for women.'"

December 31, 1917

"Our fourth War Christmas is over. ~~And now w~~We are trying to gather up some courage wherewith to face ~~the spring~~ ^**another year of it**^. Germany has, for the most part, ~~has marched from victory to victory~~ ^**been victorious**^ all summer. And now they say she has all her troops from the Russian front ready for a 'big push' in the spring. Sometimes it seems to me that we just cannot live through the winter waiting for that.

"I had a great batch of letters from overseas ~~to-day~~ this week. Shirley is at the front now, too, and writes ~~quite~~ about it all as coolly and matter-of-factly as he used to write of football ~~at Queen's~~ at Queen's. Carl wrote that it had been raining for weeks and that ~~it also~~ the nights in the trenches always made him think of the night of long ago when he did penance in the graveyard for running away from Henry Warren's ghost. Carl's letters are always full of jokes and bits of fun. They had a great rat-hunt the night before he wrote – spearing rats with their bayonets – and he got the best bag and won the prize. He has a tame rat that knows him and sleeps in his pocket at night. ~~He says he is~~ Rats don't worry Carl as they do some people – he was always chummy with all little beasts. He says he is making a study of the habits of the trench rat and means to write a treatise on it some day that will make him famous.

"Ken wrote a short letter. His letters are all rather short now – and he doesn't often slip in those dear little sudden sentences I love so much. Sometimes I think he has forgotten all about the night he was here to say good-bye ~~– the~~ – and then ~~sometimes~~ there will be just a line or a word that makes me think he remembers and always will remember. ^[*Note*] **D9**^ He is a captain now~~; Captain Ford~~. I am glad and proud – and yet 'Captain Ford' sounds so horribly far away and high up. 'Ken' and 'Captain Ford' seem like two different persons. I may be practically engaged to Ken – mother's opinion on that point is my stay and bulwark – but I can't be to 'Captain Ford!'

"And Jem is a lieutenant now – won his promotion on the field. He sent me a snap-shot, taken in his new uniform. He looked thin and old – old – my boy-brother Jem. I can't forget mother's face when I showed it to her. 'That – my little Jem~~,' was all she said.~~ ^**– the baby of the old House of Dreams,' was all she said.**^

"There was a letter from Faith, too. She ~~writes hopefully~~ is doing V.A.D. work in England and writes hopefully and brightly. I think she is almost happy – she ~~is so near Jem that she can go to him~~ saw Jem ~~in~~ ^**on**^ his last leave and she is so near ~~sh~~ him she can go to him, ~~if – if –~~ if he were wounded. That means so much to her ~~that she can bear~~. Oh, if I were only with her! But my work ~~seems to be~~ ^**is**^ here at home ~~and I must~~. I know Walter wouldn't ^**have**^ wanted me to leave mother and in everything I try to 'keep faith' with him, even to the little details of daily life. Walter died for Canada – I must live for her. That is what he asked me to do."

January 28, 1918

^[*Note*] ~~**C8**~~ **C9**^

"^**But**^ Susan is a somewhat disgruntled woman ~~these days~~ ^**at present**^, owing to the ~~Gover~~ regulations regarding cookery. ~~The~~ Her loyalty to the Union Government is being sorely tried. It surmounted the first strain gallantly. When the order ~~came to use~~ about flour came Susan said, quite cheerfully,

"'I am an old dog to be learning new tricks, but I shall learn to make war bread if it will help defeat the Huns.'

"But the later suggestions went against Susan's grain. Had it not been for father's decree I think she would have snapped her fingers at Sir Robert Borden ~~and But As it was, she has a grievance~~.

"'Talk about trying to make bricks without straw, Mrs. Dr. dear! How am I to make a cake without butter or sugar? It cannot be done – not cake that is ~~a~~ cake. Of course one can make a slab, Mrs. Dr. dear. And we cannot ^**even**^ camooflash it with a little icing! To think that I should have lived to see the day when a government at Ottawa should step into my kitchen and put me on rations!"

"Susan would give the last drop of her blood for her 'king and country,' but to surrender her beloved recipes is a very different and much more serious matter. ^[*Note*] **R10**^ [*This is the third use of the indicator "R10" in the manuscript of the text.*]

"I was down to see little Dog Monday to-day. He has grown ~~very~~ quite stiff and rheumatic but there he sat, waiting for the train. He thumped his tail and looked pleadingly into my eyes. 'When will Jem come?' he seemed to say. Oh, Dog Monday, there is no answer to that question; and there is, as yet, no answer to the other which we are all constantly asking 'What will happen when Germany strikes again on the Western front – her one great, last blow for ~~world –p~~ victory!'

March 1, 1918

"'What will spring bring?' Gertrude said to-day. 'I dread it as I never dreaded spring before. ~~I wish it were possible to take some magic draught and go to sleep for the next three months – then waken to find Armageddon over.~~ Do you suppose there will ever again come a time when life will be free from fear? For almost four years we have lain down with fear and risen up with it. It has been the unbidden guest at every meal, the unwelcome companion at every gathering.'

"'Hindenburg says he will be in Paris ~~by Ap~~ on April first,' sighed Cousin Sophia

"'Hindenburg!' There is no power in pen and ink to express the contempt which Susan infused into that name. ~~"~~'Has he forgotten what day the first of April is?'

"'Hindenburg has kept his word hitherto,~~"~~' said Gertrude, as gloomily as Cousin Sophia herself could have said it.

"'Yes, fighting against ~~foreigners~~ ^**Russians and Roumanians**^,"' retorted Susan. ~~"~~'Wait you till he comes up against the British and French, not to speak of the Yankees, who are getting there as fast as they can and will no doubt give a good account of themselves." ^[*Note*] **E9**^

"'Hindenburg says he ^[*Note*] **E8**^ will spend a million lives to break the Allied front,' said Gertrude. ~~"~~'At such a price he must purchase some successes and how can we live through them, even if he is baffled in the end. These past two months ^[*Note*] **A9**^ have seemed as long as all the preceding months of the war put together. I work all day feverishly and waken at three o'clock at night to wonder if the iron legions have struck at last. I wish there was no such hour as three o'clock at night. It is then I see Hindenburg in Paris and Germany triumphant. I never see her so at any other time than that accursed hour.~~"~~'

"Susan looked dubious ^**over Gertrude's adjective,**^ but evidently concluded that the 'a' saved the situation.

"'I wish it were possible to take some magic draught and go to sleep for the next three months – and then waken to find Armageddon over,' said mother, ^**almost impatiently.**^

"It is not often that mother slumps into a wish like that – or at least the verbal expression of it. Mother has changed a great deal since that terrible day in September when we ~~heard~~ ^**knew**^ that Walter would not come back; but she has always ~~kept~~ been brave and ~~hopeful~~ patient ~~and~~. Now it seemed as if even she had reached the limit of her endurance.

"Susan went over to mother and touched her shoulder. ~~There are times when Susan can be so gentle and tender.~~

"'~~Don't~~ ^**Do not you**^ be frightened ^**or downhearted**^, Mrs. Dr. dear,' she said gently. 'I felt somewhat that way myself ~~M~~ last night, ~~Mrs. Dr. dear,~~ and I rose from my bed and lighted my lamp and opened my Bible; and what do you think was the first verse my eyes lighted upon? It was 'And they shall fight against thee but they shall not prevail against thee, for I am with ~~thee~~ thee, saith the Lord of Hosts, to deliver thee.' ~~And~~ ^**I am not gifted in the way of dreaming, as Miss Oliver is, but**^ I knew then and there, Mrs. Dr. dear, that ~~I had been led~~ it was a manifest leading, and that Hindenburg will never see Paris. So I read no further but went back to my bed and I did not waken at three o'clock or at any other hour before morning.[22]'"

"I say that verse Susan read over and over again to myself. The Lord of Hosts is with us – and the spirits of all just men made perfect – and even then won legions will ^**legions and guns that Germany is massing on the Western front must**^ break against such a barrier. This is in certain uplifted moments; but when other moments come I feel, like ~~Gertrude~~ ^~~**Miss Oliver**~~ **Gertrude**^, that I cannot ~~face the spring.~~ [*Montgomery puts a line across the page here to indicate the original end of the entry.*]

~~bear~~ ^**endure any** ~~**more**~~^ ^^**longer**^^ ^**this awful and ominous hush before the coming storm.**^"

March 23, 1917

"Armageddon has begun! ^~~**B8**~~ **Note B9**^ Yesterday I went down to the post office ~~wi~~ for the mail. It was a dull, ~~hard,~~ bitter day. The snow was gone but the gray, lifeless ground was frozen hard and a biting wind was blowing. The ~~whoele~~ whole Glen landscape was ugly and ~~rep~~ hopeless.

“Then I got the paper with its big black headlines. ~~Day before~~ Germany struck on the twenty first. She makes big claims of guns and prisoners taken. General Haig reports that ‘severe fighting continues.’ I don’t like the sound of that last expression.

“We all find we cannot do any work that requires concentration of thought. So we all knit furiously, because we can do that mechanically. ~~At least the dreadful waiting is over and a short A week from to-morrow will be Easter Sunday.~~ At least the dreadful waiting is over – the horrible wondering where and when the blow will fall. ~~I think even this is easier to bear – and~~ It has fallen – but they shall not prevail against us! ~~– ‘they shall not pass.’~~

“Oh, what is happening on the Western front tonight as I write this, sitting here in my room with my journal before me? Jims is sleeping in his crib ~~and the night outside is still and wind is wailing about the window; and away over there in France – does the line hold?~~ and the wind is wailing ~~ab~~ around the window; over my desk hangs Walter’s picture, looking at me with his beautiful deep eyes; the Mona Lisa he gave me the last ~~lovely~~ Christmas he was home ~~su~~ hangs ~~beside~~ **^on one side of^** it, and on the other a framed copy of ~~that wonderful p~~ ‘~~“~~The Piper.~~”~~’ It seems to me that I can hear Walter’s voice repeating ~~its lines~~ it – that little poem into which he put his soul, and which will therefore live for ever, carrying Walter’s name on through the future of our land. Everything about me is calm and peaceful and ‘~~“~~homey.~~”~~’ Walter seems very near me – if I could just scrub aside the thin ~~wavering~~ **^wavering^** little veil that hangs between, I could see him – just as he saw the Pied Piper the night before Courcelette.

“Over there in France to-night – does the line hold?”

Chapter 28

Black Sunday

In March of the year of grace 1918 there was one week into which must have crowded more of searing ^**human**^ agony than any seven days had ever held before in the history of the world. And in that week there was one day when all humanity seemed nailed to the cross; on that day the whole planet must have been agroan with universal convulsion; everywhere the hearts ^**of men were failing them for fear.**^ It dawned calmly and ~~colly~~ coldly and grayly at Ingleside. ~~Rilla and~~ Mrs. Blythe and Rilla and Miss Oliver made ready for church in a suspense tempered by hope and confidence. The doctor was away, having been summoned during the wee sma's to ~~a~~ ^**the Marwood**^ household in the Upper Glen, where a little war-bride was fighting gallantly on her own battleground to give life, not death, to the world. Susan announced that she meant to stay home that morning – a rare decision for Susan.

"But I would rather not go to church this morning, Mrs. Dr. dear," she explained. "If Whiskers-on-the-Moon were there and I saw him looking holy and pleased, as he always looks when he thinks the Huns are winning, I fear I would lose my patience and my sense of decorum and hurl a Bible or hymnbook at him, thereby disgracing myself and the sacred edifice. No, Mrs. Dr. dear, I shall stay home from church till the tide turns and pray hard here."

"I think I might as well stay home, too, for all the good church will do me to-day," Miss Oliver said to Rilla, as they walked down the hard-frozen red road to the church. ~~"No matter where my body is my soul seems to be somewhere else in a dark little torture chamber of its own.~~ "I can think of <u>nothing</u> but the question, 'Does the line still hold?'"

"Next Sunday will be Easter," said Rilla. "Will it herald death or life to our cause?"

Mr. Meredith preached that morning from the text, "He that endureth to the end shall be saved," and hope and confidence rang through his inspiring sentences. Rilla, looking up at the memorial tablet on the wall above ~~the Blythe~~ their pew, "sacred to the memory[22] of Walter

Cuthbert Blythe," felt herself lifted out of her dread ~~into~~ and filled anew with courage. Walter~~, and~~ could not have laid down his life for naught. His had been the gift of prophetic vision and he had foreseen victory. She would cling to that belief – the line would hold.

In this renewed mood she walked home from church almost gaily. The others, too, were hopeful, and all went smiling into Ingleside. There was no one in the living room, save Jims, who had fallen asleep on the sofa ^**Note S10**^ No one was in the dining room either – and, stranger still, no dinner was on the table, which was not even set. Where was Susan? ~~Had she been taken~~

"Can she have taken ill?" exclaimed Mrs. Blythe ^**anxiously**^. "I thought it strange that she did not want to go to church this morning."

The kitchen door opened and Susan appeared on the threshold with such a ghastly face that ~~the three women all called out together in sudden terror~~ Anne Blythe ~~called~~ ^**cried**^ out ^**in sudden ~~terror~~ panic.**^

"Susan, what is it?"

"The British line is broken and the German shells are falling on Paris," said Susan dully.

~~Mrs. B~~ The three women stared at each other, stricken.

~~"It can't be true – it can't be~~ ^**"It's not true – it's not**^ true," gasped Rilla.

"The thing would be – ~~ridu~~ ridiculous," said Gertrude Oliver – and then she laughed horribly.

"Susan, who told you this – when did the news come?" asked ~~Mrs. Anne~~ ^**Mrs.**^ Blythe.

~~"It~~ "I got it over the long-distance 'phone from Charlottetown half an hour ago," said Susan. "The news came to town late last night ~~and Dr~~. It was Dr. ~~Graham~~ ^~~**Graham**~~^ ^^**Holland**^^ phoned it out and he said it was only too true. Since then I have done nothing, Mrs. Dr. dear. I am very sorry dinner is not ready. It is the first time I have been so remiss. If you will be patient I will soon have ~~it on the~~ something for you to eat. But I am afraid I let the potatoes burn."

"Dinner! Nobody wants any dinner, Susan," said Mrs. Blythe wildly. ~~"If the Germans are shelling Paris they must have crashed through everywhere and be at its very gates."~~ ^**Oh, this thing is unbelievable – it must be a nightmare."**^

"Paris is lost – France is lost – the war is lost," gasped Rilla, amid the

~~utttr~~ utter ruins of hope and confidence and belief.

"Oh God – Oh God," ~~moamed~~ moaned Gertrude Oliver, walking about the room and wringing her hands, "Oh – God!"

Nothing else – no other words – nothing but that age old plea – the old, old cry of supreme agony and appeal, from the human heart whose every human staff has failed it.

"Is God dead?" asked a ~~grave~~ ^**startled**^ little voice from the doorway of the living room. Jims stood there, flushed from sleep, his big brown eyes filled with dread, "Oh, ~~Miss O~~ Willa – oh, Willa, is God dead?"

Miss Oliver ~~paused in her tragic~~ stopped walking and exclaiming, and stared at Jims ~~who was on the point of tears, so convinced was he that some supre~~, in whose eyes tears of fright were beginning to gather. ^**Rilla ran to his comforting, while**^ Susan ~~suddenly~~ bounded up from the chair upon which she had dropped ~~her~~.

"No," she said briskly, with a sudden return of her real self. "No, God isn't dead – nor Lloyd George either. We were forgetting that, Mrs. Dr. dear. Don't cry, little Kitchener. Bad as things are, they might be worse. The British line may be broken but the British navy ~~isn't~~ ^**is not. Let us tie to that.**^ I will take a brace and get up a bite to eat, for strength we must have."

~~Susan got~~

They made a pretence of eating Susan's "bite," but it was only a pretence. Nobody at Ingleside ever forgot that black afternoon. ~~Miss~~ Gertrude Oliver walked the floor – they all walked the floor; except Susan, who got out her gray war sock.

"Mrs. Dr. dear, I must knit on Sunday at last. I have never dreamed of doing it before for, say what might be said, I have considered it was a violation of the third commandment. But whether it is or whether it ~~isn~~ is not I must knit to-day or I shall go mad."

"Knit if you can, Susan," said Mrs. Blythe restlessly. "I would knit if I could – but I cannot – I cannot. ~~Oh, is this unbelievable thing a nightmare?~~"

~~Gertrude~~ "If we could only get fuller information," moaned Rilla. "There might be something to encourage us – if we knew all."

"We know that the Germans are shelling Paris," said Miss ~~Oiver~~ Oliver bitterly. "In that case they must have smashed through everywhere and be at its very gates. No, ~~let us face the fact – we are – we are defeated~~ ^~~**conqu**~~ **we have lost**^ – let us face the fact as other peoples in the past have had to face it. Other nations, ^**with right on their side,**^ have given their best and bravest – and gone down to defeat in spite of it. Ours is

> "'but one more
> "To baffled millions who have gone before.'"

"I won't give up like that," cried Rilla, her pale face suddenly flushing. "I won't despair. We are not conquered – no, if Germany overruns all France we are not conquered. I am ashamed of myself for this hour of despair. ~~I'm going~~ You won't see me slump again like that. I'm going to ring up town at once and ask for particulars."

But town could not be got. The long-distance operator there was submerged by similar calls from every part of the distracted country. Rilla finally gave up and slipped away to Rainbow Valley. There she knelt down on the withered gray grasses in the little nook where she and Walter had had their last talk together, with her head bowed against the ^**mossy**^ trunk of a fallen tree. The sun had broken through the black clouds and drenched the valley with a pale golden splendor. The bells on the Tree Lovers twinkled ~~wildly~~ ^**elfinly**^ and ~~sweetly~~ ^**fitfully**^ in the gusty March wind. ~~The little paths where childish feet had run in olden days, still wound in and out among the firs and spruces and birches.~~

"Oh God, give me strength," Rilla whispered. "Just strength – and ~~hop~~ courage." Then like a child she clasped her hands together and said, as simply as Jims could have done, "Please send us better news to-morrow."

She knelt there a long time, and when she went back to Ingleside she was ~~qu~~ calm and ~~cheerful~~ ^**resolute**^. The doctor had arrived home, tired but triumphant, little ~~Lloyd George ^Burr~~ ~~^**Reuben**^~~ ^^**Douglas Haig Marwood**^^ having made a safe landing on the shores of time. Gertrude was still pacing restlessly but ~~Anne~~ Mrs. Blythe and Susan had reacted from the shock, and Susan was already planning a new line of defence for the channel ports.

"As long as we can hold them," she declared, "the situation is saved. Paris has really no military significance."

"Don't," said Gertrude sharply, as if Susan had run something into her. She thought ~~Susan's new born confidence~~ ~~^**remarks**^~~ ^**the old worn phrase 'no military significance'**^ nothing short of ghastly ^**mockery**^ under the circumstances, and more terrible to endure than the voice of despair would have been.

"I heard ^**up at ~~Burr's~~ Marwood's**^ of the line being broken," said the doctor, "but this story of the Germans shelling Paris seems to be rather incredible. Even if they broke through they were fifty miles from Paris at the nearest point and how could they get their artillery close enough to shell it in so short a time? Depend upon it, girls, that part of the message ~~is~~ can't be true.[22] ^**I'm**^

~~"I didn't think of that," said Gertrude, looking a little foolish. After all, had her tragic afternoon been over nothing. But in the line was broken. That was~~

going to try to try a long-distance call to town myself."

The doctor was no more successful than Rilla had been, but his point of view cheered them all a little~~. And~~, and helped them through the evening. And at nine o'clock a ~~"If it were only morning," sighed Gertrude. "I dread the night" – for I shall not close~~ ~~"Susan I think the emergency justifies it," I'll give you all a newel tablet," said the doctor. "I can't have all my women folk coming down with nervous prostration."~~

~~Post an age~~

long-distance message came through at last, that helped them through the night.

"The line broke only in one place, before St. Quentin," said the doctor, ^**as he hung up the receiver,**^ "and ~~the~~ the British troops are retreating in good order. That's not so bad. And as for the shells that are falling on Paris, they are coming from a distance of seventy miles – from some ^**amazing**^ long-range gun the Germans have invented and sprung with ~~the~~ opening of the offensive.[22] That is all the news to date, and Dr. ^**Holland**^ says it is reliable."

"It would have been dreadful news yesterday," said Gertrude, "but compared to what we heard this morning it is almost like good news. But still," she added, trying to smile, "I am afraid I will not sleep much to-night."

"There is one thing to be thankful for at any rate, Miss Oliver, dear," said Susan, "and that is that Cousin Sophia did not come in to-day. I really could not have endured <u>her</u> on top of all the rest."

Chapter 29

"Wounded and Missing"

"Battered but not broken" was the headline in Monday's paper, and Susan repeated it over and over to herself as she went about her work. The gap caused by the St. Quentin disaster had been patched up in time, but the Allied line was being pushed relentlessly back from the territory they had purchased in 1917 with half a million lives. On Wednesday the headline was "British and French[22] check Germans"; but still the retreat went on. Back – ~~and back~~ and back – and back! Where would it end? Would the weakened line hold or would it ~~burst~~ break again – this time disastrously?

On Saturday the headline was "Even Berlin admits offensive checked," and for the first time in that terrible week the ~~household of~~ Ingleside ^**folks**^ dared to draw a long breath.

"Well, we have got one week over – now for the next," said Susan staunchly.

"I feel like a prisoner on the rack when they stopped turning it," Miss Oliver said to Rilla, as they went to church on Easter morning. "But I am not off the rack. The torture may begin again at any time."

"I doubted God last Sunday," said Rilla, "but I don't doubt him to-day. Evil cannot win. Spirit is on our side and it is bound to outlast flesh."

Nevertheless her faith was ~~sorely~~ often tried in the dark spring that followed. Armageddon was not, as they had hoped, a matter of a few days. It stretched out into weeks and months. Again and again Hindenburg struck his savage, sudden blows, with ~~temporary and~~ alarming, though futile success. Again and again the military critics declared the situation extremely ~~critical~~ ^**perilous**^. Again and again Cousin Sophia agreed with the military critics.

"If the Allies go back three miles more the war is lost," she wailed. ~~"I read it~~

"Is the British navy anchored in those three miles?" demanded Susan scornfully.

~~"You may~~ "It ~~was~~ ^**is**^ the opinion of a man who knows all about it," said Cousin Sophia solemnly.

"There is no such person," retorted Susan~~, unconsciously plagiarizing~~. "As for the military critics, they do not know one blessed thing about it, any more than you or I~~, Sophia Crawford~~. They have been mistaken times out of number. Why do you always look on the dark side~~?", Sophia Crawford?"~~ Sophia Crawford?"

"Because there ain't any bright side, Susan Baker."

"Oh, is there not? It is the ~~seventeenth~~ ^**twentieth**^ of April, and Hindy is not in Paris yet, although he said he ~~was~~ would be there by April first. Is that not a bright spot at least?" ~~^[*Note*] **F9**^~~

"It is my opinion that the Germans will be in Paris before very long and more than that, Susan Baker, they will be in Canada."

"Not in this part of it. The Huns shall never set foot in PE Island as long as I can handle a pitchfork," declared Susan, looking, and feeling quite equal to routing the entire German army single-handed. "No, ~~Susan Baker~~ ^**Sophia Crawford**^, to tell you the ~~"It is easy~~ plain truth I am sick and tired of your gloomy predictions. ~~I do not want to quarrel with anyone, least of all at a time like this, but if you cannot keep from croaking I will speak my mind out plainly and tell you that your absence is better than you company.~~

I do not deny that some mistakes have been made. The Germans would never have got back Passchendaele if the Canadians had been left there; and it was bad business trusting to those Portuguese at the Lys River. But that is no reason why you or anyone should go about proclaiming the war is lost ^~~**We**~~^. I do not want to quarrel with you, least of all at such a time as this, ^**but our morale must be kept up, and**^ ~~but~~ I am going to speak my mind out plainly and tell you that if you cannot keep from ^**such**^ croaking your ~~absence~~ ^**room**^ is better than your company."

Cousin Sophia marched home in high dudgeon to digest her affront, and did not reappear in Susan's kitchen for many weeks. Perhaps it was just as well, for they were hard weeks, ~~with ever recurring~~ when the Germans ~~struck~~ ^**continued to strike,**^ now here, now there, and ~~the~~ seemingly vital points fell to them at every blow. And one day in early May, when ~~the~~ wind and sunshine frolicked in Rainbow Valley and the maple grove was golden-green and the harbor all blue and dimpled and white-capped, the news came about Jem.

There had been a trench raid on the Canadian front – a little trench raid so ~~insignf~~ insignificant that it was never even mentioned in the dispatches and when it was over Lieutenant James Blythe was reported "~~wounded and~~ ^**wounded and**^ missing." ~~believed killed."~~

~~On went the days – for days go on even if hearts break.~~

"I think this is even worse than the news of his death would have been," moaned Rilla through her white lips, that night.

"No – no – 'missing' leaves a little hope, Rilla," urged ~~Mis~~ Gertrude Oliver.

"Yes – torturing, agonized hope that keeps you from ever becoming quite resigned to the worst," said Rilla. ~~"Oh, Miss Oliver~~ "Like poor Mrs. Abbey at Lowbridge. Her son has been 'missing' for a year. Everyone but his mother believes he is dead. She clings to the hope that he lives and the suspense is killing her.~~" Oh, truly, I'd rather think Jem was dead than suffering and tortured as so many of the prisoners taken by the Germans have~~ Oh, Miss Oliver – ~~we must~~ ^**must we**^ go for weeks and months – not knowing whether Jem is alive or dead – perhaps we will never know. I – I cannot bear it – I cannot. Walter – and now Jem. This will kill mother – look at her face, Miss Oliver, and you will see that. She ~~never cries – not even at night.~~ ^**hasn't cried.**^ ~~She's~~ ^**She will**^ bleed~~ing~~ to death inwardly! ~~Jem was her first born son –~~ ^**And Faith – poor Faith – how can she bear it?**^"

Gertrude shivered with pain. She looked up at the ~~Mona Lisa~~ ^**pictures**^ hanging over Rilla's desk and felt a sudden hatred of Mona Lisa's endless smile.

"Will not even this blot it off your face?" she thought savagely.

~~"If Jem isn't dead he's a prisoner," Rilla went on restlessly. She must talk out her pains to someone – it helped – and she must not talk of it to her mother who had said,~~

~~"Jem isn't dead – I won't believe it – I shall hope on," but who had looked despair while she voiced hope. "And the Germans have used some of their press~~

~~To Rilla~~ ^**But**^ she said gently,

"No, it won't kill your mother. She's made of finer mettle than that.

Besides, she refuses to believe Jem is dead; she will cling to hope and we must all do that. ^**Faith, you may be sure, ~~will do it."~~ will do it.**^"

~~"I can't,"~~ **"I cannot,"**^ moaned Rilla. ~~"I wish I could – it would help I suppose. But hope seems dead in~~

[*Error in ms: page number "449" appears on two consecutive pages.*]

~~me. I can't hope without some reason for it and this is no reason."~~ "Jem was wounded – what chance would he have? Even if the Germans found him – we know how they have treated wounded prisoners. I wish I could hope, Miss Oliver – it would help, I suppose. But hope seems dead in me. I can't hope without some reason for it – and there is no reason."

~~Later~~ When Miss Oliver had gone to her own room and Rilla was lying on her bed in the moonlight, praying desperately for a little strength, Susan slipped in like a gaunt shadow and sat down ~~by the bed.~~ beside her.

"Rilla, dear, do not you worry. Little Jem is not dead."

"Oh, how can you ~~believe that say~~ ^**believe**^ that, ~~so~~ Susan?"

"Because I know. Listen you to me. When that word came this morning the first thing I thought of was ~~Little~~ Dog Monday. And to-night, as soon as I got the supper dishes washed and the bread set, I went down to the station. There was Dog Monday, waiting for the night train, just as patient as usual. Now, Rilla dear, that trench raid was ~~five~~ ^**four**^ days ago – last Monday – and I said to the station agent, 'Can you tell me if that dog howled or made any kind of a fuss last Monday night?' He thought it over a bit, and then he said, 'No, he did not.' 'Are you sure?' I said. ^**'There's more depends on it than you think!'**^ 'Dead sure,' he said. 'I was up all night last Monday night ~~with the wife and there was never a sound out of him. I would have heard it if there had been for the windows were also open.' You know, Rilla dear, the poor man's wife is far gone in consumption and if and on~~ because my ~~horse~~ ^**mare**^ was sick, and there was never a sound out of him. I would have heard if there had been, for the stable door was open all the time and ~~it~~ his kennel is right across from it!' Now Rilla dear, those were the man's very words. And you know how that poor little dog howled all night after the battle of Courcelette. Yet he did not love Walter as much as he loved Jem. If he mourned for Walter like that, do you suppose he would sleep sound in his ~~kne~~ kennel ~~if~~ the night after Jem had been killed? ~~No,~~ No, Rilla dear, little Jem is <u>not</u> dead, and that you may tie to. If he were, Dog Monday would have known, just as he knew before,[22] and he would not be still waiting ^**for the trains."**^

It was absurd – and irrational – and impossible. But Rilla believed it, for all that; and Mrs. Blythe believed it; and the doctor, though he smiled faintly in pretended derision, felt an odd confidence replace his first despair; and foolish and absurd or not, the^**y all**^ ~~household of Ingleside~~ plucked up heart and courage to ~~go on~~ carry on, just because a faithful little dog at the Glen station was still watching with unbroken faith for his master to come home. Common sense might scorn – incredulity might mutter "Mere Superstition" – ~~but in their hearts the Blythe ho~~ but in their hearts the folk of Ingleside ~~believed that~~ stood by their belief that Dog Monday knew.

Chapter 30

The Turning of the Tide

Susan was very sorrowful when she saw the beautiful old lawn of Ingleside ploughed up that spring and planted with potatoes. Yet she made no protest, even when her beloved peony bed was sacrificed. But when the Government passed the Daylight Saving law Susan balked. There was a Higher Power than the Union Government ~~and to that Power Susan~~, ^**to which Susan owed allegiance.**^

"Do you think it right to meddle with the arrangements of the Almighty?" she demanded indignantly of the doctor. The doctor, quite unmoved, responded that the law must be observed, and the Ingleside clocks were moved on accordingly. But the doctor had no power over Susan's ^**little**^ alarm ~~clock~~.

"I bought that with my own money, Mrs. Dr. dear," she said firmly, "and it shall go on God's time and not Borden's time."

Susan got up and went to bed by "God's time," and regulated her own goings and comings by it. She served the meals, under protest, by "Borden's" time, and she had to go to church by it, which was the crowning injury. ~~"But I say my prayers by my own clock,"~~ But she said her prayers by her own clock, and fed the hens by it; so that there was always a furtive triumph in her eye when she looked at the doctor ~~that summer~~. She had got the better of him by so much at least.

"Whiskers-on-The-Moon is very much delighted with this daylight saving business," she ~~said~~ told him one evening. "Of course he naturally would be, since I ~~am told~~ ^**understand**^ that the Germans invented it. I hear he came near losing his entire wheat-crop lately. Warren Meade's cows broke into the field one day last week – it was the very day the Germans captured the Chemang-de-dam, which may have been a coincidence or may not – and were making fine havoc of it when Mrs. Dick Clow happened to see them from her attic window. At first she ~~made no move to~~ ^**had no intention**^ of letting Mr. Pryor know. She told me she had just <u>gloated</u> over the sight of those cows ~~deva~~ pasturing on his wheat. She felt it served him exactly right. But presently she reflected that the wheat-crop was a matter of great importance and that ‘save and serve’ meant that those cows must be routed out as much as it meant anything. So she went down and phoned over to ~~Miranda~~ Whiskers about the matter. All the thanks she got was that he said ~~d---n, right out to her over the phone~~ something queer right out to her ~~over the phone~~. She is not prepared to ~~say what~~ ^**state that**^ it was actually swearing for you cannot be sure just what you hear over the phone; but she has her own opinion, ~~Only~~ and so have I, but I will not express it for here comes Mr. Meredith, and Whiskers is one of his elders, so we must be discreet.”

“Are you ~~trying to read lo~~ looking for the new star?” asked Mr. Meredith, joining Miss Oliver and Rilla, who were standing ~~on the narrow path to the gate, which was all the doctor would allow~~ among the blossoming potatoes, gazing skyward.

“Yes – we have found it – see, it is just above the tip of the tallest old pine.”

~~“They say it is caused by some collision that probably took place~~

“It’s ~~something~~ wonderful to be looking at something that happened five thousand years ago, isn’t~~”~~ it?” said Rilla. “That is when astronomers think the collision took place which ~~resulted in the~~ produced this new star. It makes me feel horribly insignificant,” she added ~~wistfully~~ under her breath.

“Even this event cannot dwarf into what may be the proper perspective in star systems the fact that the Germans are again only one leap from Paris,” said Gertrude restlessly.

“I think I would like to have been an astronomer,” said Mr. Meredith dreamily, gazing at the star.

“There must be a strange pleasure in it,” agreed Miss Oliver, “an unearthly pleasure, in more senses than one. I would like to have a few astronomers for my friends.” ~~Fancy talking the gos~~

“Fancy talking the gossip of the hosts of heaven,” laughed Rilla.

“I wonder if astronomers feel a very ~~pure~~ ^**deep**^ interest in earthly affairs?” said the doctor.

“Perhaps students of the canals of Mars would not be so keenly sensitive to the significance of a few yards of trenches lost or won on the Western front.”

"I have read somewhere," said Mr. Meredith, "that Ernest Renan wrote one of his books during the siege of Paris in 1870 and 'enjoyed the writing of it very much.' I suppose one would call him a philosopher."

"I have read also," said Miss Oliver, "that ~~just before~~ ^**shortly before**^ his death he ~~voiced~~ ^**said that**^ his only regret in dying ~~as being~~ was that he must die before he had seen what that 'extremely interesting young man, the German Emperor,' would do in his life. If Ernest Renan 'walked' to-day and saw what that interesting young man had done to his beloved France, not to speak of the world, I wonder if his mental detachment would be as complete as it was in 1870."

"I wonder where Jem is to-night," thought Rilla, ~~^**and suddenly**^~~
^^**in a sudden bitter inrush of remembrance.**^^

It was over a month since the ~~word~~ ^**news**^ had come about Jem ~~and since then there had had been only silence~~. Nothing had ~~trans~~ been discovered concerning him, in spite of all efforts. Two or three letters had come from him, written before the trench raid, and since then there had been only unbroken silence. Now the Germans were ~~pressing~~ ^**again at the Marne, pressing**^ nearer and nearer Paris; now rumors were coming of another Austrian offensive against the Piave line. Rilla turned away from the new star, sick at heart. It was one of the moments when hope and courage failed her utterly~~. But she kept it to herself, it was an understood thing at Ingleside that summer spring that no fears were to be expressed in words. Morale is a ticklish thing, easily broken under sudden strain, and anything that tended to weaken it~~

– when it seemed impossible to go on for ~~another~~ ^**even one more**^ day. If only they knew what had happened to Jem – you can face anything you know. But ~~an army of fears and doubt~~ a beleaguerment of fear and doubt and suspense is a hard thing for the morale. Surely, if Jem were alive, some word would have come through. He must be dead. Only – they would never know – they could never be quite sure; and Dog Monday would wait for the train until he died of old age. ~~Dog~~ Monday was only a poor, faithful, rheumatic little dog, who knew nothing more of his master's ~~faith~~ fate than they did.

Rilla had a "white night" and did not fall asleep until ~~the gray of morning crept into her room~~ ^**late**^. ~~When she wakened Miss Oliver was sitting on the foot of her bed.~~

~~"Rilla, I've had another dream."~~

~~"Oh – no!" cried Rilla ^**shrinking**^ Miss Oliver's dreams had always foretold some coming disaster.~~

~~"Rilla, dearest, it was a good dream. Listen – I dreamed, just as I did four years ago, that I stood on the veranda steps and looked out over the Glen. And it was still covered by waves that~~

When she wakened Gertrude Oliver was sitting at her window leaning out to meet the silver mystery of the dawn. ~~The early~~ Her clever, striking profile, with the masses of black hair behind it, came out clearly against the pallid gold of the eastern sky. Rilla remembered Jem's admiration of ~~Miss Oliver's~~ the curve of Miss Oliver's brow and chin, and she ~~sighed~~ shuddered. Everything that reminded her of Jem was beginning to ~~be~~ ^**give**^ intolerable pain. ~~Her grief~~ Walter's death had inflicted on her heart a terrible wound ~~the scar of which must remain forever~~. But it had been a clean wound and had healed slowly, as such wounds do, though the scar must remain forever. But the torture of Jem's disappearance was another thing: there was a poison in it ^**that**^ kept it from healing. The alternations of hope and ~~dread~~ ^**despair**^, ~~with the days of dull, times of dull,~~ the endless watching each day for the letter that never came – that might never come – the ~~la~~ newspaper tales of ill-usage of prisoners – the bitter wonder as to ~~what Jem's~~ Jem's wound – all were increasingly hard to bear.

Gertrude Oliver turned her head. There was an odd brilliancy in her eyes.

"Rilla, I've had another dream."

"Oh, no – no," cried Rilla, shrinking. Miss Oliver's dreams had always foretold coming disaster.

"Rilla, it was a good dream. Listen – I dreamed just as I did four years ago, that I stood on the veranda steps and looked down the Glen. And it was still covered by waves that lapped about my feet. But as I looked the waves began to ebb – and they ebbed as swiftly as, four years ago, they rolled in – ebbed out and out, to the gulf; and the Glen lay before me, beautiful and green, with a rainbow spanning Rainbow Valley – a rainbow of such splendid color that it dazzled me – and I woke. Rilla – Rilla Blythe – the tide has turned."

"I wish I could believe it," ~~said Rilla.~~

'"Sooth was my prophecy of fear
Believe it when it augurs cheer,"'

quoted Gertrude, almost gaily. "I tell you I have no doubt."

Yet, in spite of the great Italian victory at the Piave that came a few days later, she had doubt many a time in the hard month that followed; and when in mid-July the Germans crossed the Marne again despair came ~~again~~ sickeningly. It was idle, they all felt, to hope that the miracle of the Marne would he repeated.

But it was: again, as in 1914, the tide turned at the Marne. The French and the American troops struck their sudden smashing blow on the exposed flank of the enemy and, with the almost inconceivable rapidity of a dream, ~~the~~ the whole aspect of the war changed.

"The Allies have won two tremendous victories," ~~Rilla read the Enterprise headline~~ said the doctor on ~~July~~ the twentieth of July.

"It is the beginning of the end – I feel it – I feel it," ~~said~~ ^**cried**^ Mrs. Blythe.

"Thank God," said Susan, folding her trembling old hands. Then she added, under her breath, "But it won't bring our boys back."

Nevertheless she went out and ran up the flag, for the first time since the fall of Jerusalem. As it caught the breeze and swelled gallantly out above her, Susan lifted her hand and saluted it, as she had seen Shirley do. ^**Note T10**^ The wind whipped her gray hair about her face and the gingham apron that shrouded her from head to foot was cut on lines of economy, not of grace; yet, somehow, just then Susan made ~~a heroic~~ an imposing figure. She was one of the ~~^**millions of**^~~ women ~~wh~~ – courageous, unquailing, patient, heroic – who had made victory possible. In her, they all saluted the ~~flag~~ symbol for which their dearest had ~~died~~ fought. Something of this was in the doctor's mind as he watched her from the door.

"Susan," he said, when she turned to come in, "from first to last of this business you have been a brick! ~~There ought to be a special medal for your kind.~~"

Chapter 31

Mrs. Matilda Pitman

Rilla and Jims were standing on the ^**rear**^ platform of their car when the train stopped at the little Millward siding. The August ~~afternoon was so~~ evening was so hot and close that the crowded cars were stifling. ^[*Note*] **F9**^

Rilla was on her way into Charlottetown to spend the night with a friend and the next day in Red Cross shopping; she had taken Jims with her, partly because she did not want Susan or her mother to be bothered with his care, partly because of a hungry ~~feeling~~ ^**desire**^ in her heart to have as much of him as she could before she might have to give him up forever. James Anderson had written to her not long before this; he was wounded and in the hospital; he would not be able to go back to the front and as soon as he was able he would be coming home for Jims.

Rilla was heavy-hearted over this, and worried also. She loved Jims dearly and would feel deeply giving him up in any case; but if Jim Anderson ~~had been~~ were a different sort of a man, with a proper home for the child, it would not be so bad. But to give Jims up to a roving, shiftless, ~~though~~ irresponsible ~~man~~ ^**father**^, however kind and good-hearted he might be – and she knew Jim Anderson <u>was</u> kind and good-hearted enough – was a bitter prospect to Rilla. It was not even likely Anderson would stay in ~~Four Winds~~ the Glen; he had no ties there now; he might even go back to England. She might never see her dear, sunshiny, ~~brown-eyed~~ carefully brought-up little Jims again. With such a father what might his fate be? Rilla meant to beg Jim Anderson to leave him with her, but, from his letter, she had not much hope that he would.

"If he would only stay in the Glen, where I could keep an eye on Jims and have him often with me I wouldn't feel so worried over it," she reflected. "But I feel sure he won't – and ~~he is so~~ Jims will never have any chance ~~– or a decent education~~. And he is such a bright little chap – ~~and~~ he has ambition, wherever he got it – and he isn't lazy. But his father will never have a cent to give him any education or start in life. Jims, my little war-baby, whatever is going to become of you?"

Jims was not in the least concerned over what was to become of him. He was gleefully watching the antics of a striped chipmunk that was frisking over the roof of the little siding ~~and Nobody ever knew why the train stopped at Millward siding. Nobody was ever known to get off there or to get on. It was in the woods, ^**it was**^ at least three miles from the nearest house and was surrounded by acres of blueberry barrens and scrub spruces and firs~~. As the train pulled out Jims leaned eagerly forward for a last look at Chippy, pulling his hand from Rilla's. Rilla was so engrossed in wondering what was to become of Jims in the future that she forgot to take notice of what was happening to him in the present. What did happen was that Jims lost his balance, ~~and fell fell~~ shot headlong down the steps, hurtled across the little siding platform, and landed in a clump of bracken fern on the other side.

Rilla shrieked and lost her head. She sprang down the steps and jumped off the train.

Fortunately, the train was still going at a comparatively slow speed; fortunately also, Rilla, retained enough sense to jump the way it was going; nevertheless, she fell and sprawled helplessly down the embankment, landing in a ditch full of a rank growth of golden-rod and fireweed.

Nobody had seen what had happened and the train whisked briskly away around a curve in the barrens. Rilla picked herself up, dizzy but unhurt, scrambled out of the ditch, and flew wildly across the platform, expecting to find Jims dead or broken in pieces. But Jims, except for a few bruises, and a big fright, was quite ~~unhurt~~ ^**uninjured**^. He was so badly scared that he didn't even cry, but Rilla, when she found that he was safe and sound, burst into tears and sobbed wildly. ~~So it was Jims after all who enacted the part of comforter, with sundry hugs and kisses.~~

"Nasty old train," remarked Jims in disgust. "And nasty old God," he added, with a scowl at the heavens.

~~Rilla~~ A laugh broke into Rilla's sobbing, producing something very like what her father would have called hysterics. But she caught herself up before the hysteria could conquer her.

"Rilla Blythe, I'm ashamed of you. Pull yourself together immediately. Jims, you shouldn't have said anything like that."

~~"Why~~ "God ~~threw~~ frew me off the twain," declared Jims defiantly. "Somebody frew me; you didn't frow me; so it ~~must have been Go~~ was God."

"No, it wasn't. You fell because you let go of my hand and bent too far forward. I told you not to do that. So that it was your own fault."

Jims looked to see if she meant it; then ~~he~~ glanced up at the sky again.

"Excuse me, ^**then,**^ God," he remarked airily.

Rilla ~~looked up at~~ ^~~**scarmed**~~ **scanned**^ the sky also; she did not like its appearance; a heavy thundercloud was appearing in the north-west. What in the world was to be done? There was no other train that night, since the nine o'clock special ran only on Saturdays. Would it be possible for them to reach Hannah Brewster's house, ~~three~~ ^**two**^ miles away, before the storm broke. Rilla thought she could do it alone easily enough, but with Jims it was another matter. Were his ~~slim~~ ^**little**^ legs good for it?

"We've got to try it," said Rilla desperately. "We might stay in the siding until the thunderstorm is over; but it may keep on raining all night and anyway it will be pitch dark. If we can get to Hannah's she will keep us all night."

Hannah Brewster, when she had been Hannah Crawford, had lived in the Glen and gone to school with Rilla. They had been good friends then, ~~but Hannah had made a~~ though Hannah had been three years the older. She had married ~~when she was~~ very young and had gone to live in Millward. What with hard work and babies and a ne'er-do-well husband, her life had not been an easy one, and Hannah seldom revisited her old home. Rilla had ^**visited her once soon after her marriage, but had not**^ seen her or even heard of her for ~~four~~ ~~^**three**^~~ years; ~~but~~ she knew, ^**however, that**^ she and Jims would find welcome and harborage in any house where ~~Hannah lived~~ rosy-faced, open-hearted ~~Hannah lived~~, generous Hannah lived.

For the first mile they got on very well but the second one was harder. ^[*Note*] **G9**^ Jims grew so tired ~~durin~~ that Rilla had to carry him for the last quarter. She reached the Brewster house, almost exhausted, and dropped Jims on the walk with a sigh of thankfulness. The sky was black with clouds; the first ^**heavy**^ drops were beginning to fall; and the rumble of thunder was growing ~~any~~ ^**very**^ loud.

Then she made ~~a discovery that~~ an unpleasant discovery. The blinds were all down and the doors locked. Evidently the Brewsters were not at home. Rilla ran to the little barn. It, too, was locked. No other ~~re-furge~~ refuge presented itself. ~~There was~~ ^**The bare whitewashed little house had**^ not even a veranda or porch.

It was almost dark now and ~~the~~ her plight seemed desperate.

"I'm going to get in if I have to break a window," said Rilla resolutely. "Hannah would want me to do that. She'd never get over it if she heard I came to her house for refuge in a thunderstorm and couldn't get in."

Luckily she did not have to go to the length of ~~breaking into Hannah's ho~~ actual housebreaking. The kitchen window went up quite easily. Rilla lifted Jims in and scrambled through herself, just as the ~~rain came~~ storm broke in good earnest.

"Oh, see all the little pieces of thunder," cried Jims in delight, as the hail ~~pelted~~ ^**danced**^ in after them.

Rilla shut the window and with some difficulty found and lighted a lamp. ~~She found herself~~ ^**They were**^ in a very snug little kitchen. Opening off it on one side was a trim, nicely furnished parlour, and on the other a pantry, which proved to be well stocked.

"I'm ~~just~~ going to make myself at home," said Rilla. "I know that is just what Hannah would want me to do. I'll get a little snack for Jims and me, and then if the rain continues and nobody comes home I'll just ~~find~~ go upstairs to the spare room and go to bed. There is nothing like acting sensibly in an emergency. If I had not been a goose when I saw Jims fall off the train I'd have rushed back into the car and ~~pushed the~~ got some one to stop it. Then I wouldn't have been in this scrape. Since I am in it I'll make the best of it.

"This ~~place~~ ^**house**^," she added, looking around, "is fixed up much nicer than when I was here before. Of course Hannah and Ted were just beginning housekeeping then. But somehow I've had the idea that Ted hasn't been very prosperous ~~and~~. He must have done better than I've been led to believe, when they can afford furniture like this. I'm awfully glad for Hannah's sake."

The thunderstorm passed, but the rain continued to fall heavily. At ~~ten~~ ^**eleven**^ o'clock Rilla decided that nobody was coming home. Jims had fallen asleep on the sofa; she carried him up to the spare room and put him to bed. Then she undressed ~~and~~ ^[*Note*] **H9**^ and scrambled sleepily in between very nice lavender-scented sheets. She was so tired, after her adventures and exertions, that not even the oddity of her situation could keep her ~~asleep~~ awake; she ~~fell asleep~~ was ~~so~~ sound asleep in a few minutes.

Rilla slept until eight o'clock the next morning and then wakened with startling suddenness. ~~A harsh gruff vo~~ Somebody was saying in a harsh, gruff voice,

"Here, you two, wake up. I want to know what this means."

Rilla did wake up, promptly and effectually. She had never ^**in all her life**^ wakened up so thoroughly ~~in my ^**her**^ life~~ before. Standing in the room were three people, one of them a man, ~~upon whom she had never in her life laid her eyes~~ ^**who were absolute strangers to her**^. The man was a big~~, gray-hai~~ fellow with a bushy black beard and an angry scowl. Beside him was a woman – a tall, thin, angular person, with violently red hair and an indescribable hat. She looked even crosser and more amazed than the man, if that were possible. In the background was another woman – a ~~tiny~~ tiny old lady who must have been at least eighty. She was, in spite of her tinyness, a very striking-looking personage; she was dressed in unrelieved black, had snow-white hair, a dead-white face, and snapping, vivid, coal-black eyes. She looked as amazed as the other two, but Rilla realized that she didn't look cross.

Rilla also was realizing that something was wrong – fearfully wrong. Then the man said, more gruffly than ever,

"Come now. Who are you and what business have you here?"

Rilla raised herself on one elbow, looking and feeling hopelessly bewildered and foolish. She heard the old black-and-white lady in the background chuckle to herself. ^**Note U10**^

"Isn't this Theodore Brewster's place?" ~~she gasped.~~

"No," said the big woman, speaking for the first time, "this place belongs to us. We bought it from the Brewsters last fall. They moved to ~~Charlott the other end of the~~ to Greenvale. Our name is Chapley."

Poor Rilla fell back on her pillow, quite overcome.

"I beg your pardon," she said. "I – I – thought the Brewsters lived here. Mrs. Brewster ~~a~~ is a friend of mine. I am Rilla Blythe – Dr. Blythe's daughter from Glen St. Mary. I – I was going to town with my – my – this little boy – and he fell off the train – and I jumped off after him – and nobody knew of it. I knew we couldn't get home last night and a storm was coming up – so we came here and when we found nobody at home – we – we – just got in through the window and – and – made ourselves at home."

"So it seems," said the woman sarcastically.

"A likely story," said the man.

"We weren't born yesterday," ~~said~~ ^**added**^ the woman.

Madam Black-and-White didn't say anything; but when the other two made their pretty speeches she doubled up in a silent convulsion of mirth, shaking her head from side to side and beating the air with her hands.

~~Rilla thought she must be crazy. But~~

Rilla, stung by the disagreeable attitude of the Chapleys, regained her self-possession and lost her temper. She sat up in bed and said in ~~what she was accustomed to call her "cold pal~~ her haughtiest voice,

"I do not know when you were born, or where, but it must have been somewhere where very peculiar manners were taught. If you will have the ~~due~~ decency to leave ~~our~~ my room – er – this room – until ~~we~~ ^**I**^ can get up and dress I shall not transgress upon your hospitality" – Rilla was killingly sarcastic – "any longer. And I shall pay you ~~anply~~ ^**amply**^ for the food we have eaten and the night's lodging I have taken."

The black-and-white apparition went through the motion of clapping her hands, but not a sound did she make. Perhaps ~~he~~ ^**Mr ~~Chapman.~~ Chapley**^ was cowed by Rilla's tone – or perhaps he was appeased at the prospect of payment; at all events, ~~Mr. Chapman~~ ^**he**^ spoke more civilly.

"Well, that's fair. If you pay up it's all right."

"She shall do no such thing as pay you," said Madam Black-and-White in a surprisingly clear, resolute, authoritative tone of voice. "If you haven't got any shame for yourself, Robert ~~Chapman~~ ^**Chapley**^, you've got a mother-in-law who can be ashamed for you. No strangers shall be charged for room and lodging in any house where Mrs. Matilda Pitman lives. Remember that, ^**though**^ I may have come down in the world, I haven't quite forgot all ~~dec~~ decency for all that. I knew you was a skin flint when Amelia married you, and you've made her as bad as yourself. But ~~I'm boss here I've~~ ^**Mrs. Matilda Pitman has**^ been boss for a long time, and Mrs. Matilda Pitman will remain boss. Here you, Robert Chap~~man~~^**ley**^, take yourself out of here and let that girl get dressed. And you, Amelia, go downstairs and cook a breakfast for her."

Never, in all her life, had Rilla seen anything like the abject meekness with which those two big people obeyed that mite. They went ~~and~~ without word or look of protest. As the door closed behind them Mrs. Matilda Pitman laughed silently, and rocked from side to side in her merriment.

"Ain't it funny?" she said. "I mostly lets them run the length of their ~~terror~~ tether, but sometimes I has to pull them up, and then ~~they dan~~ I does it with a jerk. They don't dast aggravate me, because I've got considerable ^**hard**^ cash, and they're afraid I won't leave it all to them. Neither I will. I'll leave 'em some, but some I won't, just to vex 'em. I haven't made up my mind where I will leave it but I'll have to, soon, for at eighty ~~you can't afford to let things slide~~ ^**a body is living on borrowed time.**^ Now, you can take your time about dressing, my dear, and I'll go down and keep them mean scallawags in order. That's a handsome child you have there. Is he your brother?"

"No, he's a little war-baby I've been taking care of, because his mother died and his father was overseas," answered Rilla in a subdued tone.

"War-baby? Humph! Well, I'd better skin out before he wakes up or he'll likely start crying. Children don't like me – never did. I can't recollect any youngster ever coming near me of its own accord. ~~Even~~ Never had any of my own. Amelia was my step-daughter. Well, it's saved me a ~~lost of trouble~~ ^**world of bother**^. If kids don't like me I don't like them, so that's an even score. But that certainly is a handsome child."

~~At the~~ Jims chose this moment for waking up. He opened his big brown eyes and looked at Mrs. Matilda Pitman unblinkingly. Then he sat up, ~~smiled~~ ^**dimpled**^ deliciously, pointed to her and said solemnly to Rilla,

"P'witty lady, Willa – pwitty lady."

Mrs. Matilda Pitman smiled. Even eighty-odd is sometimes vulnerable in vanity.

"I've heard that children and fools tell the truth," she said. "I was used to compliments when I was young – but they're scarcer when you get as far along as I am. ^**I haven't had one for years. It tastes good.**^ I s'pose now, you monkey, you wouldn't give me a kiss."

^**Then**^ Jims did a quite surprising thing. He was not a demonstrative youngster and was chary with kisses even to the Ingleside people. But without a word he stood up in bed, his plump little body encased only in his undershirt, ran to the footboard, flung his arms about Mrs. Matilda Pitman's neck, and gave ~~a hearty~~ ^**her a bear**^ hug, accompanied by three or four hearty, ungrudging smacks.

"Jims," protested Rilla, aghast at this liberty.

"You ~~lev~~ leave him be," ~~said~~ ^**ordered**^ Mrs. Matilda Pitman, setting her bonnet straight. ~~"He's the only child that ever took to me."~~ "Laws I like to see some one that isn't skeered of me. Everybody is – you are, though you're trying to hide it. And why? Of course Robert and Amelia are because I make 'em skeered on purpose. But folks always are – no matter how civil I be to them. Are you going to keep this child?"

"I'm afraid not. His father is coming home before long."

"Is he any good – the father, I mean?"

"Well – he's kind and nice – but he's poor – and I'm afraid he always will be," faltered Rilla.

"I see – shiftless – can't make or keep. Well, I'll see – I'll see. I have an idea. It's a good idea, and besides it will make Robert and Amelia squirm. That's its main ~~advantag~~ merit in my eyes, though I like that child, mind you, ^**because he ain't skeered of me. He's worth some bother.**^ Now, you get dressed, as I said before, and come down when you're good and ready."

Rilla was stiff and sore after her tumble and walk of the night before but she was not long in dressing herself and Jims. When she went down to the kitchen she found a smoking hot breakfast on the table. Mr. Chapley was nowhere in sight and Mrs. Chapley was cutting bread with a sulky air. Mrs. Matilda Pitman was sitting in an armchair, knitting a gray army sock. She still wore her bonnet and her triumphant expression.

"Set right in, dears, and make a good breakfast," she said.

~~"We~~ "I am not hungry," said Rilla almost pleadingly. "I don't think I can eat anything. And it is time I was starting for the station. The morning train will soon be along. Please excuse me and let us go – I'll take a piece of bread and butter for Jims."

Mrs. Matilda Pitman shook a knitting needle playfully at Rilla.

"Sit down and take your breakfast," she said. "Mrs. Matilda Pitman commands you. Everybody obeys Mrs. Matilda Pitman – even Robert and Amelia. You must obey her too."

Rilla did obey her. She sat down and, such was the influence of Mrs. Matilda Pitman's mesmeric eye, ~~that~~ she ate a tolerable breakfast. The obedient Amelia never spoke; Mrs. Matilda Pitman did not speak either; but she knitted furiously and chuckled. When Rilla had finished, Mrs. Matilda Pitman rolled up her sock.

"Now you can go if you want to," she said, "but you don't have to go. You can stay here as long as you want to and I'll make Amelia cook your meals for you."

~~Rilla t~~The independent Miss Blythe, whom ^**a**^ certain ^**clique of**^ Junior Red Cross girls accused of being domineering and "bossy," was thoroughly cowed.

[*Error in ms: page number "478" appears on two consecutive pages.*]

"Thank you," she said meekly, "but we must really go."

"Well, then," said Mrs. Matilda Pitman, throwing open the door. "Your conveyance is ready for you. I told Robert he must hitch up and drive you to the station. I enjoy making Robert do things. It's almost the only sport I have left. I'm ^**over**^ eighty and most things have lost their flavor except bossing Robert."

Robert sat before the door on the front seat of a trim, double-seated, rubber-tired buggy. He must have heard every word his mother-in-law said but he gave no sign.

"I do wish," said Rilla, plucking up what little spirit she had left, "that you would let me – oh – ah –" then she quailed again before Mrs. Matilda Pitman's eye – "recompense you for – for –"

"Mrs. Matilda Pitman said before – and meant it – that she doesn't take pay for entertaining strangers, nor let other people where she lives do it, much as their natural meanness would like to do it. You go along to town and don't forget to call the next time you come this way. Don't be scared. Not that ~~your~~ you are scared of much, ~~I like your spunk – I liked~~ ^**I reckon, considering**^ the way you sassed Robert back this morning. I like your spunk. Most girls nowadays are such timid, skeery creeturs. When I was a girl I wasn't afraid of nothing nor nobody. Mind you take good care of that boy. He ain't any common child. ~~Mind you~~ ^**And**^ make Robert drive around all the puddles in the road. I won't have that new buggy splashed."

~~They got into the buggy~~

As they drove away Jims threw kisses at Mrs. Matilda Pitman as long as he could see her, and Mrs. Matilda Pitman waved her sock back at him. Robert spoke no word, either good or bad, all the way to the station, but he remembered the puddles. When Rilla got out at the siding she thanked him courteously. The only response she got was a grunt as Robert turned his horse and started for home.

"Well" – Rilla drew a long breath – "I must try to get back into Rilla Blythe again. I've been somebody else these past few hours – I don't know just who – some creation of that extraordinary old person's. I believe she hypnotized me. What an ~~account of this~~ adventure this will be to write the boys."

And then she sighed. Bitter remembrance came that there were only Jerry and Carl and Shirley to write it to now. Jem – who would have appreciated Mrs. Matilda Pitman keenly – where was Jem?

[*Montgomery's note on top of first page of chapter 32:*] "4 years since lighthouse dance"

Chap. 32

Word From Jem

Aug. 4,1918

"It is four years tonight since the dance at the lighthouse – four years ~~since~~ of war. It seems like three times four. I was fifteen then. I am nineteen now. I expected that these past four years would be the most delightful years of my life and they have been years of war – years of fear and grief and worry – but I humbly hope, of a little growth in strength and character as well.

"To-day I was going through the hall and I heard mother saying something to father about me. I didn't mean to listen – I couldn't help hearing her as I went along the hall and upstairs – so perhaps that is why I heard what listeners are said never to hear – something good of myself. And because it was mother who said ^**it**^ I'm going to write it here in my journal, for my comforting when days of discouragement come upon ~~in which~~ me, in which I feel that I am vain and selfish and weak and that there is no good thing in me.

"'Rilla has developed in a wonderful fashion these past four years. She used to be such an irresponsible young creature. She has changed into a capable, womanly girl and ~~has been~~ ^**she is**^ such a comfort to me. ~~I don't see how~~ Nan and Di have grown a little away from me – they have been so little at home – but Rilla has grown closer and closer to me. ^**We are chums.**^ I don't see how I could have got through these terrible years without her, Gilbert.[22]'

"There, that is just what mother said – and I feel glad – and sorry – and proud – and humbled! It's beautiful to have ~~one's~~ ^**my**^ mother think that about me – but I don't deserve it quite. I'm not as good and strong as all that. There are heaps of times when I have felt cross and impatient and ~~discour~~ woeful and despairing. It is mother ^**and Susan**^ who have been this family's ~~tower of strength~~ ^**backbone**^. But I have helped ~~her~~ a little, ^**I believe,**^ and I am so glad and thankful.

~~Mother and I are chums. We can just talk and laugh together like two girls.~~

"The war news has been good right along. The French and Americans are pushing the Germans back and back and back. Sometimes I am afraid it is too good to last – after nearly four years of disasters one has a feeling that this constant success is unbelievable.

"We don't rejoice ~~very~~ noisily over it. Susan keeps the flag up but we go softly. The price paid has been too high for jubilation. We are just thankful that it has not been paid in vain.

"~~There~~ No word has come from Jem. We hope – because we dare not do anything else. But there are hours when we all feel – though we never say so – that such hoping is foolishness. ~~And then again there are hours when we feel a strange, n.~~ ~~Th~~ ~~Such~~ ^**These**^ hours come more and more frequently as the ~~days~~ weeks go by. And we may never know. That is the most terrible thought of all. I wonder how Faith is bearing it. To judge from her letters ~~you would~~ she has never for a moment given up hope, but she must have had her dark hours of doubt like the rest of us."

Aug. 20, 1918

"^**The Canadians have been in action again and**^ Mr. Meredith had a cable to-day saying that Carl had been slightly wounded and is in the hospital. It did not say where the wound was, which is unusual, and we all feel worried.

"There is news of a ~~new~~ ^**fresh**^ victory every day now."

Aug. 30, 1918

"The Merediths had a letter from Carl to-day. His wound was 'only a slight one' – but it was in his right eye and the sight is gone for ever!

"'One eye is enough to watch bugs with,' Carl writes cheerfully. And we know it might have been oh so much worse! If it had been both eyes! But I cried all the afternoon after I saw Carl's letter. Those beautiful, fearless blue eyes of his!

"There is one comfort – he will not have to go back to the front. He is coming home as soon as he is out of the hospital – the first of our boys to return. When will the others come?

“And there is one who will never come. ~~But –~~ At least we will not see him if he does. But, oh, I think he will be there – when ~~the~~ ^**our**^ Canadian soldiers return there will be ~~an unseen~~ ^**a shadowy**^ army with them – the army of the fallen. We will not see them – but they will be there!”

September 1, 1918

“Mother and I went into Charlottetown yesterday to see ^**the ~~seven~~ moving picture,**^ ‘Hearts of the World.’ I made an awful goose of myself – father will never stop teasing me about it for the rest of my life. But it ~~was~~ all ^**seemed**^ so horribly real – and I was so intensely interested that I forgot everything but the scenes I saw enacted before my eyes. And then, quite near the last came a terribly exciting one. The heroine was struggling with a horrible German soldier who was trying to drag her away. I knew she had a knife – I had seen her hide it, ~~the night before,~~ to have it in readiness – and I couldn’t understand why she didn’t produce it and finish the brute. I thought she must have forgotten it, and just at the tensest moment of the scene I lost my head altogether. I just stood right up on my feet in that crowded house and shrieked at the top of my voice – ~~“~~‘The knife is in your stocking – the knife is in your stocking.~~”~~’

~~Imagine the sensation I made.~~ ^**“I created a sensation!**^

“The funny part was, that just as I said it, the girl did snatch out the knife and stab the soldier with it!

~~But imagine the sensation I made.~~ “Everybody in the house laughed. I came to my senses and fell back in my seat, overcome with mortification. Mother was shaking with laughter. I could have shaken ~~her~~ her. Why ~~didn’t she~~ hadn’t she pulled me down and choked me before I had made such an idiot of myself? She protests that there wasn’t time.

“Fortunately the house was dark, and I don’t believe there was anybody there who knew me. And I thought I was becoming sensible and self-controlled and womanly! It is plain I have some distance to go yet before I attain that devoutly desired consummation.”

~~Serbia has come to life and is beginning to win victories.~~

Sept. 20, 1918

“In the east Bulgaria has asked for peace, and in the west the British have smashed the Hindenburg line; and right here in Glen St. Mary little Bruce Meredith has done something ~~wonderful~~ that I think wonderful – wonderful because of the love behind it. Mrs. Meredith was here tonight and told us about it – and mother and I cried, and Susan got up and clattered the things about the stove.

“Bruce ~~has~~ always loved Jem very devotedly, and the child has never forgotten him in all these years. He has been as faithful in his way as Dog Monday has in his. We have always told him that Jem would come back. But it seems that he was in Carter Flagg’s store last night and he heard ~~Norman~~ his Uncle Norman flatly declaring that Jem Blythe would never come back and that the Ingleside folk might as well give up hoping he would. Bruce went home and cried ~~all night~~ ^**himself to sleep**^. This morning his mother saw him going out of the yard, with a very sorrowful and determined look ~~on his face~~, carrying his pet kitten. She didn’t think much more about it until later on he came in, with the most tragic little face, and told her, his little body shaking with sobs, that he had drowned Stripey.

“‘Why did you do that?”’ Mrs. Meredith exclaimed.

“‘To bring Jem back,”’ sobbed Bruce. “‘I thought if I ~~sacrificed~~ ^**~~sacrificed~~ sacrificed**^ Stripey God would send Jem back. So I – drownded him – and, oh mother, it was awful hard – but surely God will send Jem back now, ’cause Stripey was the dearest thing I had. I just told God I would give Him Stripey if He would send Jem back. And He will, won’t He, mother?”’

~~Poor~~ “Mrs. Meredith didn’t know what to say to the poor child. ~~He loved that kitten devotedly and it was heroic self- sacr~~ She just could not tell him that perhaps even his sacrifice wouldn’t bring Jem back – that God didn’t work that way. She told him that he mustn’t expect it right away – that perhaps it would be quite a long time yet before Jem came back. But Bruce said,

“‘It oughtn’t to take longer’n a week, mother. ~~I’ll just give Him a~~

~~week to If Jem isn't back then I'll know that Stripey wasn't big enough for a sacrifice~~ Oh, mother, Stripey was such a nice little cat. ~~Don't~~ He purred so pretty. Don't you think God ought to like him enough to let us have Jem?~~”~~'

"Mr. Meredith is worried about the effect on Bruce's faith in God, and Mrs. Meredith is worried about the effect on Bruce himself if his hope isn't fulfilled. And I feel as if I must cry every time I think of it. It was so splendid ~~– and devoted~~ – and sad – and beautiful. The dear ~~heroic little~~ devoted little fellow! He ~~just~~ worshipped that kitten. And if it all goes for nothing – as so many sacrifices seem to go for nothing – he will be broken hearted, for he isn't old enough to understand that God doesn't answer our prayers just as we hope – and doesn't make bargains with us when we ~~give up~~ ^**yield**^ something we love up to Him. ~~There is something in this little hap and that happening that wrings my heart.~~"

September 24~~3~~, 1918

"I have been kneeling at my window in the moonshine for a long time, just thanking God over and over again. The joy of ~~this~~ ^**last night and to-**^day has been so great that it ~~was half~~ seemed half pain – as if our hearts weren't big enough to hold it.

~~Last night I couldn't sleep and neither could Gertrude; so she came in with me and we talked together for a long time.~~

~~Last night I couldn't went to bed early but I couldn't sleep. Neither could Gertrude; so she came in with me and we sat talked~~

"Last night I was sitting here in my room at eleven o'clock writing ~~in~~ a letter to Shirley. Everyone else was in bed, except father, who was out. I heard the telephone ring and I ~~rang~~ ran out to the hall to answer it, before it should waken mother. It was long-distance calling, ~~from Charlottetown~~ and when I answered it said 'This is the telegraph Company's office in Charlottetown. There is an overseas cable for Dr. Blythe.~~”~~'

"I thought of Shirley – my heart stood still – and then ~~over the wires the message came.~~ I heard him saying, '~~“~~It's from Holland.~~”~~'

~~“Holland. Sept 21.~~
~~Escaped from Germany~~ ^**“The message was,**^

‘“Just arrived. Escaped from Germany. Quite well. Writing.
James Blythe.”’

“I didn’t faint or fall or scream. I didn’t feel glad or surprised. I didn’t feel anything. ^[*Note*] **V10**^ I hung up the receiver and turned round. Mother was standing in her doorway. She wore her ~~pale pink~~ ^**old rose**^ kimono, and her hair was hanging down her back in a long thick braid, and her eyes were shining. She looked just like a young girl.

‘“There is word from Jem?”’ she said.

“How did she know? I hadn’t said a word ^**at the phone**^ except ‘~~“~~yes – yes – yes.”’ She says she doesn’t know how she knew but she did know. ~~When she heard~~ She was awake and she heard the ring and she knew that ~~there~~ there was word from Jem.

‘“He’s ~~safe~~ ^**alive**^ – he’s well – he’s in Holland,”’ I said.

“Mother came ~~to the phone and~~ out into the hall and said,

‘“I must get your father on the ’phone and tell him. He is in the Upper Glen.”’

~~I left~~ “She was ~~quite~~ ^**very**^ calm and ~~radiant~~ ^**quiet**^ – not a bit like I would have expected her to be. But then I wasn’t either. I went and woke up Gertrude and Susan and told them. Susan said ‘Thank God,’ firstly, and secondly she said ^**‘Did I not tell you Dog Monday knew?’ and thirdly,**^ ‘I’ll go down and make a cup of tea’ – and she stalked down in her nightdress to make it. She did make it – and made mother and Gertrude drink it – but I went back to my room and shut my door and locked it, and I knelt by my window and cried – just as Gertrude did when her great news came.

“I think I know at last exactly what I shall feel like on the resurrection morning.”

October ~~4~~3, 1918

“To-day Jem’s letter came. It has been in the house only six hours and it is almost read to pieces. ~~Every~~ The post-mistress told everybody in the Glen it had come, and everybody came up to hear the news.

“Jem was badly wounded in the thigh – and he was picked up and taken to prison, so delirious with fever that he didn’t know what was happening to him or where he was. It was weeks before he came to his senses and was able to write. Then he did write – but it never came. He wasn’t treated at all badly at his camp – only the food was poor. ^[*Note*] **S9**^

“He wrote us as often as he could but he was afraid we were not getting his letters because no reply came. As soon as he was strong enough he tried to escape, but was caught and brought back; a month later he and a comrade made another attempt and succeeded in reaching Holland.

“Jem can’t come home right away. He isn’t quite so well as his cable said, for his wound has not healed properly and he has to go into a hospital in England for ^**further**^ treatment. ~~But we know he is safe.~~ But he ~~say~~ says he will be all right eventually, and we know he is safe and will be back home sometime,– and oh, the difference it makes~~.~~” in everything!

“I had a letter from Jim Anderson to-day, too. He has ~~gone and~~ married ~~and~~ an English girl, got his discharge, and is coming right home to Canada ^**with his bride**^. I don’t know whether to be glad or sorry. It will depend on what kind of a woman she is. I had ~~a third~~ ^**a second**^ letter also of a somewhat mysterious tenor. It is from a Charlottetown lawyer, asking me to go in to see him at my earliest convenience in ~~connection~~ regard to ^**a**^ certain matter connected with the estate of the ‘late Mrs. Matilda Pitman.’

“I ~~had~~ read a notice of Mrs. Pitman’s death – from heart failure – in the Enterprise a few weeks ago. I wonder if this summons has anything to do with Jims.”

October 4, 1918

“I went into town this morning and had an interview with Mrs. Pitman’s lawyer – a little thin, wispy man, who spoke of his late client with such ~~evident~~ ^**profound**^ respect that it is evident that he was as much under her thumb as Robert and Amelia were. He drew up a new will for her a short time before her death. She was worth ~~30,000~~ thirty thousand dollars, the bulk of which was left to Amelia Chapley. But she left ~~$5,000~~ ^**five thousand**^ to me in trust for Jims. The interest is to be used as I see fit for his education, ~~and~~ and the principal is to be paid over to him on his ~~18th birth 20th~~ ^**twentieth**^ birthday.

"Certainly Jims was born ~~under a~~ lucky ~~star~~. I saved him from slow extinction at the hands of Mrs. Conover – Mary Vance saved him from death by diptheritic croup ~~– Providence saved him when he fell off the train~~ – his star saved him when he fell off the train. And he tumbled ^**not only into a clump of bracken, but**^ right into this nice little legacy ~~– all because~~. Evidently, as Mrs. Matilda Pitman said, and as I have always believed, he is no common child and he has no common destiny in store for him.

"At all events he is provided for, and in such a fashion that Jim Anderson can't squander ~~the~~ his inheritance if he wanted to. Now, if the new English step-mother is only ~~the right~~ ^**a good**^ sort I shall feel quite easy about ^**the future of**^ my war-baby.

I wonder what Robert and Amelia think of it. I fancy they will nail down their windows when they leave home after this!"

Chapter 33

Victory!!

"A day 'of chilling winds and gloomy skies,'" Rilla quoted one Sunday afternoon – the 6th of October to be exact. It was so cold that they had lighted a fire in the living room and the merry little flames ~~sparkled~~ were doing their best to counteract the outside dourness. ^[*Note*] **K9**^ ~~^**"November is such an ugly month.**^~~

Cousin Sophia was there, having again forgiven Susan, and Mrs. Martin Clow, who was not visiting on Sunday but had dropped in to ~~inquire about Susan't rheumatism~~ borrow Susan's cure for rheumatism – that being cheaper than getting one from the doctor.

"I'm afeared we're going to have an airly winter," foreboded Cousin Sophia. "The muskrats are building awful big houses round the pond, and that's a sign that never fails. Dear me, how that child has grown!" Cousin Sophia sighed again, as if it were an unhappy circumstance that a child should grow. "When do you expect his father?"

"Next week," said Rilla.

"Well, I hope the stepmother won't abuse the pore child," sighed Cousin Sophia, "but I have my doubts – I have my doubts. Anyhow, he'll be sure to feel the difference between his usage here and what he'll get anywhere else. You've spoiled him so, Rilla, what with making so much of him and waiting on him hand and foot the way you've always done."

Rilla smiled and pressed her cheek to Jims' ~~curly hea~~ curls. ^**She knew**^ her sweet-tempered, sunny, ~~wonderful~~ little Jims ^**was not**^ "spoiled." Nevertheless her heart was anxious behind her smile. She, too, thought much about the new Mrs. Anderson and wondered uneasily what she would be like.

"I <u>can't</u> give Jims up to a woman who won't love him," she thought rebelliously.

~~"It's beginning to rain,"~~ ^**"I b'lieve it's agoing to rain,"**^ said Cousin Sophia. "We have had an awful lot of rain this fall already. It's going to make it awful hard for people to get their roots in. It wasn't so in my young days. We gin'rally had beautiful Octobers then. But the seasons is altogether different now from what they ~~were then~~ used to be."

Clear across Cousin Sophia's doleful voice cut the telephone bell. ~~Miss~~ Gertrude Oliver answered it. "Yes – what? What? Is it true – is it official? Thank you – thank you."

Gertrude turned and faced the room dramatically, her dark eyes flashing, her dark face ~~crimson~~ flushed with feeling. ^[*Note*] **N9**^

"Germany and Austria are suing for peace," she said.

~~Everybody went crazy for a few minutes~~

~~Everybody~~

Rilla went crazy for a few minutes. She sprang up and danced around the room, ~~waving~~ ^**clapping**^ her ~~han ha~~ hands, laughing, crying.

"Sit down, child," said Mrs. Clow, who never got excited over anything, and so had missed a tremendous amount of trouble and delight in her journey through life.

"Oh," cried Rilla, ^[*Note*] **I9**^ "It was worth living long dreary years for this minute, and it would be worth living them again just to look back to it. Susan, let's run up the flag – and we must 'phone the news to everyone in the Glen."

"Can we have as much sugar as we want to now?" asked Jims eagerly.

It was a never-to-be-forgotten afternoon. As the news spread excited people ran about the village and dashed up to Ingleside. The Merediths came over and stayed to supper and everybody talked and nobody listened. Cousin Sophia tried to protest that Germany and Austria were not to be trusted and it was all part of a plot, but nobody ~~listened to her.~~ ^**paid the least attention to her.**^

"This Sunday makes up for that one in March," said Susan.

"I wonder," said Gertrude dreamily, apart to Rilla, "if things won't seem rather flat and insipid when ~~the~~ peace really comes. After being fed for four years on horrors and fears, terrible reverses, amazing victories, ~~all news will~~, won't anything less be tame and uninteresting? How strange – and blessed – and dull it will be not to dread the coming of the mail every day."

"We must dread it for a little while yet, I suppose," said Rilla~~, with a sigh~~. "Peace won't come – can't come for some weeks yet. ~~I suppose~~

And in those weeks dreadful things ~~might~~ ^**may**^ happen. My excitement is over. We have won the victory – but oh, what a price we have paid!"

"Not too high a price for freedom," said Gertrude softly. "Do you think it was, Rilla?"

~~"No." I know no price is too high for that.~~

"No," said Rilla, under her breath. She was seeing a little white cross on a battlefield of France. "No – not if those of us who live will show ourselves worthy of ~~the price paid~~ ^**it**^ – if we 'keep faith.'"

"We will keep faith," said Gertrude. She rose ~~and went forward into the cer centre of the room.~~ ^**suddenly.**^ A silence fell ^**around the table**^, and in the silence Gertrude repeated Walter's famous ~~porm~~ poem "The Piper." When she finished Mr. Meredith ~~rose~~ stood ~~up~~ and held up his glass.

"Let us drink," he said, "to the silent army ~~– ^ To the victorious to the victorious legion ^to the boys in khaki^ who 'for our to-morrow gave their to-day.'~~ [*Error in ms: page number "502" appears on two consecutive pages.*]

to the boys who followed when the Piper summoned. 'For our to-morrow they gave their today' – theirs is the victory!"

Chapter 34

Mr. Hyde Goes To His Own Place and Susan Takes a Honeymoon

~~One day early in November Jim Anderson walked in with his~~

Early in November Jims left ~~Inglside~~ ^**Ingleside**^ ~~– with the soup tureen, though not in it~~. Rilla saw him go with many tears but a heart free from boding. Mrs. Jim Anderson, ~~No~~ ^**Number**^ Two, was ~~a dear little w~~ such a nice little woman that one was rather inclined to wonder at the luck which bestowed her on Jim. She was rosy-faced and blue-eyed and wholesome, ~~shamed and~~ ^**with the roundness and trigness of a geranium leaf.**^ Rilla saw at first glance that she was to be trusted with Jims.

"I'm fond of children, miss," she said heartily. ~~"I've left~~ "I'm used to them – I've left six little brothers and sisters behind me. Jims is a dear child and I must say you've done wonders in bringing him up so healthy and handsome. I'll be as good to him as if he was my own, ~~and you needn't~~ miss. And I'll make Jim toe the line all right. He's a good worker – all he needs is someone to keep him at it, and take charge of his money. ~~We're~~ We've rented a little farm just out of the village, and we're going to settle down there. Jim wanted to stay in England but I says 'No.' I ~~wanted~~ ^**hankered**^ to try a new country and I've always thought Canada ~~will~~ ^**would**^ suit me."

"I'm so glad you are going to live near us.~~" said Rilla.~~ ~~"~~You'll let Jims come here often, won't you? I love him dearly."

"No doubt you do, miss, for a lovabler child I never did see. We understand, Jim and me, what you've done for him, and you won't find us ungrateful. He can come here whenever you want him and I'll always be glad of any advice from you about his bringing-up. He is more your baby than anyone else's I should say, and I'll see that you get your fair share of him, miss."

So Jims went away – with the soup tureen, though not in it. ~~As he drove away beside his father, hugging the big soup tureen in his arms. Rilla thought of the day she had brought him home – a little red, wrin-~~

~~kled, motherless baby.~~ Then the news of the Armistice came, and even Glen St. Mary went mad. That night the village had a bonfire, and burned the Kaiser in effigy. ~~They even~~ ^[*Note*] **J9**^ Up at Ingleside Rilla ran laughing to her room.

"Now I'm going to do a most unladylike and inexcusable thing," she said, as she pulled her green velvet hat out of its box. "I'm going to kick this hat about the room until it is without form and void; and I shall never as long as I live wear anything of that shade of green again."

^[*Note*] **L9**^

Susan came in from the outdoor sunlight looking supremely satisfied.

"Mr. Hyde is gone, ~~Mrs. Dr.~~" she announced.

"Gone! Do you mean he is dead, Susan?"

"No, Mrs. Dr. dear, that beast is not dead. But you will never see him again.~~" He has gone to his own place."~~ ^**I feel sure of that."**^

"Don't be so mysterious, Susan. What has happened to him?"

"Well, Mrs. Dr. dear, he was sitting out on the ~~veranda~~ back veranda steps this afternoon. ~~It was lookin~~ It was just after the news came that the armistice had been signed and he was looking his Hydest. I can assure you he was an awesome looking beast. All at once, Mrs. Dr. dear, Bruce Meredith came around the corner of the kitchen walking on his stilts. He has been learning to walk on them lately and came over to show me how well he could do it. Mr. Hyde just took ~~one~~ ^**a**^ look and one bound carried him over the yard fence. Then he went tearing through the maple grove in great leaps with his ears laid back. You never saw a creature so terrified, Mrs. Dr. dear. He has never returned."

"Oh, he'll come back, Susan, probably chastened in spirit by his fright."

"We will see, Mrs. Dr. dear – we will see. Remember, the armistice has been signed. And that reminds me that Whiskers-on-the-Moon had a paralytic stroke last night. I am not saying it is a judgment on him, because I am not in the counsels of the Almighty, but one can have one's own thoughts about it. And neither Whiskers-on-the-Moon or ~~Mr.~~ Hyde will be much more heard of in Glen St. Mary, Mrs. Dr. dear, and that you may tie to."

Mr. Hyde certainly was heard of no more. As it could hardly have been his fright that kept him away the Ingleside folk decided that some dark fate of shot or poison had descended on him – except Susan, who believed and continued to affirm that he had merely "gone to his own place." ^[*Note*] **V9**^

"And now, Mrs. Dr, dear," said Susan, "since the fall house-cleaning is over and the ~~carrots and beets are in~~ ^**garden truck is all safe in cellar**^, I am going to take a honeymoon to celebrate the peace."

"A honeymoon, Susan?"

"Yes, Mrs. Dr. dear, a honeymoon," repeated Susan firmly. "I shall never be able to get a husband but I am not going to be cheated out of everything and a honeymoon I intend to have. I ~~shall be away for a fortnight~~ am going to Charlottetown to visit my married brother and his family ~~and I~~. ^[*Note*] **M9**^ shall be away a fortnight if you can spare me so long."

"You certainly deserve a good holiday, Susan. Better take a month – that is the proper length for a honeymoon."

"No, Mrs. Dr. dear, a fortnight is all I require. Besides, I must be home for at least three weeks before Christmas to make the proper preparations. We will have a Christmas that is a Christmas this year, Mrs. Dr. dear. Do you think there is any chance of our boys being home for it?"

"No, I think not, Susan. Both Jem and Shirley write that they don't expect to be home before spring – it may be even midsummer before Shirley comes. But Carl Meredith will be home, and Nan and Di, and we will have a grand celebration ~~– with," added the mother~~ ^**once more**^. We'll set chairs for all, Susan, as you did our first war Christmas – yes, for all – for my dear lad whose chair must always be vacant, as well as for the others, Susan."

"It is not likely I would forget to set his place, Mrs. Dr. dear," said Susan, wiping her eyes as she departed to pack up for her "honeymoon." [*The text of Note N9 is inserted here in the manuscript and then crossed out.*]

~~N9 All at one the sun broke through the thick clouds and poured through the big crimson maple outside the window. Its reflected glow enveloped her in a weird, unnatural flame. She looked like a priestess, performing some mystic, splendid rite.~~

Chapter 35

~~The End of Dog Monday's Vigil~~

"Rilla-my-Rilla!"

Carl Meredith and Miller Douglas came home just before Christmas and Glen St. Mary met them at the station with a brass band borrowed from Lowbridge and speeches of home manufacture. Miller was brisk and beaming in spite of his wooden leg; he had developed into a broad-shouldered, imposing looking fellow and the D.S.O. Medal he wore reconciled Miss Cornelia to the shortcomings of his pedigree~~.~~ ~~She allowed Mary's~~ to such a degree that she tacitly recognized his engagement to Mary. The latter put on a few airs – especially when Carter Flagg took Miller into his store as head clerk – but nobody grudged them to her.

"Of course farming's out of the question for us now," she told Rilla, "but Miller thinks he'll like storekeeping fine once he gets used to a quiet life again, and Carter Flagg will be a more agreeable boss than old Kitty. We're going to be married in the fall and live in the old Meade house with the bay windows and the mansard roof. I've always thought that the handsomest house in the Glen, but never did I dream I'd ever live there. We're only renting it, of course, but if things go as we expect and Carter Flagg takes Miller into partnership we'll own it some day. ^[*Note*] **Q9**^ ~~Miller's real ambitious~~ ~~^**and we mean to get on**^~~ He says he never saw a French girl worth looking at twice and that his heart beat true to me every moment he was away."

Jerry ^**Meredith**^ and Joe Milgrave came back in ~~February~~ January, and all winter the boys from the Glen and ~~Four Winds are~~ its environs came home ~~at~~ by twos and threes. None ^**of them**^ came back just as ~~he~~ ^**they**^ went away, not even those who had been so fortunate as to escape injury.

One spring ~~afternoo~~ day, when the daffodils were blowing on the Ingleside lawn, ^[*Note*] **R9**^ the little, lazy afternoon accommodation ^**train**^ pulled into the Glen station. ~~Nobody was there to meet it, except the new station agent, for very few passengers ever came on it.~~ ~~Very~~ It was very seldom that passengers for the Glen came by that train, so nobody was there to meet it except the new station agent and a small black and ~~white~~ ^**yellow**^ dog, who for four and a half years had met every train that had steamed into Glen St. ~~Mary~~ Mary ~~and who was still waiting there~~. Thousands of trains had Dog Monday met and never had the boy he waited and watched ~~for~~ ^**for**^ returned. Yet still Dog Monday watched on with ~~wistful~~ eyes that never ^**quite**^ lost hope. Perhaps his dog-heart failed him ~~some~~ ^**at**^ times; he was growing old and rheumatic; when he ~~trotted~~ ^**walked**^ back to his kennel after each train had gone his gait was very sober now – he never trotted but ~~walked~~ ^**went**^ slowly with ~~his head and tail drooping a little~~ a drooping head and a depressed tail that had ^**quite**^ lost its old saucy uplift. ~~He knew his master would come back sometime; but would he come.~~

One passenger stepped off the train – a tall fellow in a faded lieutenant's uniform, who walked with a barely perceptible limp. He had a bronzed face and there were some gray hairs in the ruddy curls that clustered around his forehead. The new station agent looked at him anxiously . He was used to seeing the khaki-clad figures come off the train, some met by a tumultuous crowd, others ~~like this one~~, who had sent no word of their coming, stepping off quietly ^**like this one**^. But there was a certain distinction of bearing ^**and features**^ in this soldier that caught his attention and made him wonder a little more interestedly who he was.

A black-and-~~white~~ ^**yellow**^ streak shot past the station agent. Dog Monday stiff? Dog Monday rheumatic? Dog Monday old? Never believe it. Dog Monday was a young pup, gone ^**clean**^ mad with ^**rejuvenating**^ joy ~~and rapture~~.

He flung himself against the tall soldier, with a ~~choked~~ bark that choked in his throat from sheer rapture. He flung himself on the ground and writhed in a ~~frenzy~~ frenzy of welcome. He tried to climb the soldier's ~~kah~~ khaki legs and slipped down and groveled in an ecstasy that seemed as if it must tear his little body in pieces. He licked his boots and when the lieutenant had, with laughter on his lips and tears in his eyes, succeeded in gathering the little ~~dog~~ ^**creature**^ up in his arms Dog Monday laid his head on the khaki shoulder and licked the sunburned neck, making queer sounds between barks and sobs.

The station agent had heard the story of Dog Monday. He knew now who the returned soldier was. ~~Jem Blythe had come home.~~ Dog Monday's long vigil was ended. Jem Blythe had come home.

~~“We are so happy that it fright~~

“We are all very happy – and sad – and thankful,” wrote Rilla in her diary a week later. ^**Note W10**^

“It is wonderful to have Jem back – and little Dog Monday. Monday refuses to be separated from Jem for a moment – he sleeps on the foot of his bed and squats ~~at his feet~~ ^**beside him**^ at meal-times. And on Sunday he went to church with him and insisted on going right into our pew, where he went to sleep on Jem’s feet. In the middle of the sermon he woke up and seemed to think he must welcome Jem all over again, for he bounced up with a series of barks and wouldn’t quiet down until Jem took him up in his arms. But nobody seemed to mind, and Mr. Meredith came and patted his head after the service and said,

“‘Faith and affection and loyalty are precious things wherever they are found. That little dog’s love is a treasure, Jem.’” ^**Note T9**^

[*Error in ms: page number “513” appears on two consecutive pages.*]

~~The station agent had heard Dog Monday’s story. He knew who the tall soldier was. Jem M Blythe had come home.~~

~~Jem~~

~~Rilla was gathering daffodils on the lawn when a wild little dog flew under the gate, barked frantically and flew back again. She looked up wonderingly, “Wasn’t that Dog Monday? Could he have forsaken his tryst? What did it mean? Then she saw Jem.}~~

“Jem is going back to college in the fall and so ~~is~~ are Jerry and Carl. ~~Nan and Di have got their B.A.’s and are going to teach.~~ I suppose Shirley will, too. He expects to be home in July. ~~Na~~ Nan and Di ~~have got their B.A.’s and are going to teach~~ ^**will go on teaching**^. Faith doesn’t expect to be home before September. I suppose she will teach then too, for she and Jem can’t be married until he gets through his course in medicine. ~~Una Meredith~~ ^**Note P9**^ They are all talking of their plans and hopes – more soberly than they used to do long ago, but still with interest, and a determination to carry on and make ~~the best~~ good in spite of lost years.

“‘We’re in a new world,’ Jem says, ‘~~“~~and we’ve got to make it a better one than the old. That isn’t done yet, though some folks ^**seem to think**^ ~~think~~ it ought to be. ~~It will be the task of years. The old world is destroyed and now we must build anew.~~ The job isn’t finished – it isn’t really begun ~~yet~~. The old world is destroyed and we must build up the new one. It will be the task of years. I’ve seen enough of war to realize that ~~war~~ we’ve got to make a world where wars can't happen. We've given Prussianism its mortal wound but it isn't dead yet and it isn't confined to Germany either. ~~We've got to create a new spirit – it isn't enough just to have~~ It isn't enough to drive out the old spirit – we've got to bring in the new.”’

"I'm writing down those words of Jem's in my diary so that I can read them over occasionally and get courage from them, when moods come when I find it not so easy to 'keep faith.’””

Rilla closed her journal with a little sigh. Just then she was not finding it easy to keep faith. ~~She was very lonely~~ All the rest seemed to have some special aim or ambition about which to build up their lives – she had none. And she was very lonely ^**– horribly lonely**^. Jem had come back – but he ^[*Note*] **W9**^ ~~belonged to Faith~~. ~~Even Jims had~~ ^**Walter would never come back.**^ She had not even Jims left. All at once her world seemed wide and empty – that is, it had seemed wide and empty from the moment yesterday when she had read in a Montreal paper ~~a~~ ^**a fortnight-old, a**^ list of returned soldiers in which was the name of Captain Kenneth Ford.

So Ken was home – and he had not even written her that he was coming. He had been in Canada two weeks and she had not had a line from him. Of course he had forgotten – if there was ever anything to forget – a hand-clasp – a kiss – a look – a promise asked under the influence of a passing emotion. It was all absurd – she had been a silly, romantic, inexperienced goose. Well, she would be wiser in the future – very wise – and very discreet – and very contemptuous of men and their ways.

"I suppose I'd better go with Una and take up Household Science too," she thought, as she stood by her window and looked down ^**Note U9**^ on Rainbow Valley, ^**lying in a ~~glamor of unset~~ wonderful lilac light of sunset.**^ There did not seem anything very attractive just then about Household Science, but, with a whole new world waiting to be built, a girl must do something.

~~Rilla was~~

The door bell rang, Rilla turned reluctantly ~~away from~~ stairwards. She must answer it – there was no one else in the house; but she hated the idea of callers just then. She went down stairs slowly, and opened the front door.

A man in ~~khk~~ khaki was standing on the steps – a tall fellow, with dark eyes and hair, ~~across his brown cheek ran a narrow white scar~~ and a narrow white scar running across his brown cheek. Rilla stared at him foolishly for a moment. ~~Then –~~ Who was it?

~~"Ken!" she said.~~

~~Kene Kenneth took the hand she held forth rather uncertainly and lo~~

She ought to know him – ^**there was certainly something very familiar about him –**^

"Rilla-my-Rilla," ~~said the~~ he said.

"Ken," gasped Rilla. Of course, it was Ken – but he looked so much older – he was so much changed – that scar – the lines about his eyes and lips – her thoughts went whirling helplessly.

Ken took the ^**uncertain**^ hand she held out ~~rather uncertainly~~, and looked at her. The slim Rilla of ~~five~~ ^**four**^ years ago had rounded out into symmetry ~~of form and feature~~. He had left a schoolgirl, and he found a woman – a woman with wonderful eyes and dented lip, and rose-bloom cheek – a woman altogether beautiful and desirable ^**– the woman of his dreams.**^

"Is it Rilla-my-Rilla?" he asked, ~~tenderly, passionately, with tender, passionate intonation.~~ meaningly.

Emotion shook Rilla from head to foot. Joy – happiness – sorrow – fear – every passion that had wrung her heart in those four long years seemed to surge up in her soul for a moment as the deeps of being were stirred. She had tried to speak; at first voice would not come. Then –

"Yeth," said Rilla.

The End

An Interpretive Transcription of Montgomery's Manuscript of Notes to Rilla of Ingleside

Notes

A. If the ~~transformation~~ change happened in the twilight all the Ingleside folk felt a certain terror of him. At such times he was a fearsome ~~best~~ **beast** and only Rilla defended him, asserting that he was "such a nice prowly cat." Certainly he prowled. ~~"He's a queer kind't of varmint," pronounced old Mr. Pryor whom he bit once on the leg.~~

~~B. He was "a great **notable** purrer; never was known a cat at had there been an Ingleside cat who purred so constantly and so ecstatically. The only thing I envy a cat is its purr," remarked Dr. Blythe once listening to Doc's resonant melody. "It is the most contented sound in the world."~~

C. He is through with Queen's now and

D. Wasn't Jem the dearest baby in the old House of Dreams~~, Miss Cornelia.~~? And now, he's a B.A. and accused of courting."

E. Are Di and Nan going too?"

"Yes, ~~there for~~ They both wanted to teach another year but Gilbert thinks they would better go to Redmond this Fall."

"I'm glad of that. They'll keep an eye on Walter and see that ~~he doesn't study all too hard~~ he doesn't study too hard.

F. "As for that little Bruce, Una just makes a ^**perfect**^ slave of herself to him. Of course, he is a darling. But did you ever seen any child look ~~so~~ as much like a ~~relative~~ an aunt as he looks like his Aunt Ellen? He's just as dark and just as emphatic. I can't see a feature of Rosemary in him. Norman Douglas always vows at the top of his voice that the stork meant Bruce for him and Ellen and took him to the manse by mistake."

"Bruce adores Jem" said Mrs. Blythe. "When he comes over here he just follows Jem about silently like a faithful little dog, gazing ^**up**^ at him from under his black brows. He would do anything for Jem, I verily believe."

"Are Jem and Faith going to make a match of it?"

G. I never take much interest in foreign parts.

H. Do you think that all those over-harbor MacAllisters and Crawfords and Elliotts could scare up a chin like Rilla's in four generations? ~~No,~~ They could not.

I. She howled dreadful at her husband's funeral but she married again in less than a year.

~~J. And his feet are as big as boats~~! ~~Note K.~~

K. He is an elder now and they say he is very religious; but I can well remember the time, Mrs. Dr. dear, twenty years ago when he was caught pasturing his cow in the Lowbridge graveyard. Yes, indeed I have not forgotten that, and I always think of it when he is praying in ~~prayer~~ meeting."

L. – not from vanity but from a haunting dread that people might come to think her too old to work.

M. who was going home that night for vacation.

N. I tell him everything – I even show him my diary.

O. Everybody at Ingleside was ~~proud~~ fond of him, even Susan, although his one unfortunate propensity for sneaking into the spare room and going to sleep upon the bed tried her affection sorely. Note T

P. "There's no use thinking about what you're going to do – ~~because~~ you are ~~so~~ tolerably sure not to do it."

"Oh, but you do get a lot of fun out of the thinking," cried Rilla. "You think of nothing but fun, you monkey. ^**Note Q**^ Well, what else is fifteen for? But –

Q. said Miss Oliver indulgently, ~~thinking~~ ^**reflecting**^ that Rilla's chin was really the last word in chins.

R. she had ^**once**^ lamented rebelliously to Miss Oliver

S. "When Walter ~~had the fl was ill~~ ^**was**^ in the hospital with typhoid last year I was almost crazy," sighed Rilla, a little importantly. "They never told me how ill he really was until it was all over – father ~~said~~ wouldn't tell them. I'm glad I didn't know – I couldn't have borne it. I cried myself to sleep every night~~. Bu~~ as it was. But sometimes," concluded Rilla bitterly – she liked to speak bitterly now and then in imitation of Miss Oliver – "sometimes I think ~~Rev~~ Walter cares more for ~~Jems Rags~~ Dog Monday than he does for me."

T. On this particular afternoon Rilla had no quarrel on hand with existing conditions. ~~She was~~

U. "Of course it hasn't been very exciting," said Rilla. "The only exciting thing that has happened in the Glen for a year was ~~Mis~~ old Miss Mead fainting in church. Sometimes I wish something dramatic would happen once in a while."

"Don't wish it. Dramatic things always have a bitterness for someone. What a nice summer all you gay creatures will have! And me moping at Lowbridge!"

V. ~~– in italics, for Rilla~~ Rilla was fond of italics as most girls of fifteen are –

W. "I dreamed last night I was at the dance, and right in the middle of things I discovered I was dressed I was dressed in my kimono and bedroom ~~slippers~~ ^**shoes**^," ~~laughed~~ ^**sighed**^ Rilla. "I woke up with a gasp of ~~horro~~ ^**horror**^."

"Speaking of dreams – I had an odd one," said Miss Oliver absently. "It was one of those vivid dreams I sometimes have – they are not the vague jumble of ordinary dreams – they are as clear cut and real as life."

"What was your dream?"

"I was standing on the veranda steps, here at Ingleside, looking down over the fields of the Glen. All at once, far in the distance, I saw a long, silvery, glistening wave ~~bra~~ breaking over them. It came nearer and nearer – just a succession of little white waves like those that break on the sandshore sometimes. The Glen was being swallowed up. I thought, 'Surely the waves will not come near Ingleside' – but they came nearer and nearer – so rapidly – before I could move or call they were breaking right at my feet – and everything was gone – there was nothing but a waste of stormy water where the Glen had been. I tried to draw back – and I saw that the edge of my dress was wet with blood – and I woke – shivering. I don't like the dream. ~~Rilla-my Rilla~~ There was some sinister significance in it. That kind of vivid dream always 'comes true' with me."

"I hope it doesn't mean there's a storm coming up from the east to spoil the party," murmured Rilla anxiously.

"Incorrigible fifteen!" said Miss Oliver ^~~**tub**~~ **dryly**^, "~~I'm~~ Rilla-my-Rilla, I don't think there is any danger that it ~~warns anything~~ foretells anything so awful as that!"

X. with its charm of bowery old homesteads, tilled meadows and quiet gardens.

Y. rustle of aspen poplars talking in silvery whispers and shaking their dainty, heart-shaped leaves,

Z. Carl Meredith was walking with ~~Jennie~~ ^**Miranda**^ Pryor, ~~out of pity for her~~ more to ~~tease~~ torment Joe Millgrave than for any other reason. Joe was known to have a strong hankering for ~~Jennie Pryor~~ ^**the said Miranda**^ which shyness prevented him from indulging, ^~~over~~ **on all occasions**^. Joe might summon ~~up~~ enough courage to amble up beside ~~Jennie~~ ^**Miranda**^ if the night were dark, but here, in this moonlight dusk, he simply could not do it. So he tailed along after the precession and thought things not lawful to be uttered of Carl ~~Mar~~ Meredith. ~~Jennie would much rather have had Joe than Carl, with whom she did not feel in the least at home. Yet it was something of an honor, too, to have one of the sons of the manse walking with her.~~ ~~Jennie~~ ^**Miranda**^ was the daughter of Whiskers-on-the-Moon; ~~and while~~ she did not share her fathers unpopularity but she was not much run after, being a ~~pla~~ pale, neutral ~~^silvery blonde^~~ little creature somewhat addicted to ^**nervous**^ giggling. ^**Note D2**^ ~~Je~~ She would much rather have walked with Joe than with Carl, with whom she did not feel in the least at home; yet it was something of an honor, too, to have a college boy beside her and a son of the manse at that.

A1. The Blythes left Ingleside to the melancholy of howls ~~by Jack~~ ~~^**Dogs**^~~ ^^**from Dog Monday,**^^ who was locked up in the barn ~~last~~ ^**lest**^ he wake an uninvited guest at the Light. They picked up

B1. Well, I won't think of that on this lovely night. ~~I'm always glad I – At~~ Do you know, Rilla, that when night-time comes I'm always glad I live in the country. We know the real charm of night here as town dwellers never do. Every night is beautiful in the country – even the stormy ones. I love a wild night storm on this old gulf shore. ~~What a And~~ As for a night like this, it is almost too beautiful – it belongs to youth and dreamland and I'm half of it."

"I feel as if I were part of it," said Rilla.

"Ah yes, you're young enough not to be afraid of perfect things. Well, here we are at the House of Dreams. It seems lovely this summer. The Fords didn't come?"

C1. – just exactly such a night as this,"

D1. resplendent in blue crepe, with lace overdress,

E1. nothing that he did mattered to her. He was ages older than she was; he chummed with Nan and Di and ~~the~~ Faith and looked upon her, Rilla, as a child whom he never noticed except to tease. And

F1. She hasn't got the sense she was born with where he is concerned.

G1. As if a Toronto boy like ~~Selwyn~~ ^**Ken**^Ford would ever ^**really**^ think of ~~a~~ a country girl like Ethel!"

H1. – always had hated her since Walter had pummelled Dan so notoriously in Rainbow Valley days, but why need she be ~~sneered at~~ ^**thought beneath** ~~**Selwyn**~~ ^^**Kenneth**^^ **Ford's notice**^ because she was a country girl, pray?

I1. with the glamour of a faraway city and a big university hanging around him.

J1. with a certain careless grace of bearing that somehow made all the other boys seem stiff and awkward by contrast. He was reported to be awesomely clever, ^**Note I1**.^

K1. If only her slippers didn't bite so! And if only

L1. "A merry ~~lit~~ lilt o'moonlight for mermaiden revelry," quoted ~~Selwyn~~ ^**Kenneth**^ lightly from one of Walter's poems.

M1. –"Hush! Hark: A deep sound strikes like a rising knell" –

N1. "My dream – my dream! The first wave has broken." ^**Note R1**^

O1. I've been trying to get Captain ~~McAllister~~ ^**Josiah**^ to hoist the flag but he says it isn't the proper caper till sunrise.

P1. who always said that when she couldn't think of anything else to say.

Q1. The cool and freakish wind of night crooning in the stiff grasses pm the crests of the dunes,

R1. She looked at Allan ~~Dale~~ Daly and tried to smile. "Is this ~~Arrma~~ Armageddon?" she asked. "I'm afraid so," he said gravely.

S1. I didn't go because it's getting rough and I knew I'd be seasick. I don't mind walking home from here. ^**It's only a mile and a half.**^ But I s'posed you'd gone.

T1. or "Kid" or "Puss", as he had been used to call her when he took any notice ^**whatever**^ of her ~~at all.~~ She did not ^**at all**^ resent his using Walter's pet-name for her; it sounded so beautifully in his low caressing tones, ^[*Note*] H2^

U1. and it was flounced from the waist to the hem. We didn't wear the skimpy things girls wear nowadays. Ah me, times has changed and not for the better I'm afraid

V1. Accordingly they hiked. But to "hike" along a deep-rutted, pebbly lane, in frail silver-hued slippers with high French heels, is not an exhilarating performance. Rilla managed to limp and totter along until they reached the harbor road; but she could go no further in those detestable slippers.

W1. "I'll tell my mother all about or – and Miss Oliver – and Walter," Rilla gasped between sniffs. "You sat for hours with Miller Douglas on that lobster trap, Mary Vance! What would ~~Miss Cornelia~~ Mrs. Elliott say to that if she knew?"

X1. Well, if she caught cold from walking home barefoot on a dew-wet road and went into a decline perhaps they would be sorry

Y1. a long, thin nose, a long thin mouth, and very long, thin, pale hands, ~~fold~~ generally folded resignedly ~~across~~ ^**on**^ her black calico lap. Everything about her seemed long and ~~pale and~~ thin and pale.

Z1. What business had an old – ~~and~~ ^**an**^ old beanpole like that to talk of anybody else being long and thin?

A2. And so did that little hussy of an Ethel Reese.

B2. I s'pose you'll all be dancing tonight – even the minister's boys most likely. I s'pose his girls won't go that far. Ah well, I never held with dancing. I knew a girl once who dropped dead while she was dancing. How anyone could ever dance again after a judgment like that I cannot comprehend."

"Did ~~she~~ ^**she**^ ever dance again?" asked Rilla pertly.

"I told you she dropped dead. Of course she never danced again, poor creature. She was a Kirke from Lowbridge.

C2. I have no talent at all and you can't imagine how comfortable it is. Nobody expects me to do anything so I'm never pestered to do it.

D2. She had silvery blonde hair and her eyes were big ~~timid~~ china blue orbs that looked as if she had been badly ~~seared~~ ^**frightened**^ when she was little and had never got over it…

E2. ~~Jean gave~~ ^**Mrs. Ford sent**^ them to use last Christmas and I've never had a chance to wear them yet. They're the dearest things."

F2. – or so it seemed at first.

G2. – or, if that be a physiological impossibility; she thought it did.

H2. with just the very faintest suggestion of emphasis on the "my."

I2. Beautiful young eyes sparkled and shone.

J2. It seemed to Rilla that she had lived as much in those six days as in all her previous life – and if it be true that we should count time by heart throbs she had.

K2. – Faith, who had cried with flashing eyes, “Oh, if I were only a man, to go too!”

L2. – just a tinkle now and then as the breeze swept-by!

M2. ~~Only~~ ^**But**^ it was – nice – to get away alone ~~once in a while~~ ^**now and then**^, where nobody ~~wo~~ could see ~~you~~ ^**her**^ and where ~~you~~ ^**she**^ wouldn’t feel that people thought ~~you~~ ^**her**^ a little coward if some tears came in spite of ~~you~~ ^**her**^.

N2. “Scorcs havc joined up already.

O2. “Oh!” as if a knife ~~thrust~~ had been thrust into her.

P2. But she never relents towards Doc. She says the minute he saw Jem in Khaki he turned into Mr. Hyde then and there and she thinks that ought to ~~show him~~ be proof enough of what he really is. Susan is funny but she is an old dear. Shirley says she is one-half angel and the other half good cook. But then Shirley is the only one of us she ~~ever spoils~~ never scolds.

Q2. And a bayonet charge! If I could face the other things I ~~couldn’t~~ could never face that. It turns me sick to think of it – sicker even to think of giving it than receiving it – to think of thrusting a bayonet through another man.” Walter writhed and shuddered. “I think of those things all the time – and it doesn’t seem to me that Jem and Jerry ever think of them. ~~But thinks it~~

R2. Mr. and Mrs. Meredith ~~were th~~ had come over from the manse, and Mr. and Mrs. Norman Douglas had come up from the farm. Cousin Sophia was there also, sitting with Susan in the shadowy background ^[*Note*] **S2**^. And of course there were all talking of the war ^[*Note*] **E3**^. When two people forgathered in those days they talked of the war; and old ~~Dave Jamieson~~ ^**Highland Sandy**^ of the Habor Head talked of it when he was alone and hurled anathemas at the Kaiser across all the acres of his farm.

S2. Mrs. Blythe and Nan and Di were away, but ~~the doctor~~ ^**Dr. Blythe**^ was still home and so was Dr. Jekyll, sitting in golden majesty on the top step.

T2. “Thank God, England’s navy is ready,” said the doctor. [*At the bottom of this page Montgomery inserts a note here:*] ^(see continuation on p.16)^

“Amen to that,” nodded Mrs. Norman. “Bat-blind as most of them were somebody had foresight enough to see to that.”

U2. It was a very calm evening with a dim, golden afterlight irradiating the glen.

V2. ~~Yet~~ Was it not the spirit that counted?

W2. ~~“How is Rilla-my-Rilla~~

“Doing the brave- smiling-sister–stunt, I see? What a crowd for the Glen to muster! Well, I’m off ^**home**^ in a few days myself.”

X2. “I have absolute confidence in Kitchener,” said ~~a~~ the over-harbor doctor.

“It’s a long, long way to Tipperary,” hummed Rick ~~Douglas~~ McAllister.

Y2. It was a dull day, threatening rain, and the clouds lay in heavy gray rolls over the sky; but

Z2. “It’s a commercial war when all is said and done and not worth one drop of good Canadian blood,” said a stranger from the shore hotel.

A3. Rilla felt as if she were in one fantastic nightmare. Were these the people who, three weeks ago, were talking of crops and prices and local ~~so~~ gossip?

B3. Rilla found herself standing alone and listening to disconnected scraps of talk as people walked up and down past her.

C3. “I think I’ll have it made with a crush girdle of velvet,” said Bessie Clow.

D3. – somebody kissed her cheek – she believed it was Jerry but never was sure –

E3. except Dr. Jekyll who kept his own counsel and looked contempt as only a cat can

F3. “I felt ^**that**^ there was to be bad news to-day,” said Susan, “for that cat creature turned into Mr. Hyde ~~to-day~~ this morning without rhyme or reason for it, and that was no good omen.”

G3. Mrs. Blythe went to Charlottetown to attend a Red Cross convention

H3. He brung that old tureen out from England with ~~it~~ him – said it’d always been in the family. ~~They never~~ Him and Min never used it – never had enough soup to put in it – but Jim thought the world of it

I3. Its shrieks could be heard over Ingleside from ~~garret~~ cellar to attic.

J3. She prepared its three o’clock ration with a grim determination that she would not call Susan. Oh, was she dreaming? Was it really she, Rilla Blythe, who had got into this absurd predicament? ~~Was she here after in the wee sma’ hours~~ She did not care if the Germans were near Paris – she ~~didn’t~~ did not care if they were in Paris – if only the baby wouldn't cry or choke or smother or have convulsions. Babies did have convulsions didn't they? Oh, why had she forgotten to ask Susan what she must do if the baby had convulsions?

K3. I doubt if it would survive ~~en~~ even if sent to an orphan's home. But

L3. She would never go to father for advice – she wouldn't bother mother – and she would only condescend to Susan in dire extremity. They would all see!

M3. Susan had learned by experience that when Dr. Blythe ~~made a decision~~ ^**put his foot down and**^ said a thing must be, ~~and put his foot down~~, that thing was.

N3. Rilla was very proud of Walter's approval; nevertheless, she wrote gloomily in her diary that night:--

O3. – and they tell me Whiskers-on-the-Moon says the same thing and is quite pleased about it.

P3. "Oh, those French women!" groaned Susan.

Q3. Would yez believe it,

R3. through her tense lips. She had one of those souls that are always tied to the stake, burning in the suffering of the world around them. Apart from her own personal ~~stake~~ ^**interest**^ in the war, she was racked by the thought of Paris falling into the ruthless hands of the hordes who had burned Louvain and ruined the wonder of Rheims.

S3. – moonlight on Four Winds – the stars twinkling through the fir trees – mist on the gulf –

T3. and a fragrant ~~darkene twilight wet with dew~~ ^**dew**^ darkness filled their little sylvan dell.

U3. without a soul expecting it. ~~It was just a special pure luck that me and Jem happened to be here.~~

V3. which had "come out of the everywhere" into such a dubious "here,"

W3. She kept on a-saying 'Oh, what will become of my pore ~~eh~~ baby' till it really got on my nerves.

X3. She is ~~one of those girls~~ the sort of girl who calls ~~people~~ any clever or handsome or distinguished people ^**she knows slightly**^ by their ~~given~~ ^**first**^ names – behind their backs. And she is sly and two-faced. Una doesn't mind, of course. She is ~~an angel and just~~ willing to do anything that comes to hand and never minds whether she has an office or not. ~~She always puts me in mind of a tea-rose~~. ^**She is just a perfect angel, while I am** ^^**only**^^ **angelic in spots and demonic in other spots**^. I wish Walter would take a fancy to her, ~~for I know she just adores him~~ but he never seems to think about her in that way, although I heard him say once she ~~reminded him of~~ ^**was like a tea-rose**^. She is, too. ~~But~~ ^**And**^ she gets imposed upon just because she is so sweet and willing; ~~But~~ ^**but**^ I don't allow people to impose on Rilla Blythe and ~~when,~~ 'that you may tie to,' or Susan says. ~~and when~~

Y3. and be sure the water is neither too hot nor too warm,

Z3. and asked herself pathetically if she could really be the same Rilla Blythe who had been so happy and carefree only a few weeks ago.

A4. And Mrs. Albert Meade ^**of Harbor Head**^ manages a pair and a half a day but she has nothing to do but knit. You know, Mrs. Dr. dear, she has been bed-rid for years and has been worrying ~~for~~ terrible because she was no good to anybody ^**and a dreadful expense,**^ and yet could not die and be out of the way. And now they tell me she is quite ~~cheerful~~ ^**cheered up**^ and ~~no~~ resigned to living because there is something she can do, and she knits for the soldiers from daylight ~~umti~~ until dark.

B4. It didn't kick or stiffen out; so I knew that, according to ~~Holt~~ ^**Morgan**^, ~~he~~ ^**it**^ wasn't crying for temper; and ~~he~~ ^**it**^ wasn't hungry and no pins were sticking in ~~him~~ it.

C4. Fred Arnold was at the manse and walked home with me. He is the new Methodist minister's son and very nice and clever, and would be quite handsome if it were not for his nose. It is a really dreadful nose. When he talks of commonplace things it does not matter as much, but when he talks of poetry and ideals the contrast between his nose and his conversation is too much for me and I want to shriek with laughter. It is really not fair, because everything he said was perfectly charming, and if somebody like Kenneth had said it ~~it wou~~ I would have been enraptured. ~~Howeve~~ When I listened to him with my eyes cast down I was ~~really~~ quite fascinated; but as soon as I looked up and saw his nose the spell was broken. He wants to enlist, too, but can't because he is only seventeen. Mrs. Elliott met us as we were walking through the village and could not have looked more horrified if she had caught me walking with the Kaiser himself. Mrs. Elliott detests the Methodists and all their works Father says it is an obsession with her."

D4. after ~~several fruitless~~ a wild pursuit and several fruitless dashes and pounces,

E4. "When I wake up in the night, ~~Mrs. Dr. dear~~ and cannot go to sleep again," remarked Susan, who was knitting and reading at the same time, "I pass the ~~time~~ ^**moments**^ by torturing the Kaiser to death. Last night I fried him in boiling oil and a great comfort it was to me, remembering those Belgian babies."

"If the Kaiser were here and had a pain in his shoulder you'd be the first to run for the liniment bottle to rub him down," ~~said~~ laughed Miss Oliver.

"Would I?" cried th~~e outraged~~ ^**outraged**^ Susan. "Would I, Miss Oliver? I would rub him down with coal oil, Miss Oliver – and leave it to blister. That is what I would do and that you may tie to. A pain in his shoulder, indeed! He will have pains all over him before he is through with what he has started."

"We are told to love our enemies, Susan," said the doctor solemnly.

"Yes, our enemies, but not King George's enemies, doctor dear," retorted Susan crushingly. She was as well pleased with herself over thus flattening out the doctor ~~so~~ completely that she even smiled as she polished her glasses. Susan had never given in to glasses before, but she had done so at last ~~so that she could~~ ^**in order to be able to**^ read the war-news – and not a dispatch got by her. "Can you tell me, Miss Oliver, how to pronounce M-l-a-w-a and B-z-u-r-a and P-r-s-y-m-y-s-l?"

F4. then lessening ~~soro~~ sorrowfully away down the brook.

G4. "A few months ago," said Miss Oliver, "we thought and talked in terms of Glen St. Mary. Now, we think and talk in terms of military tactics and diplomatic intrigue."

H4. And the starving Belgians!

I4. It says here that the slaughter was terrible. For all they were foreigners it is awful to think of so many men being killed, Mrs. Dr. dear – for they are scarce enough as it is.

J4. "Cousin Sophia said ^**awhile ago**^ that Serbia was done for, but I told ~~here~~ her there was still such a thing as an over-ruling Providence, doubt it who might.

K4. ~~Last night the wind kept wailing around the eaves – and I thought~~

K4. with a young silver moon hanging over her,

L4. – at the little woodland valley and the gray, lonely fallows beyond.

M4. and said, 'Does he often cry like that? – as if she had never heard a baby crying before.

"I explained patiently that children have to cry so many minutes per day in order to expand their lungs. Morgan says so. 'If Jims didn't cry at all I'd have to make him cry for at least twenty minutes, I said.' 'Oh, indeed.' Said Irene, laughing as if she didn't believe me. 'Morgan On The Care of Infants' was upstairs or I would soon have convinced her. Then she said Jims didn't have much hair – she had never seen a four-months-old baby so bald.

N4. ~~Shriek~~ Whining and shrieking and blaming Providence do not get ~~you~~ us anywhere. ~~You~~ ^**We**^ have just got to grapple with whatever we have to do whether it is minding the onion patch, or running the Government. I shall grapple.

O4. The sky was fleeced over with silvery, shining clouds.

P4. – some woman's husband a sweetheart or son – ~~or~~ ^**perhaps**^ the father of little children –

~~Q4. "I never go out these dark cold nights without thinking of those men in the~~

Q4. "~~I'm~~ ^**I am**^ rather glad when the time comes to go to bed," said ~~Miss~~ Gertrude. "I like the darkness because I can be myself in it – I needn't smile or talk bravely. ~~in it~~ But sometimes my imagination gets out of hand, too, and I see what you do – terrible things – terrible years to come."

R4. and coming back like a giant refreshed.

S4. "And I used to welcome the mornings so," thought Rilla.

T4. A shell burst near us and when the mess cleared away he was lying dead – not mangled at all – he just looked a little startled.

U4. And Mrs. Richard Elliott over harbour is worrying herself sick because she used to be always scolding her husband about smoking up the parlor curtains. Now that he has enlisted she wishes she had never said a word to him.

V4. When ever any of you go to the station be sure to give ~~Rags~~ ^**Dog Monday**^ a double pat for me. Fancy the faithful little beggar waiting there for me like that! Honestly, dad, on some of these dark cold nights in the trenches, it heartens and braces me up to no end to think that thousands of miles away at the old Glen station there is a small spotted dog sharing my ~~vigil~~ vigil.

W4. "Joe Vickers told me ~~to-night~~ ^**in the store**^ that he saw a new green-looking thing in the sky tonight over Lowbridge way. Do you suppose it could have been a Zeppelin Mrs. Dr. dear?"

"I do not think it ~~is~~ very likely, Susan."

"Well, I would feel easier ^**about it**^ if Whiskers-on-the-Moon were not living in the Glen. They say he was seen ~~walking~~ going through strange manoeuvres with a lantern in his back yard one night lately. Some people think he was signalling."

"To whom – or what?"

"Oh, that is the mystery, Mrs. Dr. dear. In my opinion the Government would do well to keep an eye on that man if ~~they do~~ ^**it does**^ not want us to be all murdered in our beds some night."

X4. "It breaks my heart to read about ~~all~~ it, Mrs. Dr. dear," went on Susan, "and I cannot console myself with the thought that ~~they're~~ ^**the tales are**^ not true. When I read a novel that makes me want to weep I just say severely to myself, 'Now, Susan Baker, you know that is all a pack of lies.' But we must carry on, Jack Crawford

Y4. – it was really like the magical pipes of the old tale which compelled all who heard them to dance.

Z4. When I saw what had been done here to homes and gardens and people – well, dad, I ~~thought of~~ ^**seemed to see**^ a gang of Huns marching through Rainbow Valley and the Glen ^**and the garden at Ingleside.**^ ^**Note A5**^ And I knew we were fighting ~~not for Su~~ to make ~~that~~ ^**those**^ dear old ~~valley~~ ^**places**^, where we had played as ~~boys~~ ^**children**^, safe for other ~~boys~~ ^**boys and girls**^ – ~~safe~~ fighting for the preservation and safety of all sweet; homey things

A5. There were gardens over here – beautiful gardens with the beauty of centuries – and what are they now? Mangled desecrated things!

B5. "And isn't the sky blue over ~~the~~ Rainbow Valley," she said, ~~falling~~ responding to his word. "Blue – blue – you'd have to say 'blue' a hundred times before you could express how blue it is."

C5. "The sky may be blue," said ~~Susam~~ ^**Susan**^, "but that cat has been Hyde all day

D5. I used to be so furious with Jem when he called me 'Spider.' And now, if he would just come whistling through the hall and call out, 'Hello, Spider,' as he used to do, I would think it the loveliest name in the world."

E5. I am not blaming Miranda exactly, but I do think she might have a little more spunk sometimes. If she put her foot down once in a while she might bring her father to terms, for she is all the housekeeper he has and what would he do if she 'struck'? If I were in Miranda's shoes I'd find some way of managing Whiskers-on-the-Moon ^[*Note*] **X5**^. But Miranda is a meek and obedient daughter whose days should be long in the land.

F5. – away ahead of it indeed, since ten months is Morgan's average for creeping.

G5. ^**As for the Lusitania**,^ it is an awful occurrence, whatever way you look at it. But Woodrow Wilson is going to write a note about it, so why worry? A pretty president!" – and Susan banged her pots about wrathfully. President Wilson was rapidly becoming anathema in Susan's kitchen.

H5. Rilla could never bring herself to ~~telling~~ ^**to tell**^ her side of it. ~~– she could not utter what Irene had reported about Walter.~~ The fact that a slur at Walter was mixed up in it tied her tongue. So most people believed that Irene had been badly used, except a few girls who had never liked her and sided with Rilla. Rilla, however, did not get much comfort out of their sympathy, ~~however~~ for it was barbed by ~~rather~~ subtle remainders of other days when she had fought Irene's battles with these very girls and snubbed them because they did not idolize her.

I5. meekly trotting through Rainbow Valley on my way to the Upper Glen Road."

J5. But all the while her thoughts were more concerned with the coming distasteful interview, and she kept rehearsing mentally her part in it.

K5. She was very thankful the interview was over. But she knew now that she and Irene could never be the friends they had been. Friendly, yes – but friends, no. Nor did she wish it. All winter she had felt, under her other and more serious worries, a little ~~sore~~ feeling of regret for her lost chum. Now it was suddenly gone ^**Note O5**^. Rilla did not say or think that she had outgrown Irene. Had the thought occurred to her she would have considered it absurd, when ~~Irene~~ she was not yet seventeen and Irene was twenty. ~~But Yet~~ ^**But**^ it was the truth. Irene was just what she had been a year ago – just what she would always be. Rilla Blythe ~~had changed~~ ^**'s nature**^ in that year ~~from an a child to a woman~~ had changed and matured and deepened. She found herself seeing through Irene with a disconcerting clearness – ^~~**through**~~ **discerning under**^ all her superficial sweetness her ~~petteness~~ ^**pettiness**^, her vindictiveness, her ~~true~~ insecurity, ^**her essential cheapness**^. Irene had lost forever her

~~fath~~ faithful worshipper.

L5. – there's even a big party coming out from town –

M5. under a tall wild ~~cherry~~ ^**plum**^ that was ghostly ~~fair~~ ^**white**^ and fair in its ~~spring bloom len fany like feathery spring bloom, mist~~ ^**misty spring bloom**^.

N5. It's perfectly sweet of you to do it when you hate children so.

O5. Irene was not, as Mrs. Elliott would say, of the race that knew Joseph.

P5. Rilla could just hear her giving Olive Kirk an account of it.

Q5. There was such a thing as self-respect.

R5. ~~and~~ She even put on a ~~silly~~ ^**grotesque**^ old Irish-woman's costume and acted the part in the dialogue which Miranda Pryor had not taken. ^**But**^ she did not give her "brogue" the inimitable twist she had given it in the practices, and her readings lacked their usual fire and appeal, ~~while her face was as white as the as pale as the milk-white crab blossoms in her hair.~~

S5. I owe life and Canada ~~that~~ that, and I've got to pay it.

T5. She was alone, the rest of the performers being in the larger room on the other side.

U5. I am always putting my foot in it, aren't I?

V5. but when – he went – away – we thought the war – would ~~soon be over~~ soon – be over – and

W5. – for I can assure you the Monroe doctrine, whatever it is, is nothing to tie to, with Woodrow Wilson behind it.

X5. – yea, verily. I would horse whip him – or bite him, if nothing else would ~~do~~ serve.

Y5. and to have wantonly kicked Miranda's ~~cat~~ ^**dog**^ as he said it.

Z5. The Piper's music rings in my ears day and night – but I cannot follow."

A6. Besides, as Rilla had told her mother one day when she was nine years old, "It is easier to behave nicely when you have your good clothes on." It was easier; it kept up the morale of the army.

B6. She had seen it coming to her – coming – coming – as one sees the shadow of a cloud drawning near over a sunny field swiftly and inescapably.

C6. but I know one thing. If I was dead and he came to my funeral I would rise up and order him out.

D6. Norman Douglas always has believed that anybody who opposed him was on the side of the devil; but a man like that is bound to be right once in a while, just as a clock that doesn't go is right twice a day.

E6. As for Una Meredith being "hateful" to anybody, the idea was so farcical that Rilla had much ado to keep from laughing in Irene's very face.

F6. And here you are as cool as a ~~cur~~ cucumber. I wish I had ~~enough~~ half your nerve.

G6. though I would never admit it to Cousin Sophia,

H6. the Grand Duke Nicholas to the contrary notwithstanding.

I6. Cousin Sophia sighed again and said, 'The Grand Duke Nicholas is not the man I took him to be.' '~~Don't~~ Do not let him know that,' said I. 'It might hurt his feelings and he has likely enough to ~~worry~~ worry him as it is.'

J6. Nan, Di and Faith had gone, ~~too~~ ^**also**^, to do Red Cross ~~won~~ work in their vacation.

K6. Everybody was trying to look very cheerful.

L6. Mary had sent her Miller off the week before, ~~al~~ with a determined grin, and now considered herself ~~a connoisseur~~ ^**entitled to give expert opinion**^ on how such ~~pa~~ partings should be conducted.

"The main thing is to smile and act as if nothing was happening," she informed the ~~Ing~~ Ingleside group. "The boys all hate the sob act like poison. Milled told me I wasn't to come near the station if I couldn't keep from bawling. So I got through with my crying beforehand and at the last I said to him, 'Good luck, Miller and if you come back you'll find I haven't changed any, and if you don't come back I'll always be proud you went, and in any case don't fall in love with a French girl.' Miller ~~swore~~ swore he wouldn't, but you never can tell about those fascinating foreign hussies. Anyhow, the last sight he had of me I was smiling to my limit. Gee, ~~that~~ all the rest of the day my face felt as if it had been starched and ironed into a smile."

In spite of Mary's excellent advice and example

M6. "Write me often and bring Jims up faithfully, according to the gospel of Morgan," ~~he~~ ^**Walter**^ said lightly, having said all his serious things the night before in Rainbow Valley. But at the last moment he took her face between his hands and looked deep into her gallant eyes. "God bless you, Rilla-my-Rilla," he said softly and tenderly. After all it was not a hard thing to fight for a land that bore daughters like this.

[*The manuscript does not contain a note numbered "N6". In the chapter "Realism and Romance", however, the indicator "Note N6" appears on page 137 of the transcript, after the sentence, "She thought perhaps she ought to resent it but she didn't." In the published version, the next sentence "(presumably Note N6) is: Instead, she glanced timidly into Kenneth's seeking eyes and her glance was a kiss."*]

O6. Besides, she was afraid Kenneth would think she was utterly unfeeling if she sat still and let a baby cry ~~let~~ like that. He was not likely acquainted with Morgan's invaluable volume.

P6. You were really the prettiest baby I ever saw, Ken, though your mother had an awful time trying to cure of sucking your thumb.

Q6. ~~barred~~ over the bars of ~~fir~~ ^**tree**^ shadows and moonlight

R6. reconstructing her rainbow castle, with several added domes and turrets.

S6. The truth was he dared not trust his voice, lest it betray his frantic desire to laugh.

T6. never, it might be to return.

U6. The step was half sunk into the earth and mint grew thickly about and over its edge. Often crushed by so many passing feet it gave out its essence freely and the spicy odor hung around thm like ~~an invisible~~ a soundless, invisible benediction.

V6. Instead, she ~~gazed~~ ~~looked~~ ^**glanced**^ timidly into Kenneth's seeking eyes and her ~~look~~ ^**glance**^ was a kiss.

W6. It was very careless of his mother to leave the fruitatives where he could get them, but she was well known to be a heedless creature. One day she found a nest of five eggs as she was going across the fields to church, with a brand new blue silk dress on. So she put them in the pocket of her petticoat and when she got to church she forgot all about them and sat down on them and her ~~clothes were~~ ^**dress was**^ ruined, not to speak of the petticoat.

X6. The great dark plumes of the firs,

Y6. or wandering through palaces of fancy

Z6. with that funny little sidelong waggle of his which always makes it seem that his hind legs are travelling ~~towards the opposite point~~ directly away from the point at which his forelegs are aiming.

A7. and the wonderful significance of the promise he had asked thrilling heart and soul,

B7. “Our concert,” said Rilla, slowly, “is in aid of Belgian children who are starving to death ~~and~~. Don’t you think you could wear a shabby dress once for their sake, Irene?”

“Oh, don’t you think those accounts we get of the conditions of the Belgians are very much exaggerated,” said Irene~~, hunorously~~. “I’m sure they can’t be actually starving, you know, in the ~~20th~~ ^**twentieth**^ century. The newspapers always color thinks so highly.”

[*The following set of numbers appear in the margin of “Notes” opposite “Note B7”.*]

65 000

52 000

117,000

C7. repenting herself of teasing Susan and

D7. Lloyd George began to heckle the Allies regarding equipment and guns and Susan said you would hear more of Lloyd George yet.

E7. To-day was dark and cloudy and to-night is wild enough, as Gertrude says, to ~~suit~~ ^**please**^ any novelist in search of suitable weather for a murder or elopement. The rain drops streaming down the panes look like tears running down a face, and the wind is shrieking through the maple grove.

F7. It’s a little he… all … [*Bottom of page is torn.*]

G7. ~~and~~ the telephone wires sang a shrill wind song in the wild. [*Note*] **K7**

H7. who is ~~very~~ as much in love with you as a china-blue girl can be with anyone and who is dreadfully ashamed of her father’s pro-German sentiments.

I7. ~~The light-hearted way in which we refer to our~~ She was especially horrified when Jem wrote in his last letter to mother ‘Tell Susan I had a fine cootie hunt this morning and caught fifty three!’ Susan positively turned pea-green. ‘Mrs. Dr. dear,’ she said, ‘when I was young, if decent people were so unfortunate as to get – those insects – they kept it a secret if possible. I do not want to be narrow-minded, Mrs. Dr. dear, but I still think it is better not to mention such things.’

J7. Serbia is being throttled and the Allies on the Western front seem able to do nothing but purchase a few paltry yards of trenches a day with the lives for which mothers have agonized.

K7. and the tall ~~withered groups~~ ^**spikes**^ of withered, ~~golden rod~~ gray-headed golden-rod in the fence corner swayed and beckoned wildly to her like groups of old witches weaving unholy spells.

L7. – the first time she hoisted it ~~that~~ since the Russian line broke and the last time . . . many dismal moons. [*Bottom of page torn*]

M7. She had wished that in a burst of romance when Jem had gone, without, perhaps, really meaning it. She meant it now. There were moments when waiting at home, in safety and comfort, seemed ~~the~~ an unendurable thing.

N7. He is a battalion runner and he did something extra brave and daring.

O7. Susan nodded slowly and portentously.

P7. The evening news is that the Grand Duke has ~~taken~~ captured Erzerum. That is a pill for the Turks. I wish I had a chance to tell the Czar just what a mistake he made when he turned Nicholas down."

Q7. "Then get Joe on the long-distance at once and tell him to bring out a license and ring tonight."

"Oh, I couldn't," wailed the aghast Miranda, "it – it could be so – so indelicate."

Rilla shut her ^**little white**^ teeth together with a snap. ~~"I'll do it, then," she said.~~ ^**Note N10**^

R7. – a beautiful, plummy, eggy, citron-peely wedding cake.

S7. accompanied by his best man, Sergeant ~~M…~~ Malcolm Crawford.

T7. While Sir Wilfrid Laurier, who had a poor opinion of lighthouses for winter residences, went to sleep in his pet nook behind the [woodbox,] a thankful dog that ~~all the d~~ ... done with war ... [*Bottom of page torn*]

U7. "Joe is coming home tonight on his last leave. I had a letter from him Saturday – he sends my letters in care of Bob Crawford, you know because of father – and, oh, Rilla, he will only have four days – he has to go away Friday morning – and I may never see him again."

V7. "Anyhow," thought Rilla, "I can write a perfectly killing account of it all to the boys. How Jem will howl over Sir Wilfrid's part in it!"

W7. ~~"The~~ "It's such a Titanic thing we can't grasp it," said the doctor. "What were the scraps of a few ~~Greek and Trojan~~ ^**Homeric**^ handfuls compared to this? The whole Trojan war might be fought ~~in a corres~~ around a Verdun fort and a newspaper correspondent would give it no more than a ~~set~~ sentence. I am not in the confidence of the occult powers" – the doctor threw Gertrude a twinkle – "but I have a hunch that the fate of the whole war hangs on the issue of Verdun. As Susan ^**and Joffre**^ say~~s~~, it has no real military significance; but it has the ~~tremd~~ tremendous significance of an Idea. If Germany wins there she will win the war. If she loses, the tide will set against her."

"Lose she will," said Mr. Meredith emphatically. "The Idea cannot be conquered.

X7. in Red Cross appeals and Government recruiting propaganda. Mothers and sisters [*Bottom of page is torn.*] ... ads thrilled to it, ... humanity caught ... of all the pain and ~~pity~~ ^**hope**^ and ~~hope~~ ^**pity**^ and purpose of the ~~great~~ ^**mighty**^ conflict, crystallized in three brief ~~stanzas~~ immortal verses. A Canadian lad ^**in the Flanders trenches**^ had written the one great poem of the war.

Y7. I could never have risen to such a height.

Z7. The fright it gave me ought to make me sensible in this respect ~~for the~~ at least for the rest of my life. I thought I had killed her – I remembered that her mother had died very suddenly from heart failure when quite a young woman. It seemed years to me before I discovered that her heart was still beating.

A8. Mr. ~~Priyr~~ Pryor had at least the courage of his convictions; or perhaps, as people afterwards said, he thought he was safe in a church and that it was an excellent chance to air certain opinions he dared not voice elsewhere ^**for fear of being mobbed**^.

B8. and he knew that the same picture was in everybody's mind.

C8. He had no desire to fall a second time into the hands of ^**an**^ avenging militarist.

D8. "I feel as if I had received a staggering blow in the face from a trusted friend," said Miss Oliver, and I think we all had just the same sensation.

E8. She listened to my tale with an expression that clearly said, 'Can it be possible that anyone has been wanting to marry this baby?' But

F8. and they cheered Foster Booth who is forty, walking side by side with ^**his**^ son Charley who is twenty. ~~Foster said when Charley~~ Charley's mother died when he was born: and when Charley enlisted Foster said he'd never yet let Charley go anywhere he ~~couldn't~~ ^**daren't**^ go himself and he didn't mean to begin with the Flanders trenches.

G8. ~~And Rita Craw~~ Mr. Meredith read an address and Rita Crawford ~~stood on a pile of lumber and~~ recited ~~“~~‘The Piper’~~”~~. The soldiers cheered her like mad and cried ‘We’ll follow – we’ll follow – we won’t break faith’ – and I felt so proud to think that it was my dear brother who had written such a wonderful, heart-stirring thing. And then I looked at the khaki ranks and wondered if those tall fellows in uniform could be the boys I’ve laughed with and played with and danced with and teased all my life. Something seems to have touched them and set them apart. They have heard the Piper’s call. ~~and and every whisper~~

H8. And every whisper of spring will be falling as a violet in Rainbow Valley.

I8. Roumania did come in – and Susan remarked approvingly that its king and queen were the finest looking royal couple she had seen pictures of. ~~And~~

J8. In the filthy trenches of the Somme front, with the roar of the guns and the groans of sticken men for the music of Ned Burr’s ~~fid~~ violin, and the flash of star shells for the silver sparkles on the old blue gulf.

K8. – of how fine and brave and splendid it was – and I said

L8. and he kept struggling with his little hands

M8. and Shirley continues to read the exploits of the aces.

N8. – she was the one brought me round when I died of pneumonia you know – she was a wonder – no doctor was a patch on her – they don’t hatch her breed of cats nowadays let me tell you –

O8. Well, all our men folk have gone now – Jem and Walter and Shirley and Jerry and Carl. And none of them had to be driven to it. So we have a right to be proud. But pride~~–” Susan clasped her hands together – “pride is poor company – sighed as she turned indoors, - “pride is poor company” – Susan gave a furtive dab at her eyes~~ – Susan sighed bitterly – “pride is ~~poor~~ cold company and that there is no gainsaying.”

P8. I wrote Jerry, too. Jerry’s getting better, you know.”

“Is he? Have you had any good news about him.”

“Yes. Mother had a letter to-day~~. They~~ and it said he was out of danger.”

“Oh, thank God,” murmured Mrs. Blythe in a half-whisper.

Bruce looked at her curiously.

“That is what father said when mother told him. But when I said ~~that~~ it the other day when I found out Mr. Meade’s dog hadn’t hurt my kitten ~~father~~ – I thought he had shooken it to death, you know – father looked awful solemn and said I must never say that again about a kitten. But I couldn't understand why, Mrs. Blythe. I felt awful thankful and it must have been God that saved ~~my~~ Stripey, because that ^**Meade**^ dog had 'normous jaws and oh, how it shook poor Stripey. And so why couldn't I thank ~~Hi~~ Him? 'Course" added Bruce reminiscently, "maybe I said it too loud – 'cause I was awful glad and excited when I found Stripey was all right. I just shouted it, Mrs. Blythe. Maybe if I'd said it sort of whispery like you and father it would have been all right. ~~Would it?"~~

"~~I think it was all right~~

Q8. I flatter myself that I am becoming quite efficient in economizing" – Susan had taken to using certain German terms with killing effect –

R8. – ay, and the dreamers, too – for if no man dreams, there will be nothing for the workers to fulfill –

S8. And I can see the moonlight shining white and still on the ~~gulf~~ old hills of home. It ~~seems so~~ has seemed to me ~~for so long~~ ever since I came here that it was impossible that there could be calm ^**gentle**^ nights and ~~unsh~~ unshattered moonlight anywhere in the world. But to-night somehow, all the beautiful things I have always loved seem to have become possible again – and this is good,~~. For it has been~~ and makes me feel a deep, certain, exquisite happiness.

T8. waiting – waiting – ~~waiting~~ waiting, while the golden years of youth passed by –

U8. When I offered to help Albert looked doubtful. 'I am afraid the work will be too hard for you,' he said. 'Try me for a day and see,' said I. 'I will do my darnedest.'"

~~Nobody said anything for a moment and Susan, mistaking the meaning~~

None of the Ingleside folks spoke for just a moment. ~~They were all~~ Their silence ~~was a tribute to~~ meant that they thought Susan's pluck in 'working out' ~~at her age~~ quite wonderful. But Susan mistook their meaning and ~~grew very red~~ her sun-burned face grew red.

"This habit of swearing seems to be growing on me, Mrs. Dr. dear," she said apologetically. "To think that I should be acquiring it at my age! It is such a dreadful example to the young girls. I am of the opinion it comes of reading the newspapers so much. They are so full of profanity and they do not spell it with stars either, as used to be done in my young days. This war is demoralizing everybody."

V8. Besides, ~~my grandson~~ ^" **said the doctor gravely, "our said grandson**^ will have ~~to manage his aeroplane and~~ give most of his attention to the aeroplane – he ~~can't~~ won't be able to let the reins lie on its back while he ~~give does his~~ gazes into his lady's eyes. ~~and makes honeyed speeches to, Besides,~~ ^**And**^ I have an awful suspicion that you can't run an aeroplane with one arm. No" – the doctor shook his head – "I believe I^**'d still**^ prefer Silverspot after all.

The Russian line broke again that summer and Susan ~~bitterly~~ said bitterly that she had expected it ever since Kerensky had gone and got married.

"Far be it from me to deny the ~~wh~~ holy state of matrimony, Mrs. Dr. dear, but I felt that when a man was running a revolution he had his hands full and should have postponed marriage until a more fitting Season. The Russians are done for this time and there would be no sense in shutting our eyes to the fact. But have you seen Woodrow Wilson's reply to the Pope's peace proposals? It is magnificent. I really could not have expressed the rights of the matter better myself. ~~I feel that I can forgive Wilson everything for it. He knows the meaning of words, and that you may tie to. Speaking of meanings,~~ ~~makes have you heard has Mrs. Oliver told you what happened this afternoon in~~ ^**I feel that I can forgive Wilson everything for it. He knows the meaning of words and that you may tie to. Speaking of meanings, have you heard the latest story about Whiskers-on-the-Moon, Mrs. Dr. dear?**^ ^[*Note*] **W8**^ [*To judge from the published version, this indicator refers to the second Note titled "W8" ("W8 #2"). At the end of that Note, Montgomery inserts the first Note titled W8 (W8#1), which follows here.*]

W8. [*The first of two notes titled "W8".*] Mary Vance came up to Ingleside that same afternoon to tell them that Miller Douglas, who had been wounded when the Canadians took Hill 70, had had to have his leg amputated. The Ingleside folk sympathized with Mary, whose zeal and patriotism had taken some time to kindle but now burned with ~~a steady~~ a glow as steady and bright as anyone's.

"Some folks~~," she said, "~~have been twitting me about having a husband with only one leg. But,"said Mary, rising to a lofty height, "I would rather have Miller with only one leg than any other man in the world~~ – unless,"~~ with a dozen – unless," she added as an after-thought, "unless it was Lloyd George.~~"~~ Well, I must be going. I thought you'd be interested in hearing about Miller, so I run up from the store, but I must hustle home for I promised Luke ~~Craw~~ McAllister I'd help him build his grain stack this evening. ~~I'm doing~~ It's up to us girls to see that the harvest is got in, since the boys are so scarce. I've got overalls and I can tell you they're real becoming. Mrs. Alec Douglas says they're indecent and shouldn't be allowed, and even Mrs. Elliott kinder looks askance at them. But bless you, the world moves, and anyhow there's no fun for me like shocking Kitty Alec." ^W8^

W8. [*The second of two notes titled "W8"*] It seems he ~~went~~ was over at the Lowbridge Road school the other day and took a notion to examine the fourth class in spellings ~~and meanings~~. They have the summer term there yet, you know, with the spring and ~~summer~~ fall vacations, being rather backward people on that road. ~~The teacher wasn't feeling well, and she having a dreadful headac~~ My niece, Ella Baker, goes to that school and she it was who told me the story. ~~Mr. Pryor~~ The teacher ~~wasn't~~ ^was not^ feeling well, having a dreadful ~~heaache~~ headache, and she went out to get a little fresh air while Mr. Pryor was examining the class. The children got along all right with the spelling but when Whiskers began to question them about ~~their~~ the meanings ^**of the words**^ they were all at sea, because they had~~n't~~ ^**not**^ learned them. Ella and the other big scholars felt terrible over it. They love their teacher so, ~~it seems~~ and it seems Mr. Pryor's brother, Abel Pryor, who is trustee of that school, is against her and has been trying to turn the other trustees over to his way of thinking. And Ella and the rest were afraid that if the fourth class couldn't tell Whiskers the meanings of the words he would think the teacher was no good and tell Abel so and Abel would have a fine handle. But ~~they couldn't do a thing to help~~ little Sandy Logan saved the situation. He is a Home boy, but he is as smart as a steel trap and he sized up Whiskers-on-the-moon right off. 'What does "autonomy" mean?' Whiskers demanded. 'A pain in your stomach,' Sandy replied, quick as a flash and never batting an ~~eeyelid~~ eyelid. Whiskers-on-the-moon is a very ignorant man, Mrs. Dr. dear; ~~and~~ he didn't know the meaning of the words himself ^**, and he said 'Very good – very good.**'^ The class caught right on – at least three or four of the brighter ones did – and they kept up the fun. Jean Blane said that 'accoustic' meant 'a religious squabble' and Muriel Baker said that an agnostic was a man who had indigestion, and Jim Carter said that 'acerbity' meant that you ate nothing but vegetable food, and so on all down the list. ~~Ella said she thought that die she would, trying to keep a straight face, but she mara managed it.~~ Whiskers swallowed it all, and kept saying 'Very good' – 'very good' until Ella thought that die she would trying to keep a straight face. When the teacher came in, Whiskers complimented her on the splendid understanding the children had of ~~the~~

~~words they spelled~~ ^**their lesson**^ and said he meant to tell the trustees what a a jewel they had. It was 'very unusual,' he said to find a fourth class who could answer up so prompt when it came to explaining what words meant. He went off beaming. But Ella told me this as a great secret, Mrs. Dr. dear, and we must keep it as such, for the sake of the Lowbridge Road teacher. It would likely be the ruin of her chances of keeping the school if Whiskers should ever find out how he had been bamboozled." [*Montgomery's note follows:*] ^**(Go back to note V8 and finish it)**^

X8. Dear old Susan! She is a perfect dynamo of patriotism and loyalty and contempt for slackers of all kinds and when she let it loose on that audience in her one grand outburst she electrified it.

Y8. Joe Milgrave was in it but came through safe. Miranda had some bad days until she got word from him. But it is wonderful how Miranda has bloomed out since her marriage. She isn't the same girl at all. Even her eyes ~~and hair~~ seem to have darkened and deepened – ~~but I think that is just because her nature they are~~ though I suppose that is just because they glow with the greatly ~~inters~~ intensity that has come to her. She makes her father stand round in a perfectly amazing fashion; she ~~h~~ runs up the flag whenever a yard of trench on the western front is taken; and she comes regularly to our Junior Red Cross; and she does – yes, she does – put on funny little 'married woman' airs that are quite killing. But she is the only war-bride in the Glen and surely nobody ~~need~~ ^**need**^ grudge her the satisfaction she gets out of it.

Z8. "This will not comfort the Kaiser much," she said.

A9. when we have been crouching and waiting for the blow to fall

B9. – 'the last great fight of all.' Is it, I wonder? ~~And who~~

C~~8~~9. "'I shall anchor my storm-tossed soul to the British fleet and make a batch of bran biscuits,' said Susan today to Cousin Sophia, who ~~was as usual full for~~ had come in with some weird tale of a new and all-conquering submarine just launched by Germany.

D9. For instance to-day's letter hadn't a thing in it that mightn't have been written to any girl, except that he signed himself "Your Kenneth," instead of "Yours, Kenneth" as he usually does. Now, <u>did</u> he leave that "s" off intentionally or was it only carelessness? I shall lie awake half the night wondering.

E9. "'You said just the same thing before Mons, Susan,' I reminded her, as gloomily as Cousin Sophia herself could have spoken. [*The word ^Note^ is written across the ending of Note E, referring to the next note, F9.*]

~~F9.~~ [*This is the first of two notes numbered F9.*] ~~I do not deny that mistakes have been made. The Germans would never have got Passendale back again if the Canadians had been left there.~~ [*NB Passendale is misspelled.*]

F9. ¶Nobody ever knew just why the trains stopped at Millward siding. Nobody was ever known to get off there or get on. ~~No living creature was ever~~ ~~It was at least three miles from the nearest house,~~ ^**There was ~~two~~ only one house nearer to it than four miles, and was ^it^** surrounded by acres of blueberry barrens and scrub spruce~~s and firs~~ trees.

G9. The road, seldom used, was rough and deep-rutted.

H9. , put on a nightgown she found in the washstand drawer,

I9. "I have walked the floor for hours in despair and anxiety in these past four years. Now let me walk it in joy.

J9. The fishing village boys turned out and burned ^**all**^ the sandhills ~~grass~~ off in one grand glorious conflagration that extended for seven miles.

K9. "It's more like November than October – November is such an ugly month."

L9. "You've certainly kept your vow pluckily," laughed Miss Oliver.

"It wasn't pluck – it was sheer obstinacy – I'm rather ashamed of it," said Rilla, kicking joyously. "I just wanted to show mother. It's mean to want to show your mother – most unfilial conduct! But I have shown her. And I've shown myself a few things! Oh, ~~Miss Oliver~~ ^**Miss Oliver**^, just for one moment I'm really feeling quite young again – young and frivolous and silly. Did I ever say November was an ugly month? Why, it's the most beautiful month in the whole year. Listen to the bells ringing down in Rainbow Valley! I never heard them so clearly. They're ringing for peace – and new happiness – and all the dear, sweet, sane homey things that we can have again~~, Miss Oliver~~ now, Miss Oliver. Not that I am sane just now – I don't pretend to be. The whole world is having its little crazy spell to-day. ~~Afterwards~~ Soon we'll sober down – and 'keep faith' – and begin to build up our new world. But just for to-day let's be mad and glad."

M9. His wife has been ailing all the fall but nobody knows whether she is going to die or not. She never did tell anyone what she was going to do ~~unit~~ until she did it. That is the main reason why she was never liked in our family. But to be on the safe side I feel that I should visit her. I have not been in town for over a day for twenty years and I have a feeling that I might as well see one of these moving pictures ^**there is so much talk of**^, so as not to be wholly out of the swim. But have no fear that I shall be carried away with them, Mrs. Dr. dear.

N9. All at once the sun broke through the thick clouds and poured through the big crimson maple outside the window. ~~The~~ Its reflected glow enveloped her in a weird immaterial flame. She looked like a priestess performing some mystic, splendid ~~rete~~ rite.

O9. She went down ~~the~~ to the end of the platform, where Sir Wilfrid and Dog Monday were sitting, looking at each other.

Sir Wilfrid remarked condescendingly,

"Why do you haunt this old shed when you might lie on the hearth rug at Ingleside and live on the fat of the land? Is it a pose? Or a fixed idea?"

Whereat Dog M to keep."

P9. Una Meredith has decided, I think, to take a course in ~~domestic~~ ^**Household**^ science at Kingsport – and ~~Miss Oliver~~ ^**Gertrude**^ is to be married to her Major and is frankly happy about it – 'shamelessly happy' she says; but I think her ~~attidu~~ attitude is very beautiful.

Q9. Say, I've got on some in society, haven't I, considering what I come from? I never aspired to being a storekeeper's wife. ^**But**^ Millar's real ambitious and he'll have a wife that'll back him up.

R9. and ~~Rainbow V~~ the banks of the brook in Rainbow Valley were sweet with white and purple violets

S9. He had nothing to eat but a little black bread and boiled turnips and now and then a little soup with black peas in it. And we sat down every one of those days to three good square luxurious meals!

Somehow that hurts me absurdly, even now when I know it's all past.

T9. ^ ¶^ "One night when Jem and I were talking things over in Rainbow Valley, I asked him if he had ever felt afraid at the front.

"Jem laughed.

"'Afraid! I was afraid scores of times – sick with fear – I who used to laugh at Walter when he was frightened. Do you know, Walter was <u>never</u> frightened after he got to the front. <u>Realities</u> never scared him – only his imagination could do that. His colonel told me that Walter was the bravest man in the regiment. Rilla, ~~do you know,~~ I never <u>realized</u> that Walter was dead till I came back home. You don't know how I miss him now – you folks here have got used to it in a sense – but it's all fresh to me. Walter and I grew up together – we were chums as well as brothers – and now here, in this old valley we loved when we were children, it has come home to me that I'm not to see him again."

U9. , through a delicate emerald tangle of young ~~hop~~ vines

V9. Rilla lamented him, for she had been very fond of her stately golden pussy, and had liked him quite as well in his weird Hyde moods as in his ~~mild~~ tame Jekyll ones.

W9. but he was not the laughing boy-brother who had gone away in 1914 and he belonged to Faith.

~~X9. "Bertha Marilla after her mother's mother and after Aunt Marilla of Green Gables;~~

Y9. Why couldn't they have called her by her first name, ^**Bertha,**^ which was beautiful and dignified, instead of that silly "Rilla"?

Z9. Then ~~Dog~~ Monday went on a hunger strike and howled like a Banshee night and day. We had to let him out or he would have starved to death.

A10. from where she sat she could see the pride of her heart – ~~her~~ ^**the**^ bed of peonies of her own planting

B10. There was another occupant of the living room, curled up on a couch, who must not be overlooked, since he was a creature of marked individuality, and, moreover, had the distinction of being the only living thing whom Susan really hated.

C10. so called because he had come into the family on a Monday ~~and~~ when Walter had been reading Robinson Crusoe.

D10. He would think only of these things and of the deep, subtle joy they gave him.

E10. right on top of Mrs. Rachel Lynde's apple-leaf spread.

F10. – which he sure will, seein' he ain't any good.

G10. "Them German men are at Senils.

H10. ~~It's been soaking in to my mind slow but – Somebody has got to~~ This thing must be fought to a finish. It's been soaking into my mind slow but I'm on now.

I10. and an over-luscious atmosphere of perfume ~~all~~ enveloping her.

J10. She would not see him again until the day broke and the shadows vanished – and she knew not if that daybreak would be ~~in this life or in~~ on the side of the grave or beyond it.
"Good-bye," she said.

K10. All at once he ~~knew~~ ^**felt sure**^ that there was nothing in that ~~story~~ ^**gossip**^ about Fred Arnold.

L10. "There was a time," she said sorrowfully, "when I did not care what happened outside of P.E. Island, and now a king cannot have a toothache in Russia or China but it worries me. It may be broadening to the mind, as the doctor said, but it is very painful to the feelings."

M10. – ~~you~~ he couldn't be let go on ~~yanmerin~~ yammering and yodelling and yawping sedition and treason –

N10. "Heaven grant me patience," she said under her breath. "I'll do it then," she said aloud.

O10. The Huns have not got all the cleverness in the world. Have you not heard the story of Alistair MacCullum's son ^**Roderick**^ from the Upper Glen. He is a prisoner in Germany and his mother got a letter from him last week. He wrote that he was being very kindly treated and that ~~every~~ all the prisoners had plenty of food and so on, till you would have supposed everything was lovely. But ~~right in~~ when he signed his name, right in between Roderick and MacCallum, he wrote two Gaelic words that meant "all lies"; and the German censor did not understand Gaelic and thought it was all part of Roddy's name. So he let it pass, never dreaming how he was diddled.

P10. The only dreadful thing he ever did was ~~nid~~ riding on the pig and it was Faith Meredith put him up to that. [*The numbers of some notes are repeated from this point.*]

Q10. but there was something in her voice which repaid Rilla for her bit of sacrifice.

~~R10. "Di is engaged – to an overseas soldier, too. Mother had a letter from her to-day, telling all about it."~~ [*Although Montgomery struck this Note out, it remains in the sequence of notes, as R10, as was the case when Montgomery struck out the Note titled "J".*]

P10 [*(P10 #2: Numbering of Notes becomes repetitive at this point. If the notes were titled in reguolar sequence, this would be "S10".*] – just like those poor Russian soldiers who had only their bare hands to ~~fight~~ ^**oppose to**^ German machine guns.

R10. [*R10#2: In regular sequence it should be "T10".*] – Mary Vance, coated from head to foot ~~in~~ ^**with**^ snow – and she brought Life, not Death, with her, though I didn't know that then. I just stared at her.

"'I haven't been turned out,' ~~said~~ grinned Mary, as she stepped in and shut the door. 'I came up to Carter Flagg's two days ago and I've been storm-staid there ever since. But old Abbie Flagg got on my last

R10. [*R10 #3: In regular sequence it should be "U10".*] – and choked and wheezed – and choked and wheezed – and I felt that he was being tortured to death – and then all at once, after what seemed to me an hour, though it really wasn't long, he coughed up the membrane that was killing him.

R10. [*R10#4: In regular sequence it should be "V10".*] I had letters from Nan and Di too – or rather notes. They are too busy to write letters, for exams are looming up. They will graduate in Arts this spring. I am evidently to be the dunce of the family. But somehow I never had any hankering for a college course and even now it doesn't appeal to me. I'm afraid I'm rather devoid of ambition. There is only one thing I really want to be – and I don't know if I'll ever be it or not. If not – I don't want to be anything. But I shan't write it down. It is all right to think it; but, as Cousin Sophia would say, it might be 'brazen' to ~~n~~ write it down.

"I will write it down. I won't be cowed by the conventions and Cousin Sophia! I want to be Kenneth Ford's wife! There, now!

"I've just looked in the glass, and I hadn't the sign of a blush on my face. I suppose I'm not a properly constructed damsel at all.

S10. [*In regular sequence this indicator should be "W10".*] and Doc, who sat "hushed in grim repose" on the hearth-rug, looking very Hydeish indeed.

T10. [*In regular sequence this indicator should be "X10".*] "We've all given something to keep you flying," she said. "Four hundred housand of our boys gone overseas – fifty thousand of them ~~to st~~ killed. But – you are worth it!"

U10. [*In regular sequence this indicator should be "Y10".*] "She must be real," Rilla thought. "I can't be dreaming her." Aloud she gasped,

V10. [*In regular sequence this indicator should be "Z10".*] I felt numb, just as I did when I heard ~~of~~ Walter~~'s~~ had enlisted.

W10. [*In regular sequence this indicator should be "A11".*] though Susan has not yet recovered – never will recover, I believe, from the shock of having Jem come home the very night she had, owning to a strenuous day, prepared a 'pick up' supper. ~~I shall never forget the and~~ I shall never forget the sight of her, tearing madly about from pantry to cellar, hunting out stored-away goodies. Just as if anybody cared what was on the table – none of us could eat, anyway. It was meat and drink just to look at Jem. Mother seemed afraid to take her eyes off him lest he vanish out of her sight.

www.ingramcontent.com/pod-product-compliance
Lightning Source LLC
Chambersburg PA
CBHW051609100726
47898CB00001B/292

* 9 7 8 1 7 7 2 4 4 0 8 2 9 *